KU-524-724

Welsh Walks and Legends

Showell Styles was born in 1908 in the English Midlands, but when his service with the Royal Navy terminated he settled in North Wales and has been resident in Gwynedd for more than 30 years.

A professional writer, more than a third of his 108 published books deal with Wales or have a background of Welsh scenery or history.

Among the more recent of these are THE MOUNTAINS OF NORTH WALES, BACKPACKING IN WALES and the GUIDES to the Glyder and Snowdon ranges.

Showell Styles

Welsh Walks and Legends

MAYFLOWER
GRANADA PUBLISHING
London Toronto Sydney New York

Published by Granada Publishing Limited
in Mayflower Books 1979

ISBN 0 583 12977 3

First published in Great Britain in two
volumes by John Jones Cardiff Ltd 1972, 1977
Revised edition copyright © Showell Styles 1972, 1977, 1979

Granada Publishing Limited
Frogmore, St Albans, Herts AL2 2 NF
and
3 Upper James Street, London W1R 4BP
1221 Avenue of the Americas, New York, NY 10020, USA
117 York Street, Sydney, NSW 2000, Australia
100 Skyway Avenue, Toronto, Ontario, Canada M9W 3A6
Trio City, Coventry Street, Johannesburg 2001, South Africa
CML Centre, Queen & Wyndham, Auckland 1, New Zealand

Made and printed in Great Britain by
Richard Clay (The Chaucer Press) Ltd
Bungay, Suffolk
Set in Monotype Plantin

This book is sold subject to the condition that it
shall not, by way of trade or otherwise, be lent,
re-sold, hired out or otherwise circulated
without the publisher's prior consent in any
form of binding or cover other than that in
which it is published and without a similar
condition including this condition being imposed
on the subsequent purchaser.

CONTENTS

	Page
Introduction	7
VALE OF LLANGOLLEN	11
Nest and her Lovers	13
The White Hart of Llangar	18
Myfanwy of Dinas Brân	21
CONWAY VALLEY	25
The Legend of the Afanc	27
The Stone Women of Moelfre	30
Taliesin the Bard	34
THE NORTH COAST	37
The End of Maelgwn Gwynedd	39
Deganwy and its Castle	44
How Prince Madoc discovered America	47
BANGOR AND MENAI	53
The Isle of St Seiriol	55
The Lake that no Bird will cross	59
The Farmer who caught a Fairy	62
LLEYN AND TREMADOC BAY	67
The Rising of the Lark	69
Helen's Spring	73
The Accursed Village	78
SNOWDON	83
The Story of Gelert	85
King Arthur's Last Battle	90
Glendower's Chimney	93
FISHGUARD AND TENBY	97
The French Invasion	99
The Lost Land of Rhys Ddwfn	102
Saint Teilo's Skull	106
The Old Maid of Kidwelly	109

SWANSEA AND GOWER   115
A Baby on Worm's Head   117
The Orgy at Pennard Castle   122
The Drowned Well of Gorslas   127
Owain of the Red Hand   131
The First Recorded Fairy-tale   136

CARDIGAN AND NEW QUAY   141
When the Cuckoo came late   143
The Mermaid of Cemaes Head   146
Introduction and Allegro   150

BRECON AND LLANDOVERY   153
Twm Shôn Catti's Cave   155
A Legend of Llangorse Lake   167
The Cave of Carreg Cennen   171
The Physicians of Myddfai   176

ABERYSTWYTH AND ABERDOVEY   181
How the Devil's Bridge was built   183
The Miraculous Cow of Llyn Barfog   188

ABERGAVENNY AND CARDIFF   193
The Giant of Painscastle   195
A Duel in the Dark   199
Doctor Price of Llantrisant   203

Reference Map   206

INTRODUCTION

This book is for visitors to Wales who want to see the best of its varied scenery and in doing so learn something of its traditions and history. It is for those who are prepared to walk short distances from the car, but who don't want to have to don mountaineering clothes and heavy boots – or leave the children behind. It tells 18 legends of North Wales and 21 legends of South Wales and helps you to see for yourself where each long-ago happening, historical or imaginary, took place. Most of the walks are short and easy, a few longer to suit the more energetic; but none of them will occupy more than half a day unless you take a picnic along.

For convenience the stories are placed under area headings. In fact, the areas overlap considerably, and in most cases the walks can be done from any of the centres mentioned, if you have a car. I shall tell the story of the legend first and then describe in detail how to reach its location. The Reference Map at the back of the book will enable you, by reference to the Map Square numbers, to spot the whereabouts of the place you are heading for. Those who carry the Ordnance Survey 1:50000 maps will find at the start of every walk-description the Grid Reference for it, preceded by the Sheet number of the map required.

When I did the Walks myself all the paths and routes described were open and public, with no access impediments. There is unlikely to be any change; but if there is, I must disclaim responsibility for any trouble that may arise. The times given for each Walk make no allowance for long halts or picnics but are a generous estimate of actual walking time.

As to the Legends, I must confess that the tales I have attached to Kidwelly Castle and Carreg Cennen Castle are based on very slight foundations, though both are perfectly feasible historically. All the rest are traditional and a few of them are factual. Several different versions of some of the Legends exist, and where this is the case I've simply picked the one I liked best.

The publishers state that the descriptions in this book do not imply a right-of-way. Walkers are urged to take all reasonable care and attention in noting private property and protecting the countryside from damage and litter.

VALE OF LLANGOLLEN

Nest and her Lovers

The White Hart of Llangar

Myfanwy of Dinas Brân

NEST AND HER LOVERS

King Henry the First of England was no more restrained in his passions than any other powerful ruler of the twelfth century. It made little difference to him that the beautiful Nest, daughter of the Welsh prince Rhys ap Tudor, had been placed in his care as a Royal Ward; he fell in love with Nest and seduced her, and she bore him a son.

In those days, however, there was an accepted way of dealing with such a situation. Nest's baby son was named Duke of Gloucester and King Henry gave Nest in marriage to one of his barons, Gerald de Windsor – who, it seems, was in love with her himself. Gerald was Earl of Pembroke, and took his new wife with him to South Wales, where the fame of her beauty soon spread far beyond those parts – as far, even, as the kingdoms of Gwynedd and Powys in the north. Though Gerald was a Norman baron and maintained an armed force in Pembroke Castle, he was on terms of slightly uneasy peace with Prince Cadwgan, Welsh ruler of this land of Ceredigion as well as of Powys, and the Earl and Countess lived in peace and happiness for a year. Then came a Christmas when Cadwgan ordained a great Eisteddfod in South Wales, to which everyone of distinction flocked, including the Welsh countess. And with the guests came Cadwgan's daredevil son Owain.

Now Owain lived in his father's second kingdom of Powys, in a hunting-lodge called Plas Eglwyseg at the head of a secret glen north of the Dee. Here he had gathered about him a band of reckless fighting-men, with whom he would sally forth by the path he called his war path to hunt, or raid, or harass King Henry's men-at-arms. He was accustomed to take for himself whatever he wanted. And when he came to his father's Eisteddfod and set eyes on the lovely Nest he determined at once to carry her off. That very night he and his men broke into the castle of Pembroke, set it on fire, and dragged Nest from the bed where she was sleeping with her husband. The Earl, naked and unarmed, escaped with his life by way of a drain-pipe. Nest was borne away across the mountains to Owain's retreat at Plas Eglwyseg, where (it appears) she lived quite happily with her captor for some time.

But the mad action of Owain ap Cadwgan brought terrible consequences. King Henry, appealed to by Gerald de Windsor, ordered Prince Cadwgan to restore the stolen countess on pain of losing his kingdoms. Cadwgan's attempts to comply met with flat defiance from his son, who eluded all efforts to capture him; and war broke out through the whole of Wales. Norman barons aided Cadwgan's Welsh rivals to take Powys from him and others robbed him of much of his southern kingdom. The new rulers of Powys disinherited Owain and at last succeeded in driving him out of his refuge at Plas Eglwyseg, whence he fled to Ireland, leaving Nest homeless. The deserted beauty made her way southward and after a long and hazardous journey reached Pembroke Castle, where Earl Gerald – now the most powerful lord in South Wales – took her in his arms and once more established her as his wife and countess.

And now, for a year or more, there was a period of peace. It was broken by the arrival of a raiding force from Ireland, which was opposed by the Earl of Pembroke in alliance with the Welsh. Owain had accompanied the raiders, but now elected to change sides and fight for his native land. In the midst of the battle Gerald recognized the man who had wronged him fighting on the same side as himself. Changing the direction of his attack, he and his bodyguard fell upon Owain and slew him, thus wiping out, to the satisfaction of everyone who counted in those days, the dishonour he had suffered at Owain's hands.

Gerald de Windsor ended his warlike career by dying peacefully in his castle of Carew, but his wife's career was not finished thereby. Though her children were now grown up and married, Nest still had her beauty – and plenty of love to spare. She transferred her affections first

'Plas Uchaf', 10 miles from Llangollen at 'World's End'

to Stephen, Constable of Caernarfon Castle, and then to the Sheriff of Pembroke, presenting each of them with a son. All her children, legitimate or illegitimate, founded great families; and if you are a Fitzgerald, a Carew, a Barry, or a Fitzstephen you are very probably of 'the race of Nesta'.

| THE WALK:
TO PLAS EGLWYSEG
AND WORLD'S END | MAP SQUARE F2
O.S. reference 229479
Suitable for the Under
Eights, being a short walk
at the end of a car ride. |

Out of the holiday season it's a quiet 10-mile walk from Llangollen to World's End and back, but in summer there are likely to be a fair number of cars making the trip and the lanes are narrow. Take the car, then, and start from Llangollen.

If arriving by the A5, turn through the town and cross the bridge over the Dee. On the far side turn right for a few yards only, then left, uphill, crossing the Llangollen canal by a bridge and turning left again, with the School (Ysgol Dinas Brân) on your right. The lane you are on mounts gently for ¼-mile, then you bear right – signpost WORLD'S END 4. From here onward the lane is narrow and winding, with occasional passing-places. The limestone escarpment called Eglwyseg Rocks is sighted, and soon you are driving along the foot of it and entering a steep-sided glen. The lane becomes narrower still, requiring slow and careful driving. When a spectacular limestone precipice is seen towering above the glen in front, you are close to the site of the hunting-lodge to which Owain ap Cadwgan carried off the lovely Nest.

On today's Ordnance Survey maps the place is named 'Plas Uchaf', the Upper Hall. An Elizabethan manor house, black-and-white half-timbered, stands on the foundations of the old hall, with a large inscription across the front: LX III ELIZABETH REGINA. According to the present owner Queen Elizabeth I once stayed here, reputedly to have a baby. He also asserts that Winston Churchill and General Goering stayed here on a shooting holiday in 1936/37. It's not easy to say whether these tales are more, or less, historical than the story of Owain and Nest!

A few yards uphill beyond the house is an iron gate. The lane goes on uphill beyond the gate, climbing a more open section of the glen, and the car can be turned and parked here close to the stream that comes down below a forested slope. The limestone crag already mentioned rises splendidly overhead; its name is Craig-y-Cythraul – the Devil's Crag.

For a short walk (20 minutes to half-an-hour) walk on up the hill for 5 minutes, to where the lane turns sharp left and goes through a ford. There is a stile on the right leading into the forest. You may be surprised at the signpost beside it, a carved oaken board with the words LLWYBYR CLAWDD OFFA. Llwybyr is the Welsh word for a footpath, and clawdd means 'dyke'. By crossing the stile you can go a little way along the ancient line of Offa's Dyke, that extraordinary boundary of bank-and-ditch built by the King of Mercia four centuries before Owain's love-affair with Nest.

The path through the forestry trees is pleasant and easy to follow. In a few hundred yards you come to a stile crossing a fence, where an older and sparser wood begins. Go over the stile and turn steeply downhill beside the fence. At the bottom a log footbridge takes you across the stream and so back to where you left the car.

THE WHITE HART OF LLANGAR

Long ago in the peaceful valley of the Afon Dyfrdwy, which Saxons call the River Dee, the pious dwellers in the district of Edeirnion resolved to build a church. It would not be very big (for at that time there were not many people in those parts) but it would be the Church of All Saints, they decided, and built in a place where the Christian folk of the valley could all get to it on Sundays.

Three greyheaded elders took charge of the work and many younger men helped in the carrying of stones and the clearing of the ground. They had chosen a place where the paths from several villages met, a level site that had building materials in plenty ready to hand, and by mustering every man capable of work and starting at dawn of a summer day they made amazing progress. The first course of huge stones was already in place when darkness fell.

Next morning the builders met again on the site, eager to raise the church walls two or three courses higher. To their utter astonishment there was no sign of the work they had so well begun the day before. The pile of raw material was still there, but all the stones they had placed in position with so much labour had vanished. It would have needed an army of men to carry the great stones away, so the builders knew that some kind of supernatural agency was at work. After a grave discussion, the three elders gave the word to start building the church again. The workers succeeded in regaining all the ground they had lost by this mysterious interference, and went home at nightfall weary but well-content.

On the second morning there was again no sign of their day's work. Every stone had vanished. And again, stubbornly refusing to be frightened or discouraged, they rebuilt the first course of the church walls. On the third morning things were exactly the same – all their work was undone. But this time the three greybeards, after an excited conference, told the church-builders to go to their homes and await word from them. For the elders had discovered that in the night each of them had received the same vision – a bright light shining from above, and a voice saying 'Seek the white hart, and where you see him, there build your church.' None of the three doubted that only by following this command would they succeed in getting their church finished, and with one accord they set off in different directions to look for the hart, or stag, of this unusual colour.

All that day they wandered, searching, through the woods and thickets that clothed the Berwyn slopes along the valley of the Dyfrdwy river; all that day until darkness was falling, with many a glimpse of the tawny-hued deer but never one of a white hart. They had arranged to meet at a place in the river valley near where the Alwen stream flows into the Dyfrdwy, and here at dusk the three came together, tired and despairing. With little spoken, they were about to make their way to their homes when, suddenly, they all saw a great White Hart standing on the hillside a little way above the river bank. For an instant he stood, seeming to look down at them; then he vanished, never to reappear.

Next morning, at the summons of the elders, the workmen began to carry the building materials to the place where the hart had stood. When they began to build, the work seemed twice as easy as before and was never interfered with. The walls rose with remarkable speed, the roof seemed almost to grow from the walls, and soon the church was finished.

It was duly sanctified as the Church of All Saints. But to all the people of Edeirnion it was known as Llan-Garw-Gwyn – garw meaning 'stag' and gwyn meaning 'white'. In after years the name was shortened, becoming first Llangarw and then Llangar. And to this day the old church, standing in its curious place remote from villages and with no road to it, is called Llangar.

MAP SQUARE E2
O.S. reference 063424
Short and easy walk; ½-hour,
could be extended to an
hour.

*This walk is based on Corwen, and could be done on foot
from a car parked at the disused railway station. However,
this would involve ¾-mile along a fairly busy road and it's
probably more reasonable to do the road part by car.*

*If you come into Corwen from the Llangollen direction,
bear left off the A5 before crossing the river bridge at the end
of the town. If you come from the Betws-y-coed direction,
cross this bridge; don't enter the town, but at once turn sharp
right, uphill, on B4401.*

*In about half-a-mile this road curves to the right across a
stone bridge. Beyond the bridge it has wide grass verges, and
when these show themselves look out for a lane on the right –
the first you come to. The car can be parked on the verge.*

*Walk down the lane, towards the river, passing a farm on
the left. 50 yards past the farm turn right, across a brook
and through an iron gate. The rough way beyond is the old
approach to the church and soon ends at an ancient lych-
gate. The church is tiny, and is now disused. Its churchyard
is a chaos of extremely aged tombstones, some of which have
stone rests near them for the comfort of those offering prayers
for the dead. The tall yewtrees that overshadow it must also
be an immense age.*

*[Note: In November 1972 the church was entirely encased
in corrugated iron, pending repairs, and looked like a large
barn. No one could tell me how soon the repairs would be
complete.]*

*If someone is willing to take the car back to Corwen, or if
you have got this far on foot, you could return as follows: go
back through the iron gate and gain the disused railway
track by a stile; turn right, and with slightly rough walking
– the river close on your left – you can reach the ruinous
station at Corwen in 25 minutes.*

MYFANWY OF DINAS BRÂN

The old story-spinners told of a hero named Brân who built a dinas, or city, on the great mound above the Dyfrdwy vale; and that was as long ago as the Bronze Age. The centuries rolled by, and there came one of the Lords of Ial (a forerunner of the Yale who founded the great American college) to make a more habitable fortress on the ditches and parapets of the old dinas. But about the year 1250 a stone castle began to rise on the great mound, every stone of its walls carried to the summit by gangs of serfs or prisoners. Castell Dinas Brân was the work of the Norman barons who were determined to subdue the rebellious Welsh.

But there were treaties and agreements – even inter-marrying – between the great Welsh families and the Norman nobles. And a hundred years after the building of Castell Dinas Brân the fortress was held by a Vychan of the house of Tudor Trevor, whose overlord was the Norman Earl of Arundel and whose daughter Myfanwy was the most beautiful maiden in all the land of Powys.

Myfanwy was well aware of her beauty. But like many a pretty girl before and since, she liked nothing better than to hear her beauty praised. Many men, young and hand-some, warriors and of good birth, thronged the hall of Castell Dinas Brân to seek her favour. Myfanwy Vychan spurned them all, for they lacked the thing she most desired – the gift of weaving poetry and music that reflected as in a mirror her wondrous beauty. The one man who possessed this gift was a youthful bard, pen-niless and of lowly birth, who dwelt in the valley below the castle. His name was Hywel ap Einion.

Hywel had fallen madly in love with Myfanwy, and every day he toiled up the long, steep ascent to the castle with his harp, hoping to be admitted to the hall where he could play and sing to Myfanwy Vychan. Sometimes he would be allowed to enter, sometimes he was sent away. But whenever he was admitted to Myfanwy's presence he played and sang to her so wonderfully – always praising her unrivalled beauty in a flood of wild words and enchanting music – that she would neither listen to nor look at any man of those around her, but Hywel ap Einion. And the young bard came to believe that she returned his love.

Too soon his hope was shattered. A suitor more handsome, more powerful, and (perhaps) more articulate than the others came wooing. The match was a suitable one for the heiress of the Tudor Trevors and in the ensuing betrothal festivities the poor bard was quite forgotten. There was not a word for him, nor even a look, from the beauty of Castell Dinas Brân by way of farewell.

Hywel climbed no more to the castle on the hilltop. Broken-hearted, he wandered through the Dyfrdwy forests with his harp; and as he went he composed the Ode which was to live for more than four hundred years as one of the best-loved Welsh poems. It was a very long Ode,

Castell Dinas Brân, Llangollen

and of its many lines four can be translated into English
thus:

> 'Far from Myfanwy's marble towers
> I pass my solitary hours.
> O thou that shinest like the sky,
> Behold thy faithful Hywel die!'

But Hywel did not die of his broken heart. And as for the
cruel Myfanwy Vychan, to whom he sang –

> 'Fairer thou and colder too,
> Than winter snow on Aran's brow' –

her undeserved reward was to be made famous by her
humble lover's poem. So that to this day, when Castell
Dinas Brân is a lifeless ruin, her story lives on.

THE WALK: MAP SQUARE F2
TO CASTELL DINAS BRÂN   O.S. reference 223431
                        Steep paths, fine views.
                        Allow 1½ hours up and down.

*Start on foot from the public car park in Llangollen. (To
drive to this car park, turn off the A5 at the traffic lights
halfway through the town, and take the first street on the
left.) From the car park make for the bridge across the Dee,
cross it, and turn right. Almost at once turn left up Wharf
Hill, a lesser road that ascends over the canal bridge. Opposite the bridge you'll see a signpost showing the start of the
path to Castell Dinas Brân.*

*First the path mounts past the school (called Ysgol Dinas
Brân) and then becomes a lane for a short time. Beyond a
second signpost it climbs to an open hill-ridge with the ruined
castle above on the right. Parents should keep a wary eye on
younger children from now on; the hillsides are scarcely
precipices, but there are steep places below the ruined wall
where a tumble could have nasty results.*

*There's not a great deal left of the old castle, and it's
anyone's guess where the castle hall used to be that saw*

Hywel ap Einion's musical courtship of cruel Myfanwy Vychan. The chief charm of the place is its magnificent situation and views. From this height of 1,060 feet above the sea you can see eastward into England as far as the Wrekin and westward to Snowdon – but for Snowdon you'll need an exceptionally clear day.

The quickest way down is the way you came up. But a pleasant alternative that takes about 10 minutes longer is to go down on the opposite side. Keep the distant Dee and its companion the Llangollen canal on your right front as you start down from the castle, and you'll quickly see a stile over the fence below. Cross this, keep on steeply down for a couple of minutes, and you reach a stile that gives access to a lane. Turn right on the lane, which has delightful views on the left as you curl rightward round the hill and descend to a house entrance. Opposite this entrance a Public Footpath sign guides you across fields on the right – keep quite level for the first 5 minutes – and this brings you back into your route of ascent at the second 'Dinas Bran' signpost. Turn left here, and you can be back at the car in 20 minutes.

CONWAY VALLEY

The Legend of the Afanc

The Stone Women of Moelfre

Taliesin the Bard

THE LEGEND OF THE AFANC

Long ago, before histories began to be written, the people of the Vale of Conway were sorely troubled by a monster who lived in a pool of the river. This afanc, as he was called, was an enormous beast that possessed super-natural powers, which he used (when he was in a vicious mood) to cause disastrous floods, ruining the crops and drowning the cattle. Spear and dart and sword had been tried against him by the bravest of the young men, but no weapon forged by man could make any impression on the afanc's scaly hide. The greybeards held conference, and decided that there was only one thing to do: the monster must be got out of his pool and taken far away to some other lake beyond the mountains.

Preparations began at once. Strong iron chains were forged, and the two mightiest oxen in the land – the giant long-horned animals belonging to Hu Gadarn – were brought to Betws-y-coed, for the afanc pool was close to this place. But the problem of how to get the afanc out of the pool, so that he could be chained to the oxen, had still to be solved. Now the monster was known to be very partial to beautiful maidens, showing in this at least one human quality; and when this was remembered, a cour-ageous damsel was found who agreed to act as decoy. The lake to which the afanc was to be dragged was chosen – Llyn Ffynnon Las, under the peak of Snowdon – and all was ready.

The giant oxen and the men with the chains hid them-selves in the woods near the pool while the damsel sat by the water's edge and called softly to the afanc. By-and-by the hideous monster came wallowing up out of the depths, and – yielding to the girl's enticements – heaved himself ashore and laid his ugly head in her lap. Now, or never, was the moment! The men leaped from their con-cealment and deftly wound the chains round the afanc, who saw too late the trick that had been played upon him. Furious, he struck at the girl with his great claws, tearing her breast, and hurled himself back into the pool.

But the chains were already harnessed to the oxen, and slowly, with every man present lending his strength to help, the afanc was drawn out. All up the rocky Lledr valley they dragged him, as far as the spot where Dolwyddelan stands now; and striking north-west over the shoulder of Moel Siabod they crossed the watershed and came into the head of the Gwynant valley. So great were the efforts of the oxen that the eye of one of them dropped out, causing it to shed floods of tears which formed the pool called ever afterwards Pwll Llygad yr Ych, the Pool of the Ox's Eye.

The last part of the oxen's labour was the hardest. They dragged the afanc up into Cwm Dyli, past Llyn Llydaw, and at last reached the lake, 1,970 feet above sea-level, which is now called Glaslyn but whose proper name is Llyn Ffynnon Las, the Lake of the Blue Fountain. On the shores of the lake, with Snowdon summit frowning overhead, the men loosed the chains. The monster plunged headlong into Glaslyn at once, and sank from sight in the immensely deep blue water. And there, the old folk in Beddgelert village will tell you, he dwells to this day.

THE WALK: MAP SQUARE D2
TO THE AFANC POOL   O.S. reference 798546
Easy and short (¾-mile) but can be extended to the Fairy Glen.

The walk starts in Betws-y-coed. Though the car could in fact be taken right to the Afanc Pool (called the Beaver Pool in some guidebooks) it's a pleasant walk on a minor road, through trees and beside the river for much of the way. If you're staying in Betws you'll want to walk anyway; if you drive in, park in the car park by Betws-y-coed station. There is a restaurant here, by the way.

When you come out of the station drive, turn left along the main road for about 200 yards. Just before the road crosses the railway, a minor road turns uphill to the right. Follow this. It quickly leaves the houses behind and becomes a leafy lane. You pass under a railway bridge that carries the single-track line to Blaenau Ffestiniog (one of the most beautiful rail trips in Britain) and soon afterwards the lane is running along the bank of the River Conway. There is more than one fine pool, but the Afanc Pool is the big one near the junction of the lane with a bigger road, A496, which crosses the river by a stone bridge just here, ¾-mile from the start of the lane.

The Afanc Pool is large and deep and rather gloomy under its big trees. No description of an afanc has been left by the people who claimed to have seen one, but no doubt he was a horrific monster, and on any but the brighter days the pool looks a suitable home for him. A little scrambly path leads down to its shore, and as there is no afanc there now it's quite safe to go down and do a bit of minor exploration.

This walk has occupied about half-an-hour so far. It's well worth extending it to see the Fairy Glen.

The entrance to this deservedly famous beauty-spot is only a couple of minutes' walk from the Afanc Pool. Go to the junction with A496, turn left across the bridge, and turn right up a signposted lane immediately beyond the bridge. The lane brings you to the Fairy Glen in an easy 15 minutes' walking, and the way can't be missed.

For those who like exploration, there is another little route that should be mentioned. Having crossed the bridge and taken the Fairy Glen lane, look for a narrow gap in the right-hand wall just 50 yards up the lane. If you go through the gap, a steep little path takes you down to the river bank. Turn left here, and you will come to some waterworn rock scenery by the big pool where the Lledr joins the Conway; or turn right, and in a few yards you can scramble under the arch of the road bridge to a fine rock seat out on the other side, overlooking the Afanc Pool.

THE STONE WOMEN OF MOELFRE

In the fields by the shores of Conway Bay the corn had been harvested. The oxen had trodden the grain from the ears, and the chaff and the grain lay together waiting to be winnowed. The winnowing was done by the women, who would have to work for hour after hour, tossing up the chaff and grain into the wind so that the lighter chaff would be blown away and the heavier grain left ready for the miller. But for days there had not been a breath of wind in the fields by the sea. Only on the tall hills that curved round to the headland of Penmaenmawr was there any wind.

The women grew impatient. The rain might come, soaking grain and chaff together, and rob them of the good flour from which they made their bread.

'There's plenty of wind up on Moelfre,' said one woman, who wore a red kirtle. 'Let's carry the corn in sacks and winnow it up there.'

She said this on a Sunday. And in Wales no man, woman, or child was ever to be seen working on a Sunday.

'We would be breaking the Sabbath,' said another, whose kirtle was white.

'What then?' retorted her neighbour. 'Doesn't the wind blow on a Sunday, and shall we waste it and lose the good flour?'

'That's sense,' nodded a third woman, in a blue kirtle. 'I'll get three sacks and we three will carry the corn up to Moelfre.'

So the three women filled the sacks and started up the hillside, bent beneath their loads. They passed a cottage, and here an old man called loudly after them, warning them that they sinned in breaking the Sabbath and would be punished. Higher up they passed a farm, and here the farmer came out to give them the same solemn warning. The three laden women laughed at the warnings and toiled on.

They climbed the steep glen where once men had used the hard Graig Lwyd stone to make primitive axes. They gained the lofty crest where the Meini Hirion – the Long Stones – stood in a wide circle. There was still no wind, but the round summit called Moelfre was not far away and they knew there would be wind up there. They carried their sacks to the very top of the hill, emptied them in a heap, and began the winnowing, throwing up the corn into the steady breeze that was blowing there.

And then came the dreadful happening which Sir John Wynn recorded in his book published in the seventeenth century. 'These faythles women, regardynge there profytt more than the obsearvynge of God's commandements,' were instantly turned into three stones, one red, one white, and one blue.

There are no coloured stones on the top of Moelfre now. But a little searching will reveal, sunk in the turf of the summit, the tops of three grey rocks; as if the Stone Women of Moelfre had at last been permitted to sink into the very ground.

THE WALK:
TO MOELFRE AND
THE DRUIDS' CIRCLE

MAP SQUARE D1/2
O.S. reference 716745
The longest walk in this book, including a climb to 1,423 feet. 4 hours up and down. Leave the Under Eights behind.

The start is in Penmaenmawr, 3½ miles west of Conway on A55. The free car park is near the centre of the town, just off A55; on your left if you come from the Conway direction, on your right if you come from Bangor. Park here. At the car park exit turn sharp right and follow the uphill road called Y Berllan, which curves right and then left, ending at the upper limit of houses where there is a fork of two narrow lanes. Take the left-hand (stony) lane.

This lane or bridle-path mounts gently into a green valley under steep hillsides. High on your right are the Graig Lwyd quarries, working noisily if it is a weekday. In 5 minutes or so the bridle-path comes to a wider road crossing it – Craig Lwyd Road. Turn to the right up this road. In 200 yards you come to a farmhouse on the left, with a gate leading to a footpath (signposted) going up on the left of the house.

The footpath climbs along the side of the green valley, zigzagging when it gets steep. Down on the left are the mounds and scars where, archaeologists say, primitive man extracted the stone for the 'Graig Lwyd' axes; stone axes that undoubtedly came from Penmaenmawr have been found all over Britain. Up in the head of the valley the path goes to the left, crossing a boggy patch by a concrete causeway and just afterwards passing through a wall by a gap with a signpost above it. Go up beside the wall, and join a broader pathway a few yards higher, turning to the right along it. In two or three minutes you will reach a level space on the crest of the hills, with a domed hill standing above. The hill is Moelfre, and an easy climb of about 200 feet brings you to the summit and a very fine view. The height here is 1,423 feet above the sea, which stretches to the far horizon on the north. Anglesey is in sight to westward, and east and south are mountains.

The non-appearance of the Stone Women may be disappointing, but the Meini Hirion will make up for it. The so-called Druids' Circle (the stones were placed here long before the Druids) is one of the finest of its kind in Wales, and is only about ten minutes' walk from Moelfre. Descend from the hill and follow the grassy path that runs level – or nearly so – along the crest, with the sea down on your left. Soon you will come to a circle of rocks, close on the right of the path; these are also primitive remains, but the Meini Hirion themselves are a short distance farther. The circle, of quite large rocks, may be as much as 4,000 years old, and was probably an early form of observatory. However, it was undoubtedly used as a place of sacrifice in the early Bronze Age, for investigators discovered, in an urn at the centre of the circle, the cremated remains of a child, together with a bronze knife.

There are several ways of extending this walk. By turning back from Meini Hirion, for instance, and following the path westward, you would come down into Llanfairfechan by way of Nant-y-pandy. Rather than walk along the coast road for 2½ miles, though, most people will prefer to go down by the way they came up: return to the wall below Moelfre, go through the signposted gap, and down to the Craig Lwyd road and so to the car park.

TALIESIN THE BARD

Elphin, son of Gwyddno Garanhir, was the unluckiest prince in all the history of Wales. His father, who ruled over Mid Wales in the sixth century, gave him a large province as his estate; and almost immediately the sea broke the defensive dams of that estate and it was lost beneath the waves. By way of comforting him, Gwyddno presented this unfortunate young man with the annual salmon-netting of the Dovey river, which was the equivalent of giving him a large present of money, so vast was the number of salmon usually caught. But Elphin's bad luck stayed with him. As he watched the river-keeper and his servants working the nets, he saw that there was not a single fish in them. Indeed, the only object to emerge from the river was a large leather bag that had lodged on the edge of the weir. It was a thousand chances to one that there was nothing of worth in the leather bag, but Elphin bade the river-keeper bring it to him. This was done and the bag was opened. Inside was a small boy, hardly more than a babe but very much alive.

'Tal-iesin!' exclaimed the river-keeper; which means 'How radiant is his brow!': for the child's forehead seemed to shine with a strange lustre.

'Taliesin let him be called,' said Elphin, and set the boy on his horse and rode homeward with him, sadly at first but soon in wonder and amazement.

As they rode, the child began to speak, holding forth in an impassioned ode. This miraculous poetry told Elphin that the boy had been sent to guide him; that he was to be not only a great poet but also a great prophet, and before him all Elphin's enemies should fall.

The years passed, and from that time Elphin prospered in all he did. As for Taliesin, he became the most famous bard of Britain. Among his prophecies was that which foretold the end of the wicked king Maelgwn Gwynedd, but his most inspired odes were those that urged on the warriors of Britain in their struggle against the Saxon invaders.

Many places in Wales became associated with the name of Taliesin, especially the beautiful lake called Geirionydd, on the forested heights above the Conway valley. Here in his later years the bard used to come to meditate and seek inspiration.

To this day the sayings of this first and greatest of bards are remembered in Wales, and none more so than the famous prophecy he made, towards the end of his life, about the British of that time and their fate:

> Their Lord they shall praise,
> Their language they shall keep,
> Their land they shall lose –
> Except wild Wales.

THE WALK:	MAP SQUARE D2
TO TALIESIN'S MONUMENT	O.S. reference 765616
BY LAKE GEIRIONYDD	Steep forestry roads, mountain lake. About 4 hours excluding halts.

This is longer than most of the Legend-walks and makes a good picnic excursion. It's easy to combine it with a visit to Gwydir Castle (Elizabethan, famous for its peacocks) or with Legend-walk No. 4, the Legend of the Afanc.

From Llanrwst on A496 – 4 miles from Betws-y-coed – cross the bridge over the Conway river and so gain the cross-roads on the opposite side of the valley, where B5106 is joined. This point can be reached from Conway by following B5106 southward through Dolgarrog. Gwydir Castle is 150 yards from the crossroads in the direction of Betws-y-coed. For the walk, you cross B5106 and drive up a minor road signposted LLYN GEIRIONYDD 2½m., which ascends into the steep forests. Follow this road for ¼-mile only. When you reach a large red-lettered notice – FOREST FIRE DANGER AREA – park on the roadside near it, or turn the car and park 50 yards back down the hill, opposite a narrow lane signposted LLYN GEIRIONYDD 2¼m. This lane starts the walk.

(N.B. the whole walking-route is motorable – just – but in general the lanes are very narrow and very steep, and walking is a less anxious business.)

The lane is easy walking at first, then climbs steeply up into the forest. 20 minutes of this, and the angle eases as you emerge into an upper land of fields and streams. Here is the tiny hamlet called Tai, where a signpost directs you: *LLYN GEIRIONYDD* 1¼. In 10 minutes a right turn, also signposted, brings you past a farm and downhill to the lake. This last bit is delightful walking – mountains in the distance, the Crafnant glen far down on the right, and Geirionydd lake coming slowly into view on the left.

The lake beneath its fine crags and forests looks more Tyrolean or Bavarian than Welsh. At the nearer end is seen the tall stone monument to Taliesin, erected here on the place where the bard is said to have lived for a time. You reach the monument in five minutes from the road, crossing a stile on the right. There's no inscription to tell you what it is, and on some old maps it's marked Bedd Taliesin – Taliesin's Grave, though traditionally the bard was buried above the Dovey estuary where Elphin found the child genius.

Along the lake shore now, with lots of good picnic places halfway and an 'official' forestry picnic site with tables and benches at the south end. Here turn left opposite the farmhouse (*Tal-y-llyn*). This lane climbs uphill, past some old lead mines, with fine backward views. At the top of the longish ascent there's a glimpse of Moel Siabod on the right, and then for the next 15 minutes you walk between forestry plantations with very little up or down. Now you reach a T-junction of lanes and turn left (signpost *LLANRWST*) for a last bit of uphill past another old lead mine. At the top of this you're at your highest point of the walk and it's worth climbing the heathery bank on the right to look at the views. In ½-hour from here you'll be back in the car.

Downhill now, curving past a small lake, a large lead-mine chimney, and a chapel. Then more steeply down, 1¼ miles, to your parking-place.

THE NORTH COAST

The End of Maelgwn Gwynedd

Deganwy and its Castle

*How Prince Madoc
discovered America*

THE END OF MAELGWN GWYNEDD

Of all the princes who have ruled over Gwynedd, as North Wales was once called, the most wicked was Maelgwn. Maelgwn was Prince of Gwynedd thirteen centuries ago, and this is his story.

In those days there were four petty kingdoms in Wales, and the four rulers wished to decide which of them should be Brenhin Pennaf, or chief king. It was agreed that they should meet on the sands of the Dovey estuary, bringing their thrones with them; that the thrones should be placed in a row fronting the incoming tide, with their royal owners sitting on them; and that whichever of the four stayed longest on his throne when the sea came racing in to submerge them should be declared Brenhin Pennaf.

Now Maelgwn had a cunning counsellor, Maeldav the Elder, who was determined that his master should triumph. 'Maeldav,' says the old chronicle, 'secretly prepared a throne made of wings' – and we can take it as pretty certain that these were inflated skins, to act as water-wings. At any rate, the spring tide came roaring and foaming in, and the sea rose higher and higher, until the princes from Powys and South Wales took fright and splashed their way to safety. But Maelgwn rode the waves on his floating throne, and so became chief ruler of Wales.

It was an age when men were accustomed to harsh treatment from their overlords, but Maelgwn Gwynedd overstepped all bounds of cruelty. The people of his own land cursed him for the blackness of his deeds, but there was no one strong enough to oppose him and it seemed as if the sufferings of his many victims would never be avenged. He built himself a palace close to the north coast, within bowshot of a hill-fort that had been the stronghold of his ancestors hundreds of years earlier, and here at Llys Rhos (as it was called) Maelgwn lived a life of drunkenness and excess, with other evil-doing too horrible to be told.

At last the great bard and prophet Taliesin foretold an end to the suffering of Gwynedd. This was his prophecy: 'A wondrous beast shall come up from Morfa Rhianedd, the Sea marsh of the Maidens, to avenge the iniquities of Maelgwn. Its hair and its teeth and its eyes shall all be yellow, and this beast shall be the end of Maelgwn Gwynedd!'

The prophecy of Taliesin was fulfilled in the year 547. In that year the deadly plague which some called the Yellow Death was ravaging Europe, and spread northward into Britain. As the plague's trail of death approached the land of Gwynedd, Maelgwn's terror of it grew until he was almost mad with fear. He shut himself in his palace of Llys Rhos with a few favourite courtiers and forbade anyone to pass in or out, and for a little while it seemed that he had escaped the fate that was overtaking so many of his subjects in the world outside. But one day, hearing his name loudly called from the outer gateway, Maelgwn looked through the keyhole of the great door. A moment later he fell to the ground, writhing in agony; and his only words before he died were 'The Yellow Beast!'

The terrified courtiers fled, leaving their dead prince in the palace. And it was long indeed before anyone would venture in to bring out the body of the Brenhin Pennaf for burial; which gave rise to a saying that is remembered to this day: Hir hun y Faelgwn yn Llys Rhos – 'the long sleep of Maelgwn in the palace of Rhos'.

Llys Rhos fell into ruin. But from its stones a new palace named Llys Euryn was built, on the very spot where Maelgwn Gwynedd wrought – and paid for – his evil deeds.

THE WALK:	MAP SQUARE D1
TO LLYS EURYN AND	O.S. reference 833803
BRYN EURYN	Easy. 1 hour, if halts are short.

The start of the path to Llys Euryn, Rhos-on-Sea

Whether you are staying in Rhos-on-Sea or coming from Llandudno or Colwyn Bay, the starting-point for this walk is the seafront at Rhos. You could walk from there, or save 1 mile ($\frac{1}{2}$-mile out, $\frac{1}{2}$-mile back) by using the car as I shall now describe.

From the centre of Rhos seafront, Rhos Road runs uphill past the shops and in about 700 yards reaches the traffic lights on the Llandudno–Colwyn Bay road, A546. Cross this main road and continue along the secondary road opposite. This soon comes to another crossroads, where the continuing road opposite is only a narrow lane with a gravel surface. Take the car 50 yards up this lane to where it widens near the entrance of an ancient quarry. Here the car can be turned and parked and the walk begins.

At the start of the narrow lane there are two signposts. One says BRYN EURYN and points up the lane, the other says LLYS EURYN and indicates a little footpath at the side of the lane. Go back a little way from where you leave the car and take the LLYS EURYN path. It's a narrow uphill path and you need to walk single-file between the thickets. After going along it for less than 5 minutes you come to all that is left of Llys Euryn – once Llys Rhos – a mediaeval hall built on the site of a Dark Ages palace. The ruins are overgrown with grass and creepers, but the tall old chimney still reaches high above the cavernous stone fireplace.

On your left as you face the fireplace there is a gap which allows you to get behind the ruined wall on that side. Here you'll find an intriguing little path that leads you safely round the rim of the ancient quarry, up past some pretty gardens, and under a fallen tree into the narrow lane bound for Bryn Euryn. Turn right up the lane, and soon it curls to the left on to open grass slopes. From here a short steep path mounts to the summit of Bryn Euryn, where there is an Ordnance Survey cairn and a superb view.

The height is only 428 feet above the sea, but the splendid panorama over the River Conway, the Little Orme, and Colwyn Bay make it seem much loftier. Flower enthusiasts

*will notice (in summer) the limestone flora up here, including
Rock Rose, Scabious, Harebell, and Traveller's Joy — common in southern England but rare in North Wales. You need
to use some imagination to trace the blurred outlines of the
hill fortress that occupied Bryn Euryn in primitive times;
but anyone can see that it must have been an impregnable
defensive position before the days of gunpowder.*

*For the descent, follow the broad track all the way down.
It brings you straight to the car.*

DEGANWY AND ITS CASTLE

Sometime in the early centuries A.D. two holy women of Ireland, Modwenna and Bride, were sitting in a meadow close to the Irish shore with their servants Luge and Athea. Suddenly all four found themselves at sea – for the portion of the Emerald Isle they were on had broken away from the mainland. They floated eastward for a day and a night before their drifting island grounded on the shores of Britain at the mouth of a river. The river was the Conway, and the piece of Ireland (which quickly became part of the coast) was the peninsula of Deganwy.

Modwenna settled in Mercia, where as Saint Modwenna of the Forest of Arden she wrote the story of this miraculous journey. Saint Bride – or Sant Ffraidd, which is the Welsh form of her name – stayed in western Britain, and is commemorated by the village two miles farther up the estuary, Llansantffraidd Glan Conwy.

Many hundreds of years later the Norman conquerors of Britain built a castle on the rocky hill above Deganwy. For a long time Deganwy Castle was the limit of the Norman advance against the rebel Welsh princes, the object of fierce attacks and desperate defences. One of the first Norman lords to occupy it was Robert, Earl of Rhuddlan, who was sent there with a small force of men-at-arms to establish the Norman idea of law and order. One morning – it was July 3rd 1088 – news reached the castle of a marauding force raiding from the mountains higher up the Conway. The Earl sent his tiny army to deal with it, under command of his lieutenant, while he himself remained in the castle with one knight and a few servants.

At noon of that day Robert of Rhuddlan 'was taking his midday sleep in the Castle, with no thought of danger or of warlike alarms', when a frightened messenger toiled up to the castle gate to beg the Earl for help. Three ships, Welsh raiders from farther along the coast, were beached on the sands below Great Ormes Head. The men from them had seized women and cattle and were only waiting for the tide to carry them off with their plunder. Earl Robert leaped from his bed and ordered all his retainers to follow him to the shore without a moment's delay. But when he rode sword in hand out of the gateway, wearing no armour, only his one knight followed him. They galloped down the steep path to the shore, came up to the three ships just as the tide was beginning to lift them, and demanded that the cattle and prisoners should be put ashore. The pirates replied with a shower of arrows and javelins. And Robert of Rhuddlan and his brave companion fell from their horses, dead.

For nearly two centuries after this event Deganwy Castle was attacked and defended, destroyed and rebuilt. Not until the year 1284, when King Edward I completed the building of Conway Castle on the opposite shore of the estuary, did the invading armies from England make much progress against the stubborn bravery of the Welsh. And by that time the little fortress on the rocky hill had fallen into disuse and was soon to become a ruin.

THE WALK:	MAP SQUARE D1
TO DEGANWY CASTLE	O.S. reference 782794
	Easy. 1 hour. Care needed
	with small children in party.

Deganwy is five miles from Colwyn Bay via A55 and Llandudno Junction; a mile and a half from Conway, across the river bridge; and two miles from the centre of Llandudno, following Gloddaeth Road and the West Parade. There is a free car park at Deganwy immediately below the front of the Castle Hotel. Just above the Castle Hotel is York Road, turning off A496 to curve uphill. Go up this road for 5 minutes and look out for a PUBLIC FOOT-PATH sign on the left. This marks the path to the Castle ruins. (The car could be brought as far as this, but it is preferable to leave it in the authorized car park.)

The public footpath goes through a white gate on to open grassy hillside with crags above. If you expect to see a castle

45

like those at Conway or Harlech, you'll be sadly disappointed. What you are visiting is a much older fortress; and what you are seeing is the ghost of a castle that was built here a thousand years ago.

The best way is to take the fortress in rear – go straight uphill, keeping the crags on your left, until an easy gap on that side, with a fragment of old wall on the right, enables you to mount into the grassy court or saddle between the rock horns. You can see now that this was a natural fortification. The turrets of crag on each side were there long before Man came, and all the Normans had to do was to build walls enclosing the space between the rock towers, and crown the towers themselves with stone battlements. The little crag on your left (if you enter as I've described) is easy to climb, by a narrow path. BUT I advise you to lead the way yourself and not to allow any small children to go up first. The summit is not very big, and drops in a sheer cliff from the farther edge.

There are no battlements left now, and what use the excavations and ledges were put to is anyone's guess. But the view alone (if the weather is clear) is worth the climb. Conway Castle and anchorage looks like a child's model, and among the Carnedd mountains that loom beyond is the second highest summit in Wales, Carnedd Llewelyn. Looking the other way, northward, Llandudno is spread like a town plan with Great Ormes Head protecting it like another and bigger fortress.

For the descent, go down from the crag by the same narrow path but turn left at the bottom. If you descend a little way from the 'courtyard', down grass slopes in the direction of Llandudno, you will quickly come to a narrow path running round the slopes. Go to the left along it. Soon the precipitous wall of the Castle crag appears above on your left, showing the largest area of man-made wall still remaining. From the blocks of stone that lie half-buried beside the path below, it is easy to deduce what happened to the battlements.

The path finishes close to the gate of the public footpath, by which you regain York Road.

HOW PRINCE MADOC
DISCOVERED AMERICA

Owain Gwynedd, ruler of North Wales in the twelfth century, had nineteen sons. One of them was Idwal, whose story is told later in this book. Another was Madoc, who loved the sea better than the mountains of his own land. But the two princes of greatest importance were Howel and Dafydd, for Owain their father had resolved that between them they should rule Gwynedd after his death.

Owain died in December 1169; and the recorded date reminds us that he and his sons were historical persons. On his death Howel and Dafydd, like many other kings' sons in history, quarrelled as to which should be the more powerful force in the kingdom and began a civil war, turning Gwynedd from a peaceful country into a land of strife. Now Prince Madoc was a peace-loving man, a thinker and a poet rather than a warrior. His courage and hardihood had been shown by several daring voyages, but he had no mind to win fame in battles, least of all by joining with Dafydd or Howel to fight against a brother. Each of the warring princes wished him to declare himself on their side, for Madoc was well loved by all who lived on the coasts of Gwynedd. To escape from this unhappy situation, Madoc determined to carry out an adventure he had long meditated. This was to sail westward beyond Ireland (where his brother Riryd had an estate) until he came to another land beyond the ocean, or – which was just as likely – until his ship met her fate in the unknown waters of the edge of the world.

So Prince Madoc at once rigged and manned the famous Gwennan Gorn, a ship of which little detail is known except that her planks were joined with stag's horns instead of nails and that Madoc had voyaged in her to distant islands in the northern sea. She was built of oak from the forests of Nant Gwynant, says one bard; and another, Gynfric ap Gronow, wrote:

Gwennan Gorn, brought to the Gele
To be given a new mast,
Was taken then to the quay of Afon Ganol
For Madoc's famous voyage.

For in those days the north coast of Gwynedd (where Colwyn Bay and Abergele stand today) had two small seaports at the river-mouths of the Gele and the Ganol. And from the quay of the Afon Ganol in the year 1170 the Gwennan Gorn sailed on her great venture.

It is recorded that Madoc's brother Riryd joined the ship at Lundy Island. Then she departed westward, and for several years nothing was heard of her. Then – and no one can be sure how long afterwards – the Gwennan Gorn came back. She had barely enough men on board to sail her, for all the rest had been left in the new land Madoc had discovered many weeks' sail across the western ocean. The Prince stayed in Gwynedd only long enough to gather a fleet of ten small ships and fill them with volunteers, both men and women, who would sail with him to the new land and make a new Gwynedd there.

The ten ships sailed, having collected at Lundy Island. And this time they were never heard of again . . .

. . . Unless the evidence of six hundred years later is to be believed. For during the seventeenth and eighteenth centuries, when the wilderness of North America was being opened up by the pioneers, reports began to come in of a large tribe of 'Red' Indians – the Mandans – whose skins were white and who spoke a language very similar to Welsh. This began a long period of exhaustive research which brought other old records to light; and on the testimony of these a great many people believe that Prince Madoc landed in Alabama in 1170, thus discovering North America more than 300 years before Columbus. And in 1953 a large memorial tablet was erected on the shore of Mobile Bay, Alabama, bearing these words:

'IN MEMORY OF PRINCE MADOC, A WELSH EXPLORER,
WHO LANDED ON THE SHORES OF MOBILE BAY IN 1170
AND LEFT BEHIND, WITH THE INDIANS, THE
WELSH LANGUAGE.'

THE WALK:
TO THE QUAY FROM
WHICH MADOC SAILED
FOR AMERICA

MAP SQUARE D1
O.S. reference 829815
Very easy pavement walking
but worth doing on foot.
1½ hours out and back,
including stops.

*For this simple trip you need to know where to look rather
than where to go. Nothing is the same as it was when Madoc
sailed.*

*Start from Rhos-on-Sea. The free car park in Colwyn
Avenue, just behind the sea-front, makes a good base. Turn
right at exit from car park and in 200 yards you come to the
Marine Drive and turn left with the open sea on your right.
If you have to walk along a 'prom' the Rhos Marine Drive is
as nice as any I know. Look out after 200 yards of it for
what must be the smallest chapel in Wales, down on the
right. A notice says:*

PARISH OF LLANDRILLO-YN-RHOS
ALL REVERENCE IS DUE TO THIS SACRED SPOT
THIS ANCIENT CHAPEL
IS BUILT OVER THE HOLY WELL OF SAINT TRILLO
A CELTIC SAINT OF THE SIXTH CENTURY
PILGRIM TURN IN AND OFFER PRAYER
THE LORD BE WITH YOU.

*Even if you're not a pilgrim, don't fail to 'turn in' — it's
worth a look, at least.*

*But for the memento of Madoc, walk on for another five
minutes, with good views on your right of the Little Orme's
Head jutting out beyond Penrhyn Bay. Soon you see the
golf course on the landward side, opposite the raised
pavement of the sea-front (for golfing fans, there's a grand-*

The garden of the house 'Odstone', Rhos-on-Sea, where Madoc left for America

stand view of the 9th-hole green from here). The last house before you come to the golf course is a big one, named Odstone. Looking into its garden, you see two ornamental pools. These are in what was once the river-bed of the Afon Ganol, where Madoc's ship lay alongside the quay. On the left as you look into the garden is a massive old wall or embankment of stone, now made into a rockery with the entrance drive running along its top. This is the old quay. There's an inscribed tablet on it, visible but not legible from the road. The garden is private, of course — so here is the inscription:

PRINCE MADOC SAILED FROM HERE
ABER-KERRIK-GWYNAN, 1170 A.D.
AND LANDED AT MOBILE, ALABAMA
WITH HIS SHIPS
GORN GWYNANT AND PEDR SANT

It will be noticed that this version speaks of two ships, and has a different spelling for 'Gwennan Gorn'. Still – now you've seen the actual place he sailed from, don't you feel that Prince Madoc may have beaten Columbus to it after all?

BANGOR AND MENAI

The Isle of St Seiriol

*The Lake that no Bird
will cross*

*The Farmer who caught
a Fairy*

THE ISLE OF ST SEIRIOL

No two Saints were ever more friendly than St Cybi and St Seiriol. Both these holy men lived on the Isle of Anglesey (Ongul's Ey as it was then called) in the sixth century; but Cybi lived in the north-west, where Holyhead now stands, and Seiriol lived in the extreme eastern corner nearly thirty miles away. It is told of them that for many years they met every day at the Wells of Clorach, halfway between Caer Gybi – where Cybi was building a church – and Penmon where Seiriol had his cell. Cybi walked fifteen miles south-eastward, with the sun of morning and noon on his face, and Seiriol walked fifteen miles north-westward with the sun behind him. When they parted to walk home again, the sun had crossed the sky. And as a consequence Cybi became dark and sunburned while Seiriol remained pale and fair. To this day they are called in Wales Cybi Felyn (Cybi of the Tawny Hue) and Seiriol Wyn (Seiriol the Fair).

In their later years these meetings ceased, for Cybi was increasingly devoted to his church in the north. So famous had the man and his work become that the northern headland was called Holy Head by the outlanders, though to the Welsh it was still known as Caergybi.

Seiriol, meanwhile, was equally renowned for his holiness and his inspired teaching. It is said that the Norse settlers who then inhabited much of Anglesey flocked to hear him speak and to be baptized, and no doubt as his fame spread the Saint was inconveniently besieged by daily crowds of disciples. He had his humble dwelling by a well (in time a Benedictine Priory was to be built here) but now Seiriol sought a more retired hermitage. Half-a-mile off-shore was a small island, and here he built himself another cell to which he could retreat when he wished to meditate apart from his followers. And so the island was given its first name – Priestholm – by the Norse Christians of Anglesey. Later, after Seiriol's death, it was named Ynys Seiriol by the Welsh; and later still the swarms of puffins – which still come here – earned it the English name of Puffin Island.

Seiriol also had a chapel or hermitage on Penmaenmawr, five miles away beyond the shallows of what is now Conway Bay. And the ancient record that tells of this seems to confirm what some geologists hold to be true: that there was once a tract of sea-marsh and sand between Puffin Island and the mainland of Wales. 'This Seiriol' (says the document) 'hadd an hermytage at Penmaen Mawr, and there hadd a chappell where hee did bestowe much of his tyme in prayers . . . and made from Priestholm to Penmaen Mawr a pavement whereupon hee might walke drye from his church at Priestholm to his chappell at Penmaen Mawr, the vale beynge very lowe grownde and wette, which pave^t may bee discerned from Penmaen Mawr to Priestholm when the sea is cleere, if a man liste to goe in a bote to see itt.'

Of St Seiriol's other accomplishments there is little record. Perhaps, though, it ranks as a very great achievement to be remembered in place-name and story for fourteen hundred years.

THE WALK: MAP SQUARE C1
TO ST SEIRIOL'S WELL   O.S. reference 631808
AND THE COAST   Path, lane, sea-coast. Easy.
BY PUFFIN ISLAND   1½-2 hours.

To reach the start of this little walk, get to the mainland end of the Menai Suspension Bridge first, and cross it – A5 – on to Anglesey; or, as a sign informs you: MON, MAM CYMRU ('Mona, Mother of Wales'). Turn sharp right at the island end of the bridge, on A545. A delightful 7-mile drive follows, through Menai Bridge village and Beaumaris. The ruined Beaumaris Castle, which you see close on the left as you pass through the little town, has a picturesque moat but no battles or sieges in its humdrum history. 1½ miles beyond Beaumaris look out for a right turn signposted PEN-MON 2. The curly lane brings you to another right-turn signpost – PRIORY, BLACK POINT – in about a mile, whence the lane runs right into the precincts of ancient Penmon Priory. (Car parking, 5p fee; by paying three times as much you can take the car right through to the coast, but you'll miss St Seiriol's Well if you do.)

The Priory buildings are interesting, and so is the huge dovecote on the right of the entrance gates beyond. Ministry of Works notices are there to tell you their history in brief. For the Well, go through the lane entrance and turn sharp left (signpost) on a narrow path. A stone doorway in a wall overgrown with massive ivy brings you to St Seiriol's Well, where the holy man used to baptize the converted heathen. The foundations of his cell are a few yards away on the left. On this side also an iron ladder-stile over the wall marks the start of a 20-minute pilgrimage which isn't signposted, to visit a stone cross 1,000 years old. Note that this is an out-and-back pilgrimage, returning past the Well.

Crossing the stile, continue 100 yards with an old limestone quarry face close on your right hand. You join a grassy track going uphill, and a short way up this you'll see the tall cross standing in the middle of a field. The notice beside it says that some of the much-worn carving on it is 'thought to represent the Temptation of St Anthony', and this (to my mind) represents a remarkable flight of imagination on someone's part.

Retracing your steps past St Seiriol's Well to the lane by the entrance, turn left uphill and follow the lane over and down to the point – an easy 15-minute walk. The views are tremendous. From the shores of Black Point, where you'll find the Pilot House Restaurant, you look across half-a-mile of treacherous strait to Ynys Seiriol – or Priestholm, or Puffin Island – and its tower, reputed to stand where Seiriol built one of his hermitages. Penmaenmawr, where he had a second hermitage, can be seen far away to the right; and we assume that Seiriol's causeway connecting the two is sunk below the intervening waters. If you 'list to goe in a bote to see itt', you'll have to hire one at Beaumaris.

Limestone quarries prevent return along the coasts to left and right, but a small variant of the return route can be made. From opposite the lighthouse (whose solemn warning bell has a melodious chime) go left along the tops of the little cliffs – fine picnic places – for 5 minutes and then strike uphill on the crest of a low-relief limestone ridge, thus regaining the lane 10 minutes' walk from the car.

THE LAKE THAT NO BIRD WILL CROSS

In the year 1140 Owain, son of Cynan, was Prince of Gwynedd, a country corresponding to the modern Caernarfonshire and Merionethshire. Owain Gwynedd, as he was called, had nineteen sons, and one of them named Idwal was a very beautiful child. At the time when Idwal was a young boy the Prince of Gwynedd was engaged in a fierce war with Howel King of Powys, and as there was a possibility that the forces of Powys would make murderous foray into Gwynedd, Owain resolved to find some place of safety where Idwal could be hidden. At the same time, he wished to have the boy educated in the arts of poetry and the harp.

After taking the advice of his counsellors and friends, to no avail, he remembered a distant relative who lived in a small mansion in the midst of the craggy wilderness not far from St Curig's Chapel. Nefydd was this man's name, and Owain recalled that he was a bard and harpist of no common order. So young Idwal was sent as foster-son to Nefydd, to live and be instructed among the huge peaks that stand around Llyn Ogwen.

Now this Nefydd was a very handsome man who had grown vainer with the years, so that he called himself Nefydd Hardd – Nefydd the Beautiful. He had a son of Idwal's age, named Dunawt. It was another of Nefydd's vanities to boast that Dunawt would grow up as beautiful as himself, though in fact Dunawt was a very plain youth and as dull in mind as he was homely in countenance. When he and Idwal sat together, as they often did while Nefydd gave them instruction, no one – not even a vain and wilfully blind father – could fail to see that Idwal was incomparably the better-looking of the two. And it was very quickly made clear to Dunawt that his foster-brother was far more clever than he could ever be.

As the days passed into weeks and the weeks into months, the envy and jealousy of both father and son smouldered more hotly until at last it burst into flame.

Taking Dunawt aside, Nefydd suggested that he should lead Idwal into one of the wild mountain recesses to show him the lake that lay there beneath some of the grimmest precipices in Cambria.

'By its west shore the water is deep,' he added. 'If Prince Idwal were to fall in, Dunawt, he would drown, for neither he nor you are able to swim.'

Dunawt was not so dull but he could understand what was proposed. He and Idwal set off up the mountainside and came to the big and gloomy lake between the precipices. They walked along the stony strand and then along the west shore, where smooth rocks overhung the water. A brutal thrust, a few moments of helpless agony, and the thing was done.

When the report of Idwal's death reached Owain Gwynedd he caused inquiry to be made, as a result of which it appeared certain that Idwal had been murdered at Nefydd's order. But the deed could not be proved against him. The Prince of Gwynedd then decreed that Nefydd and his posterity should be degraded from their rank of gentlemen and be bondsmen for ever.

As for the lake where his handsome son was drowned, it was called Llyn Idwal from that time forth, and because of the foul deed that was done there no bird will fly across its dark waters.

THE WALK: MAP SQUARE D2
TO LLYN IDWAL   O.S. reference 645595
                          Rough track, magnificent
                          scenery. 20 minutes to lake.

The walk starts from the top of the Nant Ffrancon pass, at the western end of Llyn Ogwen. This point is just over 9 miles from Bangor on the A5, at a Mountain Centre (Ogwen Cottage) and Rescue Post where the main road reaches 993 feet above sea-level. It's probably best to park a short distance along the lakeside and walk back to the Mountain Centre, which is maintained by the City of Birmingham. At the west side of the building note a *Public Footpath* sign in Welsh and English; *Llwybyr Cyhoeddus,* the Welsh form, is often taken by visitors to signify TOILETS, with sometimes embarrassing consequences.

Follow the direction of the sign, past the building, up a rocky incline, and through a gate. The broad and very stony path beyond mounts gently over open hillside, gradually entering the jaws of a great dent in the flank of the Glyder range of mountains. In about half a mile you pass through another gate and stand at the end of the lake, with Cwm Idwal's giant walls rising round you.

Nowhere in the British Isles can the heart of wild mountains be reached so easily. Llyn Idwal is popular with climbers, walkers, and nature students, but its many visitors can't spoil its grandeur. Y Garn towers above on the right, Glyder Fawr on the left, both mountains over 3,000 feet. The line of cliffs above the farther end of the lake is split down the centre by the giant cleft called the Devil's Kitchen. On your left as you face in this direction are the smaller crags known as the Gribin Facet, where you'll probably see rock-climbers engaged in their sport. The Idwal Slabs, a classic climbing ground, are farther away beyond the head of the lake.

It's possible to walk right round the lake. But in any but the driest weather you're likely to cross boggy bits — fair enough in mountain boots but not in ordinary shoes. My guess is that Dunawt administered the fatal push to Idwal over on your right, where a grey wall of rock drops steeply into the lake. It's a good place to swim from — or to sit and keep watch for any lake-crossing birds who haven't heard of the legend.

THE FARMER WHO CAUGHT A FAIRY

The young farmer of Ystrad, the farm under the sheep-pastures of Moel Eilio, discovered where the fairy maidens used to dance on moonlit nights. It was a small field between the farmhouse and the river. One night he was in his usual hiding-place, watching them, when the most beautiful of them all danced very near to where he was hidden. He sprang out, caught her up in his arms, and ran with her to the house. With shrill cries of despair the rest of the fairies vanished.

The captured fairy was well treated although she was firmly held prisoner, for the young farmer was deep in love with her and wished her to marry him. But for all his protestations, she would grant him nothing. At last she told him that she would be his servant, but only if he could guess what her name was. He tried all the girls' names he could think of, but in vain. Then he bethought him of the dancing-place, and hid himself there once more. As he had hoped, the fairy maidens were dancing that night, and talking together as they danced.

'If only she could be with us!' he heard one of them sigh. 'But she is a prisoner of the humans. Alas, poor Penelope!'

If he had tried for a hundred years the young farmer would never have guessed that name, but now he had it. Hurrying to the house, he greeted the fairy maiden triumphantly by her name, and once more asked her to marry him. Still she would not, though she now undertook to be his servant as she had agreed. With this he had to be content – and indeed there was soon no more contented farmer in all Gwynedd. Everything prospered for him and his fairy servant. The cows gave a full milking three times a day, the flocks and herds multiplied with magical speed, and in a year he was farming (besides his own freehold of Ystrad) all the lands on the north side of Nant-y-Bettws to the top of Snowdon and all Cwmbrwynog in Llanberis, an extent of 5,000 acres.

'Where the fairy maidens used to dance on moonlit nights'

Every night and morning the young farmer asked the fairy maiden to marry him. And at last she consented, with just one condition.

'You must never, never strike me with iron,' she told him. 'If that happens, I must leave you for ever and return to my own people.'

He laughed at that strange condition, for such a blow could not pass between him and his true love. So they were married, and lived happily for several years. Then, one day, the young farmer went to the field to catch the pony, for he and his wife intended to ride to Caernarfon fair that day. The fairy wife went to help him. The pony was mischievous and would not come near the man who held the bridle and bit in his hand, and when the beast had played his tricks for a while the man lost his temper and hurled the bridle at him. It missed the pony and struck his wife.

The instant she felt the cold iron on her cheek she vanished. The last the husband knew of her was a wailing voice, very faint and growing fainter, imploring him to look after their children.

That was the end of the farmer's fairy marriage, but the children of the fairy Penelope grew up and had children of their own. The people of that valley had never been able to get their tongues round the fairy wife's strange name and turned Penelope into Pelling, and now her descendants were called Pellings. As long afterwards as the nineteenth century there were highly-respected Welsh folk who claimed fairy blood, and declared proudly that they were descended from the Pellings of Ystrad.

THE WALK:	MAP SQUARE C2
TO THE MEADOWS OF	O.S. reference 535576
YSTRAD AND NANT MILL	Easy path across fields, pretty
WATERFALL	river garden. About
	1½ hours.

Caernarfon is the setting-out place for this expedition. Take A4085, the Beddgelert road, passing through Waunfawr.

Five miles from Caernarfon you cross a bridge over the little river Gwyrfai, and just beyond it on the left you'll see the church of Betws Garmon. Stop here (roadside parking) opposite a licensed farm-restaurant which has a small caravan park nearby.

The most pleasant way of doing this very short and easy walk is for the car to meet the walkers at the other end, one mile farther along the road where there is a small layby on the right. However, on a sunny day the walk there-and-back by the footpath is enjoyable enough.

There is a green Public Footpath sign beside the buildings of the farm-restaurant. Go through the gate below it, and through the second gate, beyond which is a bridge that once crossed the old narrow-gauge line of the Welsh Highland railway. Don't cross this bridge, but turn left and in 40 paces reach a third gate on the left. Go through this. In about 100 yards you can step through the fence on the left and walk along the old rail track, now a grassy path.

The 'small field between the farmhouse and the river' where the fairies used to dance must have been somewhere here, for if you look across to the left you'll see the old farmhouse of Ystrad a little way up the slopes of Moel Eilio, with trees round it. You can also see, higher up and to the left, the gaping shafts of the disused mines, whose opening no doubt chased away the last fairy from Ystrad.

Soon you cross Afon Gwyrfai by an iron railway bridge from which you can look down into the clear water and (perhaps) see brown trout or even a salmon. Ahead the flat river meadows begin to narrow. You pass in front of a house, then along a straight stretch of stone embankment. Just above on the right there is a moss-grown 'strongpoint', relic of the invasion fears of World War Two; young explorers usually find this exciting. Go under the bridge beyond, stepping over a barrier, and at once turn left, with a step over a wire fence. This brings you in a few yards to a lane and a very old bridge crossing the river. Down on your left are the gardens of the Nant Mill waterfall, miniature indeed but really charming. When you emerge on the main road in a few more paces (*the layby already mentioned is to your right*) turn left, and you can enter the gardens.

A notice on the gate says '*PRIVATE, BUT YOU ARE INVITED TO PASS THROUGH*', and the word *Welcome* is set in white pebbles on the path. In these days of access squabbles and enclosure of National Park land it's a heartening thing to find a private owner opening his land freely to visitors. The foaming river and the pretty paths are not the only attractions here. A famous sight from May onwards are the elvers, immature eels, here to be seen wriggling up the waterfall on their way to Cwellyn Lake, after (*believe it or not*) a 3-year journey from the Sargasso Sea where they were born.

If you walk back to the starting-point, do so by the same route and not by the road, which is unsafe for walkers in the holiday season. If a car is in the layby to meet you, you could drive on along the shore of Cwellyn Lake – only ½-mile from Nant Mill waterfall – where there are places for a picnic.

LLEYN AND
TREMADOC BAY

The Rising of the Lark

Helen's Spring

The Accursed Village

THE RISING OF THE LARK

They say that when David Owen, a young and gifted Bard, lay dying, he called for his harp, saying that he had just heard one of the sweetest songs of heaven. The harp was brought. And in the short time before he died the harpist played the famous tune Dafydd y Garreg Wen, 'David of the White Rock', to which in after years Sir Walter Scott wrote the English words. That was in the year 1749, and David Owen was then 29 years old. A less melancholy story is told of his earlier years, and concerns another of his famous compositions.

The name 'Borth-y-Gest' signifies 'the port of the land of Gest'; for the district westward along the coast from the mouth of the Glaslyn river was called Gest. In the eighteenth century small coasting vessels plied to and from Borth-y-gest, many of them hailing from France or Spain and carrying wines and silks, tobacco and spirits – cargoes that would show a very handsome profit if they could be sold without passing through the Customs. (Some of this contraband, it is said, found its way as far inland as Chirk, where it stocked the cellars of the great Sir Watkin Wynn.) In these days there lived at Borth-y-gest a retired sea-captain named Captain Williams, who grew fat on the profit from the contraband trade and was always known as Captain Williams the Smuggler. The Smuggler's house, Plas-y-Borth, was more like a tavern than a private house on most evenings, for he loved to hold a noson lawen, a 'merry evening', at which there would be music and dancing, and the wine and cwrw da (good ale) would flow freely. The heart and soul of the noson lawen was David Owen, the young harpist and composer of songs.

David's home was the farm Y Garreg Wen, so named from the big pale-coloured rock that stood solitary on the hill just above it. The hill was between the farmhouse and the little port, and David was accustomed to walk that way on his visits to the Smuggler's house. One night in

Borth-y-Gest. The 'White Rock' is on the hillside to the right of the picture

late Spring the noson lawen at Plas-y-Borth was over and David Owen was making his way back home by the familiar path over the hill. There had been song after song, and dance after dance, until the harpist's fingers were weary; but his skill had won him clamorous applause – and innumerable mugs of ale provided by his admirers. Indeed, his cargo of cwrw da impelled David to lie down and go to sleep, though he had reached the top of the hill and had only a few hundred yards to go to reach the farmhouse.

When he woke it was near sunrise of a May morning. He was lying on the dewy grass close to the side of the White Rock, with the distant mountains ranged against the glowing east. High above his head a lark, its wings tipped with golden light, was carrying its song far into the misty blue of the sky. In that moment of wonder David

conceived the melody and words of Codiad yr Ehedydd,
'The Rising of the Lark', a song whose gaiety and tune-
fulness quickly made it popular through all Wales. You
will hear it sung at a noson lawen today. And it was
adopted as the regimental march of the Welsh Guards.

THE WALK: MAP SQUARE C2/3
TO THE WHITE ROCK   O.S. reference 560374
                              Moderately short and easy.
                              1 hour, or 1½ if extended as
                              suggested.

*Borth-y-gest, from which this walk starts, is less than a mile
from Portmadoc, with delightful sandy coves (care needed
with children bathing) just beyond the small bay. No through
road. Leave the car in the car park (fee for parking) on the
west side of the bay, and walk from the car park entrance up
the steep hill of Mersey Street, which has a shop and post
office on the right near the bottom and the village school at
the top. When you are nearly at the top, turn right, with the
wall of the school playground on your left. The broad lane
turns sharply left round the corner of a school annexe and
becomes a narrow path, between bushes and then up a brackeny hillside. It leads to a stone wall with a large wooden
gate, padlocked. For some time it has been intended to erect a
stile here and by the time you reach the spot one may have
been provided. In any case, it is easy to climb over the gate;
which, incidentally, commands a glimpse of the open sea on
the left.*

   *Beyond the gate, take the faint path that goes straight on
for 100 yards to strike a broad curving track connecting
caravan emplacements. Turn left up this, and in a dozen
paces you will see, close on your right, a wooden stile crossing
a barbed-wire fence. Go over the stile. The White Rock is 50
yards ahead on the open green hill-crest.*

   *The view from the Garreg Wen is worth more than a
quick glance. If it is clear, you can see the Lleyn Peninsula
and the Rivals; Moel Hebog; Moel Ddu and the shoulder of*

Lliwedd above the wooded hill on the north; the tip of Cnicht, and the Moelwyns; Borth-y-gest below with Manod Mawr and the Ffestiniog valley beyond; and across the estuary the Rhinog range with Harlech Castle below. There used to be a tablet on the White Rock inscribed with the opening line of David Owen's song – Cwyd, cwyd, ehedydd, cwyd – but some years ago it was destroyed by vandals.

To vary the return route, try the slightly longer way that follows. Go back over the stile to the broad caravan track and turn to the right along it – Criccieth Castle is seen straight ahead, four miles distant – but only walk for a few paces. You will see, sharp on your left, half-a-dozen caravans in a small glen. Go down the glen between the caravans. There is a lookout rock with a fine sea view at its lower end, and from below this a steep and narrow path drops down through the thickets to emerge on a broad lane opposite a cottage gate with the name BORTH FECHAN. Turn left along this lane for 50 paces, then turn right down another narrow path heading for the coast. Bear left when this forks. You will quickly come to the Beach Cafe and the coastal path that runs above the Borth-y-gest beaches. Turn left along this path and you can reach the car park in 10 minutes.

HELEN'S SPRING

It is related that in the fourth century A.D. the Roman legions in Britain were commanded by Magnus Maximus, who in defiance of Rome declared himself Emperor of Britain. In the Roman city of Segontium, which stood where Caernarfon now stands, the Emperor Maximus wooed and won the beautiful Welsh princess Elen, afterwards known as Queen Helen of the Hosts because of her fondness for marching with her husband's legions. Helen was anxious that her countrymen throughout all Wales should be able to communicate freely with each other, and to this end she persuaded the Emperor to construct a paved road through the mountains from north to south of the country. Parts of that road were to endure for fifteen hundred years, known to the Welsh as Sarn Elen, or Helen's Causeway; and as Sarn Elen it appears on the Ordnance Survey maps of the twentieth century.

Queen Helen had two sons, both of whom grew up to hold command in the Emperor's army. Her favourite was the younger. One day Helen was journeying southward from Segontium with a large escort of legionaries, passing Llyn Cwellyn and marching thence through the Pass of Aberglaslyn in the direction of Ffestiniog. A separate body of soldiers followed some distance behind, as a rearguard. This rearguard was commanded by Helen's younger son.

Beyond Aberglaslyn the Roman road climbed from Nantmor over the foot of Cnicht. Then, as now, it was a toilsome ascent, and when the Queen's party reached a spring a little way down on the other side Helen sat down to rest and drink the pure cold water. While she was still resting here, a breathless man came clattering down the stony trail, bringing tragic news from the rearguard.

What had happened was this: the track along the shore of Cwellyn lake passed below a grim crag called Castell Cidwm, where the giant Cidwm was reputed to live as in a fortress. No sign of the giant had been seen by Helen

73

From Croesor, to Helen's Spring. Take the lane and go through a gate
on the left

and her escort, and they had journeyed on unmolested.
But as the rearguard came beneath the frowning precipice
an arrow – presumably shot by Cidwm – had sped down
from the crags and killed Helen's favourite son.

There were many who whispered, afterwards, that it
was the jealous elder brother who had shot the arrow,
trusting that the fabled giant of the crag would be
blamed. Perhaps Queen Helen herself suspected that this
might be the terrible truth, for a great cry broke from her
in her native tongue: 'Croes awr – croes awr i mi!'
('Cursed hour – cursed hour to me!') And from this cry
the spot took its name of Croesawr or Croesor; so that
when – centuries later – a small village sprang up near
Ffynnon Elen, as the spring was called, the name Croesor
was transferred to the village. And both Croesor and
Ffynnon Elen are there at the foot of Cnicht mountain,
overlooking Traeth Mawr, to this day.

Helen's spring appears to have dried up!

THE WALK:
TO FFYNNON ELEN

MAP SQUARE C2
O.S. reference 629448
Short and easy. ½-hour –
but worth extending for a
picnic.

*To reach the village of Croesor by car from Portmadoc, take
A498 as if for Beddgelert but turn right on B4410 two miles
beyond Tremadoc. This joins A4085 at the village of
Garreg. Turn left at the junction, through the village, and
look out for a mediaeval-seeming archway on the right
rather less than ¼-mile from the junction. (There is a signpost, Croesor.) Turn right here and follow the charming
uphill lane, narrow but with passing-places, for 2½ miles. At
the top of a steep hill the village appears suddenly on the
left, and is reached by turning left at a crossroads of lanes.*

If driving from the north (Beddgelert) direction, turn left

The cattle-trough is said to be supplied with water from Helen's Spring across *Aberglaslyn* bridge and left again when you reach the archway three miles farther on.

The car can be left in *Croesor* village, which has no motorable through road. A lane turns off below the conspicuous chapel, heading towards a pointed mountain in the distance – *Cnicht*; the village post office is on the corner of this lane. Go along it for 30 yards, then go through an iron gate on the left that leads to a green slope between the cottages. The slope soon narrows to a pathway curling round a knoll into a small field. Cross the field to a gap in the wall, by an iron gate, and turn right, on a stony lane beneath trees. (The animal drinking-trough in the field is supplied from *Ffynnon Elen*.) A little iron gate on the right guards a sunken water-tank, put there when the old spring was diverted to make a water supply for *Croesor* village. Go on 36 yards past the gate, and in the wall on your left you will see the mossy mouth of the spring from which Queen Helen of the Hosts drank long ago.

In dry weather no water flows here now; the diversion has sent the flow of the spring underground, and only after plenty of rain does the small mossy opening show itself as an active *ffynnon*.

You could return to the car in 10 minutes by going back to the gap in the wall and instead of turning through it taking the metalled lane beyond the iron gate. But this short walk is well worth extending by continuing up the stony track beyond Helen's Spring. In 5 minutes or a little more you emerge on a miniature pass, with a grand view of *Moel Hebog*, the *Eifionydd* mountains, and – nearer on your right – the heathery crags of *Yr Arddu*. You could picnic near here. Or, better still, go on for another 10 minutes along the same track, downhill to an ideal picnic spot by the little river *Dylif*, where a bridge of huge stone slabs crosses the water.

THE ACCURSED VILLAGE

A very long time ago three holy men, barefooted monks from the neighbourhood of St Beuno's shrine, clambered down the craggy defile leading to Nant Gwrtheyrn, intending to preach the Christian gospel to the villagers in the remote hamlet at the sea's edge. Now the chief man of Nant Gwrtheyrn village was a pagan, and he would have none of the monk's gospel. Instead, he and his henchmen drove the three holy ones with stones and curses back up the glen to its precipitous rim. Then it was the turn of the monks for cursing, and each of them placed his own curse on the village at the foot of the glen. No one who was born in the village, cried one monk, should ever lie in consecrated ground after death. No male and female born therein should ever be able to marry each other, said another. And the third monk declared that at last the village of Nant Gwrtheyrn would decay and die, to become for ever a deserted ruin.

The years and the generations passed, and time showed that the first two of these curses, at least, were effective. The men of Nant Gwrtheyrn, who were mostly fishermen, died by drowning or by falling from the cliffs into deep water, and their bodies were not recovered. By similar chances the women, too, failed to achieve burial in the only consecrated ground in those parts, namely, St Beuno's churchyard at Clynnog. By now they were all Christians at Nant Gwrtheyrn, and the women – fearful of the curses – customarily left the village when they were of an age to marry; while the men sought their wives from places outside the valley.

There came a time, two or three hundred years ago, when a youth and a maiden who had both been born in the village resolved to defy the curse and marry. All went well at first. The two exchanged presents on their wedding-morning (the bride's present to her man was a puppy-dog) and the sun shone brightly down through the branches of the ancient oaks which then grew near the

78

village. The old tradition was followed – that the bride should feign bashfulness and hide herself, so that the bridegroom and his friends could seek her out and carry her off to the church. But when the groom's party came to look for the girl she was not to be found. They hallooed, they sought for hours. At nightfall she was still missing. Next day the distracted bridegroom and all the villagers sought high and low; and the next day; and the next. But she was gone, and for ever. It was thought she had fallen from the cliffs into the sea, and was drowned, so that the curse should remain unbroken.

The poor bridegroom, broken-hearted and bereft of reason, paced every day up and down the shore with the dog, her wedding gift, in his arms. Month by month, year by year, he spent his time in this way; until the people of the village discovered that the dog he had carried about for so long was dead. They flung the body into the sea. And next day the man, too, was gone – drowned.

The years passed, but the tragic story was still remembered in Nant Gwrtheyrn. There came a night of terrible storm, with lightning smiting the cliffs above the village and rocks crashing down. A thunderbolt struck one of the old oaks near the village, splitting it open. In the morning, when the folk came to look at it, they saw that the tree had been hollow, and that a skeleton was gripped, as in a vice, by the narrow depths of that hollow trunk: a skeleton with long silky hair. They knew, then, where the bride in the old story had hidden herself.

The skeleton was placed reverently in a coffin, and a horse was harnessed to drag it up the precipitous ascent so that it could be taken to St Beuno's church for burial. But at the very top of the ascent, where the path ran along the cliff edge, the horse stumbled and fell down the precipice. The coffin was smashed into matchwood. And the bones of that skeleton were so scattered and lost among the boulders that there was no possibility of burial in ground consecrated or unconsecrated.

Still the years passed. Roads and quarries brought new

Nant Gwrtheyrn

life to the north coast under the heights of Yr Eifl, and a thriving new village sprang up in Nant Gwrtheyrn. There were fine stone cottages, fertile gardens, a school, and a chapel. When the nineteenth century turned into the twentieth this was a happy community, fortunately situated and caring little for the old dark legends of centuries gone by. What, then, of the third curse?

Go to Nant Gwrtheyrn today, and see. The fine stone cottages, the school, the chapel, the gardens – they are still there; the gardens all brambles and nettles, the buildings all broken and uninhabited. The curse of the third monk has come upon Nant Gwrtheyrn, and it is a dead village, a deserted ruin.

THE WALK: TO NANT GWRTHEYRN	MAP SQUARE C2/3 O.S. reference 350450 Good track but very steep. 900 feet to go down and come up again. Leave high heels and the Under Eights in the car.

The village of Llithfaen, on the southern slopes of the Rivals (Yr Eifl, their Welsh name, means 'the fork') is the first objective for this walk. To reach it from Portmadoc and Criccieth, follow A497 through Llanystumdwy but bear right 1¼ miles farther on, taking B4354 through Chwilog to Four Crosses where you keep straight on across A499. From Pwllheli, leave the town on A499 and at Four Crosses (3 miles) turn left on B4354. Three miles beyond Four Crosses is a crossroads where Llithfaen is signposted, to the left on a minor road heading towards the bold shapes of the Rivals. Two and a half miles of this bring you uphill to Llithfaen; keep straight on over the village crossroads, steeply uphill. The lane, unfenced now, emerges on heathery slopes above the sea ½-mile beyond Llithfaen. A right fork mounts along the hillside, but take the short left fork to an obvious parking-place on the left of the lane, and leave the car here.

You are 922 feet above sea-level. The highest peak of the Rivals, 1,949 feet, rises above and you may just make out, on its summit, part of the Iron Age hill-fort called Tre'r Ceiri, the Town of the Giants. Walk on from the parking-place, downhill, through a gateway with a cattle-grid in it, and Nant Gwrtheyrn opens quite suddenly below you.

At the first corner of the steep descent it is clear that the notice higher up – UNSUITABLE FOR MOTORS – is no exaggeration! Except from the sea and the beach, this is the only approach to the deep glen below and that could be the real reason why the village is uninhabited today. In 20 minutes you are down at the village, and as you approach it the place looks (like the farmhouse higher up) as though it is lived in and cared for. A few paces nearer, and you perceive that the sturdy stone cottages are windowless and desolate. The chapel – Seilo – bears the date 1878. In 1948 there was still a congregation here on Sundays, and children attending the village school. Then the quarrymen and their families left, and only one cottage remained inhabited – by the coast-guard. A dozen years ago he, too, found another home; and the only inhabitants since then have been the 'hippies' who made Nant Gwrtheyrn their temporary residence in 1970.

Only the disused quarries and their debris prevent the glen from being both scenic and charming. As it is, the beach – 5 minutes below the village – gives excellent bathing and there are good picnic spots.

It took one middle-aged couple 35 minutes to get up again from the village to the car.

SNOWDON

The Story of Gelert

King Arthur's Last Battle

Glendower's Chimney

THE STORY OF GELERT

Llewelyn, the son of Iorwerth Drwyndwn, was a Prince of Wales in the twelfth century, a man as renowned for his skill in battle as for his delight in hunting. In summer he would often reside with his family in a hunting lodge at the foot of Snowdon, near where the village of Beddgelert now stands. He had many dogs, but his favourite was Gelert, who was not only courageous in hunting the boar and the wolf but also a friend of the whole family – 'a lamb at home, a lion in the chase'.

One day the Prince and his Princess went out hunting with their followers, leaving their baby son in charge of a nurse and one servant. The nurse, as it turned out, was a scatterbrain unworthy of trust, for no sooner had her master and mistress ridden away to the sound of cheerful noises from the huntsman's horn than she and the servant went off for a walk on the hills. The baby, son and heir to Prince Llewelyn, was left in his cradle, quite alone.

Meanwhile the hunt ranged far and wide, until it was noticed that Gelert was no longer among the dogs. The Prince was uneasy. Gelert was always foremost on the scent and first into the attack. Why had he abandoned the party – and where would he go, except back to the house? Llewelyn commanded an end to the chase and bade his followers return with him and his wife. They rode swiftly back and reached the hunting-lodge. And as they were dismounting, Gelert came running out of the house, covered with blood and wagging his tail.

The Princess, shrieking the name of her child, swooned away. Llewelyn rushed into the room where the baby had been – to find the cradle overturned, the bedclothes piled in a bloodstained heap, and no sign of his infant son. It seemed to him that the dog must have killed the child. Blind with sorrow and fury, he drew his sword and drove it through poor Gelert, who gave a piercing yell as he died. Like a small echo, there came a shrill crying from beneath the cradle. One of the Prince's followers lifted

The beginning of the path to Gelert's grave

the cradle, and there beneath it, quite unhurt, was the baby. Then Llewelyn pulled aside the pile of bedclothes, revealing the lifeless carcass of an enormous wolf, terrible even in death.

The Prince wept tears of remorse at this discovery. He owed his child's life to Gelert's keen instinct and courage,

Gelert's grave is to the left of the picture, this side of the church

and he had rewarded the faithful dog with a fatal sword-stroke. Resolving that Gelert should be remembered as long as there were men and dogs on this earth, he caused the dog to be buried in a green meadow nearby, and the place marked with stones and shown to all who came.

A village sprang up in later years, and this was called Bedd Gelert, the Grave of Gelert. And eight hundred years after Prince Llewelyn's over-hasty deed there may still be found, every year, a few visitors who fulfil his wish:

> 'A pious monument I'll rear
> In memory of the brave;
> And passers-by will drop a tear
> On faithful Gelert's grave.'

THE WALK: MAP SQUARE C/D2
TO GELERT'S GRAVE   O.S. reference 592478
                            Short and easy. 45 minutes;
                            or 1½ hours if extended.

Beddgelert is at the junction of A487 and A498, 4 miles south of Snowdon. The free car park is close to the Royal Goat Hotel, where A498 heads south from the village towards Portmadoc. Park the car here, and turn left at the car park entrance to walk down through the village to the bridge by which the road crosses the River Colwyn. Turn right immediately before the bridge, along a broad lane that has the river on its left just beyond the wall. This lane quickly ends at a footbridge crossing the River Glaslyn (into which the Colwyn stream flows here) with a small gate on the right, before you step on to the footbridge, signposted TO GELERT'S GRAVE.

Through the small gate is a delightful path following the riverside downstream, under trees. After going along it for 250 yards take the path on the right – the only one – running straight between wire fences and leading to the grave of Gelert, which can be seen from the turning. Beneath a small sycamore tree, fenced by railings, is a large slate slab inscribed with a brief version of the legend.

Modern research has discredited the story of Gelert, and prefers the theory that the village is named for a saint or hermit called Kelert, who was buried near here. However, archaeologists are quite often wrong. And as you read the words carved on the slab you will probably find yourself deciding that this really is the grave of poor Gelert – even if you don't drop a tear on it.

This very short walk is well worth extending. Return as far as the river bank and there turn right, downstream, along the bank of the Glaslyn. This is a public right-of-way. In 10 minutes you come to the iron girder bridge by which the old narrow-gauge Welsh Highland Railway used to cross the river. Cross this (it is a footbridge now) and turn left on the other side, to follow the river upstream by its true left bank. There are many good picnic places on this side. If not stopping for lunch, allow about 20 minutes for the walk from the girder bridge to the footbridge, which you cross to the GELERT'S GRAVE *signpost where you started the footpath part of the walk. From here to the car park is 5–10 minutes.*

The extended walk could be rewarding for any bird-lover who keeps his eyes open. The last time I did it was in mid-September, and I spotted heron, grey wagtail, dipper, and (believe it or not) a goldcrest, smallest of all European birds.

KING ARTHUR'S LAST BATTLE

The great days of the Round Table were over. Arthur and his knights had succeeded in driving the pagan Saxons back into England, and the mailed champions who had charged under the Red Dragon banner were dispersed. King Arthur himself was no longer young; and there were those, among them the treacherous Sir Modred, who whispered that it was time a new king ruled in Britain. Modred sent a message secretly to the leader of the Saxons, in eastern England, appointing a meeting-place in the mountains of North Wales. If the Saxon army would join him there, he said, he would raise a second army and together they would make an end of King Arthur and his power.

Arthur was in his palace at Caerleon-upon-Usk when news of the renewed Saxon invasion was brought to him. Swiftly he gathered as many of his knights as he could find, including the faithful Sir Bedivere who had never left him, and marched northward. When he reached Dinas Emrys, a mile beyond Beddgelert up the Gwynant valley, a man of the valley told him that the great host of Saeson was encamped beneath the walls of the old city of Tregalan, in the upper part of Cwm Llan. So King Arthur and the remnant of his chivalry advanced up this deep valley that lies under the central summit of Snowdon.

The battle that followed lasted all that day. It was a winter's day, and from grey morning to grey evening the clash of steel and the battle-shout and the moans and screams of wounded men filled the wide cwm and echoed dismally from its crags. Hour by hour, foot by foot, the King's warriors forced their enemies farther into the cwm, and up the rocky hillside towards the crest of the precipice between Snowdon and Lliwedd. At nightfall the struggle had reached the crest. But it was a small and weary struggle now, for very few men were left alive. And here, in the gathering darkness of winter, King Arthur met his death.

Some say that a chance arrow slew Arthur, one of a last volley shot by the Saxons; and that Bwlch-y-Saethau, the Pass of the Arrows, was so called because of it. Others say that it was Modred himself that killed the King. Both, it seems, were sorely wounded when they met in the twilight on Bwlch-y-Saethau. Modred got in his blow first, and it was a death-blow. But Arthur lifted his own sword, Excalibur, and with one last great stroke clove through steel helm and skull and brain. Modred fell. And Arthur, near to death, fell beside him.

Then Sir Bedivere carried him precariously down the crags to the shores of Llydaw, and there a black barge, wherein sat three beautiful women, waited. The dying King was borne away into the night mist, while such of his warriors as survived the battle made their way into a cave on the precipice-face of Lliwedd, there to await the second coming of their royal leader.

THE WALK:	MAP SQUARE D2
TO LLYN LLYDAW	O.S. reference 628544
	Easy. About 3 miles out and
	back. Allow 2 hours.

The top of the Llanberis Pass is on A4086, six miles from Llanberis and five miles from Capel Curig. From Beddgelert, following A498 and turning left at Pen-y-gwryd, the distance is nine miles. There is a large car park (fee) but it is as well to get there early at holiday time because the cars of those starting out to climb Snowdon are parked here. This walk, on a broad track all the way, takes you as far into the heart of Snowdon as you can reasonably go without proper boots and clothing for mountains.

From the car park (near which there is a restaurant) follow the wide, gently-climbing track across the mountainside. There are sure to be other people on it, for this is the Miners'

Path that leads to the ascent of Snowdon by 'The Zigzags', above Glaslyn. The track gives a downward glimpse of the upper Gwynant valley before it curls round the flank on the right. Now it descends slightly past a small lake, Llyn Teyrn, beside which you see the ruins of the tiny houses where the men who worked the old copper-mines of Snowdon used to live, going home at weekends. Beyond Llyn Teyrn it climbs again, still curving into the high glen walled by steep mountains that slowly opens ahead. When you come to Llyn Llydaw you see one of the grandest of all views of Snowdon summit, for Yr Wyddfa – as the highest point in England and Wales is called – rises magnificently beyond the far end of the lake.

The track goes to the right, crossing an arm of the lake by a stone causeway. (In winter, or after very heavy rain, the causeway may be partly under water.) Follow the track round the lake shore past the old copper mine and halt where it begins to climb steeply from the waterside. This is your terminus, for the return is made by the same route. And from here you can see the setting for the final acts of the King Arthur legend.

The huge precipice of Lliwedd looms opposite across the lake; its crest is 2,947 feet above sea-level. The lower crest to the right of it, separating it from the upsurge of Snowdon summit, is Bwlch-y-Saethau, the Pass of the Arrows, where the heathen hordes were driven back over the edge and where Arthur and Modred fought their last fight. It must have been by that precipitous way down the ridge to your right that Bedivere carried his dying master to the lake shore and the waiting barge, for the crags under Bwlch-y-Saethau are too steep for such work.

As for the last of the Round Table knights, they must have been good rock-climbers as well as stout fighters. The cave they are supposed to have entered is in the groove to the right of the central part of the precipice (hardly to be seen from below) and even a mountain goat would find it difficult to reach it from the crest where King Arthur's last battle was fought.

GLENDOWER'S CHIMNEY

'Glyndwr's Gully. 250 feet.
First Ascent, Owain Glyndwr, circa 1400.'

This entry in the rock-climbing guidebook to Moel Hebog seems to confirm that the great Welsh leader, head of the rebellion against Henry IV of England, did the first recorded Welsh rock-climb. Here is how it happened.

Owen Glendower (to use the English form of the hero's name) was at the lowest ebb of his changing fortunes. His makeshift army was dispersed, his lands were in the possession of his enemies, and he himself was being hunted through Snowdonia by bands of King Henry's soldiers. Giving his pursuers the slip, he crossed the mountains into Nant Colwyn, and there found refuge in the house of an old friend named Rhys Goch – Red Rhys.

Hafod Garegog was the name of the house, and it stood in a lonely glen facing across the valley towards Moel Hebog, with no other dwelling near it. Before long, however, the news leaked out that a distinguished stranger was the guest of Red Rhys, and those who sought to kill or capture Owen Glendower heard it. There came a day when a servant of Rhys Goch dashed up to Hafod Garegog to report that a large party of soldiers in light armour and carrying swords was approaching the house. Rhys and Owen swiftly dressed themselves in servants' clothing and made for the open mountainsides, Rhys heading for Nantmor and Owen running towards Aberglaslyn and the sea. But if they had hoped to puzzle the pursuers their hope was swiftly disappointed, for Owen was recognized at once and the men-at-arms concentrated on cutting off his escape.

The Welsh rebel leader had now no chance of using the sea to win his way to freedom. He must turn for help to his native mountains. The wide semicircle of his hunters was almost within bowshot behind him as he clambered at top speed up the mountainside above the woods of Aberglaslyn. Close above frowned the line of precipices

Moel Hebog from Beddgelert

rimming the crest of Moel Hebog, the Hill of the Hawk, and Owen made for the left-hand end of these where a bald shoulder offered the only safe way over the mountain. Before he could reach it there was a hoarse, triumphant yell and he found his way barred by half-a-dozen soldiers. Desperate now, he made straight upward at the best of his failing speed, at last reaching the sloping walls of scree that buttressed the vertical crags overhead. The breathless shouts of his pursuers sounded close below him.

There was only one chance of escape now, and that an unlikely one: the vertical precipice was split by a cleft or chimney, nearly three hundred feet from top to bottom. If Owen could not get up it he was a dead man. He toiled up the scree with the hunt at his heels and launched himself at the steep rock. It gave Owen Glendower safe hold for hand and foot, but none of the pursuing soldiers would dare an ascent where one slip meant death. While their quarry climbed on up the chimney, King Henry's men scrambled off to the left to gain the crest by an easier way. And when they reached it, there was no sign of Owen, on the ridge or on the summit of Moel Hebog. Certain that he had fled downwards into Cwm Pennant on the farther side of the mountain, the soldiers hurried down and spent the rest of the day searching that valley.

They searched in vain. For Owen, after emerging at the top of his chimney, had run along the ridge to the verge of the northern precipice, Y Diffwys, and climbing down it a little way had hidden himself securely in a cave. And so the bold Welshman lived to fight another day.

THE WALK:	MAP SQUARE C2
TO THE SCENE OF	O.S. reference 585475
GLENDOWER'S ESCAPE	Easy. Allow 1½ hours. Fine views on a clear day.

This walk starts (like the Gelert's Grave walk) from the free car park at Beddgelert, which is close to the Royal Goat Hotel. Turn right when you come out of the car park and go straight up through the open yard of the hotel – a right-of-

way – passing through gaps in two walls just above it. A grassy track mounts gently beyond, quickly reaching a small bridge over the cutting once used by the little Welsh Highland Railway. Climb over the wooden stile at the other end of the bridge. As you do so, you see Moel Hebog directly above. The cliffs up which Owen Glendower escaped are those to the left of the highest point, and a 'step' in their skyline marks the top of Glendower's Chimney.

Beyond the stile, turn to the right between stone walls. The grassy track bends left in a few minutes, to go through an iron gate, cross a small bridge over a stream, and join a metalled lane. (If you turned right here you could be back at the car in 15 minutes.) Turning left up the lane brings you to a pine glade. When the lane emerges from it you will see, peering down from high above, the upper part of Y Diffwys where Owen hid in a cave after his chimney climb.

Now the lane bends left round the old farmhouse of Cwm Cloch Uchaf, and 150 yards farther on up the hill it curls left and then right to get past some farm buildings. Here the peaks of the Moelwyn range come in sight ahead. In a few minutes more the lane ends at a gate with a Private notice on it; but a large signpost on the left, BEDDGELERT, shows you the way, which is straight down the rough field below the lane. As you begin the descent there is a noble view before you – the graceful peak of Moel Siabod framed between the rocky sides of Nant Gwynant, with Beddgelert's houses in the trees below.

A little way down the slope, bear right through a gap in the stone wall. There is only a faint track here, but by keeping straight down you can't go wrong. The way goes under trees and down by two narrow wall-gaps where there is a path with steps. 100 yards below the second gap there is an iron post and sign, CWM CLOCH, and close to it a small iron gate. Go through the iron gate and to the left, keeping near the wall on your left until a track bears slightly to the right. In less than 5 minutes from the post and sign you reach the wooden stepladder at the bridge. And from here it is a 5-minute downhill stroll to car park and car.

FISHGUARD AND
TENBY

The French Invasion

The Lost Land of Rhys Ddwfn

Saint Teilo's Skull

The Old Maid of Kidwelly

THE FRENCH INVASION

The British Isles were doomed. So declared the Directory of the seven-year-old French Republic. England could not stand against the combined fleets of France and Spain which (when certain delays had been overcome) would surely sweep every British warship from the seas. Meanwhile, the cowardly British aristocrats and their slavish peasants should have a foretaste of the Terror that was in store for them. A powerful raid, the most brutal that could be devised, should be made on the western coasts. To make it extra terrifying, the raiding army should be called the Black Legion and wear black uniforms.

On February 17th 1797 this fearsome force sailed from Brest in a lugger and a corvette escorted by two frigates. It consisted of several hundred released jailbirds and galley-slaves under the command of an American adventurer of blood-curdling reputation named Colonel Tate, who was ordered by the Directory to land and 'burn Bristol, the second city in England for riches and commerce', and thereafter to land in Wales, march across the mountains, and do the same to Chester and Liverpool. His collection of blackguards was to have a free hand in raping and looting.

Into the Bristol Channel sailed the raiders – to turn tail at the first sight of what they thought was a warship but what was in fact the Dublin packet-boat. On, then, for Wales! Off the lonely village of Fishguard they anchored on February 22nd and the boatloads of ruffians pulled ashore to land in a rocky cove below Carregwastad Point and prepare for their programme of killing and burning. The four vessels had been seen, however, and the alarm given. The local British aristocrat, Lord Cawdor, mustered his 'slavish peasants', who had been formed into the eighteenth-century equivalent of the Home Guard. Castle Martin Yeomanry, Cardigan Militia, and Fishguard Volunteers they called themselves, and as they marched hastily seaward from the village of Llanwnda the women of the village, donning their red flannel shawls to protect them against the cold February wind, hurried after them to see the fighting.

By now Colonel Tate had got his Black Legion to the stony crest of Carregwastad Point. As the volunteers advanced they saw that the black-clad army outnumbered them by three to one, but they came on boldly, handling their muskets like men who meant business. Colonel Tate, looking beyond them across the hilly countryside, saw what he took to be the red coats of the regular infantry coming up in the rear. He told his Black Legion to stand firm, walked forward to meet Lord Cawdor, and surrendered himself and his army unconditionally – 'upon principles of humanity', he explained afterwards. (One can't help thinking that he was hardly the man for the job.) After that, the main problem of the volunteers was to prevent the enraged Welsh villagers from cutting the throats of their unwieldy crowd of prisoners as they were marched away to Cardigan jail.

This is history. Where then is the legend? Well, historians have been able to prove – to their own satisfaction – that the surrender of the French was *not* due to their mistaking the red shawls for red uniforms. For my part, I think the legend makes more sense than the proof against it, for it gives a reason, of a kind, for Tate's surrender. At any rate, the tale of the red shawls is no more incredible than the farcical adventures of the Black Legion.

THE WALK:	MAP SQUARE A6
TO CARREGWASTAD	O.S. reference 157/926406
POINT	Easy lane and path.
	1 hour there and back.

This Walk starts from Tre-Howel, a beautiful old farmhouse in the network of lanes behind Strumble Head. To find it is quite simple. Drive through Fishguard nearly to Fishguard Harbour, turning left, signpost 'Llanwnda', up the steep hill through Goodwick. Now follow the signposts for Strumble Head until you reach one reading 'Strumble Head 2¼', a little over three miles from Fishguard Harbour. A quarter of a mile uphill beyond it you come to a wide gateway on the right plainly marked TRE-HOWEL. Park the car on the lane verge by the gate.

All this Walk is a public right-of-way but there are no signs. Going down towards the front of the farmhouse, turn right through a gateway and cross a concreted farmyard to a gate on the other side, which opens on a lane. Follow this lane, bearing left in 100 yards and then straight on towards the sea. At the end of the straight stretch bear right, to arrive at the end of the lane where there are two gates. Go through the left-hand gate and up the edge of a field to the two gaps you can see just above. Passing through the left-hand gap, you come to a gorse-y common, pathless. Keep up slightly to the right, and in a few paces you will see the upright stone of the French Invasion Memorial a little distance away on your left front. A wooden stile farther to the right gives access to it. Erected in 1897, its inscription (in Welsh and English) reads:

'MEMORIAL OF THE LANDING OF THE FRENCH,
FEBRUARY 22 1797.'

This is Carregwastad Point, and a good place for lunch and exploration – with due care that the Under Eights don't explore too near cliff edges. The view of the rocky coast stretching away north-eastwards is a grand one. In returning, don't be tempted to take the path to the left from the stile; it's overgrown and very muddy. The best plan is to go back to Tre-Howel by the way you came.

THE LOST LAND OF
RHYS DDWFN

In North Wales as well as in South Wales there exists the tradition that a once populous and fertile land lies sunk beneath the waves of Cardigan Bay. Its coastline, they say, extended from St David's Head in Pembrokeshire to Aberdaron at the tip of Lleyn. In the north they call this lost land Gwaelod, and say that it was through the fault of Prince Seithenin that its twenty towns and rich country-side were overwhelmed by the sea; for Seithenin was a drunkard, and in his drunkenness allowed the sea-wall that was in his charge to become so weak that the waters broke through and put an end to Gwaelod and all who dwelt there. All, that is, except the fairies. In Pembrokeshire at least, they know that the land where fairy folk live cannot be destroyed.

Not so very long ago, when Milford Haven was already a port for ships and Haverfordwest was a busy market-town, many a fisherman and farmer had the tale of green isles rising out of the sea-mists off the coast where no islands had been seen before. There were sailors who claimed to have landed on these islands, not knowing they were fairy territory; when they were back on board, they said, there was nothing to be seen but empty sea. At that time, too, strangers of unusual appearance could be seen on market-days in Haverfordwest and other Pembrokeshire towns. They were handsome people but remarkably small in size, saying little or nothing while doing their marketing but paying always in silver pennies; which (as some complained) sent market prices up. These small folk favoured certain tradesmen more than others, especially a butcher in Milford Haven, who got used to their way of indicating by signs what they wanted and handing over their silver pence. Little by little the rumour spread that these were fairy folk, who came from the mysterious 'green isles' by subterranean passages that connected the islands with the mainland.

To the questions of the curious the small folk answered nothing. Yet as time went by a little more became known about them, in one way or another. For instance, there was a girl, very pretty but very small in stature, who fell half in love with a handsome young man of the small folk; and no man, fairy or human, can withstand a pretty girl when she asks him about himself. So the news spread that the strangers called themselves *Plant Rhys Ddwfn*, the Children of Rhys Ddwfn, because their prince or patriarch was a wise old man of that name. It was also told that the Lost Land of Rhys Ddwfn was invisible to mortal's eye because there grew there instead of grass a herb that prevented anyone other than a native of that land from seeing it; a herb that grew only in one place on the mainland of Britain, and that was a small patch about a square yard in area on the headland of Saint David.

There was a man of great curiosity and persistence living between Haverfordwest and the headland. When he heard this tale he considered awhile and formed a conclusion: if a mortal could tread the ground where this magic herb grew, then surely the invisible land would become visible. To Saint David's headland he went, and for many days paced and stood, and stood and paced, without avail. Then, just as he was about to give up his experiment, he stepped upon a patch of turf that was to all appearance the same as the other green places about him, and at once the sea that stretched northward from the cliffs below him vanished. In its place was a fair countryside of fields and winding roads, woodland and rounded hill – the Lost Land!

For a long time he stood motionless, staring. Then, wild excitement rising in him, he turned and ran as fast as he could to bring others to see the sight. But he had failed to take note of the exact place where he had been standing. When he returned with his companions he could not find it again, and though they shifted their ground a thousand times and repeated their search again and again no fair countryside appeared in place of the grey-green sea. Nor, from that day to this, has the Lost Land of Rhys Ddwfn been seen by mortal eye.

THE WALK:
TO ST DAVID'S HEAD

MAP SQUARE A6
O.S. reference 157/721279
Easy cliff path; reasonably
safe but look after younger
children. 1 hour there
and back.

Drive to St David's, on A487. (Incidentally, one version of the legend says that the magic square yard is in St David's churchyard; and in any case you'll want to see the famous little cathedral.) Continue beyond the village for three miles on B4583 to Whitesands, a good bathing-beach where there is a car-park. From the telephone kiosk opposite the car-park a sandy path starts, climbing to the right to bend left-ward round the edge of low cliffs towards St David's Head. It's a good path but unfenced, so take care of the Under Eights.

After the first short ascent it levels out with fine views of coast and islands on the left, then bends to the right away from the cliffs passing a stone pillar with a National Trust badge and collecting-box. (This is a good place to remember that but for the National Trust beautiful places such as St David's Head would be private property instead of being freely open to us all.) Now the path descends to a charming rocky cove with a sandy beach, easily accessible, and then rises gently for the last 10 to 15 minutes to reach the rocky top of the headland. As you approach the final crest you pass through the remains of a stone rampart that once encircled an Iron Age fort.

The views from St David's Head, the most westerly head-land of Wales, are of course immense. To the south is big Ramsey Island, westward lie the smaller rocky islands called the Bishops and Clerks, and on a clear day you can look northward across the vast expanse of Cardigan Bay and see Snowdon, 100 miles away. On dark and rainy days the headland looks bleak and barren, but in spring the slopes are covered with pink thrift, yellow ladies-fingers, and white sea campion. As for the magic square yard where the mysterious herb of Rhys Ddwfn grows, you must allow more than one hour for this Walk if you intend to search for that.

There are cliff-edge paths going farther on from the north side of the headland but a family party will probably prefer to retrace the path back to Whitesands.

SAINT TEILO'S SKULL

Teilo was once regarded as being as holy a man as David
or Cadog, who also became saints. He was the founder of
many churches and a Bishop of Llandaff, and was further
celebrated by being buried in three graves. When he died
(so the story goes) three churches contended for his
remains, so that his grave should be within their
precincts: Penalun, the place of his birth; Llandeilo in
Carmarthenshire; and the cathedral at Llandaff. After
much debate they agreed to spend a day and night of
fasting and prayer, sitting beside the body. Morning
came, and instead of one body there were three – so
everyone was satisfied and Teilo had three burials.

But the legend of the saint's well and the method of
drinking its waters is more convincing, for up to a
hundred years ago many folk in South Wales believed in
it. For this tale we have to accept that Saint Teilo was
buried near the church of Llandeilo in Carmarthenshire.

When Teilo was on his death-bed he called to him a
devoted maidservant and charged her straitly to perform
for him this last service: a year from the day of his burial
she was to take his skull from Llandeilo to a small church
he had built at Llandilo in Pembrokeshire beside a spring
of clear water, so that all ailing folk who drank the water
from the skull should be cured of their infirmities. The
girl did as she was told, and for hundreds of years the
well-water drunk in this way wrought cures of all kinds of
ailments, including the whooping-cough. In the nineteenth century the little church fell into disuse and
decay, and the skull was kept at a more recently-built
farmhouse where a Welsh family by the unusual name of
Melchior had long been settled; traditionally, the
Melchiors were descendants of Teilo's maidservant.

In 1850, and even later, sick people were travelling
from distant parts to take the miraculous cure, for which
it was necessary that a member of the family should fill
the skull and hand it to the invalid – though oddly enough

the Melchiors did not believe in the cures or make any charge for the service. Apparently the virtue lay not so much in the well-water as in the holy skull. A man brought his son from Glamorgan so that the water could cure the boy's mysterious internal ailment but went straight to the well without applying to the Melchiors. They returned none the better for their journey. Then, thinking that the ritual of the skull might after all have something to do with it, they travelled again from Glamorgan and the boy drank the water according to the saint's instructions; the result being that this time the boy was completely cured.

It is sad to record that a legend so old, yet persisting so nearly to our own times, has now lost its hold on the folk of South Wales, and that *Penglog Teilo*, Saint Teilo's Skull, has disappeared. About the turn of the century Miss Melchior, the last of the family, sold the skull for £50 to 'a person representing himself as acting on behalf of some museum or other', and it has never been heard of since.

THE WALK: TO ST TEILO'S CHURCH	MAP SQUARE B6 O.S. reference 145/099270 Through a rather muddy farmyard – about 15 minutes. Allow one hour if extended to Llandilo village.

The Walk to the few remains of Saint Teilo's Church is one of the shortest in this book, but the car drive is fairly adventurous.

Maenclochog is a straggling hillside village on B4313, a road of fine open views crossing the ridge of Mynydd Preseli (Prescelly Mountain) between Fishguard and Narberth. At Maenclochog turn eastward on a minor road heading for Mynachlogddu and Crymmych, and turn right 350 yards along it at a signpost 'Llandilo 1'. The lane is a beautiful one but extremely narrow. One mile from Maenclochog turn right again, at a signpost 'Llanycefn 3', and stop at a large farmhouse 100 yards down it on the left. The car can be parked opposite.

First asking permission of the farmer (it will probably be Mr Owen) go through a gate on the right of the house. A little way beyond, among some trees on the right, you will find the ruined walls of the ancient church of Saint Teilo, now only a few feet high, with the ruin of a smaller building – probably the original chapel – within them. Several gravestones are lying about, some of them very old. In a field to the left as you come through the gate is the well of Saint Teilo; but it is not now to be seen, for it has been built over to supply the farm with water.

Llandilo, or Llandeilo Llwydiarth, is itself worth a visit, for it must be about the smallest 'village' with a name in the whole of the country. Walk back to the lane junction and turn right, and in ten minutes you are down in a leafy hollow where a stream babbles under low branches. Llandilo chapel, newish and ugly, and two cottages almost hidden in the thickets constitute the village.

THE OLD MAID OF KIDWELLY

Hen fenyw fach Cydweli
  Yn gwerthu losin du
  Yn rhifo deg am ddime
  Ond un-ar-ddeg i mi
  Wel! dyma'r newydd gore ddaeth i mi
  I mi
  Yn rhifo deg am ddime
  Ond un-ar-ddeg i mi.

This is a very old Welsh nursery-rhyme. In English it would go something after this fashion:

  The little old maid of Kidwelly
    A seller of sweeties is she
  She's counting out ten for a ha'penny
    But always eleven for me.
  Well! that's the best news that I ever did see –
    Counting out ten for a ha'penny
    But always eleven for me.

Most nursery-rhymes, nonsense though they sound, have their foundation in some forgotten happening or person of long ago. No one knows who the original 'old maid of Kidwelly' was; but she could have been the Lady Hawise de Londres.

The Lady Hawise was as good as she was beautiful, which is to say a great deal. She had lived all her childhood and youth in the Norman castle of Kidwelly, for her father was Castellan and held the fortress under King Henry the Third, and though she was of the purest Norman blood she had many friends among the Welsh folk in Kidwelly village and spoke their language as fluently as her own Norman-French. Kidwelly Castle was much involved in the wars and politics of that unruly time, when the Welsh princes alternately bargained with or fought against the rulers of England who sought to rule Wales. Indeed, when Hawise was a small girl the fortress had been besieged and captured by a Welsh chieftain named Rhys Grug; she and her father, with a few of the garrison, had escaped with their lives. This was in the year 1215, and for five years Rhys Grug held Kidwelly Castle. Then Llywelyn ap Iorwerth, called the Great, became overlord of Wales and married King Henry's sister the Princess Joan, making himself responsible to the King of England for the maintenance of peace and order in his country. Llywelyn restored the castle to the De Londres family, giving them a parchment declaring their possession under his overlordship. Hawise came back to her home and her friends in Kidwelly.

But Wales still seethed with rebellion against the English sovereignty. In a skirmish with the rebels Hawise's father was killed, and shortly afterwards Meredydd ap Rhys, a high-born Welshman who had sworn eternal enmity against all who had Norman blood in their veins, attacked Kidwelly Castle with a large force and succeeded in taking it despite a valiant defence. Once more Hawise escaped. She took refuge in the stronghold at Carmarthen, where romance came to her; for she married a noble knight named Patrick de Chaworth. Marriage did not entirely content her, however. Since she had no brothers she was the heiress of Kidwelly, and it sorted neither with her pride nor with her affections that she should be dispossessed. She resolved to appeal to Prince Llywelyn, who was then at Dryslwyn Castle with Joan his wife.

De Chaworth had been sorely wounded in a fight with outlaws and lay in the care of the monks of Whitland, so Hawise went to Dryslwyn alone. It was an unpropitious time to make such an appeal to the prince of Wales. Llywelyn had just quarrelled with King Henry and was preparing to oppose him, and at first refused to hear Hawise or take any notice of the deed of possession bearing his seal, which she had brought with her. Then the Princess interceded for her.

'Your honour will be impugned, my lord, if you

repudiate this deed given under your own hand,' she told her husband.

The Prince frowned and considered. Hawise's demand was just; but he needed Meredydd ap Rhys's help if he was to oppose the English king. At length he sent for his clerk, bade him write a message, and attached his seal.

'This will content you, my lady Hawise,' he said, handing it to her. 'It is my command to Ap Rhys to surrender Kidwelly Castle to yourself, when you shall give the parchment to him with your own hand.'

He smiled in his beard as he said it. And when Hawise, who hurried at once to Kidwelly, reached the little township she understood the meaning of his smile. She could not possibly go to the castle, the Welsh folk told her; Meredydd ap Rhys had sworn that any person of Norman blood who came within reach of his spearmen or range of his archers would be instantly slain.

Hawise was not daunted, however. She sought out an old friend of hers, Angharad the seller of cakes and sweetmeats, who was now a withered old maid but still plied her trade between village and castle. And next morning, dressed in Angharad's red cloak and the frilled linen hood that concealed her face, she shambled with an old woman's bent and crouching gait to the door of the castle. The spearmen on duty there let 'old Angharad' through with a jest and she went on into the inner ward and the hall, where Meredydd and his men-at-arms were breaking their fast. Hawise made a round of the lower benches with her basket of sweetmeats, croaking her praise of her wares in Welsh to the men who sprawled there. Then she advanced to the dais where their lord sat and taking the parchment from her basket laid it in front of Meredydd, who started when he saw the seal of his prince and the words of the unwelcome command.

'Who are you?' he demanded, glaring at the woman before him.

Hawise straightened her body and threw back her hood.

Kidwelly Castle

'I am the Lady Hawise,' she said in Welsh, 'rightful castellan of Kidwelly – as your prince's command will assure you.'

Meredydd sprang to his feet, with hand on hilt of dagger. Then he bowed his head.

'I would not retract what I have sworn for any man,' he said. 'But your courage and beauty, lady, have gained the day. By this time tomorrow I and my men will be gone and the castle will be yours.'

So the Lady Hawise came into her own once more. And it is said that the chief lady-in-waiting at the castle of Kidwelly was a little old maid named Angharad.

THE WALK:	MAP SQUARE C6/7
TO KIDWELLY CASTLE	O.S. reference 159/409071
AND THE	Castle and river-bank path,
RIVER GWENDRAETH	easy. Allow at least 1 hour.

Kidwelly is a pleasant little town on A484 midway between Carmarthen and Llanelli. There is a parking-place (for castle visitors only) right in front of the castle. If you explore this very fine old stronghold thoroughly you will do a fair amount of walking and climb up and down a lot of steps. There is also a little Walk of about 30 minutes which will show you a different aspect of the castle, though in wet weather the route is muddy and is best left out.

On the side of the parking-place that overlooks the river there is a Public Footpath sign. Go down the little path below this, round a rather rubbishy corner. A wooden stile crosses the wire fence on the right at the bottom, and by it you gain a path along the bank of the Gwendraeth river. There are good photographic viewpoints for the castle from this path, which you follow downstream for a short distance. Nearing the road bridge, you edge round the corner of a deserted house. Here is the site of the ancient castle mill where corn was ground for the garrison; the only remaining signs of its original walls are on the side facing the castle. A Public Footpath sign now directs you to the bridge, where you turn right along the road and again right to pass below the arch of the castle gatehouse. The parking-place is just ahead.

SWANSEA AND GOWER

A Baby on Worm's Head

The Orgy at Pennard Castle

The Drowned Well of Gorslas

Owain of the Red Hand

The First Recorded Fairy-tale

A BABY ON WORM'S HEAD

A more unlikely place for a baby's upbringing than the weird, wild headland of Worm's Head in Gower could hardly be found. And a more unlikely upbringing than that of the child Cenydd could hardly be imagined. This was the way of it.

King Arthur ruled Britain in those days and held his court at Loughor. To him they brought an infant of a few days, sorely crippled in one leg, who was the child of great sin; for a father had seduced his own daughter. The king's counsellors advised him that a child so conceived must be evil and should be put to death, but Arthur's judgement was that God alone should decide the babe's fate. So the little thing was put into a wicker cradle and placed in the current of the Loughor river, which bore cradle and baby down to the Burry estuary and out to sea. That very night a great storm arose. A northerly gale it would be, for the tiny craft, skimming across the white wave-tops, was carried south to be smashed to splinters against the great gaunt cliffs of Worm's Head. But before that happened the seagulls (who throng there by thousands to this day) had caught up the child in their strong talons and carried it to the top of the cliffs. There they made for it a bed of their own feathers and shielded it from wind and rain with their wings. And so they did for a week and a day.

On the ninth day down came an angel from heaven bearing a great brass bell and placed it beside the baby. In after years this bell was preserved in the chapel at Burry Holms and called by the folk of those parts the Titty Bell. For it had a brazen breast, and when the baby was hungry he turned his mouth to the bell and sucked a baby's proper nourishment. Later there came a hind on Worm's Head who suckled the growing baby. And when it was the weaning-time and the hind's milk was no longer sufficient, down came the angel again to tell the boy God's will as to his diet, which was to be the five kinds of herbs

Worm's Head, near Rhossili, Gower

that grow on that headland. Moreover, the angel informed him that God commanded that he should stay in that place until he was given leave from heaven to depart.

Eighteen years passed away. Every day of them the angel came to instruct Cenydd in all things holy and good, and every year Cenydd grew in holiness as he grew in stature. Then came a day when the angel brought him God's command to leave Worm's Head. He was to cross to the mainland (for the Head is islanded at high water) and walk four miles northward along the coast to another rocky headland jutting from the sands, where he would find a spring of fresh water. Here he was to build a chapel and dwell there with prayer and fasting as his portion, preaching God's word to any who should come to him. So Cenydd waited for the next time of low water and set off scrambling across the jagged rocks to the mainland, with pain and labour because of his crippled leg. He came limping and weary to the rocky headland and found the spring, as it had been foretold. There he built a chapel of rocks and made his dwelling.

It was not long before rumour of the holy man on Burry Holms reached those who lived in the neighbourhood, and within the year there was a constant stream of folk coming to hear his wise words and receive his blessing. To all he gave water from the spring, which was undoubtedly a holy well. The fame of his wisdom and holiness spread until pilgrims from all over the south of Wales, and many too from the north, made long journeys to see and hear Cenydd. Nor did Cenydd live all his life on Burry Holms. In later years he was summoned by Saint David to aid him in spreading the Word, and together they wrought much good and built many churches.

Such is the story of Saint Cenydd. His chapel on Burry Holms is a ruin now, but his name is perpetuated in the church and village of Llangennith, from whose overshadowing hill you may see the Worm's Head where he was saved by seagulls and an angel for the greater good of the world.

THE WALK: MAP SQUARE C8
TO WORM'S HEAD   O.S. reference 159/385877
                             A splendid expedition, rather
                             rough and steep; not for the
                             Under Eights. 3 hours.

The village of Rhossili, at the south-west corner of the tip of Gower, is the base for this exciting Walk. Driving on A4118, which links Swansea to Port Eynon, turn right on B4247 1½ miles short of Port Eynon. The road ends at Rhossili, where there is a large car-park (fee) with a grand sea view from it.

In bad weather, especially in a gale of wind, the Worm's Head walk should not be attempted. An alternative walk, easy but much longer, is along the magnificent beach of

*Rhossili Bay to Burry Holms – Saint Cenydd's route –
where you can see the few remains of the saint's chapel. This
is 8 miles there and back. In calm settled weather, though,
Worm's Head should not be missed.*

At the car-park and lower down towards the sea there are
notice-boards showing the times when it is safe to cross to
Worm's Head. These are necessary because every high water
the sea fills the wide rocky gap separating the Worm from
the mainland. Three hours is a very generous allowance for
getting out to the tip of the headland and back again. Having made sure that you are all right for time and tide, go
down to the headland by the much-trodden path and steeply
down to the rocks opposite the Inner Head of the Worm.
There is of course no path across these sea-bed rocks, and you
pick your own way, sometimes with a little difficulty, across
nearly half-a-mile of very rugged territory to the green
hump beyond, where a narrow but well-worn path begins.
The Inner Head rises in a long narrow ridge, sheer-sided on
the north but less steep on the south; you can either scramble
up and walk along the crest or keep along the easier path
round its flank. Next you come to the Low Neck, where there
is impressive rock scenery down on your right. Connecting
the Low Neck with the Outer Head is a geological freak
called the Devil's Bridge, an arch of rock across which the
path runs. The crossing is easy and the path reasonably
broad, but those who prefer to avoid it can do so by scrambling down on the left and up again to rejoin the path beyond
the bridge – a rather toilsome alternative.

Ahead and above, the towering rock of the Outer Head
rears up intimidatingly, looking almost inaccessible. It's not
nearly so difficult as it looks. The path, which you can't
miss, tackles it from the left, mounting rightward and up
round a rocky corner. Near the top it's fairly steep, but no
one of average agility will have any trouble with it. Then
you are on the summit of the sheer-walled rock tower, the
terminal point of what will certainly be a memorable little
expedition.

It's a fine place to stand and stare, or even to sit and

picnic, but now is the time to look at your watch and recall the time-limit noted on the mainland boards. A 'night out' on Worm's Head could be memorable too, but not many of us are as hardy as Saint Cenydd.

THE ORGY AT PENNARD CASTLE

In Edmund Vale's book *The World of Wales* the author lists 76 Welsh castles with notes on their history. Of Pennard Castle he has only this to say: 'A ruin about which nothing appears to be known.' The story told by Gower folk has an explanation for this lack of information.

In the dark age when the fiercest warrior was the greatest man in the land Pennard Castle was held by a chieftain who lived only for fighting. He had gathered round him a band of men as bloodthirsty as himself, and the fame of their skill and ruthlessness in battle spread far and wide through the lands of Dyfed and Powys. Indeed, the name of this chieftain was in men's mouths whenever there was talk of war; though – for a reason that will appear – his name cannot be told here. He was famous as far north as Gwynedd, and when a king in that country was threatened by a neighbouring prince whose army was twice the strength of his own a messenger was sent to Pennard with the king's promise of unlimited reward if the Pennard chieftain would come to his aid. With hardly an hour's delay the warriors from Gower rode northward.

In the battle that took place on the borders of Gwynedd the king and his ally were heavily outnumbered. But so savagely did the Pennard swordsmen hew and thrust, and so swiftly and cunningly did the Pennard archers shoot, that the opposing warriors fell back and at last fairly turned tail and ran for their lives. The day was won, largely by the leadership and example of the Gower chieftain, who had slain more foes than any three of his men and had twice saved the life of the king. When the time came for him to claim the promised reward he demanded, not gold or silver as the king had expected, but the king's daughter, whom he had desired as soon as he set eyes on her.

Now this princess was beautiful and gentle, a lover of flowers and birds and a favourite (so it was said) of the fairies. Alas, she was also a fool. For though she hated men of violence and bloodshed she was pleased and flattered that so famous a warrior should look on her with desire. With no real love for him in her heart, she willingly agreed to marry him.

In due time the Pennard band came riding back to their castle behind the chieftain and his bride. All the way southward he had boasted to her of his bloody deeds and of mighty feats of drinking and eating, and especially of the feasting and revelry that should celebrate their arrival at Pennard Castle.

'Mountains of meat and seas of ale!' were his words. 'Girls for my lads – and you, my love, for me!'

Already she was doubting her wisdom in mating with such a man; and the feast in the castle turned her doubt to horror. The flaring rushlights shone with a fitful glow on a horde of reeling, yelling drunkards, some trying vainly to dance, some brawling with daggers until the blood spurted, others – men and women – rolling together on the floor of the hall. Sick and nearly deafened by the savage uproar, the princess was at the point of creeping away to hide herself when a shout so loud that it rose above the tumult halted her.

'Foemen advancing on the castle!' It was the sentinel from the castle wall who shouted. 'A great band of them!'

'To arms!' roared the chieftain, brandishing his sword. 'Enough of ale – let us drink blood!'

He rushed from the hall. Such of his men as could stand (and all of those were more than half drunk) rushed after him. The princess ran to a lancet window from which she could look down on the moonlit valley below the castle rock, and saw what the sentinel had seen – only *she* knew what it really was. The troop of small figures, pale and transparent as moonbeams, were fairies coming to dance at her wedding.

Swords flashed in the moonlight as the Pennard warriors charged out from the shadow of the slope they had just descended at breakneck speed. Shrieking their war-cries, they hurled themselves upon the fairies, striking and thrusting without mercy. Their blades met empty air. The princess saw the fairy troop fade and vanish and heard a great voice like the voice of the wind: 'Chieftain! You have assailed those who would not have harmed you and yours. Hear now your doom. The men of Pennard and the castle of Pennard shall be buried and lost, and your name and fame buried with them.'

Pennard Castle

These were the last words the unfortunate princess was ever to hear. The night had been calm, but now black clouds hid the moon and a tremendous gale burst suddenly on valley and castle, raising a whirlwind of sand. Sand choked the fighting-men and their leader and rose layer on layer above their lifeless bodies. Sand engulfed Pennard Castle and everyone in it. When morning came, still and bright, the rising sun lit a lifeless valley flanked by a great mound of sand.

THE WALK: MAP SQUARE D8
PARKMILL TO   O.S. reference 159/545886
PENNARD CASTLE   Easy woodland and hill paths;
suitable for all the family in
dry summer weather. Allow
2 hours.

Nature and Man between them have unearthed the ruins of Pennard Castle. Much the nicest way of visiting it is to walk there from Parkmill, a distance of less than a mile.

Parkmill is a pretty hamlet on the Swansea–Port Eynon road, A4118, about 8 miles from Swansea. There is free parking at the side of the Gower Inn, on the right as you enter the village. Coming out of the car-park, turn right along the road for 150 yards, then left over the lane bridge close to the bus stop. This bridge crosses the little River Pill, whose course you'll be following. Immediately you are across the bridge, go to the right on an indistinct path for about 40 paces, looking out for a way up the steep bank on the left. You'll see a fifteen-foot scramble with projecting stones for steps. Climb up it (small children will need help) and gain a narrow but easy path going through charming woodlands where there are many wild birds. Soon the Pill brook is seen below through the trees. At a fork of the path, bear right and descend to the stream at a footbridge connecting with the main road. Keep on along the woodland path, which is wider now and stony in parts. It mounts and descends, quickly emerging into a delightful open glen where Pennard Castle suddenly appears, perched romantically on its cliff at the side of the glen.

Follow the banks of the Pill if you want to see small flatfish (and perhaps a water-rat) and then storm the castle by one of several sandy paths. The climb will take 10 minutes at a slow and steady pace. As you begin it Pobbles Beach in Three Cliffs Bay comes in sight on your right. The crumbling walls of the castle, which have been strengthened with modern masonry, show that it was built about the thirteenth century; it's quite a small fortress, but still impresses one as a formidable stronghold – though with little space for the kind of revelry described in the legend.

It took you perhaps an hour to get here. There is an alternative return route that will take little more than half-an-hour. Leave the castle by the green track from its landward gateway and bear left, skirting the golf course. You will come to a signpost, 'Parkmill', from which a narrow path descends, with one short steep bit, to join the woodland path you came by. The footbridge over the Pill is seen below, but unless you prefer to walk back along the main road turn right on the path and clamber down the miniature 'rock-climb' at its end. Then you have only two or three minutes of road-walking before you regain the car-park.

THE DROWNED WELL OF GORSLAS

The name Gorslas signifies in English 'the green marsh', and in old time the shepherds and cowherds whose beasts cropped the herbage on the hills above Gorslas could find no safe place here to water them. For water they had to go down the valley beyond Cwm-y-glo where the stream of the Gwendraeth river began. It was not strange that the shepherds should grumble about this from time to time, but they were mostly a contented lot and had never done anything to offend the fairies who lived in the hills, and it came about that the fairies decided to help them.

'We will make you a well,' the shepherds were told, 'and we will look after it and keep the water pure. It shall be right on the top of the hills, so that your beasts can drink without going down to the valley. We make one condition. The well will be covered with a slab of stone, and every time you use it you must be sure to replace the stone over it – otherwise, the well will vanish for ever.'

The shepherds willingly agreed to this condition, and the well duly appeared, a spring of purest water on the top of one of the highest hills in that district. And for many years, because no one forgot to replace the stone, all went well.

Sir Thomas Malory has recorded in his book *Morte D'Arthur* how King Arthur sent forth his best knights of the Round Table to search for the Holy Grail, each riding alone on the quest. One of the knights, Sir Owen, rode far to the westward from the court at Caerleon-upon-Usk and on the seventh day of his wanderings found himself at a ford not far from Gorslas. The ford was guarded by a pagan knight who challenged all who came that way, and with him Sir Owen fought fiercely and long, unhorsing and disarming his opponent only after he himself had suffered many wounds. Weary and in need of food and shelter, he let his horse take him whither it would, knowing that the animal could scent straw and stable if there were any such nearby. Night was falling and in his exhaustion he took little note of the way they went. When he was roused by the stopping of his mount he found himself on a wide hilltop pasture, with no house or inn anywhere in sight and at his feet a slab of stone from beneath which came a small trickle of water. His horse, more thirsty than hungry, had led him to the well of Gorslas.

Sir Owen made the best of it. Dismounting, he exerted his waning strength to drag aside the stone and both he and his horse drank from the crystal spring that bubbled up beneath it. Then he led the horse some distance away to a thicket where it could be tethered, intending to lie down and sleep beside it. But the water of the spring had somewhat revived him, and he resolved to cross the hilltop pasture and look down the hillside to see if he could discern, in the darkling countryside below, any dwelling where he might still find shelter for the night. Before he had gone a bowshot from the thicket his weariness overcame him altogether, and he sank down on the turf and fell instantly into a deep and healing sleep.

Sir Owen was awakened by the distant neighing of his steed. He sat up, with the rays of the new-risen sun warming him, and perceived that he was still asleep and dreaming. For he was sitting on a very small green island in the middle of a considerable lake, on the margin of which was his horse, tethered to a thicket.

While he was yet rubbing his eyes, several shepherds came running along the lake shore wailing and wringing their hands. The noise they made assured Sir Owen that he was not dreaming but was indeed on an island in a lake that had come into being while he slept. What was more, he saw that the lake was still rising, for his island was rapidly shrinking and would soon be submerged. Getting to his feet, he plunged in and swam to the shore, where he was confronted by the angry shepherds.

'Our well has vanished for ever, as the fairies warned us!' said one, glaring at him.

'It was you, sir knight, who failed to replace the stone!' accused another.

Llyn Llech Owen near Gorslas

Sir Owen quickly perceived how matters lay.

'That is true, good sirs,' he said pleasantly. 'A stranger, and ignorant of your rule, I removed the stone to drink from your well and omitted to put it back. But I myself am not unacquainted with the fairies, and I think that in this matter I may have acted with their goodwill. For, as you see, if I have indeed drowned your well I have presented you with a fine lake in place of it.'

The shepherds looked at each other and smiles began to appear instead of frowns. When Sir Owen made himself known to them the last of their ill-humour vanished, for they had heard of his courage and good deeds. They bade him mount and follow them to the hamlet at the foot of the hill, where their women dressed his wounds and the knight and his horse were fed and cared for. So Sir Owen rode away from Gorslas on his long quest, and ever since his going the lake on the hilltop has been called Llyn Llech Owen, the Lake of Owen's Stone.

THE WALK: MAP SQUARE C7
TO LLYN LLECH OWEN   O.S. reference 159/568152
                           Lane and path, easy.
                           ½-hour.

The Drowned Well still gives a plentiful supply of water, and – as might be expected – Llyn Llech Owen is now a reservoir for Gorslas and district. The short walk to it is worth doing, however, for its views as well as for a look at the site of the legend.

Gorslas is on A476 one mile north of Cross Hands. At the five-way crossroads in the village take the uphill road, unsignposted, opposite the Union Tavern. Threequarters of a mile up this near the brow of the hill you'll see a waterworks building on the right with a stone seat by its entrance gate. The car can be parked on the grass verge close to the entrance.

Go through the gateway and along the straight metalled lane, which is barred to vehicles. In five minutes you reach a belt of trees where a rougher lane leads to the left. Follow this. It bends to the right and in another five minutes reaches the lake on its hilltop shelf, with a small water-tower jutting from its fenced-in shore. If you go to the left up a little path opposite the gate of the water-tower you will gain in a couple of minutes the summit of a heathery knoll with panoramic views of the surrounding countryside.

The lake shores are too boggy for a complete circuit of Llyn Llech Owen to be made. But you can go on along the path for about ¼-mile through heather and conifers, reaching an open glade overlooking the country to northward. If you were looking for a spot to picnic, this or the heathery knoll by the water-tower would do quite nicely.

The gate below the glade leads only to cottages and a farm lane, so you return to the car by the way you came.

OWAIN OF THE RED HAND

Of all the legendary figures of Wales none is more mysterious than Owain Lawgoch, Owain of the Red Hand. Tales are told of him in the north of the country as well as in the south, sometimes with Owain as the hero and sometimes as the villain but always picturing him as inhabiting a cave with his followers. In the fourteenth century, when he is supposed to have lived, the English law imposed on Wales was unpopular with a good proportion of the Welsh; so it may be that to some Welshmen the outlaw Owain Lawgoch was a heroic leader of revolt while to others he was a murderous ruffian who needed suppressing. In either case he would need to be in continual hiding from the king's officers, and he seems to have preferred caves to any other form of refuge.

The next Legend-Walk in this book concerns Craig-y-Ddinas in Mid Glamorgan, and one of Owain's caves was in the face of this crag. It has since been quarried away. Another was as far north as Nant Gwynant in Caernarvonshire and yet another on the high moors of central Wales, a hidden cave wherein Owain and his men lie sleeping with their weapons by their side until the time shall come when they will rise and lead Wales to victory against the oppressor. But the majority of legends about him, most of them very vague, centre on the limestone country in the neighbourhood of Llandybie, where there are certainly a fair number of likely caves.

It seems that Owain Lawgoch got his nickname in the course of an exploit by no means heroic. An old woman living alone in a hillside cottage began to miss bread and meat from her larder. Though she padlocked her door the robberies continued, so one night she stood patiently waiting beside her larder window with a large carving-knife in her hand. Sure enough, the window was eased open and a hand and arm were thrust inside. With all her strength the old woman hewed at the hand with her knife,

The cave of Owain Lawgoch is in the rock, to the right

half severing it at the wrist, and with a howl of pain the intruder – who was thenceforward called Owain Lawgoch – ran away.

According to the tale told long ago in Llandybie, the folk of those parts were for some years harassed by Owain and his little band of robbers, whose lair was a cave in a limestone precipice a mile north of the village. At last the villagers determined to rid themselves of this nuisance. A concealed watcher was posted to inform them when all the robbers were inside the cave, and as soon as this was certain the villagers marched up in a body. Two of them armed with bows shot arrows at any outlaw who showed himself, while the rest piled boulders against the cave entrance in such quantity that the barrier could not be shifted by those inside. So Owain Lawgoch and his gang were finally starved to death; or so boasted the Llandybie men. Confirmation of a sort, to prove the truth

The entrance to Owain Lawgoch's cave

of their tale, came five centuries later. In 1813, when quarrymen began work on the big limestone quarry which may be seen today from A483 north of Llandybie, they came upon a cave in which were the skeletons of several very tall men.

The whisper of a sequel to the Llandybie story comes from the hamlet of Carmel, three miles away on the other side of the hills. Highway robberies on the hill road to Llandeilo (now A476) were said to be the work of Owain Lawgoch – and this was after the outlaw had supposedly been walled-up and starved to death. The rumour grew that the men immured in the Llandybie cave had been hostages held there by the robbers, and that Owain had escaped by a secret entrance while the villagers were triumphantly walling-up his front door. His new lair, it was said, was another cave near to Carmel and conveniently close to the highway.

If you look carefully at the Ordnance Survey map (as I did) you will see, just south of Carmel, a wooded hill overlooking A476 from the east; marked on its western flank is the word *Cave*. So well concealed is this cave that it took me a whole morning to find it. But when it was found it seemed to me that if I were Owain Lawgoch I could hardly have found a more roomy or suitable refuge.

THE WALK:	MAP SQUARE D6
TO THE REFUGE CAVE	O.S. reference 159/591163
	Track (private land) and easy
	scramble. 45 minutes.

Start by driving on A476 to the small hillside village of Carmel, 3 miles from Cross Hands on the Llandeilo road. Right at the top of the hill by the uppermost house of the village is a bus shelter and a space where the car can be parked.

Walk down the road southward, in the direction of Cross Hands, for 200 yards – single file and keeping to the right, of course. When you come to the village sign, CARMEL, you'll see on the other side of the road an iron gate. Go through this; it's not a right-of-way but if you keep to my route you'll be doing no harm. The broad track between hedges beyond the gate bends rightward to a rusty iron barn about 3 minutes from the road, and here you'll see on the left a fine limestone cliff 200 yards away. In a sort of miniature glen leading to its foot there are many wild flowers and plants, and cotoneaster growing wild. A rubble of rocks lies across the entrance to this glen but is easily traversed. From the far side of the rocks go towards the cliff counting 50 paces, then look to the right at the low rock-wall on that side. A narrow and apparently insignificant crack will be seen a few feet up the rock-wall, easily reached by a step or two on the rock. Peering over the rim of the crack, you look into a fine underground chamber with a passage running into the rock from its bottom.

But – don't attempt to climb down. Below is the hazardous territory of cavers and potholers. The lower cave runs far into the rock until further progress is barred by a massive boulder, which the caving clubs intend to remove by blasting in the hope that other underground passages run beyond it.

THE FIRST RECORDED FAIRY-TALE

Tales of the fairies have been handed down by word of mouth ever since men began to tell stories round winter fires; but the first fairy-story to appear in a book was written – in Latin – about the year 1190, by the son of a Norman baron and a Welsh princess. Giraldus Cambrensis, Gerald of Cambridge, accompanied Archbishop Baldwin on a tour of Wales in 1188 to preach the Crusades, and on their return Giraldus wrote an account of the journey in *Itinerarium Cambriae*, since published many times in translation. In the part of the *Itinerarium* that records his travels in the upper Vale of Neath Giraldus tells of an account left by one Elidorus, a priest, concerning a strange happening that befell him when he was a boy.

Elidorus, being destined for the priesthood, was made to learn his letters, and as he was not the most apt of pupils he received many stripes from the rod of his teacher. He was twelve years old when, to escape such punishment, he ran away and hid himself under the hollow bank of the Neath river. For two days he stayed there fasting, and then there came to him two little men who promised to lead him to a land of delights and sports. He went with them along an underground passage and found himself in a most beautiful country where it was always twilight, for there was no sun to shine on it. The people of this country were extremely small, but handsome and well-proportioned, as were their horses and greyhounds. They were all of a fair complexion, with long golden hair like that of women, and lived on milk and saffron.

Elidorus was brought before their king, who held his court on a high place above the river where also his people used to dance and sport. When he had questioned the boy for some time the king delivered him to his son, who was of the same age as Elidorus, and the two boys played games with a golden ball. After a time the human boy found his way back to the river bank and to his home, where he told only his mother of his adventures; but so happy had he been in the twilight world of the Little People that he returned there almost at once, and thereafter made frequent journeys along the underground passage from the river-bank.

Now Elidorus had told his mother of the furniture and utensils of the Little People and how these were often made of gold, and one day as he was departing she desired him to bring her a present of this same gold. So on that visit, while he was at play with the king's son, he stole the golden ball and ran with it down the underground passage. He was not unpursued, however. When he was almost at the tunnel's end on the river-bank he stumbled on the threshold, and the two little men who had first welcomed him there seized the ball from him and turned him out of the passage with every mark of contempt.

Though he tried again and again to find the entrance to the country of delight, Elidorus never succeeded. He returned to his studies and in due time became a priest. 'And,' says Giraldus, ending his account, 'whenever David II, Bishop of St David's, talked to him in his advanced state of life about this event of his boyhood days, Elidorus could never relate the particulars without shedding tears.'

Apart from its location in the upper Vale of Neath, which places it somewhere near the junction of the rivers Neath and Mellte, Giraldus's story gives no definite landmarks for identification. The description of the fairy king's court 'where his people used to dance and sport' has a parallel in another old tradition of the Neath valley, which is that the last court of the kings and princes of fairydom was held on Craig-y-Ddinas, above Pont Nedd Fechan where the Neath joins the Mellte. My own deduction (which I hope you will confirm by investigation) is that Craig-y-Ddinas with its lovely surroundings is the site of the Elidorus story, fount and source of so many other British fairy-tales.

THE WALK:
TO CRAIG-Y-DDINAS

MAP SQUARE D7
O.S. reference 160/916081
Rough track, all right for the
Under Eights, with care.
1½ hours if extended.

This Walk starts from the village of Pont Nedd Fechan, 9 miles north-east of Neath. The drive takes you through the transition characteristic of the South Wales valleys, from industrial areas to grand river-glen scenery. A465(T) and A4109 join in the town of Glyn Neath at the head of the Vale of Neath, and here you take B4242 for 1 mile to Pont Nedd Fechan. In the village bear right off B4242 and follow an unsignposted road running level, with steep woodland on the left. After about ¼-mile this fairly broad road ends by some houses, and a narrower lane goes on to the right, descending to cross the river by a small bridge. Once over the bridge, drive left to the foot of the bold precipice of Craig-y-Ddinas; a small disused quarry here now forms a parking-place for cars.

Follow – on foot – the track which goes up the crest of a low ridge on the left of Craig-y-Ddinas and soon becomes a ledge-like path rising along the steep flank of the crag with the Mellte stream down below. At the top of the path bear round to the right to the summit of the Dinas. The crag, precipitous on three sides, has an almost level top, grassy and spacious; certainly big enough for a court or a dance. In the time of Giraldus the view down the Vale of Neath had no pylons in the middle distance, but despite these it is still a fine one.

Probably the climb to the top of Craig-y-Ddinas will have taken no more than 15 minutes. There is a worthwhile stroll which will take half-an-hour out and back and show you more of the beauties of this region. With your back to the Vale of Neath, walk along the green track that runs eastward along the crest of this narrow promontory between the River Mellte and its tributary stream the Sychryd. Soon the track comes near the river-gorge on the right, an impres-

sive viewpoint; use care here, for the cliff below is true ver-
tical. Just beyond, bear left on a smaller path through the
bracken leading to the left-hand rim of the promontory and
then skirting it – all quite safe and easy. At one point this
path commands a grand view into the wooded upper gorge of
the Mellte. About 15 minutes from Craig-y-Ddinas summit
the trees begin to thin out and you find yourself on the open
lower slopes of Foel Penderyn, a southern outlier of the wild
mountain region called Fforest Fawr. Here, not being
equipped for mountain walking, you turn back. It would be
genuinely dangerous to attempt a descent from Craig-y-
Ddinas by any route other than the one you came by, so you
go down the rocky path again to the car.

CARDIGAN AND
NEW QUAY

When the Cuckoo came late

The Mermaid of Cemaes Head

Introduction and Allegro

WHEN THE CUCKOO CAME LATE

Gwcw glame, cosyn dime, says an old Welsh proverb; literally translated it means 'A May cuckoo, a ha'penny cheese', implying that when the cuckoo came late folk might expect poor crops and small rations. (Incidentally, it's interesting to note that the Welsh word for a ha'penny is spelt, though not pronounced, the same as the American word for a ten-cent piece.) So the folk of Pembrokeshire watched each Spring for an April cuckoo, and none more eagerly than the villagers of Nevern, whose church is dedicated to a saint of the sixth century named Saint Brynach.

Outside the old church of Nevern stood a tall stone pillar older than the church; older, some thought than Saint Brynach himself would have been if he was still alive, though it was always called the Stone of Saint Brynach. Every year as far back as memory and tradition could trace, the first cuckoo of Spring had arrived in Nevern on Saint Brynach's Day, April 7th, and perched on the Stone. It was thought that this unfailing regularity resembled a religious duty among the cuckoos, who selected one of their number to be God's messenger on that special day. For this reason it had become a hard-and-fast rule that the priest of Nevern should not say Mass on Saint Brynach's Day until the messenger-cuckoo had arrived and perched on Saint Brynach's Stone.

There came a year of long winter and late spring. April 7th was a cold day and windy, but all the people of Nevern gathered outside the church with their priest to await the accustomed messenger. For hour after hour they waited. Midday came and passed and the waiting throng grew chilled and weary. Afternoon began to darken towards evening and still the messenger had not arrived. Some whispered to the priest that since the cuckoo had failed them this time it would be well to go into the church and celebrate Mass without more delay, but the priest would not yield to them.

'God cares for all his creatures,' he said, 'and He will neither disappoint us nor let the cuckoo fail.'

As he spoke, they all heard a faint and feeble call near at hand: *cuckoo!* And fluttering between the old yew-trees before the church came a very tired bird, to alight unsteadily on top of the tall stone. Very much relieved, priest and people gave brief thanks to God and hastened into the church to celebrate Mass.

The cuckoo remained on his perch for only a little while longer. Perhaps he remembered the long battle with the northerly winds, the icy breath of snow-covered European mountains, and the last frantic struggle across storm-swept waters that had brought him here at last, faithful to his trust. Then his head drooped and he fell to the ground. When the folk of Nevern trooped out of church they found a dead cuckoo lying at the foot of Saint Brynach's Stone.

THE WALK:	MAP SQUARE B6
TO ST BRYNACH'S CHURCH	O.S. reference 145/083400
AND ALONG THE RIVER	Lane, riverside paths and
NYFER	woodland track, fairly easy.
	1½ hours.

Nevern is a delightful hamlet on a wooded and winding stream, 2½ miles from Newport and 8 from Cardigan. It is reached from A487 in a little more than ½-mile on B4582, which leaves the major road at the hamlet of Velindre. In Nevern there is parking-space beside the inn on the south side of the river bridge, and the Church of Saint Brynach is a few minutes' walk up the road on the other side of the bridge.

The Stone of the legend stands close to the church wall, on the right as you approach up a short avenue of very ancient yews. It is one of the most beautiful old stone carvings of Wales, but contrary to mediaeval belief it commemorates not Saint Brynach but a much-revered chieftain of later date – probably tenth century – whose name is not preserved. Its 13 feet of height are covered with an interlacing pattern that is surprisingly clear considering its ten centuries of existence.

To see the Stone and take a look into the church involves a very short walk indeed; and a rather longer one is recommended.

Returning from the church, turn right before you approach the bridge, following a lane opposite the telephone kiosk. This lane bends sharply uphill to the left, and on the right-hand bend higher up you see a signboard: THE PILGRIM'S CROSS. Cross the stile beside this sign and go up the little path beyond. Thirty yards up it, look out on the right for a Cross carved in low relief on a small rockface. This was a place of prayer for mediaeval pilgrims leaving Nevern on their way to St David's, and you'll see a ledge below the Cross worn smooth by the knees of those who knelt to pray.

Continuing up the path and over a stile above, you enter a field and skirt its edge. Two more stiles are crossed, and then the path goes along a wooded flank with the river close below before emerging by another stile into an open field with some cottages below on the left. Don't descend to the cottages, but strike straight across the field – there is no distinct path here – to a rough lane that descends to them. Go only a very few paces down this and then take a narrow path that dives down to the right through bushes to a concrete 'plank' bridging a stream. Now the path, still narrow but quite plain, passes behind a white cottage and continues as a beautiful riverside track along the Nyfer, in 10 minutes coming to another cottage beyond which it rises and descends. You enter a broad track that crosses the River Nyfer by a fine stone bridge. This is about 35 minutes from Saint Brynach's Church.

Turn left and go across the bridge. The track rises beyond it, first along the edge of woodlands and then joining a lane that runs behind a riverside hotel and caravan-park. About 80 paces past the hotel entrance-gate bear left up a wide grass track and cross a stone stile beside an iron gate. The track runs on through woodland with very little up-and-down, and in 15 minutes it will bring you out across a riverside meadow to the bridge at Nevern.

THE MERMAID OF CEMAES HEAD

At St Dogmaels, on the Teifi estuary, they tell this story as a real event that happened in the eighteenth century.

On a sunny afternoon in September the inshore fishing-boats of St Dogmaels put out past Poppit Sands and hauled away nor'-westerly to round Cemaes Head. That's the time of year you'll find good fishing close in under the cliffs of the Head and it's every man for himself. One of the men, Pergrin by name, was alone in his own boat this once, and it was he who came nosing round a corner of the rocks out of sight of the rest, with his gunwale no more than a fathom clear of the cliff-face, to see a mermaid sitting in a bit of a cleft above the water and combing her long golden hair. A rare pretty piece she was, and Pergrin, who was never backward with the girls, sheered his craft alongside in a jiffy and pulled her aboard.

Maybe he'd thought of having a bit of fun with her, but she gave him no time for that. Soon as she was rightways up (for he'd capsized her in his lusty violence) she began pleading with him very piteous, in good Welsh.

'Let me go, let me go! If you keep me, Pergrin, no good will come of it. But let me go, and I'll save you from the doom I see hanging over you.'

'What doom's that?' demanded Pergrin.

But she only pleaded louder than before. 'Let me go — and I promise to give you three shouts when you need them most.'

Well, Pergrin was in two minds. Very beautiful she was, specially with naught to cover her top half but her golden hair, but there was that long shiny tail. More than one problem with that tail. He was holding her with both hands, and he raised one hand to scratch his red head, and in that instant she slipped clear of him and was overside. Pergrin peered into the blue-green water but all he saw was a silvery flash far down under his boat. The shore's very steep-to below the cliffs of the Head.

Pergrin said nothing about the mermaid to his pals, not wanting to be laughed at. And day after day went by with no sign of the doom she had talked about. Calm and still was that late summer, and calmest and stillest was a day when twenty St Dogmaels men put out north of the Head in their fishing-boats. Pergrin was one, and this time he had another man with him in the boat to help him with the nets. Flat as a table was the sea and the horizon like a line of blue paint, with the clearest sky you ever saw in your life. The boats had their nets out a mile west of Cardigan Island and the haul looked like being average good. All of a sudden, and not three fathom from Pergrin's craft, a flurry appeared on the surface of the sea and up popped a head of long golden hair. The pretty face underneath the hair was well remembered by Pergrin.

'Pergrin! Pergrin! Pergrin!' shouted the mermaid – three times, like that. 'Take up your nets! Take up your nets! Take up your nets!'

And she dived and was gone before he could ask her why. But Pergrin remembered about his doom, and though there still wasn't a cloud in the sky he reckoned a mermaid must know more about the sea and the weather than he did.

'Get the nets aboard and the oars out,' he told his pal, who was gaping thunderstruck at the wonder he'd just witnessed.

In a couple of minutes they were pulling for the shore, with Pergrin at the stroke oar giving his pal at the bow oar a real hard time of it. They'd won the lee of Poppit Sands before the storm broke. The oldest fisherman in St Dogmaels had never seen a storm like it. Wind and sea rose in a twinkling and the waves that broke on the rocks of the Head sent their spray flying clear up to the top of the cliffs. There was no hope, in a storm like that, for the boats that had stayed out fishing. Eighteen St Dogmaels men were drowned, that day. But Pergrin was safe and snug in the taproom of his favourite inn, drinking toasts to the mermaid of Cemaes Head.

THE WALK: MAP SQUARE B5
FROM POPPIT SANDS O.S. reference 145/132502
TO CEMAES HEAD Lane and unfenced cliff-top
paths: not for the Under
Eights. 2½ hours.

Poppit Sands, where this Walk starts, is a handy spot if some of the party including the younger children have to be left behind. To reach Poppit from Cardigan town, turn off A487 at the south end of the bridge across the Teifi and follow B4546 through St Dogmaels and 1¾ miles beyond. The road virtually ends at the Sands – good safe bathing here – and you can generally find parking space.

Turn left up a lane opposite a telephone kiosk close to the Sands. This lane has a NO THROUGH ROAD sign and ends at a hillside farm where you could park the car and save about a mile of uphill walking; but it is steep and narrow with few places where cars can pass, and – especially in the blackberry season – it's better to walk it. After an initial steep bit the lane levels out, with fine views of Cardigan Island and the mouth of the Teifi. Another rather milder ascent follows and then it begins to go gently downhill. Look out here for the sign COAST PATH, where you bear right through a muddy farmyard and over a stile. The little path that now begins to round the brackeny slopes towards Cemaes Head is part of the Pembrokeshire Coast Path, 167 miles long, and its signs and stiles make the way unmistakable.

So far there have been only wide sea views. The splendid cliff scenery suddenly bursts upon you at a stile on a dizzy corner, and after this there are magnificent views of the great cliffs with their contorted strata and the sea lapping the rocks at their base far below. If you have binoculars with you keep a watch on these rocks for grey seals, who are particularly fond of this coast. The seals may well have been the real origin of the mermaid legend, as they probably were for a very similar mermaid tale located at Nefyn on the Lleyn Peninsula.

The path curls along the edge of the cliffs, safe enough to tread but narrow and unfenced above a 600-foot drop (you'll be glad you left the Under Eights behind). It passes a coastguard lookout post and mounts gently beyond it to a high point from which you have a view of the coast to southward and of the sheer-sided inlet of Pwll y Granant ahead and below. Where the path begins to descend to this inlet is the terminal point of the Walk.

There's no practicable route for a short cut back over the top of the headland, despite a right-of-way marked on the map. It would be possible to go on down to Pwll y Granant and find a laborious way back through the farm of Granant and the hamlet of Cippyn, but this takes nearly two hours and is less interesting than returning by the Coast Path and the lane, a route that is all downhill and takes well under an hour.

INTRODUCTION AND ALLEGRO

The connection between the man who has been called the greatest British composer and the little village of Llangranog is fact, not legend. And the tradition that one of his best-loved compositions had its origin on the coast overlooking Ynys Lochtyn is vouched for by the composer himself.

Edward Elgar, born twenty-five miles from the Welsh border, was always a lover of Wales. In his younger days he used to go on cycling holidays in the Betws-y-Coed neighbourhood, and in later years he often visited central Wales and the southern coasts. It will be remembered that national recognition of his genius did not come until he was 42 years old. Three years later, in 1902, Elgar and his wife came to stay for a short holiday at Llangranog, then a very quiet and little-known place, on the Cardigan coast between New Quay and Aberporth. He was plain Mr Elgar then; knighthood, the Order of Merit, and international fame were still to come. His habit of jotting down scraps and fragments of music whenever he thought of them and wherever he happened to be had been with him for thirty years, ever since the days when he had knocked together little pieces and tunes for amateur music societies in Worcester.

One of Elgar's favourite walks from Llangranog was along a hillside path to the headland overlooking the rocky islet of Ynys Lochtyn. He was at this time occupied with the idea of writing a piece of music for string orchestra and his thoughts recurred to it from time to time. One calm and sunlit morning he walked along the path to the cliff above Ynys Lochtyn and sat down to rest and enjoy the view. It happened that on this day some local singers were gathered on the beach at Llangranog, little more than five hundred yards from where he was sitting, and as he dreamily considered the making of his *Introduction and Allegro for Strings* – which was to become known and loved by music-lovers the world over

– their voices drifted up to him on the still air. 'On the cliff, between blue sea and blue sky,' Elgar wrote later, 'thinking out my theme, there came up to me the sound of singing. The songs were too far away to reach me distinctly, but fitting the need of the moment I made the little tune which appears in the *Introduction*.'

Three years were to go by before Elgar's *Introduction and Allegro for Strings* received its first performance. It was instantly popular and quickly became famous. For many English people its evocation was of an English landscape, the quiet hills and fields of Herefordshire and Shropshire. But the fact remains that some singers of Llangranog unknowingly sang their way into it.

THE WALK:	MAP SQUARE C5/6
TO YNYS LOCHTYN	O.S. reference 145/314556
	Lane and track, easy.
	Allow 1½ hours.

Llangranog is reached by turning off A487 at Brynhoffnant, which is 10 miles from Cardigan and about the same distance from New Quay. A 3-mile drive along B4334 brings you to the village, tucked away in a deep and narrow glen that ends in a rocky cove with a sandy beach. Though more popular and frequented than in Edward Elgar's day, it is still a charming spot.

The Walk is quite short and easy, and strongly recommended whether you like Elgar's music or not. It starts half-way down the steep street by which you enter Llangranog. The public car-park is at the very bottom of the hill close to the beach, and a useful alternative is to park the car opposite the sign 'LLANGRANOG' at the top of the hill, where there is an ample space. St Carannog's Church is a few minutes down the hill from here. 200 yards downhill from the church go uphill by a concreted lane on the right that has a No Through Road sign. It forks at the top where there are two gates. Go left through the gate marked KEEP CLOSED and follow the broad track round to Lochtyn

Farm, with grand sea and coastal views. A National Trust sign ushers you through the farmyard and on to a green contouring track above. 5 minutes after crossing a wooden ladder-stile you see the rocky point of Ynys Lochtyn below, with a path leading down to it via another ladder-stile. Behind you the Llangranog cove is just in sight, and it seems likely that it was somewhere here that Edward Elgar was sitting when the voices of the singers came to his ears.

It's safe and easy, and well worth the small effort, to make the 15-minute divergence down to the headland and back, especially in early summer when the sea-pink and other flowers are at their best. The cliffs dropping from this grass-topped promontory are not very high but they are steep and crumbly, so keep the youngsters well back from the edges. The sheer-sided islet of Lochtyn is separated from the tip of the headland by a narrow chasm which the sea does not fill at low water and is thus only an island when the tide is in. You are advised not to attempt the crossing on to Ynys Lochtyn; it isn't difficult, but you need to be very agile, footsure, and steady-headed.

Returning from the headland and mounting to the contouring track above, follow the track round the seaward slopes below Pendinaslochdyn, with a rocky inlet steeply below on the left, until a grassy saddle appears above on your right. Go up the easy slope to the saddle, where you will find a concrete-surfaced lane that climbs the little hill on the right. Less than 5 minutes of steep plodding up this will bring you to the coastguard lookout on the summit of Pendinaslochdyn, where once there was a fortress built by men of the Iron Age. On a clear day you can see right across Cardigan Bay to Bardsey Island in the north, nearly 50 miles away.

Return by the concrete lane to a gate and straight on down the broad track. In 20 minutes from the summit it brings you to the KEEP CLOSED gate and so back to Llangranog.

BRECON AND LLANDOVERY

Twm Shôn Catti's Cave

A Legend of Llangorse Lake

The Cave of Carreg Cennen

The Physicians of Myddfai

TWM SHÔN CATTI'S CAVE

Sometime towards the end of the sixteenth century a son was born to Catherine Jones of Tregaron, who named the boy Thomas John. Surname he had none, for Catherine was unmarried; it was generally believed that the father was none other than the great Sir John Wynn, of the noble family of Gwydir in the north. So just as an English brat of that condition might have been called 'Cathy's Tommy John', this Welsh lad became known as Twm Shôn Catti – widely known, indeed, throughout southern Wales. For when he reached man's estate Twm chose the trade of thief and robber, and his rogueries were told of in every tavern between the sea and the Severn. They were told of and laughed at, too. Twm was a prince of jokers, and though he had strength and daring enough for three he preferred impudence to violence, and cunning – of which he had plenty – to the use of force.

Twm was a master of disguises, and not only of his own handsome face and figure. A dozen times he stole horse or cow, used scissors and dye, and sold the beast to the man he stole it from. None could sing a better song than Twm or crack a merrier jest in Welsh or English, and many a gentleman who knew well enough that the King's officers were looking for the rogue would ask him to sup in his house for the sake of his witty talk. With poor folk he was just as popular, for he was one of those outlaws (like the English Robin Hood) who never took a bag of gold from a rich man but he gave half of it to a poor one. Every kind of thievery from cattle-lifting to highway robbery suited Twm; and in all of it he never lost his vanity, being mighty proud of the sprinkle of noble blood in his veins and swearing now and then that one day he would be the equal of the best in the land. But if he could put on the fine gentleman when he cared to, he could also make himself the lowest of the low – as they tell in Tregaron to this day.

Twm had stolen the prize bull of the wealthiest farmer

To Twm Shôn Catti's cave go through this gate and turn right. Walk through the wood

At the end of the wood, take the lower path along the river

Turn left up through the wood, following the arrow painted on a stone

The cave is surrounded by trees and boulders

in the district, and well the farmer knew it, though he had seen not a glimpse of the thief. Mounting his horse, and with a brace of pistols in his belt, he rode straight to Tregaron and reined-in outside Catti Jones's house. There was an old ragged beggar-man sitting in the gutter.

'Is this Twm Shôn Catti's home?' the farmer demanded.

'Ou, aye, it's Twm Shôn Catti's home,' replied the beggar, blinking up at him.

'Is he within here?'

'Ou, aye, he's within.'

'Will you hold my horse and my silver-handled whip while I go in and speak with him?'

'Ou, aye, I'll hold your horse and your silver-handled whip.'

So the farmer took a pistol in each hand and strode into the house. As soon as he was inside the beggar jumped up, threw off his rags, mounted the horse and galloped away. He galloped to the farmer's house and banged on the door, which was opened by the farmer's wife.

'Oh, ma'am – your husband's in grave trouble!' panted the beggar. 'He sent me on his own horse, saying you're to ask no questions but to send him fifty pounds without delay. I was to show you his silver-handled whip to prove I'm his messenger.'

The farmer's wife gave him the fifty pounds without hesitation, and away he galloped, hell-for-leather. But if you think Twm Shôn Catti returned to Tregaron you're wrong. He rode to London, on the way composing a great many *pennillion* which are sung to this day in the shires of Brecon, Carmarthen, and Cardigan. And when he got there, what with the fifty pounds and the money he got for the horse, a rare good time he had.

It was highway robbery that put an end to Twm's career of thieving. Dressed in his handsomest finery, on a blood horse and with a sword at his side, he stopped a coach on the Llandovery highway. In it was a rich squire of those parts and his lovely daughter. Twm fell in love

To get into the cave, you need to crawl on hands and knees

From inside the cave, looking out through the crack which is the entrance

Inside the cave, part of the roof has fallen in. It is now more of a crevice than a cave

with the girl on the spot, and though he took the squire's money-bags at pistol-point he returned all her jewellery to the daughter. Whether on account of the jewellery or because of Twm's good looks, the young woman took a sort of liking for him – but not so the squire, who raised all the forces of law and order against Twm the moment he got back to his Hall, which was not far from Llandovery. Twm had to flee for his life. But being in love he didn't flee very far. He hid in a cave among the rocks where the Tywi river comes out of the mountains, and from this refuge he pestered the squire's daughter night and day with messages proposing marriage.

As often as he proposed she returned a message refusing him. But at last she relented a little. A message reached Twm Shôn Catti's cave bidding him come at midnight to the Hall and she would stretch her hand from her window so that he might kiss it in a last and absolute farewell. So at midnight, with a full moon to light his way, Twm crept up to the Hall. Her window he knew, and as he came below it the girl's hand and white arm were reached out to him. Twm caught the hand and kissed it, but he didn't let it go.

'You shall give me this hand in marriage before I loose it,' said he. 'Your promise, and quickly.'

'Never!' cried the girl.

'Then I'll take the hand without the marriage,' Twm said between his teeth, and drew his sword, '*This* shall part you from it.'

The girl gave a bit of a scream. 'You would never do such a thing!'

'You think not? You shall feel the edge for a start.'

And he ran his blade across her flesh, drawing a thin line of blood.

'I promise – I promise!' cried the girl then; and in a moment Twm was binding his kerchief round the arm and kissing it at the same time.

Well, she kept her promise. Twm married the squire's daughter, and if you think he was ever allowed to go

Carvings on the rock inside the cave. One date reads '1832'

thieving again you're much mistaken. His wife obtained for him a general pardon, and before two years were out Twm Shôn Catti was a justice of the peace, a commission which he held until his death at a ripe old age.

THE WALK:	MAP SQUARE D5
TO TWM SHÔN	O.S. reference 146/782469
CATTI'S CAVE	Woodland path, rough in places but fairly easy. Allow 1 hour at least.

In Llandovery, drive past the railway station on A40, across the bridge over the Tywi, and turn up the lane on the right immediately beyond the bridge for Cilycwm, 4 miles, and carry straight on. Turn right at Bridge Inn, crossing the Tywi again, and immediately after crossing the bridge bear left (marked Llyn Brianne Dam) for 2½ miles, until the road climbs away from the river and comes close to steep woodland on the left.

Here there is a parking place in a dip just off the road, with a gate leading into the woodland. Park here.

Go through the gate and turn right on a waymarked path through the woods, rounding the slope of the hill. This is a Nature Reserve, and you are asked to keep to the path, which makes a complete circuit of the wooded height above. First mounting slightly, the path bends leftward and descends to a green space on the bank of the Camddwr stream, with precipitous crags on the opposite side. The valleys of the Camddwr and the Tywi which converge and meet a little farther on contain some of the grandest scenery in Wales. The path now keeps close to the river but soon mounts over rocks to maintain its level as the river rushes downward in its picturesque gorge. The steeper path going up on the left to Twm Shôn Catti's Cave is clearly marked all the way, and though it is something of a scramble the ascent is worth making — if only to marvel how Twm could have lived in such a place for any length of time. The surroundings are

View from Twm Shôn Catti's cave

165

extremely wild and beautiful but except as a refuge from the hangman the cave has no attractions.

The steep ascent has to be descended again and the circuit path rejoined. Turn left on the lower path. The river is now far down under the wooded hillside, where it plunges into the Tywi. The path soon bends to the left away from the river and leads, always clearly marked, back to the gate and the parked car.

A LEGEND OF LLANGORSE LAKE

The best-known legend of Llangorse Lake, also called Llyn Syfaddan or the lake of Brecknock, concerns a wicked city that was overwhelmed by floods and now lies at the bottom of the lake. More interesting, because more nearly historical, is the story told by Giraldus Cambrensis, the wandering scholar who recorded the first British fairy-tale. The events Giraldus relates must have occurred less than twenty years before he wrote them down.

King Henry I, who had made himself liege-lord of the royal Welsh princes, sought to appease these rightful rulers of the land by giving them small territories to hold under him. For instance, Gruffydd, son of Rhys ap Tewdwr and heir to the kingdom of Deheubarth (as southern Wales was called) was summoned to the king's court and given the lordship of one commote in his own country. On his return Gruffydd was accompanied by two barons, privy counsellors to the king: Milo earl of Hereford, and Payn Fitz-John, lord of Ewyas. Their way led along the shore of Llangorse Lake, which Giraldus calls 'the famous lake of Brecheinoc', adding that it supplied all the country with 'pike, perch, excellent trout, and eels'.

The two Normans and the Welshman who was in effect their captive rode in apparent amity, their gay surcoats worn over light chain-mail and their steeds splendidly equipped. Behind them at a distance rode the Norman men-at-arms. The lake at that season was covered with all kinds of water-fowl, and it was perhaps this that incited Earl Milo to make a jeering remark.

'There is a saying in Wales, I am told,' he said to Gruffydd, 'that if the true ruler of Deheubarth comes to this lake and orders the birds to sing, they will obey him.'

'In that case,' returned Gruffydd coolly, 'you Normans, who certainly hold dominion over the land, had better give the command.'

Llangorse Lake

More in jest than in earnest, Milo first and then Payn Fitz-John raised their voices and bade the birds sing. The crowd of water-fowl went on paddling and diving without taking any notice. And now Gruffydd, who had small faith in the old saying but full faith in his right over these foreign conquerors, threw himself from his horse and knelt facing the east, as if making prayer before battle.

'Almighty God, and Lord Jesus Christ, who knowest all things,' he prayed in a voice that all might hear, 'declare here this day thy power. If I am the true ruler of Deheubarth, I command these birds in thy name to proclaim it.'

As he finished speaking a great tumult arose on the surface of Llangorse Lake. All the myriads of water-fowl began to beat the water with their wings, each calling loudly in the voice of his kind, so that the noise was deafening. The two Norman barons and their followers were amazed and confounded. Milo and Fitz-John conferred hastily together and decided to send Gruffydd on his way alone while they hurried back to report to King Henry.

'When they related this singular occurrence to the king,' Giraldus ends his account, 'he is said to have replied, with an oath he was accustomed to use, "By the death of Christ!" it is not a matter of so much wonder. For although by our great authority we use much violence against these people, yet they are indeed the rightful inheritors of the land.'

For all that, the English kings never relaxed their hold on Wales. And to this very day there are Welshmen who maintain that the dominion of their country should rightly be in the hands of the Welsh.

THE WALK: MAP SQUARE E6
TO LLANGORSE LAKE O.S. reference 161/130265
                   Short and easy. ½-hour
                   or more.

Two miles out of Brecon on the Abergavenny road, A40, look out for a signpost on the left, LLANGORSE 4. Just before you enter the village LLANGORSE LAKE is signposted on the right and is reached by a short lane which emerges into open fields with the lake a few hundred yards ahead. There is a large car-park here.

Nowadays the lake is a very popular resort, with dinghy-sailing and pony-trekking in full swing at holiday seasons, but it's very well worth a visit for its beautiful setting. Placed in a wide circle of hills, it has a grand distant view of the whole Brecon Beacons range to westward and above it on the east Mynydd Llangorse rises to 1,661 feet. The largest natural sheet of water in Wales next to Bala lake, its shore-line is 5 miles long, much of it marshy, with colonies of wild-fowl of many different kinds; dinghy-sailers and holidaymakers keep these in hiding during the summer, but in the winter Llangorse Lake is almost as populous with water-birds as it was when the Norman barons and the Welsh prince rode along its shore. Rather oddly, the lake does not drain into the Usk, whose river-valley lies just below on the south-west, but sends its waters down to the Wye at Glasbury, ten miles away.

Sailing-clubs and caravan parks have appropriated much of the shore at this point but there is a pleasant short walk that will take you away from the crowds. Opposite the car-park at the end nearest the entrance lane a raised grass track runs straight across the big open field. Follow this to a foot-bridge guarded by a wooden stile, which takes you across a stream. On the other side, bear left across another field to a second stile, beyond which you have a view down the length of the lake.

THE CAVE OF CARREG CENNEN

For many days the castle high on its limestone crag had been besieged, its small garrison heavily outnumbered by the well-armed force of outlaws that ringed it round from the ravine of the Cennen river on the south to the hilly saddle on the north. The Lord Rhys, who commanded within the castle, had sworn a great oath to maintain law and order throughout this countryside and had no thought of surrendering his castle to outlaws; but he and his few men were slowly being defeated by an enemy in their midst – Thirst. The castle water-butts, previously filled from the Cennen stream, were empty now, though there was ample food in store. Two sallies led by Lord Rhys himself had failed to reach the Cennen and in both skirmishes men had fallen to the arrows of the besiegers.

One moonlit evening, while the sentinels on the walls watched keenly for a night attack, Lord Rhys sat at meat in the castle hall with his warriors. Beside him at the high board was Geraint, a brave and handsome youth who was like a son to Rhys. These two had shared the last of the water equally with their men-at-arms days ago, and though the soldiers croaked and cursed over their food no complaint had so far passed the lips of Rhys or Geraint. Tonight, however, Rhys could not eat the dry meat and bread with no drop of liquid to moisten it. He pushed the platter away.

'I thirst!' he muttered into his beard. 'God, how I thirst!'

Geraint, who had heard him, stood up and tossed back his mane of yellow hair.

'I will fetch you drink, my lord,' he said resolutely, turning from the table.

'Stay!' croaked Rhys. 'I command you, Geraint, that you shall not try to reach the Cennen stream!'

'That I swear, my lord,' returned the youth, and was gone from the hall before any there could stop him.

Lord Rhys tugged his beard and pondered awhile,

Carreg Cennen Castle, near Llandeilo

frowning. Was it possible that Geraint had some hidden flask of wine or water, concealed until now? But that was not in accordance with the frankness and nobility of the boy's character. Nor would Geraint swear an oath and then break it. Where, then, could he find water, when all knew there was not a single drop in the castle? Rhys summoned the oldest and sagest of his men and put the question to him. The grizzled warrior scratched his head and pondered in his turn.

'There's the cave, my lord,' he said at last, 'the cave in the face of the castle crag. It has a spring in it. A man can only reach it by a desperate climb, but I have seen my lord Geraint gain it.'

Rhys waited to hear no more. Springing to his feet, he rushed up to the battlements, followed by the old warrior. Peering down the vertical masonry that overlooked the Cennen gorge, they could see the sheer cliff that dropped from the foot of the wall clear and pale in the moonlight. And the moonlight glinted on the fair head of a man who edged precariously across the rock-face towards the dark opening of the cave, a leather flask gripped between his teeth. The outlaw sentinels down by the stream had seen Geraint too. Arrows hissed and rattled against the rock and one of them flew to its mark. Without a cry Geraint loosed his holds and fell. The yell of triumph from the outlaws was echoed by a cry of rage and grief from Rhys, who turned instantly and ran down to the castle hall.

'Lower the drawbridge!' he ordered, brandishing his sword aloft. 'The noble Geraint is killed! A sally – a sally to avenge him!'

Out into the moonlight rushed the garrison like a swarm of angry bees, to fall upon the outlaw force that occupied the hillside. Geraint had been dearly loved by all, and so terrible was the fury of Rhys's men, and so fierce and unexpected their onslaught, that although their enemies outnumbered them they were put to flight with heavy loss. Then Rhys, dividing his small force into two, attacked the outlaws in the river glen front and rear, and so furiously that they too were all slain or harried from the valley. Afterwards, while his warriors slaked their thirst at the stream, Lord Rhys took up the body of Geraint in his arms and carried it tenderly to the castle.

So the siege was raised. And on the very next day the Lord Rhys began the work that would ensure that no man should ever again die as Geraint had died. Near the castle gatehouse he caused pits to be dug and lined with stones to catch the rain-water, as may be seen to this day; and – as also may be seen today – he made a safe way between the castle and the spring in the cave below it. A fissure near the cliff-edge was found to lead down into the cave, and this he enlarged so that a man could reach the spring. Next he built a covered passage along the edge of the cliff to the fissure entrance. When this work was finished he had provided his fortress with an unfailing supply of water, and though Carreg Cennen Castle was attacked and taken and re-taken many times in the turbulent centuries to come, it was never again threatened by the enemy Thirst.

THE WALK:	MAP SQUARE D6
TO CARREG CENNEN	O.S. reference 159/668191
CASTLE AND THE CAVE	Short and scenic; if including the cave, take a good electric torch. 1½ hours.

To reach Carreg Cennen Castle drive on A483(T) to the hamlet of Ffairfach, only ½-mile short of Llandeilo. Here leave the main road on a lane descending eastward to cross the river, and beyond the bridge turn right (signpost CARREG CENNEN CASTLE) on a lane for 2½ miles to Trapp village. Here the castle is signposted again, uphill to the left, and again in ¾-mile where you bear right. Now look out for a Castle sign and cattle-grid on the right. They lead on to a finely-situated car-park and picnic place, with the castle looming grimly above.

The Walk consists chiefly of visiting the castle, which will take 10 to 15 minutes to reach. When you have passed through the two gates beyond the farm at the foot of the castle hill take the left-hand green track, bending right higher up to gain the two 'drawbridges'. Booklets obtainable at the castle warden's little shed inside the walls (which also stocks some good postcard views) will tell you all you want to know about the castle. It is smaller and starker than Kidwelly Castle but has a much more romantic site, its frontal wall rising straight from a vertical cliff 300 feet above the Cennen river in its glen below. The distant views are best seen from outside the walls: the Carmarthen Van to northward and gentler wooded hills and valleys rolling away to southward.

The adventurous part of the Walk (for which you'll need a torch) is the exploration of the cave of the legend. The route is only suitable for active folk and older children, and if you manage it without banging your head on the rock you'll do better than I did. The entrance to it is easily found. At first there are steep but well-made steps descending, then a covered passage with arrow-slit windows through which you catch thrilling glimpses of the drop below. Then you come to a warning notice and a steeper descent where a torch becomes necessary. From now on, mind your head!

A narrow cave, partly man-made, winds down into the heart of the cliff for about 150 feet, with rather slippery footing and a roof of uneven height. Near the bottom you come upon water oozing from the rock to collect in a hollow, but nowadays it seems hardly sufficient to supply a garrison. The cave ends in a shallow hole, which could be the blocked-up exit on to the cliff face.

When returning from the castle to the car-park, it's worth going a little way down to the right from the lower end of the wooden 'drawbridges', in the direction of the Cennen gorge. You pass the ancient lime-kiln and quarry ditch used for making mortar when the castle was constructed, and reach a flat grassy shelf above the Cennen stream. From here you have a good view of the sheer cliff on which the castle stands and of the windows lighting the covered passage on the cliff edge.

THE PHYSICIANS OF MYDDFAI

The Physicians of Myddfai figure in the historical records of seven centuries, from the Middle Ages when their odd herbal remedies were copied into the books of European doctors to the nineteenth century when their descendants were traditionally medical men. The legend of Llyn y Fan Fach tells how the ancient family of Myddfai came to possess this hereditary gift of healing. There are several versions of the legend, all with a great deal of circumstantial detail which I have had to abbreviate in re-telling the story.

The son of Blaensawdde farm, which is four miles south of Myddfai hamlet, was accustomed to graze his mother's cattle on the hill slopes round Llyn y Fan Fach, under the precipices of the Carmarthen Vans. One day he saw a most beautiful girl sitting on the surface of the lake and combing her long hair, and fell in love with her on the spot. Not knowing what else to do, he offered her the bread he had brought with him for his lunch, at the same time begging her to marry him. To his delight she came nearer to him and reached out her hand. But she withdrew it before it touched the bread, saying:

Cras dy fara
Nid hawdd fy nala!

– 'Hard-baked is thy bread – I'm not easy to catch!' – and with that she dived under the surface and vanished. The disappointed youth returned to the farm and asked the advice of his mother, who gave him some unbaked dough and told him to offer it to the girl if she appeared again. Appear she did, on the very next day; but this time her answer was:

'Unbaked is thy bread –
I will not marry thee!'

The persistent lover tried once more, taking with him new bread perfectly baked; and this time the girl came

176

The mountain lake of Llyn y Fan Fach, near Llanddeusant

out of the lake, took him by the hand, and agreed to
become his bride. She warned him, however, that she was
not an ordinary mortal, and that if ever he struck her
three times the marriage must come to an end and she
must return to the lake.

The two were married and lived happily together for
many years. The girl from the lake made a good wife and
bore her husband three sons, and the man prospered ex-
ceedingly in his farming. Then, on an occasion when the
wife had been forgetful, the husband tapped her jestingly
on the shoulder. Instantly she reminded him of the condition attached to their marriage, and repentantly he
promised to remember it in the future. Nevertheless, in a
year or two the offence was repeated in a light blow, and
the same happened two years later. On this third occasion
the lady of the lake rose up and left the house, saying:
'The last blow is struck, the marriage-contract is broken.

Farewell!' And back she went to Llyn y Fan Fach, to plunge into its waters and vanish.

Of the sorrowing husband nothing more is told. But the three sons, grieving for their lost mother, often went up to the mountain lake to gaze into its depths, hoping against hope for a sight of her. She too must have been grieving at the separation, for one day she appeared to them, bearing with her a leathern bag which she gave to Rhiwallon, the eldest son.

'The mission of you and your brothers,' she told him, 'shall be to heal the sick. In this bag are the healing secrets of the Other World.'

Then she showed them the different herbs that grew on the mountainside and instructed them in their use for the cure of all ailments. The waters of Llyn y Fan Fach closed over her for the last time, and the three brothers went down from the mountains full of their new mission. In time they became the most famous physicians in Wales, and were appointed as court doctors to the Prince of South Wales. For generation after generation all the sons of the Myddfai family followed the profession of medicine; and it is a fact that their last known descendant was Doctor C. Rice Williams, who had a medical practice in Aberystwyth in the year 1881.

THE WALK:	MAP SQUARE D6
TO LLYN Y FAN FACH	O.S. reference 160/804218
	Easy track.
	Allow 1½ hours
	at least.

Llanddeusant village is the starting-point for Llyn y Fan Fach, and to get there you drive on A4069 (south from Llandovery or north from Brynamman) to branch off on an eastward lane at Pontarllechau, 3 miles south of Llangadog. Llanddeusant is well signposted. When you reach the village, at the foot of a hill, turn down to the right, signpost 'Llanddeusant Church', then left at a signpost 'Llyn y Fan

Fach'. You have now about 4 miles of lane to follow, narrow and needing slow and careful driving. Pass the old church after 2 miles and go on $1\frac{1}{2}$ miles farther, passing the farm-house and riding-school of Blaenau. A short distance past Blaenau you come to a gate with a waterworks notice. Turn right here, steeply down through a gate to the riverside. The track ahead is now very rough. A sensible plan is to halt and park the car at the first likely turning-place, which is on the right just after you have crossed a bridge, and walk the rest. The total of $2\frac{1}{2}$ miles up to the lake and back will probably take about $1\frac{1}{2}$ hours.

Ten minutes or so up the stony track bring you to a build-ing, two gates, and a system of small dams and sluices. Higher up, the precipitous nose of Bannau Sir Gaer comes in sight, and a few minutes later you see the rounded crest of the highest Carmarthen Van, 2,362 feet, farther to the left. At this point you have about 15 minutes more to walk. Near the top of the track take a plain grassy path on the left to cut off a bend.

A building and a small dam can hardly spoil the wild grandeur of Llyn y Fan Fach, gleaming darkly under the sandstone precipices of the Vans. And the walk back will be grand, too – downhill every yard of the way.

ABERYSTWYTH AND ABERDOVEY

*How the Devil's Bridge
was built*

*The Miraculous Cow of
Llyn Barfog*

HOW THE DEVIL'S BRIDGE
WAS BUILT

In the early Middle Ages, when there were monks at Strata Florida Abbey and there was not a bridge across the Mynach river anywhere, an old woman named Marged lived in a cottage on the banks of the stream. She was a widow, and her only companions were her little dog Smala and her cow Malen. For her living old Marged relied on Malen, who supplied her with milk in such quantity that there was plenty for making butter, which she sold to her nearest neighbours at Pont Erwyd. The cow was accustomed to graze on the north bank of the Mynach near Marged's cottage, there being no way of getting across the gorge of the torrent; but one day of ceaseless and very heavy rain she strayed upstream and Marged saw nothing of her until that evening. Malen must have crossed the Mynach higher up, and in the morning before the water had risen. For when Marged went out with a cloak over her head at milking-time she saw her cow on the other side of the ravine, with a roaring flood separating her from her mistress. There was nothing Marged could do.

'Oh, why isn't there a bridge?' she cried, stamping her foot. 'I'd give anything for a bridge!'

No sooner had she spoken than she saw a tall monk standing on the other side of the river. He wore the long white robe of the Cistercians, and his cowl – which was oddly shaped at the top – hid his face.

'I will build you a bridge, Marged,' he said in a deep voice that came clearly above the noise of the water.

Marged clasped her hands. 'Will you indeed?' she said eagerly, and then hesitated. 'I know you holy men can work miracles,' she went on, 'but surely it will cost much money?'

'It will cost you nothing, Marged,' answered the monk. 'A bridge you shall have within the hour. As for recom-

Devil's Bridge

pense, I ask only to be given the first living thing that crosses it.'

Marged was so excited that she took little notice of his last sentence. 'Yes, yes – of course,' she said. 'Within the hour! That will be a miracle, sure enough.'

'And since my miracles must have no witnesses,' continued the monk, 'go into your cottage and wait there until I call you.'

The old woman did as she was told. To pass the time, she and the little dog Smala had their supper; and before the meal was finished she heard the voice of the monk calling in ringing tones. Marged ran out at once, a crust of bread in her hand and Smala trotting behind her. The bridge had been built! It was a fine stone bridge spanning the gorge, and on the far side the monk was standing close to Malen the cow.

'Your cow will not cross, Marged,' he called. 'You will have to come over and fetch her.'

Marged nodded eagerly and set foot on the bridge. At that moment a small gust of wind blew up the gorge and lifted the cowl from the monk's head. He pulled it on again in an instant, but not before Marged had seen what had been hidden beneath it. On either side of the monk's head there were two pointed projections. *Horns!* This was no monk, but the Devil himself!

It was now that Marged remembered the recompense she had agreed to. 'The first living thing that crosses' – the Devil was after her soul, of course! But Marged was a sharp old lady. She stayed where she was and got her wits to work.

'What's the matter?' the Devil demanded. 'Are you afraid to cross?'

'How do I know your bridge is strong enough?' retorted Marged boldly. 'I doubt if it would stand the weight of this crust in my hand.'

'Well, throw it on the bridge and see for yourself,' shouted the Devil impatiently.

So Marged threw the crust. But instead of throwing it

on to the bridge she threw it right across to the other side – and Smala at once ran across after it. As the little animal set foot on the farther shore the Devil gave a tremendous howl of rage.

'What use is a dog to me?' he yelled.

And a moment afterwards he vanished in a cloud of smoke and flame.

When Marged went across to fetch Malen, they were both glad to get back again, for there was a very strong smell of sulphur on the other side.

THE WALK:	MAP SQUARE D5
JACOB'S LADDER WALK	O.S. reference 135/742770
AT DEVIL'S BRIDGE	Path and steps, steep in places. Allow 1 hour.

To reach the small village of Devil's Bridge, drive from Aberystwyth on A44(T) turning right at Pont Erwyd (11 m.); or take the very scenic Rheidol Valley narrow-gauge railway. From Aberdovey, drive on A493 to Machynlleth, then on A487(T) for 14½ miles to Bow Street, where you bear left to join A44(T) for Pont Erwyd and the right turn to Devil's Bridge. In a quiet season you can park the car on the Pont Erwyd side of the bridge; otherwise, cross the bridge and turn left to the car-park on B4574.

The Falls of the Mynach are on ground belonging to the hotel, which has installed two turnstiles (each 20p in 1976). Both give impressive views of bridge and river, but the turn-stile admitting to the side overlooking the steep drop to the valley gives better value for money. The scenery of Devil's Bridge is unique in the British Isles and has been famous for three centuries. The Walk involves a descent of 300 feet, which has to be ascended again, and a steep flight of steps – Jacob's Ladder; elderly folk and small children may find the Ladder too steep for them. There is a Nature Trail along this route, for which descriptive leaflets can be obtained at the hotel.

Once through the turnstile, you can look up at the bridge, or bridges; there are three of them, one above the other. The Devil's Bridge of the legend (it was probably built by the monks of Strata Florida Abbey) is the lowest and smallest, with a stronger bridge built about 1700 above it and the road bridge at the top. An old paved path leads on easily for some minutes, with fine views down the forested Rheidol Valley, and then begins to descend by steps with guard rails. The final flight of these is Jacob's Ladder and goes right down to the river in the bottom of the gorge, where (if you reach it) you will have come down 113 steps. At the beginning of this last descent, by the way, is the only viewpoint where photographers can get a reasonable picture of the Falls of the Mynach, and a most impressive viewpoint it is.

An arched iron bridge crosses the torrent and beyond this you mount by more steps up the other side of the series of cascades. The ascent is thrilling as well as interesting, because there are spectacular viewpoints for each cascade. A short distance above the arched bridge a path goes down on the left to a cave by the side of the biggest fall, once the hiding-place of robbers; and about halfway up there is a welcome seat from which you have a superb distant view of the Rheidol Falls. A final ascent of 57 steps brings you to the wall supporting the road, where you turn right and gain the road by an exit door close to the hotel.

THE MIRACULOUS COW OF
LLYN BARFOG

Old Owen had farmed the land at the head of Cwm Dyffryn Gwyn, which some call the Happy Valley, for a good many years, and was known as a good farmer with plenty of sound common sense. There wasn't a better judge of cattle between the Dyfi and the Mawddach. But there's such a thing as uncommon sense, and in this, as you shall see, Owen was lacking.

Up in the hills above Owen's farm was a small lake called Llyn Barfog. According to the people of the valley the lake was a favourite resort of the Gwragedd Annwn, the noble dames of Fairyland, and more than one claimed to have seen these ladies strolling on the lake shores at the close of a fine summer's day followed by their greyhounds and three or four beautiful cows. Old Owen put little faith in such tales; fairies were outside the bounds of common sense and he didn't believe in them. All the same, he couldn't help thinking about the beautiful cows that were mentioned each time the tale was told, and wondering whether they, at any rate, were real cattle – strays from some distant farm beyond the hills. Resolving at last to put this idea to the test, he went up one warm summer evening to the lake, taking a length of hemp rope with him in case he found use for it.

Owen hid himself in the heather of the hillside above Llyn Barfog and waited. Just at sunset the surface of the lake stirred and out of the waters came three beautiful women. After them came three greyhounds and three cows of a size and shape that made Owen covet them at once. While the fairy dames walked slowly along the lake shore with the dogs gambolling round them, the cows fell to grazing the short grass by the water's edge, and since they were on the same side of the lake as the farmer in his hiding-place he had an excellent view of them close below him. So lost was he in admiration of the fairy cattle that he rose up to see them better, forgetting the fairy women.

The dames saw him instantly. Without delay but without haste, they all three glided into the lake and vanished. So did the three dogs, and so did two of the cows. But the third cow, whose grazing had taken her away from the others, was slow in reaching the water and Owen seized his chance. Rushing down the hillside, he secured his rope round her neck. To his delight, she was as gentle as she was handsome, and came willingly behind him as he led her down to his farm.

And now began a time of great prosperity for Owen the farmer. The fairy cow came near to making his fortune, for in quantity and quality her milk exceeded anything that ever was known and the butter and cheese that was made from it was just as remarkable. Moreover, she produced a large progeny, presenting the farmer with the finest herd of cattle in the whole of Wales. The fame of *Y Fuwch Gyfeiliorn*, the Stray Cow, was known far and wide, and Farmer Owen was a proud man indeed.

The years passed, and the time came when ordinary cows begin to lose their quality as milch-kine and mothers of calves. And now Owen's lack of uncommon sense was his undoing. This cow gave milk and bore calves like any other, and his common sense told him that – like any other – she must be converted into beef at the proper season, so he sent for a friend of his who was a skilled butcher. They led the fairy cow into the farmyard, where not far above them rose the craggy hill beyond which lay Llyn Barfog. The butcher had raised his knife, when suddenly a piercing cry rang out from the hilltop overhead. Instantly the butcher was held motionless with upraised arm and the farmer stood like a man turned to stone. From the hilltop the lady of Llyn Barfog called her cattle and they went to her up the winding path, not only the fairy cow but every one of her descendants, in a long file that represented most of Owen's wealth.

Not until every cow had passed the crest of the ridge and the fairy dame had vanished were Owen and the butcher released from the spell. They hurried to the crest as fast as their legs could carry them and looked down on the lake in its circle of low hills. They were in time to see the last of the herd walk into the water and vanish beneath the surface of Llyn Barfog. Nor were the cows, the greyhounds, and the *Gwragedd Annwn* seen again by anyone from that day to this.

THE WALK: MAP SQUARE D4
TO LLYN BARFOG   O.S. reference 135/653988
                                   Easy track and path.
                                   About 1¼ hours.

From the south and Aberystwyth, drive on A487(T) to Machynlleth, turn left on A493 and ¾-mile beyond Pennal bear right on the mountain road heading for Towyn. 4 miles along this there is a Parking sign on the left; park here. From Aberdovey, drive 1 mile beyond Towyn on A493 and turn left on a lane signposted 'Happy Valley and Bearded Lake', 3½ miles up which you come to the Parking sign on the right. There is a small car-park beside a lane.

Go through the gate at the far end of the car-park and follow the lane for 5 minutes to a farmhouse. The lane now becomes a track and mounts leftward through two gates. After 10 minutes a Public Footpath sign on the right marks a divergence up a grassy track, rather steeper, that curls to the left and then straight up to a gate on the skyline. If you pause halfway up, as you probably will, notice the fine backward view across the Happy Valley and its wooded hills to the sea.

At the skyline gate you can see nothing of the lake. But only 5 minutes beyond, passing through another gate, you come upon Llyn Barfog close below you, cradled in rocky hills and half-covered with water-lily plants. The water-lilies could be in flower any time from the end of June to early September. Barfog means 'Bearded', and though the name might have come from this flowery covering on the face of the lake there are learned folk-lorists who say that it commemorates one of King Arthur's knights who was sur-

named 'the bearded one'. It's possible and quite easy to walk halfway round the lake on a little path until you are stopped by a barbed-wire fence. Just above you at this point is a knob of heathery rock commanding a good view down the valley in one direction and up to distant Cader Idris in the other. This is one of many likely picnic-spots. However, if you intend to picnic bring the drinks with you; there is no running water and it's inadvisable to drink the lake water unless you boil it first.

ABERGAVENNY AND CARDIFF

The Giant of Painscastle

A Duel in the Dark

Doctor Price of Llantrisant

THE GIANT OF PAINSCASTLE

Once there was a strong castle where now only the big castle-mound stands above the little village of Painscastle. It was held by a huge and ruthless man known as the giant, with a warlike band of men-at-arms. Like the other petty lords in their castles at Hay and Old Radnor and Clifford, the giant of Painscastle deemed everything his that he could take by force, whether it was gold or cattle or some luckless maiden who had taken his fancy.

Llan Bwchllyn lake was on the western limits of the territories the giant claimed as his own, and one May morning he and two of his followers were riding past the lake when they caught sight of a young man and a girl pacing along the green shore, each with an arm round the other's waist. The giant recognized the youth as a squire named Arthur, noted for his skill as an archer, and though he had not seen the girl before he saw that she was very beautiful and instantly determined to have her for himself. Bidding his men follow, he cantered down to the lake shore. Before Arthur could disengage the short-hafted battle-axe that hung at his hip he was felled to the ground and his three attackers were galloping away, with the screaming girl flung across the giant's saddle-bow.

Half-dazed from the blow, wild with grief and fury, Arthur nevertheless acted quickly. He knew that the girl would be taken to the giant's castle and that his only hope lay in attacking it swiftly with sufficient force to make a siege successful. He ran to the farm of Llanbwchllyn and thence dispatched messengers on speedy ponies to the local chieftains he knew to be enemies of the giant – to Old Radnor Castle and to Cefn-y-Blaen where there were forty strong and sturdy fighting-men. Then he hastened to his own house for his bow and a quiverful of arrows, and with half-a-dozen of his men at his back set out to keep watch on the castle. Arthur did not doubt that the giant of Painscastle would expect him to do just what he had done, and would himself have sent messengers to

Hay Castle and Clifford Castle whose overlords would take his side in the inevitable fight. Likely enough, these messengers were on their way; but if by good fortune even one of them could be intercepted it might make the difference between victory and defeat in the forthcoming battle. So Arthur, approaching the walls and turrets of the castle stealthily, posted his six men to watch the main gateway while he took himself to a thicket from which he could see the small postern door in the flank of a tower a bowshot away.

Now as soon as the giant had arrived back at the castle with Arthur's lady-love on his saddle-bow he had given the half-fainting girl into the care of an aged dame, threatening the woman with death if she failed to keep the prisoner safe. Then he hurried away to muster his men-at-arms. The beldame was toothless and ugly but soft-hearted. When the captive sobbed out her sad story and begged for help she resolved to contrive the girl's escape and risk the giant's displeasure. Knowing every corner of the castle as she did, it was easy to lay hands on doublet and hose, a cloak, and a leathern casque such as the men-at-arms wore. When the girl had changed into these clothes the old dame led her quickly across the hall where men were hastily arming themselves, gained in safety a chamber in the foot of the tower, and drew the bolts of a little door in the outward wall. It was the postern door.

Crouched in his thicket, Arthur saw the door begin to open, slowly and cautiously. So the giant was sending out his messengers this way! He fitted an arrow to the bow-string and drew it to his ear. He was a master bowman and he would aim for the heart. Out from the doorway stepped a figure in cloak and casque. There was a sharp *twang!* and the figure collapsed with an arrow in its breast – and with a dying shriek that was certainly not the voice of a man. Arthur rushed forward and saw that he had killed his love. Springing up like a madman, he was in time to thrust in through the postern before the old woman could close it; and after him dashed his six men, who had come running at the sound of the shriek. Yelling their war-cries, they gained the castle hall where the giant and his men were arming.

Five to one were the odds in that brief and bloody fight, but Arthur and his men had the advantage of surprise. Using their short axes, for here was no space for archery, they slew some and put the rest to flight. Arthur, ducking below the sweep of the Painscastle leader's great sword, brought his battle-axe down in a blow that cleft the giant's skull.

In their flight from the castle the giant's surviving men soon joined forces with the fighting-men marching from Hay and Clifford. And Arthur found himself reinforced by the Cefn-y-Blaen men and those from Old Radnor Castle. The two opposing troops met at the ford of the Bach Howey stream half-a-mile south of Painscastle, and here at Rhyd-lydan the Painscastle faction was defeated with great slaughter, in which Arthur (as some say) sought death and found it.

THE WALK: MAP SQUARE F6
TO THE CASTLE MOUND   O.S. reference 148/167462
                                 Lane and fields.
                                 Allow 1 hour.

Readers of Kilvert's Journal *will recognize this story as the tale told to the Reverend Francis Kilvert by one of his parishioners in 1870 and recorded by him in his diary.*

The hilltop hamlet of Painscastle can be reached in a pleasant hour's drive from Abergavenny, leaving on A40 to branch right on A479 and reach the Wye Valley and Hay-on-Wye. From Hay, cross the river to Clyro and follow signposts and narrow lanes for the 4 miles to Painscastle. There are several places to leave the car, one of them opposite the Post Office. The castle has of course long vanished from Painscastle, but the huge mound and earthworks where it once stood are impressive, especially if approached by the short walk I shall describe.

At the crossroads in the village, take the lane towards Clyro for ⅓-mile, steeply downhill. Just past a ruined barn on the right at the bottom of the hill, and a few yards short of the bridge over the Bach Howey stream, go through an iron gate on the right. Keeping along by the hedge for 75 yards, you come to a second gate. Go through this and straight on in the same line across a large field, heading for another gate you can see about 500 yards ahead. There is no discernible path but this is a right-of-way.

The third gate brings you into a track. Turn right, uphill, heading for the earthworks of the castle mound above. When you reach them you'll find hardly a stone to tell you of the walls and towers that once stood here, but the size of the fortress is shown by the massive ditches and mounds. There is a fine view from here, Llanbedr Hill and Red Hill to the north and the Begwns to the south, with the quiet valleys and their little streams below.

This ancient mound is farm property, and the farm that owns it is tucked close under the slope on the north-east side. Go down and through the gate into the farmyard and out into a lane. Two minutes along this, going left, will bring you to the crossroads in the village.

If you are returning to Abergavenny from Painscastle, it's strongly recommended to take B4594 at the crossroads and follow it the 6 miles to Erwood, thence using A470 back to Abergavenny.

A DUEL IN THE DARK

In the *Llyfr Baglan*, that ancient book, it is related that Prince Gwaethfod of Cardigan had three sons, Aeddan, Bach, and Gwyn. All were great warriors, and they needed to be, for in the eleventh century the pagan Saxons were continually threatening to invade Wales. The Prince built and strengthened three castles close to the English frontier and appointed his sons to hold them; Aeddan had Grosmont, Bach had Skenfrith, and Gwyn was given the castle that became known as Castell Gwyn or the White Castle.

Many and fierce were the Saxon onslaughts, but the castles withstood them all. The years passed and at length the forays of the Saxons ceased, for their armies had to turn and face a new foe – the Normans. By now Sir Gwyn ap Gwaethfod was growing old, though he was still held to be the best swordsman for miles around, and his sight was beginning to fail. But as time went on, whitening his beard and rendering him quite blind, the old man learned that the White Castle would soon have to face another siege. The Normans, masters now of England, were preparing to conquer Wales.

The red-bearded son of the Conqueror, William Rufus, himself headed the strong army of Normans that laid siege to the White Castle. Beset by overwhelming numbers, facing the newest battle equipment, the defenders fought bravely but were at last forced to surrender. Sir Gwyn was taken prisoner and brought before William the Red, who let out a startled oath when he saw that the Welsh knight who had withstood his army for so long was an old, white-haired man with sightless eyes.

'Was there no strong warrior to command this strong castle of yours, Sir Gwyn?' he demanded jeeringly.

'None stronger than myself,' returned the old knight. 'Set me face-to-face with your best fighter, Sir Norman, and I will prove it.'

'What – old and blind as you are?' scoffed William. 'By

heaven, you shall rue that vain boast! Here is your sword and yonder stands my most skilled swordsman. If you can beat him in single combat I swear you shall keep your White Castle.'

'Agreed,' said Sir Gwyn, taking the sword. 'I ask one thing only – that this duel shall take place in a closed room without windows. It is but fair that my opponent should be sightless, as I am.'

The request was granted and the two fighting-men, Welshman and Norman, were taken to a windowless room of the castle and the door was closed behind them. Now began the sounds of conflict muffled by enclosing walls; the clash and clang of steel, the short fierce shouts of the combatants, and at length a louder cry suddenly cut short. The door opened, and Sir Gwyn came forth with his reddened sword in his hand.

'Your man fought well,' he said curtly. 'But you swore an oath, Sir Norman, and I call on you to keep it.'

'And keep it I will, Sir Gwyn!' exclaimed William Rufus. 'I and my men go from the White Castle forthwith, leaving it in hands well worthy to hold it.'

He was as good as his word. And Sir Gwyn ap Gwaethfod remained lord of the White Castle until the day of his death.

THE WALK:	MAP SQUARE F6
TO THE WHITE CASTLE,	O.S. reference 161/380167
RETURNING BY	Fields and paths, about
OFFA'S DYKE	2½ miles; allow 2 hours
	to include exploration
	of castle.

The White Castle is about 8 miles from Abergavenny and can be reached by lanes from B4521 or B4233, but it's pleasanter and more adventurous to walk to it from the nearest village, Llanvetherine, on B4521. Coming from the Abergavenny direction on the Skenfrith road, you pass Llanvetherine church on the right and go on for ⅓-mile look-

ing out for a telephone kiosk on the left. There is a roadside parking-place just beyond the kiosk on the same side.

From the parking-place, walk on 250 yards to a sign on the right saying 'WHITE CASTLE 1·2 KM'. A wicket gate gives access to a field where there is little trace of a path, but by going downhill in the exact direction indicated by the signpost you come to a wooden footbridge over a brook. Cross it and bear right, mounting to a stile, and beyond the stile go uphill beside the fence. Fine views open on the right as you follow the fence right to the crest of the hill, crossing another stile on the way. There are trees ahead, which hide the castle, and a stile at the left-hand corner of the wood. The small leafy path beyond this quickly emerges on a lane, with the White Castle entrance a few paces away on your right. You pay to enter (15p for adults in 1978) and you'll count it money well spent.

Descriptive leaflets can be obtained at the warden's hut, so I'll only say that for me White Castle is the most charming of all Welsh castles, having a real moat full of water and a battlement platform from which you look across hills and valleys unspoiled by the passage of time.

The return walk can be made by a different route. Opposite the castle entrance is a sign 'PONT GILBERT 1·3 KM'. Take this way, a broad grassy track that curves round the outer walls of the castle to a stile beside an iron gate. The long-distance footpath following Offa's Dyke uses these paths. Beyond the first stile, go along with the hedge on your right and then cross a second stile on your right, close to a barn; the sign here says 'OFFA'S DYKE PATH'. After 100 yards, turn left over a third stile and keep along the edge of a field with the hedge on your right. Stile Number Four has another Offa's Dyke Path sign. Beyond it, start by going downhill close to the fence and tall hawthorns on your left (the path, if any, is very faint) until you see, half-right and below you, a post and stile leading to a footbridge over the stream. Turn down to the bridge and cross it. 150 yards beyond is a hedge corner, where you bear right and follow the hedge (which is kept on your right) all the way round the edge of a big field. Ten minutes from the footbridge will bring you to the last stile, where you emerge on B4521 again. Turn right along the road for 5 minutes and you will regain the car.

DOCTOR PRICE OF LLANTRISANT

This is a true story, of a man who became a legendary figure in his own lifetime.

It was a cold Sunday night of January in the year 1884 and the chapel-goers of Llantrisant were coming out of chapel.

'See up yonder!' exclaimed a woman suddenly. 'Someone's lit a fire on Caerlan!'

Sure enough, there was a flickering point of bright red in the darkness overhead.

'Ten to one it's some flummery of the old doctor's,' said one of the men. 'We'd best go up to see he doesn't set himself afire.'

A crowd of people began to climb the hill, for Doctor William Price commanded affection as well as fear among the folk of the Valleys. There were those who said the old man was mad, because he claimed to be an arch-druid and practised strange rites by moonlight at the Pontypridd Rocking-Stone wearing a fox's skin on head and shoulders. But he was the finest physician that Glamorganshire had ever known, and his rule had always been to charge poor people nothing for his services and make it up by sending enormous bills to his rich patients. Also he had led the workers in the Chartist rising 45 years ago, and escaped to France disguised as a woman when a warrant was issued for his arrest. Now he was 84 years old and living with a girl, Gwenllian Llewellyn, less than a third of his age. It was believed she had borne him a child. All the same, he was the fearless champion of the hundreds of women and children who toiled long hours underground to put more money in rich men's pockets, so it wouldn't do to let him come to harm on Caerlan on a midwinter night.

As the little crowd neared the hilltop a familiar smell came to their nostrils: roast meat. They saw that some rocks had been built into a low cairn and the fire had been lit on top of it. Beside the cairn a wild figure stood to face them defiantly – an old man with snowy hair and beard, but tall and straight as a youth. But what brought them to a sudden halt was the sight of what lay on the improvised altar among the flames. It was the half-burned body of a very small child.

The cry of horror that rose among them swelled quickly into an angry uproar. Mad or sane, good or bad, Doctor Price had gone too far this time. Men grasped and held the old man, others dashed the flaming sticks from the altar and pulled the tiny corpse from the fire. Amid execrations, especially from the women, the Doctor was dragged down the hill into the village, declaring loudly as he went that the infant was his own son, called Jesus Christ, who had died a natural death. This, in fact, proved to be true, as was discovered after he had been taken into custody by the local police-sergeant. But this did not prevent him from being charged with the crime of burning a human body instead of burying it.

At Cardiff Assizes, before Justice Stephens, William Price chose to conduct his own defence against the indictment. Displaying a vast knowledge of British law and with frequent recourse to ancient documents, he succeeded in his contention that there was nothing illegal in cremating a dead body instead of burying it. The jury found him not guilty, and when he returned triumphant to Llantrisant the folk who had dragged him down the hillside of Caerlan on that Sunday night cheered him as he entered the village.

It was characteristic of the eccentric Doctor that the first thing he did after being released was to obtain the body of his infant son and re-cremate it. He continued to live with Gwenllian Llewellyn (he believed in free love and not in marriage) and had by her two more children – a boy, Jesus Christ the Second, and a girl, Penelopen. When he died at the age of 93 his body was cremated at Caerlan fields; and by that time cremation, established by Doctor Price of Llantrisant to be legal, was no longer so uncommon as it had been in 1884.

THE WALK: MAP SQUARE E8
CAERLAN AND O.S. reference 170/047834
LLANTRISANT VILLAGE A very short walk, up grassy
hillside. ½-hour.

Llantrisant is 7 miles north-west of Cardiff on A4119, a
small place with a rural charm which is unexpected so near a
great city. Where the road through it reaches the top of a hill
there is a small car-park with toilets. Park here.

Caerlan hill, where Doctor Price was interrupted in his
cremation ceremony, rises directly behind the car-park. A
wicket-gate at the side of the car-park gives access to it but
this is sometimes locked. An alternative way is to step easily
over the fence at the back of the car-park itself – I was told
'a good many folk go that way and nobody minds'.

A short steep climb up grass brings you to a projecting
knoll with a good view, where (say the locals) Doctor Price
built his altar and cremation fire. In full view down below is
the Tabor Baptist Chapel, and it would be characteristic of
William Price to perform his dubious rites where the chapel-
goers could see them.

The walk can't be extended from here; it is perhaps more
a pilgrimage to the site of the first cremation than a walk.
But a stroll round Llantrisant is recommended afterwards,
for the place has a certain quaintness and can have changed
very little since Doctor William Price's day. If you look
towards Caerlan from the tiny central square called the Bull
Ring you can see the Doctor's house standing solitary on the
hill crest, looking slightly sinister.

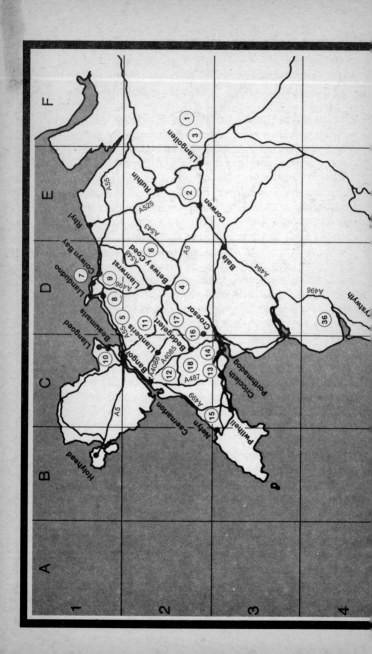

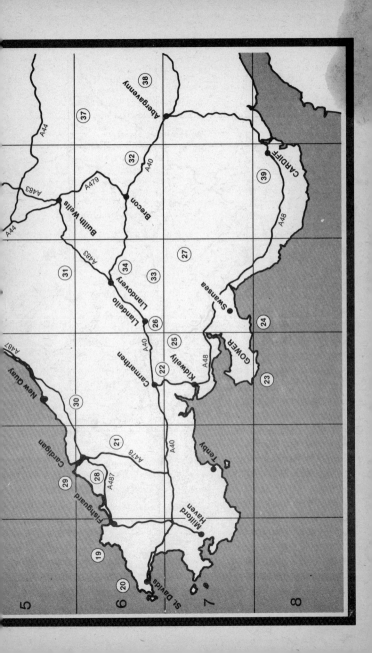

KEY TO REFERENCE MAP

Area	Map No.	Legend	Page
VALE OF LLANGOLLEN	I	Nest and her Lovers	13
	2	The White Hart of Llangar	18
	3	Myfanwy of Dinas Brân	21
CONWAY VALLEY	4	The Legend of the Afanc	27
	5	The Stone Women of Moelfre	30
	6	Taliesin the Bard	34
THE NORTH COAST	7	The End of Maelgwn Gwynedd	39
	8	Deganwy and its Castle	44
	9	How Prince Madoc discovered America	47
BANGOR AND MENAI	10	The Isle of St Seiriol	55
	11	The Lake that no Bird will cross	59
	12	The Farmer who caught a Fairy	62
LLEYN AND TREMADOC BAY	13	The Rising of the Lark	69
	14	Helen's Spring	73
	15	The Accursed Village	78
SNOWDON	16	The Story of Gelert	85
	17	King Arthur's Last Battle	90
	18	Glendower's Chimney	93
FISHGUARD AND TENBY	19	The French Invasion	99
	20	The Lost Land of Rhys Ddwfn	102
	21	Saint Teilo's Skull	106
	22	The Old Maid of Kidwelly	109
SWANSEA AND GOWER	23	A Baby on Worm's Head	117
	24	The Orgy at Pennard Castle	122
	25	The Drowned Well of Gorslas	127
	26	Owain of the Red Hand	131
	27	The First Recorded Fairy-tale	136
CARDIGAN AND NEW QUAY	28	When the Cuckoo came late	143
	29	The Mermaid of Cemaes Head	146
	30	Introduction and Allegro	150
BRECON AND LLANDOVERY	31	Twm Shôn Catti's Cave	155
	32	A Legend of Llangorse Lake	167
	33	The Cave of Carreg Cennen	171
	34	The Physicians of Myddfai	176
ABERYSTWYTH AND ABERDOVEY	35	How the Devil's Bridge was built	183
	36	The Miraculous Cow of Llyn Barfog	188
ABERGAVENNY AND CARDIFF	37	The Giant of Painscastle	195
	38	A Duel in the Dark	199
	39	Doctor Price of Llantrisant	203

Accession no.
36186686

THE NEW PUBLIC HEALTH

KU-453-731

THE NEW
PUBLIC HEALTH

Health and self
in the age of risk

Alan Petersen and
Deborah Lupton

LIS - LIBRARY

Date	Fund
17/09/15	xg-shr

Order No.

2652717

University of Chester

SAGE Publications
London • Thousand Oaks • New Delhi

ISBN 0-7619-5403-1 (hbk)
ISBN 0-7619-5404-X (pbk)
© Alan Petersen and Deborah Lupton, 1996
First published 1996 by
Allen & Unwin, Australia
Reprinted 2000

Apart from any fair dealing for the purposes of research or private study,
or criticism or review, as permitted under the Copyright, Designs and
Patents Act, 1988, this publication may be reproduced, stored or
transmitted in any form, or by any means, only with the prior permission
in writing of the publishers, or in the case of reprographic reproduction,
in accordance with the terms of licences issued by the Copyright
Licensing Agency. Inquiries concerning reproduction outside those
terms should be sent to the publishers.

 SAGE Publications Ltd
1 Oliver's Yard, 55 City Road
London EC1Y 1SP

SAGE Publications Inc
2455 Teller Road
Thousand Oaks, California 91320

SAGE Publications India Pvt Ltd
B–42 Panchsheel Enclave
PO Box 4109
New Delhi 110 017

British Library Cataloguing in Publication data
A catalogue record for this book is available from the British Library

Printed digitally and bound in Great Britain by
Lightning Source UK Ltd., Milton Keynes, Bedfordshire

Contents

Acknowledgments   vii

Introduction   ix

1 The new public health: a new morality?   1

2 Epidemiology: governing by numbers   27

3 The 'healthy' citizen   61

4 Risk discourse and 'the environment'   89

5 The 'healthy' city   120

6 The duty to participate   146

Conclusion   174

References   182

Index   199

Acknowledgments

This book was made possible with the assistance and support of many people and institutions. Alan would like to thank Andrew Lyon (Co-ordinator, Glasgow Healthy City Project), Ruth Stern (Coordinator, Camden Healthy Cities Project), Julie Taylor (Coordinator, Liverpool Healthy City 2000), Dr Greg Goldstein (WHO, Geneva), Heather McDonald (WHO, Geneva), Stephen Barton (Faculty of Health Sciences, Flinders University of South Australia), Antoinette Ackermann, and Linda Petersen and staff at the Healthy Cities Project Office in Copenhagen for giving willingly of their time and for providing items of information on the Healthy Cities project. He would particularly like to acknowledge the generosity and support of Dr Margaret Reid and the Department of Public Health at the University of Glasgow for allowing him the opportunity to share some of his early ideas with others at the Lilybank Seminar and for providing office space during the period of his stay in Glasgow. Lynne Hunt, of Edith Cowan University, Western Australia, introduced him to Margaret, for which he is grateful.

Alan would also like to thank the following people with whom he discussed aspects of the work while in the UK in 1995: Dr Robin Bunton, Dr Lesley Jones, Dr Sarah Nettleton, Roger Burrows, Dr David Armstrong, Professor Nikolas Rose, Dr Ade Keans, Jill Russell, Dr Graham Hart and Dr Simon Carter. Closer to home, he would like to thank everyone in the Sociology Program, Murdoch University, Western Australia, for providing such a supportive and stimulating environment; Associate Professor Patricia Harris for reading and offering feedback on his earlier draft chapters (the usual disclaimer applies); Dr Charles Waddell (Department of Anthropology, University of Western Australia) for his constant encouragement; and Murdoch University, which funded a period of study leave in which he was able to undertake research and meet the above people. Finally, he would like to thank Ros Porter, who has accompanied him on his journeys and has been a constant source of support.

Deborah thanks her previous place of work, the University of Western Sydney, Nepean, for granting study leave for the first semester of the 1995 academic year, during part of which she wrote the first drafts of her chapters. She also thanks Gamini Colless for his continuing support of her work. We both thank Elizabeth Weiss from Allen & Unwin for her guidance on this project.

Both authors contributed in equal measure to this book. Alan wrote Chapters 5 and 6 and most of Chapter 1 and Deborah wrote Chapters 2, 3 and 4, with each of us editing drafts of the other's work. The Introduction and Conclusion are joint efforts.

Introduction

'Lose weight!' 'Avoid fat!' 'Stop smoking!' 'Reduce alcohol intake!' 'Get fit!' 'Practise safe sex!' 'Play safe!' In contemporary Western societies the health status and vulnerability of the body are central themes of existence. Individuals are expected to take responsibility for the care of their bodies and to limit their potential to harm others through taking up various preventive actions. Increasingly they are also expected, as part of their responsibilities of citizenship, to manage their own relationship to the risks of the environment, which are seen to be everywhere and in everything. With the emergence of concerns about ecological crisis, we have all been forced to confront the global nature of threats to both self and society and to consider what we, individually, can do to protect our health and that of our fellow citizens. Everyone is being called upon to play their part in creating a 'healthier', more 'ecologically sustainable' environment through attention to 'lifestyle' and involvement in various collective and collaborative endeavours. All these concerns, expectations and projects come together in, and are articulated through, an area of expert knowledge and action that has come to be known as 'the new public health'.

The new public health takes as its foci the categories of 'population' and 'the environment', conceived of in their widest sense to include psychological, social and physical elements. With the development of this perspective, few areas of personal and social life remain immune to scrutiny and regulation of some kind. Given the scope of the new public health, and its impact on virtually all aspects of everyday life, there has been surprisingly little critical analysis of its underlying philosophies and its practices. The new public health has been warmly embraced by people of diverse backgrounds and political persuasions. It has been represented as the antidote to all kinds of problems linked to modern life, particularly problems of the urban milieu. The uncritical acceptance of the basic tenets of the new public health is disturbing in light of the increased potential for experts to intervene in private lives and for established rights to be undermined. We suggest that this reticence is in itself indicative of the power of the discourse of the new public health to shape public opinion. In this book, we highlight what we believe are some important dimensions of the new public health and critically appraise their implications for concepts of self, embodiment and citizenship.

Although the sociology of medicine, health and illness is a burgeoning field, and has been so for some time, very few sociocultural analyses of public health have been published (recent exceptions include Bunton et al. 1995; Lupton 1995; Petersen 1996). Sociologists working in public health areas have generally taken a consensual view of public health, engaging in a type of 'social epidemiology' in gathering data on people's health-related practices, beliefs and behaviours; or they have adopted an interpretive phenomenological approach, seeking to identify the 'authentic' lived experience of health and illness. These approaches therefore tend to work within the goals and discourses of new public health, servicing it rather than challenging it. While numerous Marxist and feminist critiques of public health have appeared over the past two decades or so, they have generally focused on specific aspects such as deficiencies in the provision of preventive services for underprivileged social groups, or the 'victim-blaming' approach in health education. Little attention has been paid to analysing the fundamental principles, discourses and practices of public health from an epistemological position, or to exploring public health as a sociocultural practice and a set of contingent knowledges. While we would not argue that other types of research should necessarily be cast aside by sociologists, we maintain that there is room for a more theoretically informed perspective on contemporary public health.

Over the past decade or so, there has been an upheaval in the humanitie and social sciences instigated by the adoption of poststructuralist theory. In its emphasis on the ways in which language, knowledge and power interact to construct and reproduce our way of experiencing our selves, our bodies and the social and material worlds, poststructuralist theory has challenged many of the assumptions about truth and knowledge previously held dear by scholars and researchers in the humanities and social sciences. No area of study, whether it be sociology, psychology, education, philosophy, cultural studies, geography, literary studies, history or anthropology, has remained impervious to this challenge. Indeed, these recent developments in sociocultural theory have blurred the boundaries between the disciplines. All of the above fields now include scholarship into the construction of knowledge and experience in the context of power relations. Such concepts as discourse, embodiment, spatiality and subjectivity are now ubiquitous in writings on humanity, culture and social life.

Despite the enormous influence of poststructuralist thought on the humanities and social sciences, the fields of academic inquiry and practice that have traditionally focused on the health of the human body—medicine, nursing and public health—have remained relatively impervious. This is due in no small part to the traditional exclusion from medicine, nursing and public health of the perspectives offered on embodiment, health and disease by the humanities and social sciences. These fields have tended to present themselves as scientific disciplines, built upon an objective knowledge base unsullied by questions of power. Medical and nursing students, therefore, have traditionally spent most of their time studying such subjects as anatomy, biochemistry and physiology, which represent the human body as an atomised collection of chemical and physical relationships—little time has been given over in the curriculum to exploring the body in its sociocultural, political and historical contexts. Similarly, students of public health, their gaze diverted from the human body as a single entity to human bodies in groups, have traditionally been trained in the rationalised, quantifiable techniques of epidemiology, biostatistics, health promotion, health economics and demography; again, they are given little time to explore the sociological or cultural dimension of public health. In the health sciences, the perspectives offered by the humanities and social sciences, poststructuralist or otherwise, have been frequently marginalised, at best treated as 'add-ons' to an already crowded curriculum (Lupton 1993; Petersen & Winkler 1992).

We decided to collaborate in the writing of this book after discovering our common interests and perspectives in relation to the social and cultural aspects of public health. Although this book is a joint effort, it complements and extends ideas we originally developed independently elsewhere, especially in our books, *The Imperative of Health: Public Health and the Regulated Body* (Lupton 1995) and *In a Critical Condition: Health and Power Relations in Australia* (Petersen 1994). These previous books share similar concerns, and to some extent, similar theoretical approaches, with the present book. *The Imperative of Health*, while adopting a poststructuralist analysis similar to the one presented here, was primarily focused on the historical antecedents of public health and the strategy of health promotion, whereas *In a Critical Condition* covered a far broader range of topics in less detail than the present analysis. We therefore see this joint work as both complementing and extending our previous writings by focusing on a particular range of discourses and strategies supporting the ideals of 'the new public health' that we had not examined in detail in the past.

In this book we demonstrate the ways in which contemporary sociocultural theory throws light upon the new public health as a domain of knowledge and an arena of practice. We explore how new public health knowledges and practices are constructed and reproduced and examine certain dominant assumptions that underpin them. In particular, we focus upon the new public health as a new morality system in ever-more secularised Western societies, a means of establishing a set of moral tenets based on such oppositions as healthy/diseased, self/other, controlled/unruly, masculine/feminine, nature/culture, civilised/grotesque, clean/dirty, inside/outside and rational/emotional. A number of themes run throughout the book. These include the importance of risk as a sociocultural concept in the new public health discourses and practices; the reliance upon the 'rationality' and 'objectivity' of science to contain disorder that pervades public health; the representation of the human body, the subject and social groups within the new public health; the notion of citizenship as it is constructed through new public health objectives and discourses; and the effects on the new public health of the globalising tendencies of modern societies.

Our analysis begins in Chapter 1 with the recognition of the fact that the new public health is at its core a moral enterprise, in that it involves prescriptions about how we should live our lives individually and collectively. Although professional experts justify their interventions in the name of objective, 'disinterested' science, they selectively order knowledge in such a way that some categories and some utterances and actions are privileged above others, and therefore seem more natural and logical. As we explain in this chapter, belief in the powers of science, in progress through science, and in rational administrative solutions to problems is central to the post-Enlightenment modernist tradition and finds expression in the philosophies and practices of the new public health. Much of our critical analysis is, therefore, oriented to the new public health as a modernist project. Following Michel Foucault, we contend that in modern societies power operates not so much through repression, violence, direct coercion or blatant control as through the creation of expert knowledges about human beings and societies, which serve to channel or constrain thinking and action. Expertise plays a crucial role in modern systems of power through the creation of knowledge about the 'normal' human subject. The notion of repression implies the use of naked force to coerce subjects into adopting some officially defined line of action. It is clear, however, that in modern societies power operates largely through a diffuse and diverse array of sites, utilising the agency of subjects so that they largely govern themselves voluntarily as particular kinds of persons. In the public health arena, experts have assisted in this process of self-governance through the advice they offer and through seeking to promote social institutions that facilitate 'healthy' choices. The area of citizen rights and responsibilities is an important terrain in the playing-out of these relations of power and knowledge, and can be seen to reflect changing relations of power in modern societies.

In the following chapters, then, we examine different aspects of the new public health in terms of citizen rights and implied reciprocal responsibilities and obligations. We draw particular attention to the recent emergence of the concept of the entrepreneurial self; that is, the self who is expected to live life in a prudent, calculating way, and to be ever-vigilant of risks. This concept of self, we explain, has appeared during a period of retreat from welfare interventionism and of reaffirmation of the importance of 'markets' as regulators of economic activity. The entrepreneurial self is the product and target of 'neo-liberal' forms of rule that employ technologies for 'governing at a distance' by seeking to create localities, entities and persons able to operate a regulated freedom. With the rise of 'neo-liberalism', the concept of rights, which largely took shape during the ascendancy of the welfare state, begins to appear rather limited, and flimsy at that. With the development of a 'duties discourse' in parallel with the 'rights discourse', citizens are assigned a whole range of new reciprocal responsibilities and obligations which require something of a superhuman effort to fulfil. As we point out at various points in our discussion, being a 'healthy', 'responsible' citizen entails diligence, self-control and hard work.

Chapter 2 focuses on epidemiology as it has been applied to pursue the objectives of the new public health. Epidemiological knowledge has played a key role in the construction of 'truth' about disease, risk factors, and categories of 'at risk' subjects. Further, epidemiologists have worked closely with the public health establishment in the effort to persuade people to make changes to their lifestyles so as to reduce risk at the population level. The development of national 'goals and targets' that has underpinned public health planning in a number of Western societies would not be possible without the contributions of epidemiological researchers. Given its close alignment with policy processes, it is surprising that epidemiology as a discipline has remained generally impervious to the type of critical scrutiny to which other sciences have been treated by sociologists of science. Epidemiology's pride of place within the public health establishment can be explained by the post-Enlightenment belief in the scientific theory of causation and in the ability to ultimately control problems through rational administrative control. Although epidemiology has a hallowed role in the new public health, its 'facts' are frequently disputed, both by experts and non-experts. Experts may disagree about the interpretations of findings and may be cautious in offering recommendations. Non-experts have their own lay understandings ('lay epidemiology') of health risks that may conflict with, and override, established scientific evaluations of risk. Chapter 2 explores these complexities, and highlights some implications for those who are the subjects of as well as subject to epidemiological knowledge.

Chapter 3 goes on to explore and critique the use of the discourse of citizenship in the new public health, pointing to the complexities and difficulties of adopting the notion of the 'healthy' citizen. As we emphasise in this chapter, 'health' has come to be used as a kind of shorthand for signifying the capacity of the modern self to be transformed through the deployment of various 'rational' practices of the self. Health is viewed as an unstable property, something to be constantly worked on. It is in the process of working on the self, and of demonstrating the capacity for self-control of the body and its emotions, that one constitutes oneself as a dutiful citizen, and hence as governable. Although the discourses of neo-liberalism might lead us to believe that private life is inviolable in that we have complete personal 'freedom' in choosing health-promoting behaviours, the range and kinds of practices we take up and adapt are, in the final analysis, suggested or imposed by the broader sociocultural and political context. Public health knowledges hold a privileged status as providing the 'truth' of health-promoting practices. The discourses of the new public health are deeply gendered, although this tends to be obscured by neo-liberal discourse which operates with reference to a disembodied, and therefore non-gendered, subject. As we point out in this chapter, women and men are positioned differently in relation to the discourse of 'healthy' citizenship and this has implications for how women and men experience their bodies.

Chapter 4 examines the multiple meanings of the concepts of 'the environment' and risk which have become central to the discourses of the new public health. In new public health discussions, 'the environment' and 'nature' are referred to as though their meanings were not contentious. However, as we show, both 'the environment' and 'nature' are shifting categories, inevitably reflecting assumptions about society and about human subjects. We examine these assumptions and spell out some implications of the broadening of the concept of 'the environment' in the new public health for self and citizenship. The concept of risk looms large in the contemporary period of heightened consciousness of the threats posed by 'the environment'. Risks are increasingly seen to be of a global dimension, and public health experts and environmentalists have turned their attentions to 'saving the "sick planet"'. In this endeavour, the city has become an increasingly important site for intervention. The modern city is seen as distorting the 'true nature' of humanity, and its spaces and places have become sites for controlling pathology. Contemporary concerns about the city and its spaces in certain respects represent a return to nineteenth-century understandings of the link between urban conditions and health status. As we show, however, the broad concept of 'the environment' has taken concerns far beyond the control of odour and dirt to the examination of the psychosomatic effects of urban life.

In Chapter 5 we turn our attention to the concept of the 'healthy' city which is gaining increasing currency within the discourses of the new public health. This chapter picks up and develops in more detail a number of the themes introduced in earlier chapters, in particular the influence of modernist concepts on new public health thinking and action; the focus on 'the environment', and particularly environmental risk; an emphasis on active and individual citizenship; and the tendency to pathologise certain city spaces and places through their identification as sites of risk. The Healthy Cities project of the World Health Organization (WHO), described by its proponents as the 'local expression of the new public health', reflects many of the concerns about the 'healthy' city, and provides a major focus for our discussion in this chapter. However, as we point out, the development of the Healthy Cities project gives only a partial indication of the popularity of the concept of the 'healthy' city. Many cities that are not formally part of the WHO project have adopted core principles of the new public health and are linked to one another via national and international 'networks' of Healthy Cities. We describe the context of concerns about the 'healthy' city, namely the problem of managing 'eco-crisis'. As we show, the 'healthy' city exhibits quintessentially post-Enlightenment modernist features, such as the concern with rational planning, the control of space, and the use of organic and scientific metaphors in descriptions of city functioning. Thus far there has been little critical reflection in the new public health on the concept of the city and on the political strategies deployed in advancing the ideals of the 'healthy' city.

In Chapter 6 we critically appraise the notion of 'community participation', seen by many as definitive of the new public health. Again, we
focus on the Healthy Cities project since, in new public health rhetoric,
Healthy Cities provides a key means for realising the ideals of active
citizenship and 'community participation'. For citizens, 'participation' has
become not simply a right but a duty. In the discourse of neo-liberal
democracy, participation is taken as a prerequisite of the fully democratic
society. However, in the light of many criticisms by groups who have
been excluded from participation, and of attacks on established rights
during a period of state retreat from welfare, the meaning and utility of
this concept need to be questioned. In this chapter, we draw attention
to the personal and interpersonal demands and responsibilities required
of those who are called upon to conform to the participatory ideal, and
make some critical observations on the concept of community. There is
now an extensive body of feminist and other literature critiquing the
concept of 'community', yet the term continues to be used in public
health as though its meanings and implications were unproblematic.
'Community' tends to be used in an overly restrictive way, with the
emphasis on place (the 'neighbourhood') as the basis for identity. The
effect of this is to deny the importance of other non place-based
identities that cut across, and may even conflict with, place-based
affiliations. We show how this place-based definition operates to 'fix'
identity and to exclude those who are deemed not to be members of the
'community'. The chapter concludes by calling for a critical scrutiny of
the discourse of liberation for its unacknowledged implications and its
constraining and often coercive and discriminatory effects.

In the Conclusion we draw attention again to the central themes of
the book, particularly the way that the new public health, almost in spite
of its own rhetoric and objectives, continues to rely upon a traditionally
modernist, science-based approach to dealing with health issues. This
approach, we argue, perpetuates standard binary oppositions that serve to
cast moral judgments of blame upon certain social groups, just as did
nineteenth-century public health. These moral distinctions, we argue, have
important material effects, including discrimination and the limiting of
access to resources such as health care. We end the book by reflecting
upon the ways in which individuals working in or researching the domain
of the new public health may seek to find alternative approaches that may
avoid some of the limiting, stigmatising and judgmental tendencies we
have here identified.

1 The new public health: a new morality?

All people in all countries should have at least such a level of health that they are capable of working productively and of participating actively in the social life in which they live. (World Health Organization's Global Strategy of Health for All by the Year 2000)

Health is not a 'state' to be captured and dealt with; nor is it some achievement to be attained with finality. It is rather the response of people to their environments. It is a response that allows them to go about their daily activities without personal restrictions that can be prevented. (Milio 1986)

Good health and wellbeing require a clean and harmonious environment in which physical, social and aesthetic factors are all given their due importance. The environment should be regarded as a resource for improving living conditions and increasing wellbeing. ('Principles for public policy', in World Health Organization 1990a)

Health status and the means for achieving good health are among the predominant concerns of our age. While health has always been a preoccupation to some extent in nearly all societies, the extent and intensity of health-related concerns evident in many contemporary Western societies are remarkable. Since the mid 1970s there has been a proliferation of new knowledges and activities focusing on health status, particularly the health status of 'populations'. While the increasing attention to body shape, diet and exercise is perhaps the most obvious manifestation of this concern (the 'lifestyle' focus), there is also a new consciousness of risks that are believed to lie beyond the individual's control but which are viewed as, ultimately, a result of human activity (for example pollution, hazardous chemicals, global

1

warming, the greenhouse effect, loss of biodiversity, and so on). There are, it seems, few areas of personal and social life untouched by this new health-consciousness.

The term frequently invoked to describe these developments, 'the new public health', implies the 'rediscovery' of, and some continuity with, the 'old public health' project. This 'old public health' provides a major source of identity for the contemporary field of knowledge as a whole. The 'old', or nineteenth-century, public health movement was primarily directed at controlling filth, odour and contagion, based as it was upon the miasma theory of disease and illness. It emerged at a time in which the European cities had experienced massive expansion with an influx of the working class from rural areas in search of employment. There were fears that the health and consequently the productivity of the burgeoning urban working population would deteriorate and that insurrection might occur due to the poor living conditions. The emphasis for quite some time was upon the infectious diseases that caused high mortality. It was not until the 1940s that public health practitioners, in Britain at least, began to devote their attentions to non-infectious diseases such as cancer and cardiovascular disease (Terris 1993, p. 137). These conditions are now the predominant focus of public health activities at the end of the twentieth century, with particular emphasis being placed on their prevention.

Within the new public health literature, there is a great deal of nostalgia for the 'golden age' of reform that supposedly heralded great improvements in health and in living conditions in general. The public is asked to place great store in the argument that the new public health continues this great tradition of reform and is of general social benefit. Typically, the evolution of public health is seen to comprise a series of scientific or technical 'breakthroughs': sanitary reforms are seen to have followed from the discovery of the contaminants of the physical environment; the rules of hygiene followed from the discovery of microorganisms; and (more recently) 'lifestyle' prescriptions and environmental and social changes are suggested by emerging knowledge of the personal and social 'factors of risk'. The narrative of public health emerges as a series of causal events in which the advance of science plays an independent and key role in improvements in life expectancy and population well-being (see, for example, Ashton 1992, pp. 1–12; Ashton & Seymour 1988; Martin & McQueen 1989).

This idealistic and progressionist view of public health, we argue, serves to obscure its profound moral, political and social implications.

The new public health can be seen as but the most recent of a series of regimes of power and knowledge that are oriented to the regulation and surveillance of individual bodies and the social body as a whole. This is not to say that it is simply a controlling or oppressive influence, and that there is no scope for individual autonomous action (in fact, we argue the contrary); rather it is to caution against the dominant view that the new public health is unproblematically a liberating project or 'movement'. Before proceeding with details of this argument, it is necessary to make some preliminary comments about that body of knowledge and domain of practice that has come to be known as public health.

PUBLIC HEALTH AS A BODY OF KNOWLEDGE AND DOMAIN OF PRACTICE

The term 'public health' itself is used in a number of different, and sometimes competing, ways. It is generally noted in contemporary definitions, however, that 'public health' implies a focus on the health states of populations rather than individuals; 'the public' in this case standing for 'the masses'. Emphases on the use of scientific principles, and on organisation and management also generally appear in definitions of public health, as in the following taken from public health textbooks:

> Public health is a combination of science, practical skills, and beliefs that is directed to the maintenance and improvement of the health of all the people. (Last 1987, p. 6)

> Public health is the organization of local, state, national, and international resources to address the major health problems affecting communities. (Detels & Breslow 1984, p. 20)

The term 'public health' also glosses the array of professionals and institutions who are responsible for measuring, monitoring, regulating and improving the public's health—primarily medical workers, health promoters, epidemiologists, health economists and bureaucrats working in state-sponsored organisations such as public health units; as well as academics engaged in researching public health issues, acting as consultants for the bureaucracies and training public health workers. Sometimes public health is associated with governmental action; that is, the public sector. Thus, the term 'public' health is often used simply to designate those forms of health care delivery not provided by the 'private' sector. On other occasions, it has taken on a broader connotation which includes not only these governmental actions but also the participation of the organised community; that is, 'the public'. Or it can refer to those services that are targeted not at a specific individual but at 'the environment' (for example sanitation) or the 'community' (for example health education), or to those personal preventive services oriented to especially vulnerable groups (for example maternal and child care programs). There are a number of sites at which public health is practised that are not funded by the state; for instance, the mammographic screening facilities offered by private health care services and community health advocacy groups. To further complicate matters, the term 'public health problem' is frequently used to designate diseases that are particularly frequent or dangerous; for example, AIDS or smoking-related diseases (Frenk 1993, pp. 471–2).

It is evident, however, that a comprehensive conception of public health has emerged that is directed not to specific services, forms of property, or types of problem, but rather to a level of analysis: the population (Frenk 1993, p. 472). Clearly, the category of 'population' has become the object and target for increasingly detailed knowledges and strategies. Thus, according to Ashton and Seymour,

> the new public health is an approach which brings together environmental change and personal preventative measures with appropriate therapeutic interventions, especially for the elderly and disabled. However [it] goes beyond an understanding of human biology and recognises the importance of those social aspects of health problems which are caused by life-styles. In this way it seeks to avoid the trap of blaming the victim. Many contemporary health problems are therefore seen as being social rather than solely individual problems; underlying them are concrete issues of local and national public policy, and what are needed to address these problems are 'Healthy Public Policies'—policies in many fields which support the promotion of health. In the New Public Health the environment is social and psychological as well as physical. (1988, p. 21)

This definition emphasises a number of themes to be found in conceptions of the so-called new public health: a shifting away from the biomedical emphasis on the individual towards a focus on 'social' factors, particularly 'lifestyle', in the aetiology of problems; a recognition of the multidimensional nature of problems and of required solutions; and particularly the adoption of a broad concept of the determining 'environment' that includes psychological, physical and social elements. It should be noted, however, that some definitions of the new public health are restricted to environmental concerns and exclude publicly provided personal health services such as maternal and child care, and even preventive services such as immunisation or birth control (see, for example, Nutbeam 1986, p. 122). Since the late 1980s, and especially after the 1992 United Nations Conference on Environment and Development (Earth Summit) held in Rio de Janeiro in Brazil, attention has increasingly focused on the health impacts of human intrusions into the 'natural' environment. There has been a proliferation of expert knowledges and activities (that is, publications, conferences, and governmental inquiries and commissions) focusing on the new environmental threats, or 'risks', posed in particular by industrial activities and rapid population growth, especially in urban areas; for example, the health effects of energy use and land degradation (WHO 1992a; National Commission on the Environment 1993; Ewan et al. 1991; National Health and Medical Research Council 1992). More will be said on this later in this chapter, and in other chapters. The point to be stressed at this juncture is that the dual emphases on 'population' and on a broad concept of 'environment' that goes beyond national boundaries have redefined many areas of personal life as 'health related'.

The new public health encompasses such concepts and strategies as health promotion and health education, social marketing, epidemiology, biostatistics, diagnostic screening, immunisation, community participation, healthy public policy, intersectoral collaboration, ecology, health advocacy and health economics. All of these are relatively 'new' approaches, which are used in conjunction with, or have supplanted, older methods of preventing the spread of disease such as quarantine, isolation and sanitary inspection. The new public health mainly incorporates voluntary actions on the part of citizens but also uses legislation, much of which is enshrined in public health acts, directed at the control of such activities as the wearing of safety helmets while riding a bicycle or motor bicycle, drink-driving, seatbelt use, the manufacture of foodstuffs, occupational health and safety, the use of firearms, the advertising and sale of cigarettes and alcohol, and the sale and use of drugs defined as illicit. Legislation is also directed at the control of infectious diseases, allowing the state to incarcerate individuals who knowingly spread communicable disease agents such as HIV. Emphasis is placed on cooperative relationships between state institutions and agencies, agencies and organisations in the private sector, and voluntary organisations; this is typically described as 'intersectoral' cooperation. With this expansive agenda, involving professional experts, bureaucrats and ordinary citizens, everyone is, to some extent, caught up within what has become an expanding web of power and knowledge around the problematic of 'public health'.

PUBLIC HEALTH AND MODERNITY

Public health and scientific medicine are traditionally archetypal modernist institutions. That is, both projects depend on 'science' as the bulwark of their credibility and social standing, and share a similar belief in the powers of rationality and organisation to achieve progress in the fight against illness and disease. That both public health and scientific medicine demonstrate a modernist approach is not surprising, given that they emerged at a similar time in history, the post-Enlightenment period, which was characterised by a turning away from the 'superstition' of religion to the power of human thought as a means of control over the vagaries of nature. A classical modernist approach views public health as a progressive activity, drawing on the available expert knowledges, technologies and means of calculation to further the good of members of the public by improving their health status. It relies upon the setting of goals and objectives and the measurement of 'outcomes' and 'efficacy' (as the current jargon has it). Public health, as a modernist enterprise, depends upon enumeration and surveillance as a means of countering the fear engendered by illness, disease and death, seeking to establish and maintain order in the face of the disorder of ill bodies.

Where the approaches of medicine and public health differ is in their relative focus on the health of the individual versus that of the collective. The knowledge base and philosophy of medicine privilege individual health above that of groups; doctors and other health care workers are charged with the responsibility to do their best by each patient. In contrast, public health views health states as collectivities rather than the property of individuals, tending towards a utilitarian approach favouring the interests of the many over those of the few. Hence the tensions created by the attempt of the health care bureaucracy to impose economic constraints on health care workers. The need to weigh up how best to spend limited resources at the population level—on the care of premature infants versus people requiring heart transplants, for example—conflicts with the notion prevailing in medicine that each patient, as an individual, has the right to the appropriate treatment.

While both medicine and public health are constructed upon the tenets of classical modernism, they have undergone a series of dramatic changes, as have many other social institutions, since the turn of this century. No longer are the claims of science to aid humanity accepted unproblematically. Medical practices and medical practitioners have become subject to open challenge on the part of members of the lay public over the past few decades. Critical scholars such as Ivan Illich (1976) have argued that biomedicine, rather than treating illness and disease successfully, is characterised by iatrogenesis—or illness caused by medical treatment—and fosters dependency. The green and environmental movements are examples of groups that have vociferously argued that science and medicine may be harmful, rather than beneficial, to the health and well-being of many individuals. In medicine, evidence of disillusionment with the claims of science has been shown by the emergence of self-help and patient advocacy groups, the antivivisectionist movement, the home birth and women's health movements, the growth of litigation for medical negligence and the increasing following attracted by alternative therapies (Williams et al. 1994, p. 186).

The HIV/AIDS epidemic has undermined the claims of modern medicine and public health to be able to conquer fatal infectious diseases, as there is yet to be discovered a vaccine or effective treatment for the syndrome. A discourse of fear has emerged around 'killer viruses' such as HIV and the Ebola virus, and bacteria such as necrotising fasciitis, the 'flesh-eating bug' that caused the deaths of seven people in south-western England in 1994. While the recent emergence of these 'new' diseases has also begun to throw into question the success of the modernist approaches of public health, the strategies used to deal with these diseases are themselves essentially modernist. The best measures public health can provide to deal with these epidemics are those of epidemiology and preventive health, including the centuries-old strategy of isolation and quarantine: tracking down the source of the epidemic, seeking to demonstrate how the virus spreads, suggesting ways of limiting exposure. Such activities provide a semblance of reassurance, in dealing 'rationally' with the epidemic, but ultimately demonstrate the ineffectiveness of medicine and public health in dealing with these new illnesses.

'The new public health' has been positioned by some as an evolved form of public health that goes beyond its original modernist strategies and philosophies. Burrows et al. (1995) contend, for example, that public health approaches are characterised by features of late modernity or postmodernity: in their deliberate attempt to distance themselves from hospital-centred curative medicine, in their focus on multisectoral efforts and multidisciplinary approaches, and in their emphasis on the 'active participation' of individuals rather than their passivity. Burrows et al. assert that 'health promotion and the new public health represent new forms of social mediation in relation to health and illness' in their emphasis on approaches 'based upon assumptions of contingency, a plurality of rationalities and, ultimately, to the abandonment of "truth" claims' (1995, p. 242). Some strategies of public health, however, they see as still modernist in their approaches, for example health economics, in its emphasis on rationality, costs, outcomes and systematic evaluation.

We would argue that despite these claims, the new public health still largely retains central features that may be described as traditionally modernist. It is not only the strategy of health economics that privileges evaluation; for example there is currently an emphasis upon evaluation, using rational strategies, in all activities of the new public health, including those involving community participation, to see whether they 'work' successfully. Medical, scientific, epidemiological and social scientific knowledges are routinely employed as 'truths' to construct public health 'problems' and to find solutions for dealing with them. Professional expertise remains privileged over lay expertise, as is highly evident in health educational advice to populations on how they should regulate their lives to achieve good health. Thus, while the new public health may draw on a 'postmodernist' type of rhetoric in its claims, it remains at heart a conventionally modernist enterprise.

The regulatory implications of the broad agenda of the new public health have remained largely unexplored in the academic literature on public health. This is due in large part to unshakable faith in the narratives of post-Enlightenment humanism—the ideas of scientific and social progress and of human perfectibility. The existence of pre-social human subjects who can, and should, be 'liberated' or assisted to reach their full potential through their own and others' efforts (particularly those offered by experts) has been largely taken for granted. Within this narrative, the early sanitary reformers appear as heroes who have helped to ameliorate the sources of misery in the lives of those disadvantaged by the twin processes of industrialisation and rapid urbanisation. Furthermore, they are presented as exemplars for current efforts to improve population health and well-being.

A clear example of the use of this narrative of progress is to be found in commentaries on the so-called Healthy Cities project, which was launched by the WHO in 1986 ostensibly for implementing new public health principles at the local level (see Chapter 5). In writing on the history of the Healthy Cities project, John Ashton locates the origins of 'the Sanitary idea' to the educative work in Britain of members of the Health of Towns Association in the 1840s. This largely upper-middle-class group of men are seen to have 'left behind them an approach and a menu of measures which had flowed from the sanitary idea', which included such supposed virtues as:

1. The legitimacy of working locally.
2. Resourcefulness and pragmatism.
3. Humanitarianism and a strong moral tone.
4. The recognition of the need for special skills and qualifications.
5. Appropriate research and inquiry.
6. The need to focus on positive health.
7. The value of producing reports on the state of the health of the population.
8. Populism.
9. Health advocacy.
10. The need for persistence and working with trends.
11. The need for organisation.
12. The recognition that public health needed to be the responsibility of a democratically accountable body. (Ashton 1992, p. 3)

Like much of the contemporary writing on the new public health, the form of narrative adopted here would seem to have more to do with confirming what has already become largely orthodoxy in thought and practice rather than with developing a critical understanding of fundamental assumptions. For instance, there has been no questioning of the fact that the Healthy Cities project was initiated by a group of experts and bureaucrats who have remained 'wedded to a conventional (and modernist) view that science can both liberate the human condition and provide legitimation for the political processes of so doing' (Davies & Kelly 1993, p. 7). We discuss in Chapter 5 how these modernist assumptions inform thinking about the city. In their failure to appraise critically the narratives of progress that underlie and support many of the projects of the new public health, public health advocates can be accused of leaving unexamined and intact the power relations that these narratives both reproduce and help to sustain. Given the centrality of the concept of 'empowerment' in the discourse of the new public health, health promoters have offered surprisingly little analysis of power relations as they pertain between, for instance, experts and non-experts, populations of the wealthy 'developed' countries and populations of the poor 'developing' countries, men and women, and heterosexuals and gay men and lesbians (for a critique of 'empowerment', see particularly Chapter 6).

NEO-LIBERALISM AND THE NEW PUBLIC HEALTH

Recent theoretical work in the social sciences and humanities has drawn attention to the interconnections between specific techniques of governance and particular forms of knowledge, and to the ways in which discourses such as public health have helped to shape identity and to define the limits of what might be humanly possible. Rather than theoreticians looking to knowledge to 'liberate' the 'authentic' human subject, the emphasis has shifted to an examination of the power of knowledge to define and hence govern subjects, as well as to an examination of the implications of this for the construction of self-identity, or subjectivity. Poststructuralist perspectives in particular have drawn attention to the fact that the assumed or constructed human subject of Western modernist discourse is an exclusive subject in that it is predominantly male, European, heterosexual, middle aged, and middle class.

From this perspective, the philosophies and forms of intervention of the new public health can be understood by reference to the political rationalities that characterise the societies in which the new health knowledges and practices have emerged, namely 'neo-liberalism' or 'advanced liberalism' (Gordon 1991; Rose & Miller 1992; N. Rose 1993). Since the mid 1970s, in Britain and elsewhere in Europe, the United States and Australia, the 'neo-liberalist' critique of welfarism has found increasing favour. The emphasis on individual and collective entrepreneurialism in health and welfare, and the devolution of responsibility for health care and other social services to 'communities', have received widespread endorsement across the political spectrum during a period when the limits of welfare as an economic, political and social strategy have become apparent. The features and language of neo-liberalism are described in detail elsewhere (see particularly Burchell et al. 1991; Rose & Miller 1992). Briefly put, neo-liberalism reinstates liberal principles, including the notion that individuals are atomistic, rational agents whose existence and interests are prior to society; scepticism about the capacities of political authorities to properly govern; vigilance over attempts of such authorities to govern; an emphasis on markets over planning as regulators of economic activity; and so on. Neo-liberalist rule operates not through imposing constraints upon citizens but rather through the 'making up' of citizens capable of exercising regulated freedom (Rose & Miller 1992, p. 174). Personal autonomy, therefore, is not antithetical to political power, but rather is part of its exercise since power operates most effectively when subjects actively participate in the process of governance. Neo-liberal government, then, is dependent upon technologies for 'governing at a distance', seeking to create localities, entities and persons able to operate a regulated autonomy (Rose & Miller 1992, p. 173). One of the chief mechanisms of neo-liberalism is the attempt to create and sustain a 'market'. Although the state is still seen to have a role in defending the interests of the population in the international sphere and in creating a legal framework for social and economic life, the emphasis is on '"autonomization" of the state from direct controls over, and responsibility for, the actions and calculations of businesses, welfare organisations, and so forth' (Rose & Miller 1992, p. 199).

Part of the impetus for a redefinition of state involvement in everyday life has undoubtedly originated with that loose political grouping known as the New Right, intent as it is in 'rolling back the state', particularly its welfare aspects. It is also apparent, however, that some of the social, political and cultural redefinitions that have facilitated the changing mode of rule have occurred as a consequence of the critiques and interventions arising from the so-called new social movements, such as the green movement, the peace movement, the gay and lesbian rights movement and the women's movement. The basic tenets of the new public health are fully in accordance with the 'progressive', 'democratic', and 'humane' impulse of these social movements, and indeed with the neo-liberal democratic values of the societies within which many of these movements emerged. It is significant that the new public health is frequently described as being a 'movement' for change, and that it draws heavily on the language of many other new social movements, using terms such as 'self-help', 'equity', 'access', 'collaboration', 'empowerment', 'participation', 'community control', and so on. This language has broad appeal, and its use has been an important means by which the new public health has achieved broad-based support while remaining closely wedded to official objectives (Stevenson & Burke 1991). It serves to mask shifting relations of power involving, in particular, a redefinition of citizenship rights and responsibilities.

The new public health is, if nothing else, a set of discourses focusing on bodies, and on the regulation of the ways in which those bodies interact within particular arrangements of time and space. Perhaps less obviously, the discourses of the new public health also seek to transform the awareness of individuals in such a way that they become more self-regulating and productive both in serving their own interests and those of society at large. By providing norms by which individuals are monitored and classified, and against which individuals may be measured, the emphasis of the new public health is upon persuading people to conform voluntarily to the goals of the state and other agencies. This is a crucial feature of the concept of neo-liberalism: the recognition that in modern societies the state is positioned as not domineering, repressive or authoritarian, but rather as part of a set of institutions and agencies that are directed at enhancing personal freedoms and individual development. Therefore self-government—or the regulation and discipline of the self as an autonomous individual—partly takes place through external imperatives. Given the penetration of these imperatives into everyday life, individuals come to understand themselves as citizens in relation to the sociopolitical technologies of government. As Burchell points out:

> It is in the name of our governed existence as individual living beings, in the name of our health, of the development of our capabilities, of our membership of particular communities, of our ethnicity, of our gender, of our forms of insertion into social and economic life, of our age, of our environment, of particular risks we may face and so on, that we both revile and invoke the power of the state. (1991, p. 145)

Corresponding with the emergence of this new entrepreneurial ethos has been a reconfiguring of the rights and responsibilities of the subject *qua* citizen. Roche (1992) has pointed to the undermining of the legitimacy of the concept of social rights as it has developed within the welfare state, as a consequence of New Right attacks on welfare provision and the very idea of social rights, as well as a consequence of new social movement critiques of the limitation of the established formulations of rights. Contemporary social movements of the oppressed, and the ecology movement, have drawn attention to the fact that the duties that rights imply are not all state duties, but also apply to interpersonal, international and intergenerational relations (see, for example, Evans 1993; Dietz 1994; Pateman 1994; Young 1994). Feminism, for instance, challenges men to act against the patriarchal order in which women are second-class citizens and to work towards a society of equal citizenship. The ecology movement calls upon all members of the present generation to undertake duties of 'environmental stewardship' on behalf of future generations (Roche 1992, pp. 50–2). The development of a 'duties discourse' in parallel with the 'rights discourse' has brought a stronger emphasis on social obligations and personal responsibilities that are restricted neither to national borders nor to a single generation. Thus, at the very same time as there has been an increasing emphasis on regional, corporate and individual autonomy, there has also emerged a stronger notion of globalism and global political responsibilities which makes national identity appear anachronistic (Turner 1990, p. 212). As we detail in Chapter 3, subjects *qua* citizens are increasingly being called upon to consider not only their contribution to the national health bill and their responsibilities to fellow nationals who have hitherto been denied full rights of citizenship (because of their sex, ethnicity, employment status and so on), but also their duties in respect to global environmental problems and to those people in less fortunate circumstances in other countries.

The emergence of a 'duties discourse' and a greater emphasis on the duties implied by rights is reflected in a wide variety of new public health literature, but especially in reports and charters of the WHO. Thus, the WHO's European Charter on Environment and Health acknowledges that while 'every individual is entitled to an environment conducive to health', she or he also has an obligation to 'care for a health giving environment' (WHO 1990a, pp. 29–31). As the Charter states,

> the entitlements of individuals do not exist without corresponding responsibilities, not only to protect the safety of others but to help promote a safe, health-enhancing environment for the community. Moreover, the individual is responsible to more people than those encountered from day to day in the immediate environment; public policies designed to promote the health and wellbeing of future generations and inhabitants of other countries need the assent and sometimes the active participation of individual people. Individuals are also responsible for the quality of the urban, rural and natural environments because they significantly influence health and wellbeing. (1990a, pp. 31–2)

A broadening of the concept of social citizenship, and an emphasis on 'rights implies duties', have profound implications for contemporary subjectivity in that individuals are called upon to take on responsibilities and obligations that were unimaginable when the conception of citizenship was restricted to the level of nation and welfare-state. To argue for the social rights of future generations and for remote others is to argue for new social duties and constraints on present generations and those already enjoying full rights of citizenship, with little or no possibility of reciprocity of rights claims against those generations or others (see Roche

1992, p. 242). It has brought into play an increased expectation of individual duties towards oneself and others and has given rise to new relationships, including international 'collaborative ventures' such as the Healthy Cities project. Among these relationships are those involving experts, on whom the individual depends for advice, although increasingly on a voluntary basis (N. Rose 1993, p. 296).

THE ROLE OF EXPERTISE

Expertise plays a crucial role in political rule in modern societies, by rendering a multiplicity of social fields governable through detailed documentation, classification, evaluation and calculation (Johnson 1993). Foucault has demonstrated how the human sciences emerged in the nineteenth century as part and parcel of the development of an extensive system of moral regulation of populations, which has involved making human beings the objects of the exercise of power. New specialist knowledges such as medicine, sociology and psychology, and new institutions such as prisons, schools and hospitals, were part of an expanding apparatus of control, discipline and regulation that involved micropolitical processes whereby individuals were encouraged to conform to the morals of society. These knowledges turned power from an external economic and political force into a form of rule based on 'the administration of bodies and the calculated management of life' (Foucault 1980, p. 140). Commenting on the techniques of rule in neo-liberal societies, Rose and Miller note that:

> The vital links between socio-political objectives and the minutiae of daily existence in home and factory were to be established by expertise. Experts would enter into a kind of double alliance. On the one hand, they would ally themselves with political authorities, focusing upon their problems and problematizing new issues, translating political concerns about economic productivity, innovation, industrial unrest, social stability, law and order, normality and pathology and so forth into the vocabulary of management, accounting, medicine, social science and psychology. On the other hand, they would seek to form alliances with individuals themselves, translating their daily worries and decisions over investment, child rearing, factory organization or diet into a language claiming the power of truth, and offering to teach them the techniques by which they might manage better, earn more, bring up healthier or happier children and much more besides. (1992, p. 188)

Public health expertise can be seen, then, as a particular example of a more general deployment of expert knowledge for shaping the thoughts and actions of subjects in order to make them more useful and 'governable'. In order that subjects be governable, however, social life needs to be rendered into a calculable form; for example, in the form of reports, pictures, numbers, charts, graphs and statistics. Those material conditions that enable thought to analyse an object, which Bruno Latour calls inscription devices, translate reality into a form in which it can be debated and diagnosed (Rose & Miller 1992, p. 185). Public health has developed many techniques for defining and circumscribing a governable terrain, and in this respect expert 'theories' play a decisive role.

In recent years, there have been an increasing number of public health 'theories' that posit one or more aspects of the 'conditions of modern life' as a causative factor in ill health and as an object for reform. An important development was the 'discovery' of 'unhealthy lifestyles', or rather their 'rediscovery', since the discourse of lifestylism can be traced back at least as far as the late nineteenth century (see Chapter 3). It is difficult to identify with any certainty the precise date of this 'discovery'. The mid 1970s, however, can be taken as marking the approximate beginnings of a period in which there has been a proliferation of academic and professional writings and associated practices focusing on those aspects of 'lifestyle' conducive to ill health. The recognition that it is 'lifestyles'—lack of exercise, poor diet, over-consumption of certain products, exposure to hazardous chemicals, and so on—that make people ill, has led to the adoption of a range of new education initiatives that have sought to inform individuals about how to change their behaviours in such a way as to avoid illness. The body of knowledge and practical activities that has come to be known as 'health promotion' has been largely concerned with identifying and changing 'unhealthy' or 'risky' lifestyles. Lifestyle theory posits the individual subject as a rational, calculating actor who adopts a prudent attitude in respect to risk and danger. The health promoters who want to change lifestyles are advocating similar values to those of the Protestant ethic that Weber (1976 [1930]) linked with the rise of capitalism; namely, that life should be lived rationally, in a profit-maximising way, with no room for such excesses as drunkenness, overeating, gambling, idleness, thriftlessness, and so on. Many health promoters would wish to 'turn people into calorific and cholesterol counting machines'. In this respect, they are closer to missionaries than to the disinterested scientists that they believe themselves to be (Metcalfe 1993, p. 41).

Within contemporary health promotion, it is assumed individuals have a choice in preserving their physical capacity from the occurrence of disease. In the event that one is unable to regulate one's own lifestyle and modify one's risky behaviour, then this is, at least in part, 'a failure of the self to take care of itself' (Greco 1993, p. 361). A persistent sociological critique of the lifestyle philosophy has centred on its failure to acknowledge the impact of such factors as class, gender and ethnicity both on life chances and on those individual decisions predisposing to 'unhealthy lifestyles', and on the consequent tendency to 'blame the victim' for what are seen as structurally induced problems (see, for example, Crawford 1977). This critique loses much of its potency as the domain of public health expands and everyone becomes, in effect, a 'victim'. As mentioned earlier, the theoretical project of the new public health has broadened since the late 1980s to encompass the 'total environment' as an object of study, calculation and intervention. Reflecting these concerns, the preamble to the WHO's Charter on Environment and Health stated that

> the starting point for policy on health and the environment is the recognition that, in principle, *almost every aspect of the environment potentially affects health for good or ill*. This applies not only to specific agents (microorganisms, other biological entities, physical forces and agents, and chemicals) but also to elements of the urban and rural environment: homes, workplaces, leisure facilities and the main components of the natural world (the atmosphere, soil, water, and many parts of the biosphere). A properly managed environment is therefore essential, not only to improve health but indeed to ensure human survival. (WHO 1990a, p. 21 [emphasis added])

As this suggests, there are few aspects of the environment that do not in some way or other have an impact on health status and hence are not relevant to human control or 'management'. Since the adoption of this Charter, there has been a rapid development of knowledge about the effects on health of the incursions of human beings into the 'natural' environment. A proliferation of government and academic reports has resulted as have professional meetings concerned with defining the relationship between health and environment and/or with establishing principles and guidelines for action.

Increasingly, there has been a focus on the risks associated with industrial practices and rapidly growing urban populations in both 'developed' and 'developing' countries; for example, the depletion of non-renewable resources, the increase in air and water pollution, and the generation of hazardous wastes. A growing number of expert reports and commentaries have drawn attention to the creation of unsustainable demands on the environment, and the intimate connection between current patterns of 'development', population growth, consumption and health (see, for example, WHO 1990a, 1990b, 1992a; Draper 1991; McMichael 1993a, 1993b). (This is analysed in more detail in Chapters 4 and 5.) It is within this context that a new conception of public policy has emerged. This conception is outlined by Milio:

> Simply put, public policy—the guide to government action—sets the range of possibilities for the choices made by public and private organizations, commercial and voluntary enterprises, and individuals. In virtually every facet of living, the creation and use of goods, services, information and environments are effected by government policies— fiscal, regulatory, service provision, research and education, and procedural. Public policy then becomes a prime approach to creating the conditions and relations that can nurture health. The new public health thus asserts that all public policies should take into account the health interests of the public. It advocates that policies should make healthful choices easy (less costly in various ways) and damaging choices difficult (high in monetary and other costs) to the chooser, whether a corporate body or individual. (1991, pp. 8–9)

As this quote suggests, public policy is seen as both constraining and 'enabling'. The idea of 'mak[ing] healthful choices easy' (or 'damaging choices difficult') is central in this theory, and constructs the individual subject and other entities as rational, autonomous actors whose behaviour can be guided or shaped through rational planning. Public policy is posited as a kind of tool which can be deployed in order to facilitate the autonomy of individual and corporate actors in fulfilment of their health-related obligations and responsibilities. As Milio points out elsewhere, the task of public policy has become one of 'creating environments' so that 'individuals would be better able to develop and pursue their personal views of "health"'. Although governments cannot assure that every individual attains personally defined 'health', they at least have the responsibility 'to establish environments that make possible an attainable level of health for the total population' (Milio 1986, pp. 4–5).

The shorthand term used to designate those policies designed to support the entrepreneurial actions of individual and collective subjects—'healthy public policy'—is seen by its advocates as a key part of the new public health (Draper 1991, p. 17) (see Chapter 5). According to the rhetoric, such policy is 'multisectoral' in scope; that is, it is not confined to the conventional sphere of health policy. It is also collaborative in strategy, involving many levels and areas of government, voluntary, economic and community groups (Milio 1986, p. 9). At least in principle, this has brought together and legitimated the involvement in health of a vast array of experts from such diverse areas as transport planning, engineering, architecture, agriculture, banking, social work, media studies, town planning and other areas of local government. It has also led to the emergence of a new conception of the domain of expert practice, encompassing 'political' action (for example, lobbying politicians, involvement in local action groups) as well as the production and application of 'impartial' scientific knowledge. Community action and 'community participation' have emerged as key concepts in the new public health, reflecting a more general concern with developing a non state-based sphere of 'the political' and with nurturing local autonomy (see Chapter 6).

THE PERVASIVENESS OF RISK

One of the key tasks of this expanding system of expert knowledge is to track down, calculate and eliminate the 'risks' that are seen to pervade all aspects of human life. The concept of 'risk' is central to the new public health and is therefore introduced at various points in our discussion, particularly in Chapters 2 and 4. Our approach to risk adopts the constructionist perspective espoused by writers such as Mary Douglas (1992), in which it is asserted that risks are sociocultural constructs; are always political in their construction, use and effects; and inevitably include moral judgments of blame. This focus on the social construction of risk is not to argue that there are no 'real' dangers and threats to which humans may fall prey, causing ill health, pain or death, but rather is to contend that our understanding of these dangers and hazards, including their origin and their outcomes, are constituted through social, cultural and political processes. It is through these processes that dangers and hazards become 'risks'. For instance, some dangers are singled out and labelled as 'risks', while others are not; this selection process is inevitably shaped by the sociocultural and political context.

Castel (1991) has shown the importance of risk discourse and the new prevention credo for social regulation in contemporary societies. As he observes, regulation has moved from a dependence on corrective or therapeutic interventions to the probabilistic calculation of risk and the development of risk profiles. The calculation of risks allows interventions to be legitimated not simply on the basis of the existence of actual concrete dangers, but rather on the basis of the expert assessment that an undesirable event may occur and that intervention can prevent this. This would seem to have vastly extended the possibilities for intervention since, to be suspected, one need not manifest symptoms of dangerousness or abnormality, but rather need simply display the characteristic that experts responsible for the prevention policy have identified as a risk factor (Castel 1991, p. 288). (For a more detailed discussion of risk as governance in relation to the discourse of health promotion see Lupton 1995, Ch. 3; Petersen 1996.)

A recently published public health text, *The Health of Populations* (second edition), illustrates the centrality of the concept of 'risk' within contemporary discourses of public health (Harper et al. 1994). The book is devoted almost entirely to the analysis of health 'risks': historical background to the control of risks (for example those associated with infectious diseases); the identification of contemporary 'risk factors' of personal behaviour and lifestyle (smoking, alcohol, diet, exercise, reproductive and sexual behaviour, driving behaviour, social relationships, the occupational environment, pollution, and the built environment); interventions designed to reduce risk (the production of less harmful cigarettes, cessation of smoking, changes in diet, driver education, legislation, and mass media campaigns); the search for effective therapies and changes in health care organisation for managing or alleviating the distress caused by 'risks'; and epidemiological methods of measuring risk. An elaborate body of theory, based upon the science of epidemiology, has been developed to explain associations between health outcomes and predisposing (that is, 'risk') factors. The science of epidemiology has become so integral to the public health endeavour of identifying, reducing exposure to, or eliminating 'risks' that it has become almost synonymous with the new public health enterprise itself (see Chapter 2).

Risk assessment has facilitated 'government at a distance' in such a way that health promoters are not clearly seen to be directly intervening, or coercing or punishing. Indeed, health promoters see themselves working at a distance through the efforts of others by way of forging collaborative ventures (for example 'intersectoral collaboration'), lobbying for policy change, promoting community action ('community development') and making alliances with the ecology movement (for example 'sustainable development') (Bunton 1992, p. 9). Contemporary health promoters have been at the forefront in the call for efforts to reorganise social institutions, and to implement different kinds and levels of intervention and collaboration involving public and private sectors, in fulfilment of the goal of 'health for all'. In their efforts to identify and control the 'factors of risk', health promoters have taken on the roles of expert administrators, program coordinators and 'community developers'. The 'factors of risk' they identify are distributed throughout the social body to the extent that (responsible) individuals at every turn face the task of having to monitor, regulate and change (that is, refashion) themselves to avoid, modify, control and eliminate behaviours and situations deemed 'risky'.

The construction of 'risk profiles'—analyses of the distribution of risks in given milieux of action undertaken on the basis of the current state of knowledge and conditions—has become an important task of health promoters. Since what is 'current' is constantly in flux, however, these profiles are constantly being revised and updated (Giddens 1991, p. 119). As experts identify new sources of risk, the norms for risk-avoiding behaviour change, and new forms of intervention and personal behaviours are called for. In theory, there is no limit to the number of risks that can be created and, hence, the number of interventions and personal strategies that can be employed. For the individual, it would seem, part of living in the 'risk society', to use Beck's (1992) term, is to be always aware of risk; to build risk appraisal into one's 'life-planning' (Giddens 1991, pp. 125–6).

A particularly clear example of the attempt to generalise these risks to the whole population is the development and implementation in health promotion of specified 'goals and targets'. Australia, the United States, England and Wales, and to some extent New Zealand, have in recent years developed such targets to 'guide decision-making in relation to health services provision and health promotion activities' (Nutbeam et al. 1993, p. 10). In Australia, the goals and targets were originally endorsed by the Australian Health Ministers' Conference in 1988. In 1993, however, there was a proposal to further refine these national goals and targets with the explicit aims of broadening the 'framework of action', setting in place mechanisms for accountability and the monitoring of progress, and more fully engaging the health system in health promotion (Nutbeam et al. 1993, pp. 8–9). The proposed 'extended framework' in the subsequent *Goals and Targets for Australia's Health in the Year 2000 and Beyond* included an elaborate schema identifying health goals and targets (including estimated date of achievable change) for a large range of 'preventable mortality and morbidity' in relation to different 'priority populations' (defined by age, gender, ethnicity, Aboriginality, socioeconomic status, and location of residence). It also sought to identify lifestyle and risk factors, personal knowledge and skills, and environmental determinants of health that need action in respect to each of a range of identified preventable conditions.

The ambitious nature of this agenda can be appreciated by examining just one area for action noted in the above goals and targets proposal: land transport, particularly motor vehicle transport. The dangers associated with motor transport identified in the 1993 *Goals and Targets* report include air pollution, traffic congestion, excess noise, personal injury, loss of bushland, and global warming (Nutbeam et al. 1993, p. 189). In order to develop transport systems that protect and promote health (that is, systems that minimise risks), it was contended, changes need to be made in such areas as vehicle design and safety, road safety legislation, local traffic planning, and land use planning. This calls for the involvement of a large range of regulatory agencies (for example, state and federal departments of transport, local councils, urban planning authorities), and the employment of specialised bodies and expertise to monitor the environmental and health impacts of these developments (Nutbeam et al. 1993, pp. 189–90). The goals and targets proposal acknowledged the differential impact of risks on different categories of population, and so specific strategies were proposed for specified 'at risk' groups. For example, children, older people, and people with a disability were collectively deemed to be at high risk of transport-related injury (presumably because they are more likely to be pedestrians), and a number of recommendations to minimise exposure to risk were indicated (1993, p. 191).

The complex system for monitoring and regulating populations that is indicated in the goals and targets strategy is informed, and technically facilitated, by advances in the statistical calculation of risk. Health promotion surveys, often referred to as 'lifestyle surveys', focus attention on increasingly detailed aspects of everyday life used for the calculation of risk: leisure activities; participation in exercise; the extent of social and sexual contact; intake of fats, fibre, sugar, alcohol and tobacco; body weight; blood pressure; cholesterol; and so on (Bunton 1992, p. 7). There are few areas of personal and public life that are not relevant to the calculation of risk based on such surveys. Armstrong (1983) depicts the social survey as a means of distributing the disciplinary gaze throughout society. It has expanded the concerns of medicine beyond the confines of the hospital walls, and constructed the concept of health from populations. Both the sick and the well are caught up in a web of observation. The survey has provided the possibility of dissolving the division between normal and abnormal populations. It has become an increasingly important technique for regulating populations by construct-ing the norm and allowing the measurement of individual differences; that is, for creating particular kinds of selves (Armstrong 1983, pp. 50–1).

With the advent of the survey there is no longer any need for individuals to be under the direct gaze of experts, because the construction of risk profiles largely takes the place of treatment (Castel 1991, p. 291). The need for intervention is deduced from the general definition of dangers one wishes to prevent rather than from their observation in experience. For instance, a social worker will be sent to visit a family to confirm or disprove the 'real' presence of a danger, on the basis of the 'probabilistic and abstract' existence of risks (Castel 1991, pp. 287–8). Castel believes this shift 'from dangerousness to risk' has given unprecedented power to the administrators, and that 'practitioners are made completely subordinate to objectives of management policy'. Practitioners no longer control the use of the data they produce, for administration acquires almost complete control over the new technology (Castel 1991, p. 293).

SELF-REGULATION AND BODY MANAGEMENT

The body has become the target of many of the new health risk-man-agement strategies, as both Giddens (1991) and Shilling (1993) have observed. In a context of risk and uncertainty concerns about the social and 'natural' environments are projected onto a concern about the body. A central feature of the way that health risk is currently perceived and understood is the perception that 'the world is getting smaller'; that events in one part of the world have the potential to have an impact on distant other parts. It is not only regions and countries that are linked together in this discourse, but also individual bodies: our health is now connected to social processes occurring in areas remote from where we live. This raises the issue of another feature of contemporary human existence, which has been termed 'globalisation'—the tendency towards lack of differentiation between nations or cultures in conjunction with greater diversity within nations and a concomitant fragmentation of identities (see Chapter 6). As environmental and technological risks are generalised to the point where everyone, regardless of social location, is 'at risk', there is a tendency for concern about the body to be globalised (Shilling 1993, p. 73). The body offers at least one 'island of security' in a global system of multiple and inescapable risks. Strict adherence to self-care regimes is seen as the only real means of avoiding the cancers, heart diseases and other afflictions that constantly threaten the integrity of the self in a generalised climate of risk.

In the consumer culture of modern society, the consuming body has become a key marker of identity. It provides the point of reference for subjects in constructing themselves both in conformity with social norms (the 'social self') and as separate and distinctive from other selves (the 'individual self') (Falk 1994, pp. 136–8). The discourses and practices that have emerged around 'healthy' bodies constitute probably the most clear instance of how the body has become a project to be 'worked on' as part of a person's self-identity. It is so pervasive that even those who smoke, drink, and consume other drugs cannot help but reflect on the effects of such actions on the health and appearance of their bodies (Shilling 1993, p. 6). Attention to the 'healthy' body, therefore, is not simply about warding off disease. It is also concerned with how we present our bodies to ourselves and to others. While 'old' public health strategies focused almost entirely on issues of public hygiene—the cleanliness of the streets, the regulation of industry, sanitation and water supply—the new public health has directed its attentions towards the conduct and appearance of the individual body. Treating the body as a project implies that it is open to reconstruction in line with the designs of its owner, so that one can, in effect, reconstitute the self in accordance with one's own desires. There is a certain 'open-endedness' or 'unfinishedness' about this project since the body is continually shaped by social, cultural and economic processes (Shilling 1993, pp. 4–8, 199–200). The body therefore bespeaks fashions in bodily practices emerging from both aesthetic and health-related imperatives: the plump body, the angular body, the jogging body, the taut body, the tanned body, the pale body are all testaments to changing notions of what is considered both attractive and healthy in different eras (see also Garner et al. 1980; Koval 1986).

The strategy of health promotion, in particular, adopts the conceptualisation of the body as a writing surface, subject to visible changes wrought by bodily practices:

> This metaphorics of body writing posits the body, and particularly its epidermic surface, muscular-skeletal frame, ligaments, joints, blood vessels, and internal organs as corporeal surfaces, the blank page on which engraving, graffiti, tattooing, or inscription can take place. (Grosz 1994, p. 117)

In this conceptualisation, the body is plastic, malleable, a text that may be written over and retraced, resulting in a body that is a palimpsest of bodily practices (Grosz 1994, p. 117). Indeed, some of the key concerns and dimensions of the new public health, in particular those related to health promotion, are arranged around aesthetics: the avoidance of illness and disease, the aftereffects of which are often physically unaesthetic (the blotches of Kaposi's sarcoma and the extreme thinness that accompany HIV/AIDS, the mastectomy, the scars caused by surgery, the hacking cough and spitting accompanying emphysema or lung cancer); the focus on the slender, firm, controlled body as contrasted with the 'grotesque' body of flabby obesity; the sweet breath and clear skin of the non-smoker versus the halitosis and wrinkled, nicotine-stained skin of the smoker ('Kissing a smoker is like licking an ashtray', as one health promotion sticker had it).

That the body has become a project that is seen as 'unfinished', malleable and as subject to transformation is supported by the growing knowledge and technical expertise concerned with intervening in and substantially altering the shape, look and functioning of bodies. A 'body industry' has emerged, comprising such diverse institutions as weight loss centres, gymnasiums, fashion magazine publishers, the medical establishment, and pharmaceutical and advertising companies, institutions that collectively extol the virtues of nurturing the 'healthy', risk-averting body (Koval 1986; Finkelstein 1991). Alongside this there has developed an increasingly sophisticated array of experts of both mind and body such as plastic surgeons, psychologists, psychoanalysts, aerobics teachers, dietitians and stress management consultants, available to instruct one on how to better manage one's relationship to risk. Together these experts help to produce individuals who monitor their own compliance with dietary, exercise and other body maintenance regimes and who live their life as a project to be perfected (Metcalfe 1993, p. 41).

Feminist writers such as Bordo (1993), Sawicki (1991), McNay (1992) and Diprose (1994) have drawn attention to the deeply gendered nature of the processes of body self-regulation, particularly in respect to those aspects of the body associated most centrally with female sexuality and beauty: the face, breasts and reproductive organs. These writers have spelt out the many implications for the subjectivity of women in such areas as childbirth, eating disorders, cosmetic surgery and the treatment of illness. An important development in feminist theory is the acknowledgment that women are not passive 'victims' of regulatory mechanisms of the body, but are active and willing participants in the very processes that objectify and dominate them (see, for example, Jacobus et al. 1990; Bordo 1993). Women take up forms of body management that tend to constitute them as mothers, carers and homemakers, while men engage with forms of body management that allow them scope to demonstrate their power, self-control and physical invulnerability (see Chapter 3). Both women and men, however, are to some degree caught up in the processes of body self-regulation, with attendant implications for self-identity and social identity.

The 'healthy' body has become an increasingly important signifier of moral worth, a mark of distinction that serves to delineate those who deserve to succeed from those who will fail (Crawford 1994, p. 1354). The pursuit of health through work on the body has become a crucial means by which the individual can express publicly such virtues as self-control, self-discipline, self-denial and will power—in short, those qualifications considered important to being a 'normal', 'healthy' human being. Maintaining normality is hard work in that it takes time, effort and planning. It becomes so taken for granted by all, however, that people generally need only minimal policing by experts to persuade them to monitor their own bodies for signs of potential illness (de Swaan 1990, pp. 57–71). The adoption of various regimes of health and fitness can be seen to provide opportunities to mobilise symbolic resources; to demonstrate the competence of the self both in mastering oneself and in demonstrating virtues of moderation (for example the well-toned, trim body). More than this, such regimes also provide the occasion for policing the boundaries between the normal ('healthy') self and abnormal ('unhealthy') others—for example, the poor, 'drug addicts' or 'sexual deviants'—who are imagined as embodying all the properties falling outside this health-signified self. Thus, the process of nurturing identity necessarily entails the adoption of various strategies for protecting oneself from symbolic connection to 'infected' others and the negative characteristics ascribed to them (Crawford 1994, p. 1348). This can lead to intolerance, exclusion or persecution of others who are deemed 'infected', 'contagious' or of imperfect body shape or size, or who appear unwilling or unable to engage in those activities deemed health-enhancing.

Metcalfe has drawn attention to the dangers of the preoccupation with personal health as a primary element in the definition of personal well-being; that is, 'healthism'. As he contends, healthism operates on the questionable assumption that everyone should work and live to maximise their health (1993, p. 35). Those who are unable or unwilling to subscribe to the dominant health norms are likely to be labelled in a derogatory way (for example fat, weak or lazy) and to be castigated for their lack of self-control. Metcalfe's criticisms are mainly directed against those health promoters who 'decide that their goal is to make people more health-conscious and healthier, or that their goal is to stop people's consumption of cigarettes, alcohol and unhealthy foods, to increase the amount of exercise they have, or to make them "live longer" or "get more from their life"'. Healthism, however, can also lead to a general intolerance by those who subscribe to the dominant health norms against those who do not or cannot (Metcalfe 1993, p. 35).

CONCLUDING COMMENTS

As should now be apparent, the new public health can be seen to involve much more than simply concern about 'health', as it is narrowly understood, or about achieving some 'essential' state of individual or collective well-being and happiness. Above all, it is about the exercise of a particular form of power: one that presupposes and employs the regulated freedom of individuals to act in one way or another. As such, it has implications for subjectivity that go way beyond what might generally be implied by the 'improvement of health'. In the following chapters we focus more specifically on a number of integral discourses, strategies and practices in the new public health: epidemiology, 'risk', the notions of the 'healthy' citizen and 'the environment', the 'healthy' city, and community participation.

2 Epidemiology: governing by numbers

As we observed in the previous chapter, one of the distinguishing features of public health as it has developed in the nineteenth century and into the twentieth century is its reliance upon 'scientific' and 'rational' methods of monitoring, measuring and regulating the population in the interests of improving health states. At the end of the twentieth century this preoccupation is as strong as ever. The field of epidemiology is one such 'rational' method employed as part of the apparatus of the new public health. Epidemiology is frequently defined as the 'science of epidemics'; that is, the study of disease and illness and their risk factors as they occur in groups rather than in individuals. It is a central strategy adopted in modern public health practice to identify, define and manage public health 'problems'. The British Acheshon Report on the Public Health published in 1988, for example, gave a strong emphasis to the role of epidemiology in contemporary public health practice, particularly in the monitoring of the health status of the population, in the analysis of patterns of illness in relation to its causes, and in the evaluation of health care services (Bruce 1991, p. 103). As such, the strategy of epidemiology and the accompanying sphere of knowledge of biostatistics, both of which came to prominence in Europe in the mid nineteenth century, are central features in the training and the endeavours of public health workers in most countries.

This chapter focuses in detail on the field of epidemiology as it is conceptualised and employed in new public health activities. Epidemiology, as a supposedly 'neutral' science based upon measurement and quantification, is rarely subjected to sociological analysis, particularly from within public health. To address this lacuna, particular attention is paid to the construction of epidemiological 'facts', the use of statistics, the notion of risk as it is employed and constructed through epidemiological research, and the portrayal of self and the 'other' in epidemiological discourses and practices.

THE EMERGENCE OF EPIDEMIOLOGY

The emergence of epidemiology as a specific field of research in France and England in the mid nineteenth century was associated with developments in statistical techniques, the calculus of probabilities, and methods of gathering data on social groups. The growth of the hygienic or public health movement provided a raison d'être for epidemiological research (Lilienfeld & Lilienfeld 1982). The adoption by epidemiological researchers of 'scientific' and quantitative methods of data analysis lent a certain aura of respectability to the nineteenth-century public health movement, supporting its claims to be a 'professional' discipline (La Berge 1992, p. 29). The notion of 'population' was central to epidemiology and other governmental strategies of regulation:

> The great eighteenth-century demographic upswing in Western Europe, the necessity for coordinating and integrating it into the apparatus of production, and the urgency of controlling it with finer and more adequate power mechanisms cause 'population' with its numerical variables of space and chronology, longevity and health, to emerge not only as a problem but as an object of surveillance, analysis, intervention, modification, etc. (Foucault 1984a, p. 278)

Statistical measurement and analysis emerged in the late eighteenth and early nineteenth centuries as a means of measuring, classifying and monitoring characteristics of populations in early capitalist societies. From this time onwards an 'avalanche of printed numbers' was produced as the bureaucracies of European nation-states began to collect data on various types of human behaviours (Hacking 1990). In Britain, the institution of regular censuses of the population and systems of notifying births and deaths to a centralised body in the first half of the nineteenth century allowed the construction of vital statistics, for such data provided the required numerators and denominators. These data were supplemented by technological developments in medical research during this time—including the stethoscope and the compound microscope, which moved the focus of late-nineteenth-century epidemiological research towards exploring the role of pathogens in disease patterns—and by the fieldwork carried out by epidemiological investigators into the sources of outbreaks of contagious diseases (Trostle 1986, pp. 38–40).

As Hacking (1990) points out, the systematic collection of data about populations and the use of the laws of probability to calculate statistics serve to shape individuals' subjectivity in certain defined ways, by constructing categories against which individuals and groups could be measured. Statistics is therefore a technology for defining norms and deviations from the norm (Hacking 1990, p. 2). Through these processes, individuals are 'normalised' by comparison with the 'average', with the intention of ensuring that the pathological 'abnormal' is eradicated and that individuals will engage in self-regulation. The enumeration of behaviours and the construction of statistical laws which gathered force in the nineteenth century were primarily directed at acts or behaviours considered to be 'deviant', such as suicide, madness, disease, crime, prostitution. The science of statistics was based upon the tenets of post-Enlightenment modernism, incorporating the belief that rational counting and ordering of such disorderly behaviours would help bring them under control; in other words the notion 'that one can improve—control—a deviant subpopulation by enumeration and classification' (Hacking 1990, p. 3). Through these means the 'unruly population' is rendered manageable, 'in a form in which it could be used in political arguments and administrative decisions' (N. Rose 1990, p. 6).

A case in point is the development of the life table, a means of predicting the lifespan of males and females in certain populations at different ages. The life table led to a new way of conceptualising death. Death was no longer viewed as random, striking anyone at any time, but became calculable and patterned, subject to the laws of probability, striking populations rather than individuals, resulting in 'an actuarial vision of human existence' (Prior & Bloor 1993, p. 355). Related to this new way of conceptualising death were studies exploring the influence of such factors as social class and occupation on mortality rates, further removing the concept of death from personal bodies to subgroups in the larger population (Prior & Bloor 1993, p. 359). Statistical research on populations in the nineteenth century led to findings that drew attention to differences in mortality rates that were directly related to socioeconomic conditions. Such research also identified the illnesses and diseases causing the greatest mortality, nominated the groups that were found to be particularly vulnerable to certain illnesses or early death, investigated the source of epidemics and the relationship between occupation and health states, and moved on to explore such social 'problems' as prostitution (Rosen 1973, p. 628). One of the most well known epidemiological studies published during the nineteenth century was the

English reformer Edwin Chadwick's *Report on the Sanitary Condition of the Labouring Population of Great Britain* (1842), which highlighted the ill-effects of crowded and dirty living conditions on the British poor and working class and provided a basis for the emergent public health movement to develop strategies for action.

By the mid twentieth century, epidemiology had become an academic field of knowledge for which training was provided in departments of public health within faculties of medicine. This institutionalisation was accompanied by a change in perspective (in Western countries, at least) from primarily focusing on the control of infectious diseases to monitoring and preventing chronic conditions such as cancer and heart disease (Oppenheimer 1995, p. 918). The discipline of epidemiology now constitutes the major source of the 'knowledge' and 'facts' of the new public health enterprise. Terris has defined the functions of contemporary epidemiology as:

1. To discover the agent, host and environmental factors which affect health, in order to provide the scientific basis for the prevention of disease and injury and the promotion of health.
2. To determine the relative importance of causes of illness, disability, and death, in order to establish priorities for research and action.
3. To identify those sections of the population which have the greatest risk from specific causes of ill health, in order that the indicated action may be directed appropriately.
4. To evaluate the effectiveness of health programs and services in improving the health of the population. (1993, p. 142)

Epidemiology thus performs a number of regulatory and surveillance functions: not only is it active in the 'discovery' of disease-causing factors using 'scientific' methods, but it also performs evaluative and policy roles in establishing and ordering conditions and social groups in terms of importance and greatest risk, prescribing solutions and interventions and monitoring preventive health care delivery. Epidemiological research is used as the basis for the development of health care programs, the allocation of resources and the development of relevant legislation.

THE CONSTRUCTION OF EPIDEMIOLOGICAL FACTS

Epidemiology relies upon a complex set of data from numerous sites to enumerate cases of disease and to construct and verify models of disease causation and spread: 'Careful clinical observation, precise counts of well-defined cases, and demonstration of relationships between cases and the characteristics of the populations in which they occur, all combine in the method upon which epidemiology depends' (Last 1987, p. 28). It adopts no one sphere of knowledge or method; rather, epidemiological practice relies upon what Fujimura and Chou have described as a 'mosaic framework of data, materials, technologies and knowledges produced by different expertises or methodologies' (1994, p. 1023). These include the knowledges and methods of virology, cell biology, pathology and bacteriology; sociological, psychological and anthropological research; medical research and case studies; as well as surveys and statistical analysis. Epidemiology depends upon comparisons usually expressed as 'rates', taking into account changes over time and between geographical areas or social categories. To establish rates, epidemiology uses numerators and denominators: the former comprising those individuals with the condition or experiencing the event in question ('cases'), the latter a defined broader population from which the cases come.

As epidemiologists deal with rapidly changing conditions—including the emergence of 'new' diseases such as HIV/AIDS, periodic outbreaks of infectious diseases such as legionnaires' disease, and shifts in the incidence of non-infectious diseases such as lung cancer—they must maintain the routine surveillance and analysis of populations through rationalised procedures of notification and storage of data. Major centres such as the Centers for Disease Control in Atlanta in the United States and the epidemiological sections of government departments of health have the major responsibility for data collection and analysis. Collection of vital statistics for the compilation of health status registers begins at birth, when features of infants' health status—such as their birth weight, length, colour, heart rate, respiratory function and muscle tone—and information about their mothers—including ethnicity, age and place of residence—are notified to public health authorities (in many countries, such notification is compulsory). The collection, analysis and publication of such data are therefore major components of public health as a governmental apparatus, for, as Nikolas Rose argues, 'government is dependent on knowledge . . . [it] depends upon the production, circulation, organisation, and the authorisation of truths that incarnate what is to be governed, which make it thinkable, calculable, and practicable' (1990, p. 6).

As we observed above, the credibility and claim to legitimacy of epidemiology are built upon the field's continual gathering and statistical analysis of 'scientific facts'. There is a strong focus on demonstrating the interrelationship of specific variables and health or illness outcomes, often with a preference towards identifying causal associations. The 'determinants', or 'necessary causes and enabling factors' of disease are identified and frequently broken down between 'host factors'—or those that determine individual susceptibility (such as age, gender, genetic makeup, nutritional condition)—and 'environmental factors'—or 'those that determine the host's exposure to the specific agent' (such as family size and composition, housing conditions, occupation and 'lifestyle' factors) (Last 1987, p. 29). Thus epidemiological studies seek to ascertain the extent to which such 'determining' or 'independent' variables as gender, age, social class, race, ethnicity and place of residence are related to such 'outcomes' as longevity, heart disease, cancer, respiratory disease, alcohol consumption, smoking behaviour, and so on. It is assumed each independent variable may be isolated from others and correlated with disease incidence or health indicator to demonstrate statistically the extent to which it affects outcomes. These variables are generally treated in epidemiological research as 'given' biological or social entities; there is little acknowledgment that categories such as social class, race and ethnicity are themselves subject to manifold interpretation and debate (Oppenheimer 1995, p. 919).

Epidemiology relies upon the principle of the 'web of causation', or the idea that illness and diseases are produced through a complex interaction of several risk and protective factors, both direct and indirect (Kriegler 1994). The concept therefore challenges the simple model of disease causation upon which much of clinical medicine is based, such as the germ model, which argues for a single agent causing disease or illness. According to Kriegler, the 'web of causation' metaphor first emerged in the 1950s, evoking 'the powerful image of a spider's web, an elegantly linked network of delicate strands, the multiple intersections representing specific risk factors or outcomes, and the strands symbolising diverse causal pathways' (1994, p. 890). While it is typically described as 'non-hierarchical', the 'web' construct tends to privilege some explanations over others, focusing particular attention on the risk factors that are relatively contained and closest to the outcome under investigation (Kriegler 1994, p. 890). Thus, although 'fuzzy' factors such as socioeconomic status will often be included as potential risk factors, few solutions for how to 'eradicate' these risks will be offered, simply because they are complex societal structural features compared with more discrete and therefore more approachable risk factors such as a contaminated water supply. The 'web' model also tends to be temporally unidimensional, losing sight of historical changes in disease causation. While the 'web' model acknowledges there is often no single cause of illness, it still emphasises the ways in which multiple causes combine to have an impact upon a socially atomised individual, often ignoring or playing down the social context (Kriegler 1994, p. 892).

What is routinely glossed over in the official accounts of epidemiological research—the articles published in scholarly journals and reports produced by bureaucratic organisations, for example—is the socially constructed nature of the findings. While most epidemiologists recognise the 'fuzziness' of their practice, they continue to strive after scientific objectivity. Bruce, for example, contends in relation to epidemiological practice, that '[a]bsolute scientific objectivity and purity of method are never achievable even in the most rigorous research situation, but these are nevertheless important goals to be striven for' (1991, p. 104). Biomedicine, and as a corollary, epidemiology and biostatistics, are presented as emerging from a 'neutral' knowledge base supported by scientific principles of observation and testing, untainted by the entry of the social or the cultural. Like other scientific facts, epidemiological facts gain their credence from being published in scholarly journals, in which process the historical and sociocultural dimensions of their construction, as well as the more personal imperatives such as maximising one's career opportunities, are effectively hidden. We assert that—contrary to the vision of scientific neutrality entertained by many epidemiologists—such research, like any other form of 'fact' generation (including sociological research), is a practice of constructing 'problems', defining them and proposing ways of dealing with them in the context of 'ways of seeing' which shape the 'facts' that consequently emerge. Thus the 'patterns' identified by epidemiological research are not pre-existing, simply waiting to be 'discovered' using the right tools and insights, but are constructed through the expectations and processes by which they are detected: 'Data gathered, then, is [sic] also data produced' (Jackson 1994, p. 427).

The philosopher of science Ludwig Fleck pointed out in his work *Genesis and Development of a Scientific Fact* (1979/1936) that a scientific fact is not the neutral, objective 'truth' it is presented to be in the discourses of science. 'Facts' are not autonomous entities 'out there'; on the contrary, it is through scientists' knowledge and belief systems—themselves developed and expressed in the context of professional interests, resource allocation, available technology and power relations—that scientific (and other) facts, models and theories are brought into being. Fleck refers to 'thought styles' or collective ways of thinking and acting which each individual scientist shares in, contributes to, draws upon and thereby reproduces in scientific research. For Fleck, 'facts' are collectively created, a function of thought styles, which will vary in time, space and culture. There are styles of scientific practice and reasoning in scientific disciplines that become the 'standards of objectivity' which produce these outcomes of research (Fujimura & Chou 1994, pp. 1019–21). Latour and Woolgar (1979) similarly point out in their account of 'laboratory life' that scientific knowledge is constructed from a disordered series of observations with alternative potential interpretations. Scientists respond to this disorder by imposing coherence through the use of certain limited conceptual frameworks. As Latour and Woolgar note: 'It is part of our world view that things are ordered, that order is the rule, and that disorder should be eliminated wherever possible. Disorder always has to be eliminated from politics and ethics as well as from science' (1979, p. 251). Like other scientific endeavours, epidemiology provides a means of rationalisation and ordering, of containing the disorder and chaos threatened by such phenomena as disease and death, and of rendering their uncertainties more controllable. As one epidemiologist describes his field: 'Epidemiological methods are above all an assertion of what planning theory would describe as a rational and comprehensive approach to problem solving' (Bruce 1991, p. 104).

There are a set of 'tenacious assumptions' in biomedicine that underlie its practices. These include the little-questioned assumptions 'matter is opposed to spirit', 'nature is autonomous from human consciousness', 'nature is separate from society, culture and morality', 'nature/truth is universal, autonomous from time or space' and 'the individual is distinct from, and prior to, society/culture' (Gordon 1988, pp. 19–56). These assumptions also, inevitably, underlie epidemiological practice, as a field of applied medical and public health research. Cultural understandings of the body, health and the causes of disease are all integral to the epidemiological construction of facts. Diseases and illness themselves are culturally constructed categories rather than objective 'truths', interpreted and experienced through lay, biomedical and epidemiological knowledges (see Lupton 1994a). This is not to argue there is no such thing as health or illness states, or that links between these and factors such as age, gender, ethnicity, social class, and so on do not exist. Rather it is to assert that the ways in which such variables are defined and measured (including such seemingly given categories as 'social class' or 'ethnicity') are subject to sociocultural processes which epidemiological researchers largely fail to acknowledge when undertaking their research and presenting it to others. As Wright argues, '[t]o consider a category as social-constructed is not to render it illusory, or a figment of the imagination: it is, if anything, to ground it more firmly by rooting it in the lived experience of members of a shared culture' (1988, p. 299).

Paula Treichler makes this point in relation to viruses, which are commonly understood in both biomedical and popular knowledges as natural phenomena, describable through science if not available to verification through the human eye. She contends that:

> a virus—any virus—is a constructed entity, a representation, whose legitimacy is established and legitimised through a whole series of operations and representations, all highly stylised. Each of these must be critically analysed on its own terms rather than accepted as though a scientific assertion about a virus stood for a referent rather than a sign. (1992, p. 75)

Treichler (1992, pp. 76–7) describes the particular ways in which the human immunodeficiency virus (HIV, the virus associated with AIDS) was constructed as 'scientific fact' through the practices of a small group of virologists staking out their territory by co-citing each other's work and thereby gaining control over the nomenclature of the virus, over publication in prestigious journals and over invitations to give addresses at important conferences. All of these practices served to define the field of study around HIV and AIDS and participated in the epistemology and construction of the 'history' of the virus. As a result, Treichler contends, certain researchers were able to effectively exclude others' views, competing research efforts and participation in the defining of the field of study: 'the effect is not only to help or hurt individual scientists but to set a gold standard for future discourse' (1992, p. 77). Fujimura and Chou (1994, p. 1031) further point to the participation of other social groups in the definition of HIV and AIDS, including American patient activist groups who have lobbied for revisions to the official definition of AIDS. As they argue, epidemiological and clinical definitions of medical conditions and public health 'problems' are continually subject to negotiation and revision; they are not static 'facts'.

HIV and AIDS are not the only examples. Over the past few centuries since the emergence of biomedicine, some medical conditions have disappeared, no longer accepted as 'real', while others have emerged because of changes in 'ways of seeing' which are inextricably linked to the social world. Conditions such as hysteria and chlorosis, commonly diagnosed in privileged women in the nineteenth century, are no longer deemed to be physical illnesses. They emerged as illnesses at that time in history because of a constellation of sociopolitical factors, including women's growing awareness of and frustrations about the constraints of their lives (Bassuk 1986). Much more recently, acceptance that exposure to passive smoking is harmful to human health has been influenced by the notion of diseases as separate, discrete entities, the assumption that 'doses' of chemicals in cigarette smoke could be measured in the blood or urine with the use of biochemical markers, the scientific dichotomy that was made between mainstream and sidestream smoke, the acceptance of health as an individual responsibility, and the definition of all bodies as potentially susceptible to disease (Jackson 1994). These assumptions are clearly historically based; for example, there was very little concern about the effects of passive smoking until the late 1970s, but by the late 1980s it had become a major health concern (Jackson 1994 p. 432). Changes in perception are not simply an outcome of 'new discoveries of knowledge', but are tied to broader social, cultural and political changes that shape what kinds of knowledges are considered to be important and which 'facts' should be pursued and publicised.

The importance of acknowledging the assumptions underlying the construction of epidemiological 'facts' is demonstrated in critical analyses of the ways in which the HIV/AIDS epidemic in Africa has been conceptualised. Medical tests for HIV antibodies and clinical definitions of HIV infection and AIDS were developed in Western countries, and were applied to the African context assuming 'a northern hemispheric distribution of pathogens'; that is, that conditions such as the common cold are endemic, 'ordinary' and relatively 'clean' while 'tropical' conditions such as malaria and polio are 'exotic', emerging from conditions of filth and moistness (Patton 1990, p. 26). As a result, Patton (1990, p. 26) contends, HIV/AIDS may easily have been misdiagnosed in African countries because the symptoms that have been identified as being associated with AIDS, such as night sweats, weight loss and general malaise, are characteristic of a number of conditions that are common in equatorial regions. The standard Eurocentric definition of HIV/AIDS is therefore difficult to apply in the African context. Similarly, the early HIV antibody tests could not distinguish between HIV antibodies and antibodies to the malarial plasmodium that is common in equatorial African countries, resulting in a large number of false-positive results for HIV antibodies among Africans. As a result, epidemiological data have represented HIV/AIDS in Africa as devastating the population, fitting into a pre-established discourse of the 'dark continent' as redolent with disease, poverty, filth and rampant sexuality (Patton 1990, pp. 26–7).

The ways in which epidemiological data on HIV/AIDS have been collected since the emergence of the condition in the early 1980s provide another example. The symptoms grouped together as a condition later to be called AIDS were first noted in gay men in the United States. Therefore the condition was initially called 'gay-related immuno-deficiency' or GRID, and the recreational drug-taking and sexual practices of the first group of gay men identified with GRID were noted as risk activities. As a result, it was assumed all gay men engaged in similar practices and therefore were at 'high risk' of AIDS (Levine 1992, p. 193). HIV/AIDS then became strongly associated with injecting drug users and prostitutes. The condition was therefore constructed as a disease of gay men and other 'deviant' groups, involving activities that are highly stigmatised in Western societies. Due to this construction, many people who do not see themselves as belonging to these 'deviant' groups have tended to dissociate themselves from HIV/AIDS, viewing it as a disease of stigmatised 'others' who engage in 'dirty' or 'deviant' activities. Furthermore, despite the link of HIV/AIDS with non-sexual activities (such as injecting drug use and blood transfusions), its designation as a sexually transmissible disease has had implications both for public perceptions of the condition and for the public health strategies used to deal with it. In the United States, for example, public health officials are entitled to seek follow-up information about the sexual partners of people living with HIV/AIDS in ways that may be regarded as violating personal rights to confidentiality (Volinn 1989, p. 1160).

QUANTIFICATION AND EPIDEMIOLOGICAL 'TRUTHS'

As noted earlier, forms of quantification are integral to epidemiological knowledges. The term 'ethnostatistics' has been used to describe the ways in which statistical data are socially constructed and interpreted as well as the sociocultural and political uses to which they are put as apparently 'objective' and 'scientific' phenomena (Bloor et al. 1991, p. 131). Statistics and other forms of enumeration employ the discursive device of 'quantification rhetoric', or 'the manner in which numerical and non-numerical quantity formulations are deployed when proposing and undermining argumentative cases' (Potter et al. 1991, p. 333). They are vital to the representation of statements and contentions as factual and are used to achieve specific persuasive and argumentative ends (Potter et al. 1991, p. 337).

One example is the category of 'curable cancer'. As Potter et al. point out, this category is not an unproblematic entity, but rather is subject to definition and enumeration based on the position from which an argument is being generated. The notion of 'cure' itself in relation to cancer is a highly variable concept, because cancer tends to return: people may receive treatment and be apparently cured of their cancer, yet find it returns some years later in an equally virulent form. To deal with this uncertainty, medical discourse often arbitrarily categorises those patients who survive five years from the date of first diagnosis as 'cured'. As a result, someone can die of the cancer they supposedly were cured of if their death occurs more than five years after diagnosis (Potter et al. 1991, p. 346). Individuals speaking from different positions then employ this arbitrary concept of 'curable cancer' in different ways depending on what discursive end they are attempting to accomplish. People from cancer charities, for example, may be anxious to emphasise the number of curable cancers to demonstrate the worth of their charity, and therefore employ quantification rhetoric that supports their position, while cancer researchers seeking funds for further research may choose to emphasise the 'small' number of the 'curable cancers' to make their own case. The latter may tend to use such phrases as '1 per cent of a quarter of a million' to enumerate the number of cases of cancer that are curable out of those diagnosed each year in Britain, because they are more persuasive than the same proportion described as '2 500 out of 250 000' (Potter et al. 1991, p. 341).

Quantification rhetoric using epidemiological statistics is common in news and documentary accounts of health and medical issues, being used frequently to represent certain health risks and diseases as 'serious problems'. It is also a common device in the portrayal of risk and disease in more esoteric texts—such as medical and public health journal articles and books, and public health policy documents. Visual displays of numbers and statistics, such as tables or graphs, are also central to the persuasive function of quantification rhetoric. Particularly as it is employed in epidemiological discourse, quantification rhetoric tends to suggest the figures used are not subject to doubt or uncertainty, simply by adopting a precise count and basing a network of assumptions on it. When blood tests for cholesterol became fashionable in the 1980s, for example, a certain figure denoting the level of blood cholesterol was decided upon as the point after which people would be deemed as having a 'high' cholesterol reading and as therefore being at 'increased risk' of heart disease. The 1993 *Goals and Targets for Australia's Health in the Year 2000 and Beyond* document, for instance, asserts that blood cholesterol greater than 5.5 mmol/L is the 'danger' point, and therefore formulates an ideal 'target' of reducing the percentage of the Australian population whose blood cholesterol is greater than 5.5 mmol/L (Nutbeam et al. 1993, pp. 118–19). All individuals who had the test were told their 'number' and where it fitted on the scale of 'low' to 'high' blood cholesterol levels. Those whose 'number' was above the 'danger point' were advised to take especial care to regulate their dietary intake of cholesterol and saturated fats and to increase their participation in exercise activities. Some were even prescribed drugs designed to lower their blood cholesterol level. This continual citing of the 'danger level' fails to acknowledge to those who present for testing the uncertainties around the accuracy of the blood test itself, the validity of the 'number' designated as 'dangerous', the efficacy of the remedies urged upon those who were told they were 'at risk', and the extent to which blood cholesterol levels are related to subsequent heart disease (see the discussion about the debate over cholesterol later in this chapter).

Potter et al. (1991, p. 337) argue there are two central processes that are part of the construction of quantification accounts: what should be counted and how should it be counted? In epidemiology, certain risk factors, symptoms, diseases or conditions are identified first as being 'problems', and then as requiring precise measurement, while in comparison others are ignored or neglected. The very choice of what phenomena require measurement and surveillance is a product of sociocultural processes, related to such factors as the research interests of the epidemiologists involved, current knowledge systems about the links between human behaviours or embodied characteristics and illness and disease, access to resources to fund research and surveillance strategies, the interests of the organisations in which epidemiologists are located, feasibility of measurement, and ethical and political considerations.

One example is research into the effects of tobacco use. Given the contemporary acceptance that cigarette smoking is closely associated with illnesses such as lung cancer and heart disease, and has no health-enhancing properties, research projects that set out to demonstrate or identify the positive effects of tobacco use are far less likely to be funded than those directed towards demonstrating the negative effects of smoking. Government funding bodies and researchers see tobacco as a 'dirty drug', while drug companies prefer to avoid funding research on a substance that is now regarded as an 'abusable drug' (Mundell 1993, p. 15). In the same way, because alcohol is considered a dangerous substance in public health knowledges, it is pathologised, represented as little else than a personal, social, and public health 'problem'. Particularly in the North American context, any suggestion that alcohol consumption may have beneficial effects tends to be down played or ignored, so that educational curricula attack the concept of moderate drinking as dangerous, the 'thin edge of the wedge'. Health promotional advice insists upon the negative effects of alcohol: according to one American pamphlet, alcohol 'has no net health benefit, is linked with many health problems, is the cause of many accidents, and can lead to addiction' (quoted in Peele 1993, p. 808). This is despite the findings of a number of epidemiological studies suggesting that the risk of developing coronary artery disease may be reduced by the regular intake of moderate amounts of alcohol (Peele 1993).

The socially constructed nature of epidemiological data is further evident in the ways in which the data are collected and analysed. Epidemiological research sets out to create categories into which people may be classified. This very act of categorisation inevitably shapes the data collected in certain ways. As Bloor (1995, p. 55) points out, such classificatory schemes 'have a self-fulfilling character. The ways of seeing that are endorsed by the adoption of particular classificatory schemes become themselves the basis for the everyday interpretative acts of those who compile and construct the statistical tables.'

One example is the construction of statistics on mortality via death certificates. The format of the death certificate, which by law must be filled in by a medical practitioner when someone dies, implies several rules: death is a product of pathology and is a physical event; and the cause of death is visible at postmortem, is always a singular event, is proximate to the event of death and makes sense in the context of assumptions about natural and normal death (that is, it should be a likely event given the dead person's age, medical history, and so on). Yet it is often the case that the causes of death are imprecise, or multifactorial. For instance, doctors are aware of the social need to cite liver disease rather than alcoholism as a cause of death because the former diagnosis is more precise and linked to a specific organ failure (Prior & Bloor 1993, p. 363). For similar reasons, social conditions such as poor housing, poor diet or poverty are generally not considered appropriate to cite as reasons for death on certificates. As a result, 'the causes of death may be said to reside in conceptual frameworks rather than in human cadavers—frameworks which only become visible in and through specific representational forms' (Prior & Bloor 1993, p. 371).

Therefore, Prior and Bloor (1993) argue, the accuracy of death certificate data as they are used in the construction of such epidemiological statistics as mortality rates is open to question. Such aspects as doctors' inaccurate diagnoses of cause of death, their reluctance to record socially stigmatised conditions or conditions they know will be further investigated by the authorities, and shifts in fashions of diagnosis mean that these data must be treated with caution. Even the gender and age of the person who died or their socioeconomic status appear to influence the extent to which their deaths are rigorously investigated: the deaths of men, young people and people of higher socioeconomic status, for example, are generally subject to far more investigation than are those of women, the aged and the less socioeconomically privileged. Changes in the rules for coding deaths also have an unacknowledged effect on mortality statistics. When sudden infant death syndrome was introduced as a category of death, the percentage of infant deaths attributed to other causes, such as pneumonia, subsequently fell. This did not mean fewer infants were dying of pneumonia, but rather that their illness was recategorised (Bloor et al. 1987). As these comments suggest, both the collection and interpretation of epidemiological data are subject, as is any data collection, to the interpretive frameworks and everyday practices of the actors involved and to the constraints and contingencies surrounding these practices.

Another case in point is the statistics calculated from epidemiological data that are gathered on the pattern of HIV infection and AIDS in large populations. This data collection is plagued by a number of problems, including under-reporting; changes in the definition of AIDS over time; missing, inadequate or uncertain case information; and double-counting of cases (Bloor et al. 1991, pp. 132–3). There is also the problem that the ways of reporting and representing the 'risk category' of HIV infection in many countries (including Britain, the United States and Australia) do not allow for multiple risks of infection (except for one category of 'male homosexual/bisexual and injecting drug use'). Instead, the strategy of data categorisation insists that individuals with HIV be classified as having received the virus from one activity only, such as homosexual contact (a misleading euphemism for engaging in anal intercourse), injecting drug use or a blood transfusion. If more than one risk practice is reported by the individual in question, the monitoring agency uses a hierarchy of risk practices to speculate upon which of the risk practices is the 'most likely' to have been the cause of infection. As a result, given the currently prevailing dominant construction of HIV/AIDS as a sexually transmitted disease, a gay man who might also have reported having had a blood transfusion while travelling abroad will be categorised as having received HIV through homosexual activities rather than through the blood transfusion (Bloor et al. 1991, pp. 133–4).

Not only are the classificatory schemes of epidemiologists inevitably shaped through their own ways of seeing, their attempts to 'slot' people into pre-established categories for the purposes of data collection fail to recognise that humans, sited as they are in cultural environments rather than in laboratories, do not tend to behave in expected ways. For a variety of reasons, people are not always willing to report their activities to epidemiological researchers, and may 'fudge' their answers, lie outright, simply not be able to provide an answer or refuse to answer. This is particularly the case when the behaviour in question is socially stigmatised. For example, many people are reluctant to report to others their drug-taking activities because of their status as activities that are 'disapproved' of or even illegal. So too, the difficulties in accurately measuring the kinds and quantities of foods people eat are notorious. People who are overweight may under-report the quantity and type of foods they eat, while others may overestimate the quantities of 'healthy' as opposed to 'unhealthy' foods consumed.

As is the case with any research involving human subjects, epidemiological data are therefore continually subject to 'contamination' on the part of the very people they are attempting to survey. In discussing sociological research, Giddens has termed this phenomenon 'the double hermeneutic', or the process by which

> the subjects of study in the social sciences and the humanities are concept-using beings, whose concepts of their actions enter in a consti-tutive manner into what those actions are. Social life cannot even be accurately described by a sociological observer, let alone causally elucidated, if that observer does not master the array of concepts employed (discursively or non-discursively) by those involved. (1992, p. 149)

The metalanguage and conclusions of social research thus enter the public domain, changing ways of thinking about the world. There is therefore a symbiotic or dialectical relationship between scholar/researcher and the subject of research—each influences the other. The resonances for epidemiological research are obvious. For example, men who regard themselves as heterosexual and emphatically not homosexual, but who might engage in sexual activities with other men from time to time, will often not divulge such activity in epidemiological surveys or interviews or identify with public health advice directed at gay or bisexual men. So too, the changeable nature of subjectivity means that people conceptualise themselves in different ways in different contexts. Other individuals may veer from considering themselves to be 'bisexual' to considering themselves exclusively 'gay'. At a more subtle level, the 'double hermeneutic' of epidemiological research serves to shape the data by way of the constant categorisation of and comparison between 'normal' and 'pathological' individuals or groups. As Hacking notes, under the laws of probability used in statistical analysis '[p]eople are normal if they conform to the central tendency of such laws, while those at the extremes are pathological. Few of us fancy being pathological, so "most of us" try to make ourselves normal, which in turn affects what is normal' (1990, p. 2). Most epidemiologists have yet to confront these epistemological dimensions of the data collection and analysis upon which the claims of their endeavours are predicated.

CONTESTED KNOWLEDGES

Many of the medical and epidemiological 'facts' presented as 'truths' to the lay public are not quite as free from controversy as they tend to be portrayed. Although epidemiological researchers who publish their very specific findings in medical and public health journals are generally aware of the tentative nature of the associations they have identified, and therefore tend to be cautious about making strongly worded recommendations based on their findings, the translation of their research into forums to which the majority of the population have access often dispenses with such caution. While the same 'story' continues to be given to the public on the part of public health workers, the disputes over 'truth' that appear on the pages of epidemiological, medical and public health journals are rarely acknowledged. This is evident in reports of research findings in the mass media, and in the translation of findings into public health policy and planning documents and health education programs, where strong statements are routinely made about the importance of 'health promoting' activities such as engaging in regular exercise and avoiding such substances as tobacco, alcohol and dietary fats.

The cholesterol control debate provides an example of the way in which epidemiological knowledge is often subject to dispute. The notion that high blood cholesterol levels are associated with poor cardiovascular health has been disseminated by medical and public health authorities throughout Western populations. It has been argued that high levels of blood cholesterol lead to atherosclerosis, or the clogging and subsequent narrowing of the arteries, reducing blood supply to the heart. As we argued earlier in this chapter, public health documents have subsequently tended to assert very strongly that individuals should have their blood cholesterol level regularly monitored and should take steps to reduce the level if it is deemed to be 'too high'. The dominant message emerging from public health authorities is that a high cholesterol reading automatically places an individual at 'high risk' of developing heart disease, and thus requires urgent intervention and self-regulation, often involving giving up pleasurable activities.

Atrens (1994) has pointed to the vested commercial and professional interests that surround and are reliant upon the continuation of the belief that cholesterol causes heart disease, including not only medical and public health researchers but also coronary health foundations, the 'healthy' food industry, and drug companies who market drugs to lower cholesterol. In the face of these powerful interests and 'thought styles', research that has challenged the orthodox line on the relationship between cholesterol and heart disease has often been ignored or down played. This was demonstrated in a study of the frequency of citation of research studies investigating the results of clinical trials of the effects of lowering cholesterol levels on coronary heart disease. The citation study found that researchers cited the clinical trials that supported the orthodox line almost six times more often than those that were not supportive. There was, therefore, an evident reluctance on the part of researchers working on this topic to admit the findings of dissenting researchers into academic debate (Ravnskov 1992). As one commentator has noted, 'in much of the debate facts seem to be used as missiles to defend entrenched positions' (Marmot 1994, p. 351). Yet, by sheer force of numbers, the growing body of dissent did eventually make itself known in the medical literature, to the extent that by 1992 one commentator in an editorial published in the prestigious British Medical Journal contended that intervening in the attempt to reduce individuals' cholesterol levels may do more harm than good (Oliver 1992). Researchers in a number of studies have suggested low blood cholesterol is associated not with increased longevity, but rather with an increased rate of mortality from non-cardiovascular conditions such as cancer, injury and violence, suicide, and respiratory and digestive disorders (Hulley et al. 1992). It has been hypothesised that very low cholesterol levels may be associated

LIBRARY, UNIVERSITY OF CHESTER

with depression and other 'personality disorders' associated with aggression, hence explaining the higher rate of death due to accidents, violence and suicide among those people with low levels (Kleiner 1995).

Other research has suggested cardiovascular health itself is adversely affected rather than improved by strategies directed at lowering blood cholesterol. Perhaps the most widely publicised study to record such results is the 'Finnish businessmen's study', which found after a randomised trial of ten years that cardiac deaths and total mortality had progressively increased in the men who had taken steps to reduce their blood cholesterol level, as compared with a control group (Strandberg et al. 1991). These findings, for which clinicians and epidemiologists are still trying to formulate feasible explanations, raise ethical questions around the continued screening for and treatment of high blood cholesterol (Becker 1987; Atrens 1994). While the findings, as with any other epidemiological 'facts', should not be taken simply as neutral scientific 'truths', they represent an oppositional viewpoint on the cholesterol orthodoxy which has thus far largely failed to have an impact on public health advice and practice in relation to members of the lay public. For example, in an 'information sheet' circulated in the early 1990s as a direct response to the cholesterol controversy, Australia's National Heart Foundation still continued to insist that 'in developed countries like Australia cholesterol levels are probably higher than they need to be' and 'cholesterol lowering reduces the risk of heart attack and death from heart disease'.

Epidemiological research is beset by its reliance on probabilities and post hoc observational studies that attempt to relate health outcomes (for example, cases of breast cancer) to exposure to hypothesised 'risk factors' that preceded the outcome. Thus, researchers conducting a study of women who have already developed breast cancer will develop hypotheses about the risk factors that may have caused the cancer (such as intake of dietary fat, body weight or tobacco use) and seek to determine from these women their history of exposure to such risk factors. It is clear that pre-established assumptions about the cause of a disease may shape the manner in which research is carried out to then 'prove' this causal link, in ways that neglect other factors. Indeed, Skrabanek claims that once an epidemiological 'fact' has become accepted, poor data are then manipulated by researchers using selective statistical techniques to move 'from mandated conclusion back to selected data in order to reach the mandated conclusion' (1993, p. 1502). He contends that when strange or unexpected correlations are found in epidemiological studies—for example, between hip fracture and caffeine consumption, or between premature skin wrinkling and cigarette smoking—these associations are often not dismissed as artefacts of the research process. Rather, some kind of 'plausible biological mechanism' is usually found to explain the findings and to demonstrate that they are causal, for the whole rationale of such studies is to identify causes of the disease in question. Such apparently causal relationships may be spurious, but because a plausible explanation can eventually be manufactured by the researchers, these relationships are then treated as 'fact'. Such 'facts' may then have important effects on the types of people who are classified as being 'at risk' of a condition and on the advice given such people on the ways of reducing 'exposure' to these 'risks'.

One example of this type of post hoc hypothesising is the link that was suggested at the time of the emergence of the AIDS epidemic (the early 1980s) between AIDS and the use of amyl nitrite ('poppers') by gay men as an enhancement of sexual pleasure. Before HIV was identified and accepted as the causal factor for AIDS, some epidemiological research studies indicated that there was a strong association between 'popper' use as an independent risk factor for AIDS, because many gay men with a large number of sexual partners and who had the symptoms of AIDS had used the drug. It was hypothesised that 'popper' use may affect the immune system, causing the immunodeficiency associated with the syndrome, and that the use of these drugs should therefore be avoided. Once HIV was identified and accepted as the sole cause of AIDS, this theory was generally dropped in epidemiological and medical circles, and 'poppers' were no longer linked to AIDS. They were, therefore, no longer constituted as a public health 'problem' (Davey Smith et al. 1992). In the early 1990s, the acceptance that HIV is the sole cause of AIDS was challenged by heretical dissenters such as Peter Duesberg. This dissenting opinion has been subjected to trenchant criticism on the part of other researchers who refuse to accept the challenge to the accepted 'fact' of the relationship between HIV and AIDS (Fujimura & Chou 1994). In the meantime, the 'fact' that HIV causes AIDS has resulted in a constellation of practices around the identification, treatment and prevention of HIV infection and AIDS. The sheer magnitude of what has been cynically termed the 'AIDS industry'—or the plethora of huge international and national conferences, drugs and treatment strategies, health education programs, medical and popular literature, research projects, health care workers, support groups and community organisations—is such that 'HIV has become, in short, a reality that is too costly to give up' (Treichler 1992, p. 89). There is no doubt people die from the constellation of symptoms that currently bears the name 'HIV/AIDS'. What *is* in doubt is the knowledge system operating around the causes of these symptoms, and the related issues of how best the syndrome can be treated and prevented.

EPIDEMIOLOGY AND RISK DISCOURSE

As the above discussion suggests, the discourse of risk is central to epidemiological knowledges, discourses and practices. Indeed, as observed in Chapter 1, the term 'risk' has become prevalent in medical and public health discourses in general over the past few decades. One study of medical journals published in the United States, Britain and Scandinavia found that between 1967 and 1991 there was a rapid increase in the number of articles with the term 'risk' in the title or abstract, particularly in the most recent five-year period of the study (Skolbekken 1995). The most rapid increase was found in epidemiological journals. The study's author described this phenomenon metaphorically as an 'epidemic' in its own right. He ascribed the growing frequency of risk as used in medical and public health journal articles to changes in beliefs about the causes of illness and disease and the development of such fields as probability statistics, actuarial science, computer technology, risk management, quality assurance and health promotion.

Frankenberg argues that when risk is dealt with in epidemiology, two initial choices are posed: 'which outcomes to focus upon and which risk factors ought to be given priority'. As he notes, these choices, like any others, 'are surrounded by culturally defined moral problems in which power relations always have a central position' (1993, p. 236). Thus, for example, the 'web' of causation that is often constructed to show why individuals may choose to smoke draws attention to such factors as stress, lack of knowledge about the side-effects of smoking, addiction to nicotine, low self-esteem and low self-efficacy. While the sociocultural context is clearly important here, it is generally reduced to the individual level: a person feels stress and smokes to alleviate it, lacking the self-esteem and self-efficacy she or he requires to give up. The questions of how 'stress' is generated, why that particular individual should be suffering from 'stress' in comparison with others, and the sources of that individual's lack of self-esteem and self-efficacy are often glossed over for a focus upon 'improving' self-esteem and self-efficacy and alleviating stress, so that the individual may then give up smoking. Such individualistic understandings of smoking behaviour tend to ignore or at the very least play down the whole panoply of broader sociocultural phenomena around smoking, including the cultural and symbolic meanings of smoking, the use of cigarettes as commodities to define the self, and the economics and politics of the production and marketing practices to do with cigarettes (see Lupton 1995, Ch. 5).

The term 'risk' as it is technically used refers to something that can be given a numerical value. In popular and public health discourses, however, the term takes on a far more malignant meaning, implying danger. Because epidemiology deals with groups rather than individuals, risk in this field tends to have an encompassing effect. All bodies are constructed as 'at risk' from one or more conditions or illnesses, whether it be HIV infection, cardiovascular disease, cancer or genetic disorders. The notion of 'health', therefore, has become somewhat of an abstract and liminal category in epidemiology, as all people, whether or not they are experiencing symptoms, may harbour 'risk factors' potentially leading to illness. To be labelled as being 'at risk' means entering a state in which an apparently healthy body moves into a sphere of danger. Such labelling not only has implications for an individual's subjectivity, but also has potential effects on the type of medical treatment and care she or he may encounter. Thus, for example, a woman who wishes to give birth at home who is deemed to be 'at risk' of having complications during the birth may be strongly dissuaded by medical authorities from carrying out her wish, and so end up in hospital. If she resists, she may be branded as being irresponsible and non-compliant, posing a risk herself to the health of her infant (Kaufert & O'Neil 1993).

Risk, therefore, is a sociocultural construct, its meanings developed in and through medico-scientific and epidemiological research (Lupton 1995, Ch. 3). There is a strong element of moralism and emphasis on personal responsibility in new public health discourses on risk. Public health practitioners often tend to make pronouncements implying that as long as the defined risk factors are dealt with, then the illness associated with them will be avoided. Milton Terris, for example, a well-known figure in American epidemiology and public health, has claimed that in discovering the aetiologic agents of disease, 'our epidemiologists forged powerful weapons to combat most of the major causes of death' (1992, p. 186). He went on to argue that conditions that are now the leading cause of death in Western countries, such as heart disease, cancer, cerebrovascular disease and accidents, are 'amenable to public health programs' and may be 'effectively prevented' or 'eliminated' through epidemiological knowledge applied to lifestyle change (1992, p. 187). For Terris, now that the threat of infectious diseases is eradicated in Western countries, it is the 'irrationality' of people who engage in such activities as cigarette smoking and excessive alcohol consumption that is the main target of epidemiological knowledge and practice: 'We are now engaged in the major battles of the second epidemiologic revolution, including the struggle against unhealthy lifestyles' (1992, p. 188).

Such statements suggest the possibility of human mastery over disease via the rationality of epidemiology, amounting to a virtual denial of death. As one of us has noted previously, such strategies as epidemiology 'are instrumental in categorizing death in ways that avoid direct confrontation with its reality' (Lupton 1995, p. 65). Death defies reason, in fact humiliates reason by demonstrating its ultimate failure. It mocks the ideals of modernity as it reveals the triumph of 'nature' over humanity. As a consequence, 'death has become a guilty secret; literally, a skeleton in the cupboard left in the neat, orderly, functional and pleasing home modernity promised to build' (Bauman 1992b, p. 134). When death and serious illness were common and apparently random, the notions of luck and fatalism were central to making sense of these phenomena. In our 'epidemiological age' it is now far more difficult to accept the randomness of death and serious illness: we need to be able to ascribe them a specific cause, even when they occur in very old people. Death and disease, therefore, seem more controllable because we can now identify their specific causes, which we believe may then be avoided. A further corollary of this understanding of death, illness and disease is that individuals are ascribed personal responsibility for their deaths or illnesses; by continuing to smoke, by not engaging in enough exercise, by failing to wear condoms when having sex, and so on, they have caused their own fates. This understanding draws upon the notion of the body as an unfinished project (see Chapter 1); something to be worked upon and improved throughout the lifespan, with death as the ultimate failure of self-control and rationality.

In the medical and public health context, different actors give different meanings to risk discourse, influenced by such factors as personal experience (including the individual's own embodied experience of health and ill health), professional interests and 'ways of seeing'. Gifford (1986, p. 215) refers to two ways of conceptualising risk: the 'objective' and 'scientific' approach, emerging from epidemiology, and the 'lived' or socially experienced dimension. She observes that epidemiological assessments of risk, based as they are on patterns within and between groups rather than on individuals, are depersonalised: 'Risk is about states of health which are located outside of any one particular individual' (1986, p. 217). In contrast, the experience of being diagnosed as 'at risk' is highly personal, often confronting the individual with the possibility of serious illness or death and changing notions of the embodied self. Kaufert and O'Neil (1993) have identified three stances of interpreting risk discourses: those of the epidemiologist, the medical practitioner and the lay person. These stances often conflict with or contradict, as well as sometimes overlap and influence, each other. The medical practitioner will tend to interpret data on risk through her or his own emotionally charged experience in working with individuals, having responsibility for their care and treatment, and being in the position of seeing patients die or avert death. Doctors will therefore tend to emphasise the negative nature of risk: 'Rather than being derived from statistics as in the epidemiological language of risk, clinical risk is compounded from a few cases of actual disaster and a somewhat higher number of cases in which disaster was averted' (Kaufert & O'Neil 1993, p. 46).

Epidemiologists, in contrast, often do not have the experience of dealing with individuals as 'risky bodies'. Instead they deal with abstract statistics, and do not have to face 'real' people who are suffering or dying when making their evaluations about the level of risk. Lay people, for their part, may embrace official definitions of risk at some times, while at other times they may ignore or resist such definitions in the pursuit of their own interests and goals. Thus, a woman with strong beliefs against abortion or who desperately wants a child may choose to go ahead with a pregnancy even after she has been counselled following genetic screening that the foetus has a genetic abnormality and will probably be born with serious deformities or mental retardation (Rapp 1993). It is important to recognise that the 'facts' constructed in contemporary epidemiological and medical research are major contributors to the ways in which people understand and live their bodies. The 'fact' that dietary fat leads to obesity and heart disease, for example, has meant that many people have almost a horror of fat, to the extent that the very sight or smell of it causes disgust. Should they decide to eat a food or meal that they consider particularly 'fatty', because of a craving or urge for such food, people find themselves feeling guilty and anxious about the effect the fat will have upon their bodies in terms of both health and physical appearance (Lupton 1996, pp. 82–3). Yet in other cultures, and not so long ago in Western societies, animal fat was considered as 'good for you' and even as a luxury. So too, people who are somewhat overweight are deemed archetypal candidates for heart disease, and are subject to anxiety and to discriminatory remarks from others. Another example is the emergence of the concept and discourse of 'social stress'. As Pollock (1988, p. 388) points out, the assumption which has emerged over the past few decades that stress is a condition of late industrial societies, with potential pathogenic effects on the vast majority of individuals, has been accompanied by an 'outbreak' of 'stress diseases' which are often said to be reaching 'epidemic proportions'. As a result of the high degree of attention given to the notion of stress as a health risk, the concept has become dominant in most people's understandings of the aetiology of illness and in the ways in which they think about their lives (see also Chapter 4).

It is clear from several studies undertaken in Western countries that people understand health as a personal responsibility, often ascribing moral qualities to states of health or illness. These studies have found that many people regard negatively the actions of neglecting one's health by failing to engage in health-protective behaviours, such as taking regular exercise or controlling one's weight (see, for example, Herzlich & Pierret 1987; Saltonstall 1993; MacInnes & Milburn 1994; Lupton 1996). Yet people also often reject the discourse of personal responsibility in relation to health status and risk avoidance—adopting such notions as luck, random distribution, 'God's will', heredity and chance to explain why some people become ill and others do not—or challenge the validity of medical knowledge and expert advice. Davison et al. have described a phenomenon they entitle 'lay epidemiology', or the understanding of health risk held by non medically qualified people based on 'the routine observation of cases of illness and death in personal networks and the public arena. The assessment of such cases and the circumstances surrounding them serve to support or challenge lay and scientific explanations for the causes of disease' (1992, p. 678). Thus, for example, personal experience and observation of others' health experiences construct an understanding of the ways in which diseases are patterned that recognises the difficulties of maintaining orthodox health-protective behaviours as well as the role played by chance.

An American study of crack cocaine users and their exposure to syphilis demonstrates the ways in which 'official' epidemiological knowledge may conflict with lay epidemiological knowledge. The participants discussed their choice of sexual partners as being based on whether they were 'clean', drawing upon considerations of whether the individual was well presented and groomed, with a pleasant demeanour or good family background, or how well known they were to the participant. They argued that 'fundamentally decent people are at lower risk for syphilis' (Balshem et al. 1992, p. 153). This judgment may contravene the orthodox epidemiological categorisation of people as being of 'low' and 'high' risk of syphilis, which is based largely on sexual practices such as having sex without a condom with multiple partners. For the participants in this study, it was people beyond the world of moral control, who were not well known to them or who appeared not to take care of their personal hygiene, who were regarded as being at highest risk for syphilis. This judgment of risk may or may not have included consideration of their sexual practices. Several other studies looking at the ways in which people assess their sexual partners in relation to the risk that they might have HIV/AIDS have similarly found that the apparent 'cleanliness' or 'dirtiness' of potential partners, or features such as their physical attractiveness, social class or manner (apparent 'sleaziness' for example), contributed strongly to such judgments, often in the absence of knowledge of the individual's sexual or drug-using history (see, for example, Lupton et al. 1995; Lear 1995). Such studies point to the socially constructed and symbolic nature of health risk as it is perceived and dealt with as part of individuals' everyday milieux.

It should be emphasised that 'lay epidemiology' and 'scientific' knowledges of epidemiology are not mutually exclusive. As we noted earlier in this chapter, 'scientific' epidemiological 'facts' are as socially shaped as are lay knowledges. Lay people's experiences of being 'at risk' are clearly shaped by clinical or epidemiological understandings of risk; indeed, many people would not view themselves as being 'at risk' of a medical condition unless they had been identified as such via clinical or epidemiological discourses. Epidemiologists and clinicians themselves come to their knowledges of medical risk as members of a professional body who have been trained in the scientific 'way of seeing' but who also develop their knowledges via personal experience and other sources as members of the wider society. Nonetheless, as we observed above, there are clear differences in the conceptualisation and experience of risk between the individual who has been diagnosed as being 'at risk' of a medical condition and the individual who is in the position of assessing such risk as a medical or public health professional, either for an individual patient or for social groups.

As Davison et al. (1991, p. 15) observe, the difficulty of the arguments of epidemiology and preventive health as they are employed in the new public health lie in their focus on populations rather than on individuals. The emphasis is on persuading large numbers of people to make changes to their lifestyles so there is a general diminution of risk at the population level. Hence the statements in such public health policy documents as *Goals and Targets for Australia's Health in the Year 2000 and Beyond* (Nutbeam et al. 1993), which describe 'targets' of reducing mortality or incidence rates of conditions or risk behaviours from a certain level, expressed as a percentage, to another level, in specified 'priority' populations. Thus, for example, the section on nutrition and diet sets a target of 30 per cent (from the current figure of 33.7 per cent) of average consumption of dietary fat as a proportion of total energy intake, to be achieved by the year 2000 for the priority population of 'all adults' (1993, p. 109). This means, however, that many individuals in the target population are persuaded to make small changes that may bring no obvious personal benefit. This is the 'prevention paradox', the phenomenon by which 'a preventive measure which brings much benefit to the population offers little to each participating individual' (Rose, cited in Davison et al. 1991, p. 15). Such blanket statements relating to risk modification also neglect in their simplistic reductionism the complexities of the interactions of behaviours and genetic susceptibility to illness. The proportion of dietary fat alone is not necessarily a risk factor for heart disease, but is mediated through other factors such as gender, family history of heart disease, age, and level of physical activity. In arguing that such diseases are controllable, the new public health tends to ignore the genetic aspects of chronic diseases, including (in the case of heart disease), being male, and other risk factors individuals are powerless to modify, such as age (McKinlay 1993, p. 111).

Most people, in constructing notions of 'lay epidemiology', are well aware of these complexities. They note, for example, that young adults may well drink to excess, smoke or eat 'junk food' with little detriment to their health because of their youth and their participation in exercise, while those in middle age or old age may need to accept some type of deterioration in health status as inevitable, given their position in the lifecourse (Backett & Davison 1992). Many people agree that even the most obvious 'candidate' for a heart attack (that is, someone who is overweight, eats too much, smokes or drinks excessively, or is under a lot of stress) may live to a ripe old age, while the most ascetic and virtuous individual may suddenly die young of a heart attack (Davison et al. 1991, 1992; Lupton 1996). It is also acknowledged by most people that it is extremely difficult to conform to the expectations of public health authorities, given the strains of modern life and the pleasures offered by engaging in activities that public health advice frowns upon. As one study of Scottish men found, the participants considered smoking cigarettes or drinking alcohol as an important way of dealing with the pressures of work, without which they would find it difficult to cope or relax (Mullen 1992).

A turn towards adopting explanations of ill health based on genetic factors has its own limitations, however. Recent work in genetic knowledge (for example, the Human Genome Project) has the potential to reshape epidemiological understandings of disease causation by emphasising the association of genotype with the physical expression of illness and disease. It has been predicted that genetic testing could be used to determine individuals' predisposition to such conditions as respiratory diseases, diabetes, cardiovascular disease, alcoholism, some psychiatric disorders, some cancers, and even to homosexuality or criminal activity. Genetic testing is already widely available to pregnant women, being commonly used to test for such conditions in the foetal genotype as Down's syndrome, and to members of families with a history of hereditary illness such as muscular dystrophy and Huntington's chorea.

While on the one hand it is important to recognise the link between genetic susceptibility and illness, an overemphasis can be placed on the identification of this link. This field of knowledge threatens to reduce understandings of disease causation to the individual level, as does in a similar way the single agent model of biomedicine. It is one thing to identify in an individual's genotype a gene that is associated with the development of a disease such as cancer; it is entirely another to make assumptions based on this knowledge. The mere presence of a gene is often not enough for a disease to develop, and many people who have the gene will never develop that condition. Representations of the gene–disease link, however, particularly those in popular culture such as news reports, have tended to reify the gene as the disease. They also imply that current uncertainties in medical and social life will be eradicated by identifying the genes associated with particular medical conditions (Davison et al. 1994, p. 342). These representations have implications for the ways in which people who are identified as 'carriers' of a gene associated with a condition understand and experience this risk. Some may find this labelling a stigmatising experience, influencing their relationships with prospective marital partners and others (Parsons & Atkinson 1992). The resonances of eugenics with some discourses on genetic testing are obvious in the identification of some genotypes as

'inferior' and requiring intervention, and in the singling out of characteristics such as homosexuality as 'genetic illnesses'.

SELF AND 'OTHER' IN EPIDEMIOLOGICAL DISCOURSES

The routine categorisation of social groups as 'normal' or 'abnormal' in
epidemiological practice conforms to a broader cultural tendency to
construct oppositions between self and 'other', or between 'inside' and
'outside'. As Mary Douglas argued in her book *Purity and Danger* (1980),
a community that perceives itself as threatened will tend to define 'self'
within certain boundaries, with 'other' existing outside of these boundaries, and will proceed to regulate and monitor movement in and out.
The community is conceptualised as a human body susceptible to
invasion by disease-carrying agents. As part of the process of drawing a
dichotomy between 'high risk' or 'unhealthy' groups and 'low risk' or
'healthy' groups, fears about social order, death and disease may be
projected by the latter onto the former: 'Differentiating itself from the
unhealthy group, the healthier group can experience itself as free of the
causes of disease, indeed freed of them by the availability of higher-risk
groups to act as depositories for projective phantasies' (Figlio 1989,
p. 88).

One example of this projection of 'otherness' upon stigmatised social
groups is contemporary public health approaches to the control of
alcohol consumption and illicit drug use. The discourse of war and
aggression is dominant in public health texts on such drug use, with
individuals urged to 'fight' their urges to use the drugs and the nation
represented as waging a 'war on drugs'. In the United States in the 1980s
the Reagan administration diverted many government resources towards
'The War on Drugs', which took on the flavour of a moral crusade. In
Australia, one of the current anti-drug health promotion programs is
called 'The Drug Offensive'. In these discourses, people designated as
'alcoholics' or 'addicts' are often described as 'the enemy'. Those who
use certain kinds of drugs are viewed with contempt because they fail
to conform to the hegemonic assumptions that one must 'face the real
world' without the use of drugs. They become the repository of a sense
of 'badness' felt by the majority group, partly through emphasising the
lack of control and dependency exhibited by such 'folk devils' (Stein
1990). It is commonly suggested in public health documents on illicit

drug use that drug users and drug dealers are like virulent pathogens in the body politic, destroying the morally good order from within.

Even members of stigmatised social groups themselves adopt the strategies of making moral judgments about individuals when conceptualising health risk. This phenomenon was demonstrated in the American study discussed earlier in this chapter, which interviewed users of crack cocaine, several of whom engaged in paid sex work to fund their habit. This study found that the participants presented themselves as maintaining adherence to the dominant norms of cleanliness, morality and sexual behaviour, even while they made judgments on the risk status of their sexual partners in relation to syphilis based on their apparent 'cleanliness' and 'decency' (Balshem et al. 1992). Not only, then, do the strategies of ceaseless measurement, standardisation and comparison employed in epidemiological research as part of the new public health serve as a means of mastering disorder through modernist systems of rationalisation, ordering and control—they also seek to contain disorder by clearly identifying and publicising social groups as being 'at risk'. Such groups then serve as reservoirs for shared anxieties and dreads on the part of majority groups, who are presented as members of 'the public' who require protection from 'contaminating others'.

On occasion the generally covert discrimination and stigmatisation of particular social groups in epidemiological writing becomes overt. European cultural assumptions about the sexuality of black African peoples have strongly influenced the construction of epidemiological knowledges of HIV/AIDS in Africa, in ways that parallel earlier research into syphilis in Africa at the turn of the twentieth century. In both cases, it was assumed by Europeans that the disease was more easily spread in African countries because of the imputed 'promiscuity' and 'immorality' of black Africans in their sexual behaviour, including their supposed high number of sexual partners, men's greater tendency to participate in sex with prostitutes, and the practice of anal sex among heterosexuals. As a result, alternative explanations for the spread of HIV in African countries, such as the high rate of injections given with inadequately sterilised needles in many areas or the high levels of malnutrition and poverty in many black African populations, have been little explored (Packard & Epstein 1991).

An article published on this topic in the prestigious international journal *Social Science & Medicine* in 1989 by Rushton and Bogaert demonstrated a high reliance upon racist stereotyping. In this article, entitled 'Population differences in susceptibility to AIDS: an evolutionary analysis', the authors compared the sexual behaviour of 'Mongoloids', 'Caucasoids' and 'Negroids'. They argued that, compared with Caucasians, 'populations of African ancestry' are 'inclined to a greater frequency of uninhibited disorders such as rape and unintended pregnancy and to more sexually transmitted diseases including AIDS', while 'populations of Asian ancestry are inclined to a greater frequency of inhibitory disorders such as low sexual excitement and premature ejaculation and to a lower frequency of sexually transmitted diseases including AIDS' (Rushton & Bogaert 1989, p. 1211). In drawing their conclusions the authors used such concepts as 'sexual restraint', glossed in their article as 'a lowered allocation of bodily energy to sexual functioning' (1989, p. 1213), as well as such factors as 'intercourse frequencies'; size of penis, vagina, testes and ovaries; and hormonal levels. Estimates of 'intercourse frequency' in marriage for couples in their twenties were compared for Asians, Europeans and black Africans, and the authors noted that the latter reported a higher frequency than did the other groups. Rushton and Bogaert did not explain how they categorised the different racial groups, but went on to employ sociobiological arguments, resting on assumed discrete genetic differences between races, to develop their case. They adopted an evolutionary argument to assert that because black Africans apparently produce more ova they are less progressed along the evolutionary chain. Rushton and Bogaert linked this phenomenon to a plethora of factors in which they argue that Africans are less developed, including health status, brain size and intelligence, physical and emotional maturation rate, marital stability, mental health, law-abidingness and temperament (1989, p. 1215).

Rushton and Bogaert's article thus reproduces the myths of black Africans as sexually aggressive, uninhibited and primitive, of Asians as overly sexually constrained and inhibited, and Europeans as 'normal'—the template against which other groups should be compared. They employ cultural understandings of black Africans as 'the very embodiment of dirt and disorder, their moral affliction all of a piece with their physical degradation and their "pestiferous" surroundings' that were evident in European nineteenth-century colonial discourses (Comaroff 1993, p. 306). Just as the nineteenth-century human sciences strove to provide a hierarchy of 'civilisation', based largely on skin colour and other biological or physical attributes, so too do Rushton and Bogaert attempt to demonstrate that black Africans occupy the rung of the least 'civilised' people on the ladder of human civilisation. The explanations they devise for these stereotypes are then supported with biological data, with no recognition of the cultural contexts in which such data are generated. They argue, for example, that the reason for statistics demonstrating that more African-Americans in the United States are arrested for rape than are members of the other racial groups is that they are less 'sexually inhibited' (1989, pp. 1216-17). The authors ignore the possibility that the entrenched racism that permeates the legal system in that country may be the underlying reason for these statistics, rather than African-Americans' genetic disposition towards rape.

The concept of 'risk groups' as it is employed in epidemiological discourse also betrays a set of moral assumptions that are drawn from the wider culture. The very construction of a series of 'risk groups' constitutes a way of defining the implicated from the immune, the pathological from the healthy, relying on social properties. Thus, all gay men are frequently defined as a major 'risk group' for HIV infection, as it is assumed that they all engage in similar sexual practices such as anal intercourse and having multiple sexual partners. To define a man as gay is therefore to automatically place him in a 'risk group', regardless of the types of sexual activities in which that individual may or may not participate. As a result of this categorisation, all gay men are rendered vulnerable to discrimination, based on their assumed infected status, on the part of both the wider population and members of the medical and health care professions, some of whom have refused the provision of health care to gay men because it is assumed that they are HIV positive and therefore pose a risk (Waldby et al. 1995).

Sometimes such 'labelling' may be material rather than symbolic. In Australian in 1995 at least one Sydney hospital was routinely using colour-coded wristbands for identifying or 'tagging' patients with hepatitis C and HIV infection. Such patients were identified as posing a risk to other patients and their health care workers using a manner of identification that was kept secret from them and had implications for the ways in which they were treated as patients (reported in the *Sydney Morning Herald*, 29 May 1995). Waldby et al. have also pointed out the ambiguity of the term 'risk group' used in relation to the direction of HIV infection: 'It connotes a group considered both at risk of contracting HIV, and at risk of transmitting it, either to another member of the "risk group" or outside, to a member of the "general population"' (1995, p. 9). The latter meaning tends to receive more circulation in epidemiological and popular discourses, with the implication that people deemed at 'high risk' pose a threat to others deemed at 'low risk', and therefore require careful surveillance and control. Members of stigmatised 'risk groups', such as gay men and prostitutes, are routinely portrayed as 'guilty' of contracting and spreading HIV, while those individuals assigned to 'innocent' categories, such as children, are represented as having been infected by a member of the 'guilty' risk group (Waldby et al. 1995, p. 11).

CONCLUDING COMMENTS

In this chapter we have explored from a sociological perspective the complexities surrounding the construction of epidemiological facts and the use of epidemiological data. As 'a scientific practice tied to practical action' (Fujimura & Chou 1994, p. 1024), epidemiology provides the foundation for virtually all other strategies in the new public health through identifying risk factors, risk groups and the apparent causes of disease. We have argued that epidemiology, as a highly influential plank of the new public health, performs sociocultural and political functions— such as constructing and perpetuating both material and symbolic distinctions between social groups—in ways that are rarely recognised from within public health. Despite the inevitable uncertainties and 'fuzziness' of epidemiological knowledge, it tends to be taken up by contemporary public health practitioners and presented to members of the lay public via health education and health promotion as a set of objective and given 'truths'.

This assumption of certainty has ramifications not only in discourse, but also in practice: epidemiological assessments, evaluations and projections have a privileged status as knowledge in public health, affecting policy, planning, funding and resource allocation decisions. The imperatives issuing from epidemiological knowledge also have a direct influence upon the ways in which members of the lay public come to construct their understandings of their bodies and health or illness states, upon the choices they may make in relation to protecting themselves against health risks, upon the ways in which they think of and treat others, and upon the nature of medical treatment and health care they may receive. It is not uncommon, for instance, for individuals who have been deemed 'responsible' for their illness, such as gay men with HIV/AIDS or people with lung cancer, to be denied both compassion from others and resources such as health care. While members of the public do not uncritically accept and take up these imperatives, the status of epidemiological knowledge as 'rational' and 'scientific' does much to bestow it with the values of credence and authority that are often difficult to contest.

Epidemiology is thus one of the central strategies in the new public health used to construct notions of 'health' and, through this construction, to invoke and reproduce moral judgments about the worth of individuals and social groups. What implications does this understanding of 'health' and 'morality' have for the conduct of oneself as a citizen? The next chapter goes on to explore the ways in which the concept of 'healthy' citizenship is understood and articulated in relation to the new public health.

3   The 'healthy' citizen

The concept of the 'citizen' is a central feature of the new public health. Indeed, the very term 'public health' includes within it an assumption that members of the 'public' are understood as citizens, for the term 'public' assumes a common purpose and goal, a sense of community: 'It refers to the life of a group as a commonwealth, rather than to a structure held together defensively . . . The word public identifies a phantasy of a group in which people can participate without cost to others: without privilege or deprivation' (Figlio 1989, p. 85). Citizenship as it is represented in the new public health emphasises both the rights and the obligations of individuals to take up and conform to the imperatives of 'expert' public health knowledges. A useful citizen engages in work, participates in social relationships and reproduces, he or she even goes to war to defend the country if prevailed upon to do so. Good health is deemed to be vital to achieving these activities. This chapter begins by explaining the development of the broad concept of citizenship. The discussion then focuses more specifically on the contemporary notion of the 'healthy' citizen, exploring its historical antecedents and implications for subjectivity. The chapter ends with a discussion of gender and citizenship, comparing the notion of the 'healthy' citizen as it applies differently to women and to men.

THE CONCEPT OF CITIZENSHIP

The concept of citizenship, originating in ancient thought, has undergone a number of metamorphoses over the centuries. Citizenship is thus an amorphous, rather than an easily definable, term. It should be considered as a diverse set of contingently and unevenly distributed

61

attributes and statuses which do not add up to a coherent whole, requiring a 'disaggregated' understanding of citizenship (Thomas 1993, p. 386). Citizenship is more than simply a cognitive or subjective phenomenon, but rather is lived at the site of embodiment at both the conscious and the unconscious levels. Indeed, the very fact of an individual's citizenship is founded upon his or her physical presence as 'body' within the boundaries of a country. Understandings, knowledges and practices around political identity are learnt very early in life and are experienced and manifested through the individual's body. As Scarry contends, 'the nation-state resides unnoticed in the intricate recesses of personhood, penetrates the deepest layers of consciousness and manifests itself in the body' (1985, pp. 108–9). While the extent of these processes may be hard to assess, it is clear that they occur via such phenomena as the external objects one puts inside one's body (such as food and drink) and the body's use of space through shape and form, learnt postures, gestures and gait. Such embodied forms of loyalty are more deeply ensconced, less easily shed, than disembodied forms of patriotism such as thought about national identity.

In ancient times, citizenship focused narrowly on participation in political life as part of the ideal of democracy. The move of the Western world towards modernity after the Enlightenment, with the growing focus on humanistic ideals, brought with it an increasing emphasis on the individual rather than the collectivity and on self-regulation. This change has had implications for the ways in which citizenship is understood in contemporary societies. This more individualistic concept of citizenship developed in early modern England with the dissolution of the feudal system of government. The notion of citizenship was dominant in Enlightenment thinking and in the project of modernity, centring around 'universalistic norms of participation in civil society' underpinned and justified by a rational social order (Turner 1994, pp. 155–6). It included the idea of individuals as 'free', with legal personalities and civil rights, owned by no-one but the self. This was a concept of personhood centred around property both of material possessions and one's own body (Fraser & Gordon 1994, pp. 95–6). This notion of self-possession was limited, however, as it did not apply to women and such social groups as the poor and foreigners.

The contemporary meanings of citizenship are closely aligned with notions of the civic and the civil, and are intertwined with the relationships between citizens, the common public life and the city. The civil is associated with the private sphere, with security and rights, while the civic is associated with public solidarity and obligations (Kelly 1994, pp. 30–2). The term 'civil' connotes refinement, knowledge of good manners and 'proper' social behaviour, order as opposed to rusticity, barbarism and disorder. Civility is important to citizenship because participation as a citizen in participatory democracy involves self-control of the body and the emotions, the regulation of one's demeanour and the cultivation of patience, enthusiasm and interest (Minson 1993, p. 203). Civility is generally understood as emerging from a highly reflexive self, a self who monitors his or her behaviour with due regard for others with whom he or she interacts socially. This concept of selfhood began to emerge in Europe in the Renaissance. At that time the public behaviour of individuals came to signify their social standing, a means of presenting the self and of evaluating others, and thus manners and the control of the outward self were vital (Elias 1978). The classical or 'civilised' body—the body that was able to control its tendency towards animality and emotionality—became privileged over the 'grotesque' body, that which was given over to excess, and to fleshly and sensual pleasure (Stallybrass & White 1986).

Even within the twentieth century there have been major changes to the concept of citizenship. Over the past half century alone there has developed a plethora of versions of citizenship, including cultural citizenship, global citizenship, ecological citizenship (van Steenbergen 1994, p. 3) and sexual citizenship (Evans 1993). Miller and Rose (1993, pp. 97–8) note that the citizen in the first half of the twentieth century was constituted as 'a social being whose powers and obligations were articulated in the language of social responsibilities and collective solidarities'. Diverse programs such as those arranged around social security, child welfare, physical and mental hygiene, and education were developed to serve 'needs' and to construct ideal citizens. By the early 1980s there had emerged a different concept of citizenship:

> No longer is citizenship construed in terms of solidarity, contentment, welfare and a sense of security established through the bonds of organisational and social life. Citizenship is to be active and individualistic rather than passive and dependent. The political subject is henceforth to be an individual whose citizenship is manifested through the free exercise of personal choice amongst a variety of options. (Miller & Rose 1993, p. 98)

As a result, governmental programs and regulatory technologies have diversified still more, to construct an autonomous subject whose choices and desires are aligned with the objectives of the state and other social authorities and institutions.

As we discussed in Chapter 1, under the neo-liberal approach to government it is expected that the subject *qua* citizen will conform to the goals of the state voluntarily, in most cases needing no direct coercion. Such self-discipline is vital to this mode of government. Citizens are required to become active on their own behalf: the emphasis on the role and duty of the nation-state in human progress is therefore decentred (Usher & Edwards 1994, p. 216). The concepts of rationality and self-control are central to an understanding of citizenship, because both concepts underpin contemporary assumptions of what it means to be 'human' and what the ideal modern 'self' should be. As we asserted in earlier chapters, in contemporary Western societies individuals are expected to constantly interrogate their lives and relationships in the quest for self-improvement, the achievement of authenticity, the maximisation of life chances and the exercise of choice from among alternatives. Subjectivity is created both through the techniques of governmental self-formation produced by external authorities and agencies and through the practices of ethical self-formation by which individuals come to know themselves and give meaning to their experiences. These processes are necessarily interrelated and reciprocal (Dean 1994, pp. 156–7).

Given its current linking with notions of self-control, citizenship inevitably raises moral questions in relation to what is considered 'good' or 'bad' citizenship. Judgments of morality are also related to the expectation that the practice of citizenship involves not only caring for the self but also protecting others' rights: 'To be called a good or real citizen is a particular positive judgement about the morality of one's behaviour. It implies that the person is concerned with the collective interest and its well being' (Janowitz 1994, p. 43). With the growing emphasis on health as a personal strategy of self-care and a resource for self-development, notions of citizenship have clear application to the new public health activities.

THE 'HEALTHY' CITIZEN

In contemporary Western societies, the pursuit of good health, like education, is considered both an obligation and a right of citizens. Education is an obligation because it enables individuals to prepare for citizenship, in allowing them to understand their civic duties and make use of their rights and in preparing them for productive employment; it is integral to becoming a 'good citizen' (Janowitz 1994, p. 49). So too, good health is required for a person to become a 'good citizen', for ill health removes individuals from the workforce and other responsibilities, and places an economic burden on others. It is one's duty to achieve and preserve good health, so that one might fulfil the other obligations of citizenship. As one German writer asserted in the late eighteenth century, 'Whoever neglects the precious treasure of health offends all of society, of which he [sic] is a member. Society rightly demands of him that he sacrifice a part of his energies and time to her needs and for her benefit, who every day contributes so much to his need and benefit' (quoted in Duden 1991, p. 18).

The 'right to health' was once understood to be related to enhancing the access of all citizens to health care services for the better treatment of ill health. In contemporary times, however, as the philosophies of the new public health have gathered force, the 'right to health' is rephrased as taking on personal responsibility for one's health by accepting and adopting the imperatives issuing forth from the state and other health-related agencies concerning the maintenance and protection of good health (Herzlich & Pierret 1987, p. 231). Greco has described this ethic as 'the duty to stay well', incorporating the understanding of health as 'a domain of individual appropriation through rational choice' (1993, p. 357). Managing their own relationship to risk has become an important means by which individuals can express their ethical selves and fulfil their responsibilities and obligations as 'good citizens' (Scott & Williams 1991, p. 3).

The contemporary focus on self-regulation, transformation and personal body 'maintenance' as a primary strategy to achieve public health goals is a relatively recent phenomenon. From medieval times until well into the twentieth century, public health strategies relied upon an overtly coercive element, attempting to force citizens to behave in ways deemed most appropriate for the interests of the state via legislation. Even in Britain in the nineteenth century, despite the prevailing political emphasis on laissez-faire economic production and individualism, public health acts were passed that challenged civil liberties. For example, these acts required parents to present their children for vaccination against smallpox or risk fines or imprisonment, and provided for the enforced medical inspection of prostitutes in specified towns and ports and their detainment if they were found to be infected with venereal disease. Such legislation was subject at the time to controversy and challenges based on criticisms of the state's intervention into the bodies of its citizens (Porter & Porter 1988, pp. 104–7).

A heightened concern about the health of populations emerged in the modern European states in the seventeenth and eighteenth centuries in concert with the emergence of industrialism and the breakdown of the feudal system. Health became viewed as an element of national policy and a site for the intervention of government in the interests of maintaining a robust population to support the state's endeavours. As a result, a new set of connections was generated between subject and discourse and subject and polity. The public health movement developed as a response to these new concerns privileging order and human rationality:

> The Enlightenment wrote health onto its banner as a physical–moral category. The concept was politically so effective and so double-edged because the interest of the authorities and the national economy in a self-administered objectification of the self appeared in it as a subjective need of the individual or an act of philanthropy. (Duden, 1991, p. 19)

It was during this period that governmental means of regulating the population began to shift from overtly coercive methods to those of self-regulation, assisted through the knowledges and technologies engendered in medicine, education and science. In the nineteenth century the theories of Malthus and Darwin contributed to both a concern about recording statistically the movement and reproduction of populations and a focus on constructing and monitoring norms of human behaviour. The human body, through these discourses, knowledges and practices, was constructed as a target of surveillance and regulation, subject to regular measurement and comparison against statistical norms:

> Within this set of problems, the 'body'—the body of individuals and the body of populations—appears as the bearer of new variables, not merely between the scarce and the numerous, the submissive and the restive, rich and poor, healthy and sick, strong and weak, but also between the more or less utilizable, more or less amenable to profitable investment, those with greater or lesser prospects of survival, death, and illness, and with more or less capacity for being usefully trained. (Foucault 1984a, p. 279)

By this process of normalisation, categories of 'normal' and 'abnormal' or 'pathological' bodies and social groups were constructed (see Chapter 2). Good health came to be regarded as the natural right of all citizens, which it was the duty of the state to promote and preserve (La Berge 1992, p. 16).

For some theorists, the contemporary era is characterised by the replacement of the political doctrine of liberty by the notion of consumption. The 'free' individual is conceptualised as the individual who possesses the maximum capacity to acquire goods, and consumption is a major source of meaning and moral values in everyday life. 'This makes for an aestheticised politics of civic identity', argues Miller (1993, p. 48). It is apparent that the notion of citizenship as it is phrased in the new public health discourses is centred around the consumption of commodities while also relying upon appeals to aesthetics (see Chapter 1). The unhealthy commodity (alcohol, cigarette, fatty food) is commonly represented in health promotional literature and media campaigns as producing ugliness, distorting the ideal body. Common images in these texts include the drunken teenagers engaging in fights and vomiting in front of their friends; the drink-driver in a mangled car, a bleeding passenger beside him or her; and the artery clogged by fat deposits. The commodity, in this representation, imposes itself upon the consumer, an external force of evil invading the body and taking control. Health promotion works to instil the consumer with the moral courage and fortitude to withstand this invasion. Yet consumption is not simply negated, for citizens are encouraged to engage in the consumption of commodities deemed 'healthy', such as low-fat or low-salt foods, nicotine patches, sports shoes and gym memberships.

In its overt goal of enhancing the health of citizens, the new public health directly works upon individuals' shared desires to maintain good health and demonstrate self-control through the regulated body. The health status of the individual is regarded as 'collective capital owned by the lineage, the race, or the nation' (Herzlich & Pierret 1987, p. 161). In the context of Western economies, in which expanding production and the accumulation of wealth are important, 'good health' is that condition which is least disruptive of production: the 'healthy citizen' is the citizen who can work continuously over her or his lifetime. Good health, therefore, is related to virtuous citizenship because of the benefits that extend from the individual to the social body. A healthy person is able to take part, to the best of his or her physical ability, in contributing to the nation's prosperity. A document published by the New South Wales Department of Health, entitled A State of Better Health, argues:

> Health promotion is an investment in better health for today and for future communities and populations. Health promotion is more than just

avoiding illness and disability, however. It aims to help everyone enjoy the best possible level of health. It is about giving them energy and the chance to live life to the full. It is adding life to years as well as years to life. (1991, p. 6)

The *Health for All Australians* report similarly contends that '[g]ood health is a positive state of being. It is an individual and community asset of great value' (Health Targets and Implementation Committee 1988, p. 5). The individual's state of health is thus viewed as subject to agency, an active rather than passive state that is directed at instrumental goals. Good health is represented not simply as an accomplishment of an individual, but as a general social resource.

The new public health has provided a rationale and apparatus for 'healthy' citizens to demonstrate their capacities of self-regulation as part of both their civic duty and their duty to themselves. As a result, the activities under the rubric of 'health' have proliferated. Many definitions of 'health' in the new public health literature expand to go beyond the notion of lacking physical or mental disability or pain to conceptualising health as the way in which individuals approach and deal with life in general. The capacity for economic production is not the only important outcome for the healthy self in the new public health discourses. Health is also privileged as a resource for self-fulfilment and enjoyment and as a capacity to respond in a dynamic manner to the world around oneself. For example, Ilona Kickbusch, as Director of Health Promotion and Education at the WHO, defined health as 'the extent to which an individual or group is able, on the one hand, to realise aspirations and satisfy needs, and, on the other hand, to change or cope with the environment' (quoted in de Leeuw 1989, p. 1282). Self-development and the expression of individual potential are related to 'good health'. Thus, in one 1995 magazine advertisement, the South Australian Health Foundation claims that 'to enjoy life you have to be healthy first . . . To realise your dreams the first step is to enjoy being healthy'. The advertisement lists the activities in which citizens should engage to achieve health: 'To be healthy means being active, eating the foods that make you healthy, choosing to drink less alcohol and choosing not to smoke'. The emphasis on personal enjoyment and on a purposive response to life involving 'activity', and the repetition of the notion that individuals are 'choosing' health-promoting strategies rather than being forced to undertake them, are highly characteristic of the new public health philosophy.

This concept of 'good health' recognises the experiential as well as the functional dimension of health: 'health' is the ability to realise personal goals, to exert control over one's life, to engage in self-development. It is suggested that citizens are thus acting in their own best interests in conforming to the imperatives issuing forth from the state in relation to 'healthy living': 'In effect the most recent space of surveillance has been a sort of "political awareness" which might be rendered as subjectivity. It has been the thinking, acting subject which has been both the object and effect of the new public health in its various manifestations' (Armstrong 1993, p. 407). Engaging in health-preserving and body-controlling activities such as exercise and dieting is viewed as protecting citizens from the degeneracies of contemporary society, providing a means of dispelling uncertainties and demonstrating allegiance to accepted moral norms in the interests of self-presentation. As in the discourse of war, the process of hardening and toughening individual bodies acts as a metonym for the toughening of the nation's moral fibre (Scheper-Hughes & Lock 1987, p. 25). The regulation and control of the body, it is argued in the new public health, require high levels of knowledge and self-efficacy to achieve. To this end, some public health documents have begun to refer to the concepts of 'health literacy' and 'health skills', which are seen to comprise 'personal health knowledge', 'positive attitudes towards changing behaviour', 'resilience', 'self-esteem' and 'problem solving', 'self-help' and 'coping' skills (see, for example, Nutbeam et al. 1993, p. 15).

Ideal 'healthy' citizens have their children immunised according to state directives, participate in screening procedures such as cervical cancer smear tests and blood cholesterol tests (but only when they are deemed to be in the appropriate target group), control their diet according to dietary guidelines and take regular exercise to protect themselves against such conditions as coronary heart disease and osteoporosis. Not only do they take steps to protect their own health, but they are also concerned about the health of others. This dimension of the obligations of the 'healthy' citizen is highly apparent in discourses about cigarette smoking, which currently emphasise the effects that cigarette smoke has on other people, especially children. Recent health campaigns have urged citizens to carry out surveillance in relation to cigarette smoking not only upon themselves, but upon others, in the interests of protecting the masses from 'other people's smoke', for example by insisting that others do not smoke inside one's house (Lupton 1995, p. 118). Responsibility for others' health status is also a central argument for preventive strategies relating to contagious diseases such as HIV infection and hepatitis. As one pamphlet on AIDS published by the New South Wales

Department of Health in 1989 noted: 'It is . . . important that anyone who has been exposed to HIV should adopt lifestyle and behavioural practices which help to strengthen the immune system and do not spread the virus to other people'. It is also assumed that it is the responsibility of 'healthy' citizens to be aware of their HIV status. This awareness is only the first step of a self-maintenance program. If individuals are negative for HIV antibodies, it is asserted that they should take steps to reduce their chance of contracting HIV by engaging in safer sex practices and avoiding the sharing of needles to inject drugs; if they are positive, they are exhorted to engage in activities to reduce the effects of positivity on their bodies and to avoid passing on the virus to others.

Goals and targets for public health expressed in such terminology as 'reducing mortality from lung cancer by 12 per cent by the year 2010' (see, for example, Nutbeam et al. 1993) are couched in terms that express the community's health status over that of the individual's health status. As observed in Chapter 2, such a target may be reached by infinitesimal improvements in the individual (for example, an extra month of life) but result in statistics that appear beneficial at the population level. As this suggests, in the new public health discourses devoting attention to one's health status is not only represented simply as an individual action but is also commonly sited within the context of a community, city or nation. As one writer has put it: 'Promoting the health of a community means developing and supporting the will and capacity of people to understand and work towards their own specific health needs . . . The central aim is to involve the entire community in an effort to promote the health of all groups within a geographical area' (Monaem 1989, pp. 297–8) (see Chapter 6).

The contemporary virtuous 'healthy' citizen, therefore, aligns personal satisfaction with the public good. Thus, the avoidance of drink-driving and of smoking and the adoption of the practice of seatbelt wearing are about both the health of the citizen and the citizen's needs to protect others—either their health or the public purse. The self is never lost in this discourse, however; its needs are never abandoned for those of the polity. The ethic of restraint that is phrased in this discourse is not based on the asceticism of self-denial or obedience to an authoritative imperative, but rather is supported through a narcissistic approach of 'caring for and about oneself', maximising the body's capacity for both productive labour and self-fulfilment and development (Singer 1993). Through the new public health discourses (among others), external imperatives are internalised as private interests. Discourses on dental

hygiene and care, for example, have continually emphasised the responsibility of the individual (or in the case of children, of their mothers)
to conform to expert advice consonant with the imperatives of governmentality (Nettleton 1991). These norms about dental care have
become naturalised in the family: children are taught how to brush their
teeth, and at which prescribed times, from infancy. As adults, individuals
continue to brush their teeth as an everyday habit, often with little
reflection on the reasons why they do so. The practice has become a
habit, a practice of the self perpetuated not by the dictates of external
imperatives but by the individual's habits of everyday life.

While the overt rhetoric of the new public health is directed towards
appeals to the notion of the 'civil citizen' in its emphasis on self-regulation and self-control, there remains a notion that the state should
sometimes step in to guide or even control its citizens that has resonances
with early public health philosophies. The state still takes a largely
paternalistic approach to the task of monitoring and regulating its
citizens' health, albeit cloaked in the discourse of individual and community 'voluntary participation'. Public health represents the state as the
agency responsible for guarding and ensuring the health of the populace.
As Sears notes, 'modern Public Health has, from the outset, been
identified with the state. Indeed, the very conception of "Public Health"
centres around the state, whether explicitly or implicitly' (1992, p. 64).
Most of the new public health activities are sponsored by the state on
behalf of its citizens, generally administered through bureaucratic health
departments and often enshrined in legislation that includes penalties
for non-compliance.

Many of the most obvious sites where a more directive state/citizen
relationship becomes apparent are in relation to public health concerns,
including legislation directed at preventing the use of illicit drugs (such
as heroin and cocaine), the age at which individuals can purchase licit
drugs (cigarettes and alcohol), and driving practices (seatbelt wearing
and drink-driving). A number of contemporary public health acts permit
the state to intervene in the conduct of bodies, enforcing medical
inspections, vaccinations or medical treatment upon the unwilling, and
in extreme cases allowing for the internment of individuals to prevent
them spreading disease. Some state-imposed regulations include extreme
violations of personal liberty and privacy. For instance, individuals
involved in methadone programs are often forced to engage in urine
tests (to check for opiate use) under the full observation of health

workers. In this context of enforcement, the citizen's liberty and rights as an individual become subsumed under those of the collectivity.

In many cases such enforcement has been exercised upon stigmatised or less powerful social groups: prostitutes rather than their clients, gay men and lesbians rather than heterosexuals, immigrants rather than native-born citizens, the poor or dispossessed rather than the wealthy. All these interventions are justified in the name of the good health of the public, and it is assumed that citizens will conform to state imperatives. The underlying ethic is predominantly utilitarian, in privileging the well-being of the community over that of individuals, as well as paternalistic, assuming that the state 'knows best' and should act to protect those who cannot protect themselves. Bentham's doctrine, 'that it was the duty of the legislator to secure the greatest happiness of the greatest number through the deployment of science, expertise, and legal sanctions', was particularly influential on the policies and practices of the nineteenth-century public health reformers (Porter & Porter 1988, p. 101) and remains a central plank of the new public health philosophy.

WOMEN AS HEALTHY CITIZENS

The concept of citizenship assumes that individuals have common goals and status, a common culture (Turner 1994, p. 165). The rhetoric implies that all individuals, regardless of age, ethnicity, gender, social class or sexual identity, have an equal status as citizens and similar access to and investment in the reciprocal rights and obligations of citizens. It is clear, however, that many individuals are not equal under the concept of citizenship, for example women, children, the dispossessed and minority social groups. The woman as citizen is quite a different social and historical phenomenon from the man as citizen. In fact, women have historically been denied many of the rights, privileges and responsibilities of citizens in the political sphere. As Waldby (1994, pp. 380-1) points out, women in Western societies lacked many of the features of either civil or political citizenship in the early part of the twentieth century, including the 'political' right to vote, the 'civil' right to work at an occupation of their own choice, and, if married, the 'civil' right to be free of their husband's physical coercion. Indeed, until relatively recently, women's bodies were considered the property of their husbands (Sevenhuijsen 1992, p. 168; Vogel 1994, pp. 78–9).

For centuries in Western societies the so-called private site of the family has been very much related to women's participation in citizenship, particularly as public participation was effectively denied most women. It is in relation to this private sphere that the discourses of medicine and public health have contributed to understandings of the woman *qua* citizen. They have been regularly employed to naturalise the assumption that women are not equipped to participate as citizens in the public sphere. These discourses have constructed women as passive and irrational, unequipped physically, emotionally or intellectually for a role in public life. Indeed, in the nineteenth century it was frequently postulated that women could only achieve good psychological and physical health through confining themselves to the tasks associated with marriage and reproduction (Turner 1987, pp. 89–90). Any exertion of the feminine mind, it was argued, including both intellectual effort or fierce emotion, could cause a fatal stoppage in the flow of menstrual secretions. Women should therefore concentrate on dulling the mind, avoiding any type of mental excitement so that their bodies could proceed 'naturally' (Shuttleworth 1990, p. 57). Women in the gynaecological literature were frequently compared to children, as 'incomplete adults' in their assumed physical delicacy, psychological instability and irresponsibility (Moscucci 1990, p. 31). The figure of the 'hysterical woman', for example, which was dominant in the Victorian era, represented women as controlled by their wombs, their minds being unable to regulate their bodies. Even today, women are generally represented as more prone to illness, as both physically and psychologically defective compared with men, and as dependent upon medical care throughout their lives. Illness, and its associated meanings of lack of control, dependency, passivity, physical inactivity and weakness, are thus conflated with femininity (Turner 1987, Ch. 5; Broom 1989).

Women in Western societies have been principally represented as citizens in terms of their contribution to the bearing and raising of children and the care of husbands and other family members. The woman as 'healthy' citizen, therefore, is understood as a resource for the reproduction and maintenance of other 'healthy' citizens. Such participation in citizenship does not fall into the notions of civil or political citizenship. Rather, it is an understanding of citizenship that revolves around contributing to the welfare of society through private actions (childbearing and domestic labour).

The problematising of 'the family' as a site of intervention on the part of public health authorities in the mid eighteenth century (Foucault 1984a) is central to the ways in which women, as mothers, have been constructed as citizens, particularly in their role of ensuring the health of their children. The use of medico-hygienist justification was an important element of regulating the population via the family, with particular emphasis on the role played by mothers. From the eighteenth century, the welfare of children was constituted as a 'problem' of government, and included such aspects as their survival and growth rates, education, and moral and physical well-being (Donzelot 1979). The 'private' world of the family was charged as the site within which the problem of the child—including the maintenance and development of the child's body—was largely addressed (Donzelot 1979; Foucault 1984a, p. 280).

The site of the family thus provided a link between the 'private' ethic of good health, as espoused and championed by individual families, and general political objectives regarding the health of the social or public body (Foucault 1984a, p. 281). As a leading nineteenth-century proponent of social work argued, the family was the 'nursery of citizenship', with familial affection and understandings of responsibility acting as an exemplar for ideal wider social relations (Helen Bosanquet, cited in Lewis 1992, p. 86). With the growing emphasis upon the health implications of domestic space in the late nineteenth century and into the early twentieth century, the responsibility for maintaining the hygiene of the home was directed towards women, in their roles as mothers and wives. As one American book outlining lessons for young girls in schools on the care of younger siblings argued in 1917: 'These early lessons will prepare them for citizenship, make them lovers of law and order, health and cleanliness, honesty and morality, and thus insure a happy contented neighbourhood' (quoted in Sears 1992, p. 72). In this text, the cleanliness and orderliness of the home site and of the bodies of those inhabiting the home are represented as the domain of responsibility of girls and women in their duty as citizens. At the same time as motherhood was being defined as a caring, altruistic and absorbing activity, laws seeking to punish infanticide, abortion, birth control and baby farming—activities that were viewed as highly immoral and damaging to the social order—were being enacted in Britain (Smart 1990, p. 15).

The British working-class mother in the late nineteenth century and into the early twentieth century was a particular target of these discourses, defined as little more than 'the unpaid nursemaid of the State', and subject to imperatives from a cluster of state bodies and private organisations that constituted the Infant Welfare movement. The price of non-compliance included humiliation, and fines, jail sentences or loss of child custody (Ross 1993, p. 197). The 'health visitor' system was instituted in Britain in the late nineteenth century, designed to observe and advise and to report to local medical authorities the conditions of working-class mothers and their infants; its main mission was to create 'responsible' mothers (Ross 1993, p. 209). For British middle-class women during this period, voluntary social work and other philanthropic work with the working class and the poor allowed them to fulfil their obligations as citizens by serving and caring for others outside the immediate vicinity of their own families (Lewis 1992; Bland 1992). These women were thus extending their 'civilising' and domesticating role from the home into the wider world by engaging in 'municipal housekeeping' (Bland 1992, p. 44). The emergent science of psychology was central to this endeavour, and health education at the time had similar goals and methods.

The emphasis upon women as bearing responsibility for the health and welfare of their partners, children and other family members (such as their ageing parents) by ensuring the cleanliness of the home remains strong in contemporary Western societies. For example, a concern about the level of lead found in the blood of infants and children in inner-city areas of Sydney in the 1990s has generated calls for mothers (rather than fathers) to protect their children by mopping and vacuuming the house frequently, disposing of flaking paint, ensuring that children wash their hands before eating, and covering any exposed soil around the house. The expectations concerning women's role as the primary carers for children still tend to limit women's access to playing a full role in political decision-making (Vogel 1994, p. 85). So too, the notion that women are less well equipped to participate as citizens in the public sphere continues to rely upon biological and medical discourses for support, particularly those asserting the supposed unstable emotional states of pregnant, premenstrual or menopausal women. One example is an article published in 1994 on the front page of a Sydney newspaper, which reported the findings on gender differences in sleep needs made by a male psychologist at a Sydney university. The article was headlined 'It's a biological fact: women need more sleep', and quoted the psychologist's claims that until menopause women live on a 'hormonal rollercoaster', that the biochemistry of their brains was more complex and changeable than that of men's brains and that women are therefore more susceptible to the effects of 'sleep deprivation' and depression than are men (Dayton 1994). This article is a good example of the phenomenon described by Broom, whereby '[a]ny disadvantages from which

women may suffer are [explained as the] consequences of natural defects
in women themselves, in their genes, their hormones, the "structure" of
their brains, or perhaps in the distinctively female organs and functions
of reproduction' (1989, p. 129).

Not only are women defined as abnormal and ill through notions of
femininity, they are also frequently positioned as producing ill health or
deviant behaviours in others, particularly their children and husbands
(Broom 1989, p. 130; Spensky 1992, pp. 106–7). Mothers of sexually
abused children tend to be the targets of accusations of 'poor mothering',
which includes such factors as absence from the home, sexual estrange-
ment from their partners and lack of appropriate protection of the child
(Hooper 1992, p. 68). Pregnancy is a particular site at which women's
bodies and practices of the self are constructed through the discourses
of public health. Personal responsibility for self-control and self-moni-
toring is therefore extended into another body—that of the foetus. There
is a long history in Western societies of pregnant women being represented as the containers for their foetuses. In early modern Europe,
pregnant women were advised against all sorts of activities, including
travelling in carriages, horse riding, and consuming spicy foods. It was
suggested in both lay and medical texts that women's intellectual activities, imagination and emotional states during pregnancy could cause
birth malformations and birth marks in their offspring. Pregnant women
were exhorted by medical 'experts' to avoid upsetting events in the
interests of their foetuses, for example by maintaining domestic harmony
in their households. As a result of such beliefs, the birth of a malformed
infant was held to be the fault of the mother, exposing her 'secret
passions' (Epstein 1995, Ch. 5). In the Victorian era, a woman's womb
'was figured both as a sacred font originating life, and as a crucial stage
in the machinery of material social manufacture' (Shuttleworth 1990,
p. 58). The outcome of such concerns has generally been the restriction
of women's activities.

Contemporary public health discourses frequently position pregnant
women as needful of constant self-surveillance to protect the health of
their foetus. Pregnant women are advised to monitor their diet closely
and are routinely dissuaded from drinking alcohol or smoking throughout
their pregnancy. In some contexts, the health issues around pregnancy
have been rephrased as criminal issues. In the United States, women
who use illicit drugs during pregnancy are subject to punitive legal
charges: over the past decade, more than 160 women in 24 states have
been charged with child neglect and the distribution of drugs to a minor

based on charges that they took certain drugs during pregnancy. By 1994, in seven states in the United States, there was legislation in place that ensured that if a woman delivered an infant who tested positive for drugs, or if she herself tested positive at delivery, she would be subject to arrest at release from hospital and her infant would be removed from her care by the Department of Social Services. The woman would be subsequently charged with administering the drug through the umbilical cord (Susskind 1994).

While there is not yet similar legislation in Australia, there is a continuous emphasis in popular and medical discourses on the woman's responsibility for the foetus *in utero*. One example is a newspaper article headlined 'Life in womb will be written on your tomb', in which the journalist quoted a medical researcher who argued that: 'We need to be much more focused on what happens in pregnancy . . . You are marked forever by what happens in the womb. The most important day of your life is not conception, it's the next nine months.' The researcher contended that such adult conditions as heart disease, high blood pressure and diabetes are influenced by the conditions of foetal development in the uterus and the size of the infant at birth. He conceded that it was not fully understood what factors influenced foetal development, but contended that women should pay attention to their diet even before conception to ensure the health of their child (Sweet 1994). The emphasis on women regulating their emotional states in the interests of the infant's health also remains a feature of advice to pregnant women. In self-care books, women are frequently reminded that their emotional states have a direct impact on the foetus. Such books warn, for example, that a mother who is ambivalent about her pregnancy is far more likely to have a difficult birth and that her infant will experience physical and behavioural problems, having supposedly sensed *in utero* that she or he is not wholeheartedly wanted (Shuttleworth 1993/94, p. 38).

These discourses tend to position the health and well-being of the foetus as more important than those of the pregnant woman, suggesting that a woman's refusal to engage in protective behaviours amounts to child abuse. This responsibility for another's health continues as the infant is born and grows to adulthood, with mothers being charged with the duty to ensure that the moral, social and physical development of their children is maximised. As women are placed in this role of caring for others' health and well-being, it is assumed that they need to protect their own health so as to better perform this duty. A study carried out in the English city of Bradford found that doctors caring for a middle-aged heart patient tended to invite that person's spouse for a discussion on how to meet the patient's new dietary requirements only if the patient were male: a wife, but not a husband, was considered responsible for such health care provision (H. Rose 1990, p. 214). As this suggests, 'women still carry out most of the unpaid work in the domestic task of producing, maintaining and protecting health' (H. Rose 1990, p. 215).

Women's sexuality has also contributed to their representation as citizens in public health discourses. Public health literature has traditionally portrayed women's bodies as 'risky' through their potential for intimate contact with other bodies as both seducers and nurturers. For centuries women, particularly prostitutes or other women deemed 'promiscuous', have been represented as the source of contagion for sexually transmissible diseases such as syphilis via the erotic touch: 'Female beauty only serves as a mask for corruption and death' (Gilman 1989, pp. 95–6; see also Gilman 1993). Female bodies have been marginalised as contaminating, inspiring feelings of disgust and revulsion. Their bodies are seen to threaten to contaminate other bodies, principally those of men. As a result, women's sexual activities and conduct have been subject to control and surveillance in the interests of public health to a far greater extent than have those of men. As we noted earlier in this chapter, in the last century such monitoring of women included forcible medical inspection and their detainment if they were found to have the symptoms of a sexually transmissible disease.

The portrayal of women's bodies as particularly contagious, as possessing and passing on disease, has remained strong into the twentieth century. In the middle of the twentieth century women were the primary target of tuberculosis screening. Public health films produced to persuade women to seek X-ray screening for tuberculosis positioned the female body as a key vector of contagion, the bacilli insidiously lying hidden within women's bodies and threatening the health of their lovers, family members and the public (Cartwright 1995, p. 147). In contemporary public health discourses the bodies of women continue to be portrayed as subject to lack of control over bodily boundaries. In discourses on such conditions as HIV/AIDS, for example, women's bodies remain understood as 'leaky', as contaminating objects. As a result, women are routinely charged with the responsibility for protecting both their own health and that of their male sexual partners by insisting on the use of condoms. In contrast, heterosexual men are rarely positioned as the targets of public health research or education programs in relation to HIV/AIDS (Tulloch & Lupton 1997).

Women's bodies are viewed as highly risky and contagious because they emit fluids that are potentially 'dirty'. Such fluids threaten integrity; they are embarrassing, undignified, reminding humans of their animality. As Grosz argues: 'Body fluids attest to the permeability of the body, its necessary dependence on an outside, its liability to collapse into this outside (this is what death implies), to the perilous divisions between the body's inside and its outside' (1994, p. 193). These symbolic meanings surrounding women's bodies are particularly evident in discourses on HIV/AIDS, where women function as both 'the guardians of the purity of sexual exchange' and as the threats to purity by virtue of their fluid, seeping, and therefore 'dirty', bodies (Grosz 1994, p. 197). The imagery of women as 'reservoirs' for HIV infection is often noticeable in epidemiological writing that discusses the role of female prostitutes in the HIV/AIDS epidemic. Prostitutes, it is frequently argued, harbour infection within their bodies in the shape of the semen deposited by their clients, which then poses a threat to the next customer. The prostitute's body is represented as a 'swamp' where infection breeds, or as a 'passive holding tank' that becomes infectious 'only when another penis is dipped into it' (Treichler 1989, p. 49). Men are told they should avoid sex with prostitutes or use condoms for their own protection, but not for the protection of the prostitutes. It is always assumed that men are at risk from prostitutes, not vice versa, because of the latter group's cultural construction as 'contaminating', 'immoral' and 'dirty'. The threat posed to the prostitute herself by her clients (who are, after all, the providers of the infected body fluid) is ignored in this discourse.

Women, therefore, are seen as more susceptible to ill health and as more likely sites of contamination of others than are men, and as a result are regarded as requiring greater surveillance and control, imposed both by authorities and through self-regulation. Throughout women's lifespans they are encouraged to protect their own health not simply for their own interests but because of their responsibility to others. As one Australian pamphlet on cervical screening asserted to its audience: 'So take care of yourself, and make sure you have a Pap smear every two years. Do it for the people who love you and need you. But most of all, do it for yourself.' In a newspaper advertisement published in 1995, the Sydney Breast Cancer Institute used the heading 'Some victims of breast cancer are very young' accompanied by a photograph of a little boy looking vulnerable and forlorn. The text went on to assert: 'Breast cancer is now the leading cause of death by cancer in Australian women. But some of the hardest hit victims are those who have to cope with someone they love going through this terrible disease.' The directives of such texts attempt to position women as always linked to others in a caring relationship, and as needing to protect their own health to save others' feelings. Women's participation in these health-protective activities is constructed both as their right as citizens who are due health care entitlements and as their responsibility as citizens who should not place a burden on the state or upon loved ones by becoming ill through their own negligence. The notion of citizenship, therefore, is phrased through a willingness to engage in the surveillance and bodily regulation activities offered by the state, rendering more complex the idea of active citizenship (Howson 1994).

A clear link is therefore evident between the emphasis in past regimes of public health on women's duties as citizens to protect the health and well-being of others—their husbands and children—and a similar emphasis in the new public health. This conceptualisation is clearly directed at the heterosexual woman: lesbians are notable by their absence from public health discourses. However, while women continue to be typically constructed as wives or mothers in new public health discourses, with a focus on their reproductive potential and related responsibilities, there is also a newer focus on women participating in practices of the self to achieve their individual potential, including in the roles of productive worker or alluring sex partner. In new public health discourses women are encouraged to monitor the shape and size of their bodies so as to maximise their sexual attractiveness and desirability, and to avoid practices such as smoking because men will find their breath unattractive or because it causes premature wrinkling. The feminine 'healthy' citizen, it is suggested, should seek both soundness of body and physical allure through the self-care techniques proffered by the new public health. In these discourses there is an elision between the ideals of commodity culture and public health, for both promote the slim, attractive, healthy, physically fit, youthful body as that which women should seek to attain.

MEN AS HEALTHY CITIZENS

In contrast with women, until very recently men have rarely been singled out in the new public health discourses as vulnerable to illness and needful of more health care. While women's bodies are routinely presented as the focus of the male gaze, as passive objects rather than as subjects, men's bodies tend to be represented as active and productive, participating in such arenas as politics and sport. Although men are also exhorted to maintain an attractive body, there is far less emphasis in popular and public health discourses on their physical appearance. Even in discourses of the ageing body there is a far greater focus on older women compared with older men in policy debates, the social science literature and popular culture. This disparity can only partly be explained by the fact that women tend to live longer than men (Hearn 1995). The bare flesh of men's bodies tends to be far less available to the gaze than that of women's bodies; instead men generally appear clothed in the armour of business suits or uniforms. While a woman must generally watch herself and be highly aware of her embodied presence as it appears to others, men tend to constitute the surveyors rather than the surveyed (Berger 1972, p. 46). Women, therefore, are routinely constituted as far more 'embodied' than are men.

Unlike women's bodies, which tend to be represented as 'leaky', moist and flowing, and therefore liminal and difficult to contain, men's bodies are conceptually rigidly separated from 'outside'. The male body is dominantly culturally represented and understood as 'contained', dry and controlled compared with the soft, viscous body of a woman. The hardness, resistance and tightness of the male body represents the ideal: 'A hard body will ensure that there are no leakages across the edges between inner and outer worlds . . . What holes remain must be firmly shut' (Easthope 1990, p. 52; see also Theweleit 1987). This ideal reaches its apotheosis in the practice of bodybuilding, a technology of the self and source of self-transformation directed at increasing muscular size and emphasising hegemonic masculinity. The heavily muscular body has been idealised since ancient Greek times, resembling the phallus in its hard, erect form, and denoting power. The muscular body not only stands for outward containment, but also bespeaks inner control and rigidity (Dutton 1995, p. 43). The physical and dietary routines of bodybuilding are directed at disciplining the body and denying weakness, and thus constitute a potent display of power, self-confidence, authority and self-control (Mrozek 1989; White & Gillett 1994; Dutton 1995).

In the context of medicine and illness the male body becomes even more disembodied. The ideal male body suffers no pain or weakness, is never ill and never breaks down. When men fall ill, therefore, they find the experience confronting in terms of the vulnerability they suddenly experience—the sense that they no longer have rigid control over their bodies. This experience may even challenge a man's sense of his masculinity. As one man wrote of his experience being hospitalised for a heart condition at the age of 46:

> After so many years of bodily invisibility, this period felt like a time of alien invasion, of having my body colonised and prodded by machines that penetrated far inside my body. My fear of losing masculine control and being de-armoured was acute. I had learnt to be the penetrator and the fucker. Now they were fucking me, penetrating into my secret places. My purchase on a safe, heterosexual masculine identity was being eroded. (Jackson 1990, p. 64)

The meanings associated with 'health' and 'protective behaviours' are inextricably linked with the feminised discourses of 'looking after yourself', risk avoidance and caution, and are highly embodied. Such practices are also often coded as 'homosexual' rather than 'heterosexual', in their feminised interest in physical appearance. For the male subject position, to 'give into' or betray to others feelings of weakness or illness is thus 'unmasculine' (Theweleit 1987; Grosz 1994).

Very little detailed research has been undertaken on the ways men conceptualise and use their bodies in the context of health activities, a lack which in itself demonstrates the de-emphasis on men as the subjects of the new public health discourses. One in-depth study of five British male students aged in their early twenties found that they articulated anxiety about the strength and size of their bodies, particularly remembering the embarrassment they felt about their bodies around the time of puberty (Jones 1993). The young men said that they tended to ignore orthodox public health advice, preferring self-conscious risk-taking to test and demonstrate the inherent resilience of their bodies. They also engaged in some activities, however, that enhance masculinity at the same time as they accord with health promotional discourses, for example physical exercise—including bodybuilding as well as other, less overtly narcissistic sports such as football and athletics. One of the men described his participation in sporting activities as allowing him to build up and maintain a better physique 'for myself' rather than for the gaze of others, to 'feel so much better about myself', while another played sport to enhance physical fitness and as a leisure activity. Others chose to avoid exercise, involving themselves in more intellectual or artistic pursuits. All of these young men enjoyed drinking as a means of inebriation, relaxation, socialising, of liberating the self and demonstrating their masculine identity, of temporarily disrupting the boundaries between body and ego.

In another study involving group discussions with Australian school students about solar protection and skin cancer (Lupton & Gaffney 1996), the male students articulated a disdain towards people who 'deliberately' attempted to become suntanned. They described men who sought a suntan as vain and possibly homosexual because of their evident desire to appear attractive. They suggested that while girls may choose to lie on the beach attempting to tan, boys should develop their tans through active pursuits such as outdoor sporting activities, rather than 'passively' tanning. Most of the male students were also at pains to emphasise that they 'did not care' about the possible cosmetic side-effects to tanning, such as wrinkles, and therefore did not bother with such protective strategies as applying sun block or staying out of the sun during the middle of the day.

Other research has suggested that women and men understand, talk about and experience their bodies differently in the context of health. Interviews carried out by Saltonstall (1993) with middle-class American men and women aged between 35 and 55 found that while both men and women conceptualised health as involving deliberate, intentional action, as 'taking care of yourself', as a creation and accomplishment of the thinking individual, there were clear gendered differences. The male interviewees frequently referred to 'good health' as related to 'keeping' or 'being in control', as exercising power over the body through will. The men tended to describe their bodies as 'belonging' to them, while the women were more likely to refer to their bodies as having a momentum of their own. For the men, body maintenance in the interests of good health tended to revolve around exercise and 'fuelling' the body with nourishing food, suggesting a concept of the body as medium of action, with its function and capacity most important. The female interviewees tended to refer to the physical appearance of the body as important for good health, for example slimness, thereby emphasising the 'outer' rather than the 'inner' body.

In discourses on masculinity it is often suggested that to be a man is to invite, rather than avoid, risk. As Paul Willis found in his study of young working-class men in England, their participation in drinking in pubs and getting drunk provided a means of escaping boredom, of relaxation and of participating in 'another world' in which there is a promise of adventure. The amount consumed became an indicator of 'how much of a man you are' (1990, pp. 100–1). Willis asserts that in this context:

> Risk is esteemed . . . It's almost as if some young men want to invent, through drink, their own trials by performance in uncertain situations.

> The kinds of risks they take, the way they structure these risks, the way they deal with them, indicate, of course, components of young masculinity. (1990, p. 102)

There is, therefore, a tension between the imperative towards achieving the ideal of the hard, muscular body that bespeaks hegemonic masculinity and the desire to avoid an appearance of vanity. For many heterosexual men, particularly those in their adolescence and early adulthood who are in the process of constructing their sense of masculinity, attempts to expend too much time on deliberately enhancing bodily appearance, to engage in narcissistic rituals of self-preservation, are regarded as effeminate, as the preserve of women and gay men (Watson 1993). By contrast, engaging in activities that threaten one's health, endanger one's body, are often coded as masculine. These activities include smoking, drinking and other drug taking, adventure sporting activities and reckless driving. Such activities are rituals that call into question the boundaries of the body, allowing the space for experiencing the limits of embodiment (Jones 1993).

These approaches to the body are, of course, shaped by such features as age, social class, ethnicity and religious beliefs as well as by gender. While excessive drinking bouts at the local pub may be a favoured pastime for English working-class young men, the leisure practices of older men or middle-class men living in the same area are likely to be somewhat different. There are multiple discourses surrounding the notion of masculinity (just as femininity is multiple), although some discourses may be described as more dominant than others. Mullen (1994), for example, found in his interviews with working-class, middle-aged men in Glasgow, Scotland, that they demonstrated moralist judgments about people who drank too much. Some men who held strong religious beliefs articulated a notion of the body as a temple of God, and as requiring care and protection for that reason.

While the male body is rarely singled out as a strategic target for health promotional strategies in the same way as is the female body, there is a general covert assumption that the 'public' body, the body to which public health activities are directed, is masculine. The archetypal human body in medical discourses is that of the male body. Both in visual imagery and verbal texts, medical discourses portray a masculine rather than a feminine body, implying that it is the masculine body that is the 'healthy' norm, while the feminine body is that which deviates from the norm. For example, the illustrations in contemporary medical textbooks continue to use the male body to stand for the human body, describing women's bodies as 'weaker' or 'less developed' in relation to men's bodies (Lawrence & Bendixen 1992). The new public health discourses have similarly represented the heterosexual male body as the 'normal' body, requiring less in the way of education, surveillance and monitoring activities such as screening technologies than do women's bodies. While gay men's bodies have historically been subject to intense medical surveillance, as 'deviant', feminised and pathological—particularly in the wake of the AIDS epidemic—heterosexual masculine bodies have rarely occasioned such scrutiny. As we observed above, the heterosexual male body subject to HIV infection, or dying from AIDS, is virtually absent from public discourses on AIDS, while the figures of the feminised gay male body deteriorating from AIDS and the passive female 'victim' of infection are extremely common (Lupton 1994b, pp. 130–1; Tulloch & Lupton 1997). As such, masculine bodies (particularly if heterosexual) are represented as signifying the 'body politic' that public health agencies and activities are designed to protect, for they represent the ideal of the ordered, rational, self-contained body (Waldby 1993). Other bodies, particularly those of women, threaten the 'normality' of the male body.

Save for times of war, when the health and physical fitness of the male recruit are subject to intense monitoring and measurement, heterosexual men as citizens have rarely been asked to engage in medical surveillance. There is no substantial medical equivalent to gynaecology for the study and treatment of men's bodies, for example. Rarely are men expected to take responsibility for the health of others as husbands or fathers, in the same way that women are routinely encouraged and expected to do so as wives and mothers. The implication is that the health status and physical fitness of men's bodies are important only in the public sphere in terms of sites of productive labour or as part of a defence force. Men as citizens, therefore, are not those who are charged with the responsibility of caring for others' health; rather they are represented as those who hold an entitlement of protection from others.

In the 1990s, however, a quite novel discourse, that of 'men's health', has begun to emerge, particularly among middle-class men in Western countries. This discourse, which argues that men's health has been largely neglected and that there should be better and more health services provided for men, is strongly linked to a wider 'men's movement' that has challenged the neglect its members perceive of men's rights, emotions and selfhood. In Australia the first national Men's Health Conference was held in 1995, with the objectives of drawing together interested groups and individuals to focus on men's health issues, to raise awareness of issues affecting men's health, to identify areas of particular disadvantage and to identify strategies to address these problems. The conference was followed by a series of forums in most capital cities in late 1995. A draft National Men's Health Strategy was subsequently produced and circulated in January 1996, discussing the relationship between notions of masculinity and men's health status and seeking written submissions to finalise a men's health policy program by the end of 1996 (Commonwealth Department of Human Services and Health 1996).

The main thrust of the 'men's health' discourse is that men die younger than women, seek less health care throughout their lives than do women and are more susceptible to conditions such as heart disease, stress-related illnesses, violence and accidents. It is argued that, as a by-product of the focus on women's health over the past two decades engendered by the feminist movement, men's health has been unjustly neglected. Thus, for example, some individual men and men's groups have called for prostate screening to be made widely available for men, just as breast and cervical cancer screening is provided for women (Fletcher 1994; Dow 1995). The popular media have taken up this emphasis, with more and more articles about 'men's health' published over the past few years. In December 1994, *Time* magazine published a cover feature on the issue of men's health, and one national Australian newspaper features a regular column dedicated to men's health, covering such issues as impotence and other sexual problems, prostate and testicular cancer, stress, work issues and relationships.

The newly established 'men's health' field has begun to have implications for public health resource allocation. In one Australian case in 1990, a medical doctor and bureaucrat, Dr Alex Proudfoot, filed a complaint of sexual discrimination with the Human Rights and Equal Opportunities Commission. The basis of his complaint was that the government's provision of special women's health care services in his city of Canberra was discriminating against men. Proudfoot contended that men could not gain access to such services, even though they provided health care that could be of benefit to them (other than strictly gynaecological and obstetric services); for example, services directed towards drug and alcohol addiction, depression, and eating disorders. Proudfoot drew attention to the statistics demonstrating that men have higher rates of certain types of morbidity than do women and that men die younger, and called for the immediate cessation of women's health services in Canberra and the publication of apologies in newspapers.

Proudfoot's complaint was followed by two others filed by men, arguing on similar grounds. After being heard by the Commission in 1992, their complaints were dismissed (Susskind 1992; Broom 1994).

Such calls for the expansion of health services to men are interesting in their overturning of the notion of men as disembodied citizens. The discourse of men's health draws attention to the ways in which men are weaker and more physically vulnerable than women in its quoting of morbidity and mortality statistics. It positions the male body as the site of medical intervention by such technologies as screening, suggesting that men as 'healthy' citizens should adopt the range of bodily regulation, monitoring and surveillance activities emerging from the state with which women have routinely been asked to engage for decades. As such, the men's health movement is both gendering and pathologising men's bodies, representing them as emphatically 'male' in relation to disease and death—rather than as a degendered, ideal-type 'healthy' body—and as subject to the medical gaze. The calls for greater medical screening of men's bodies rest upon the appeals to objectivity, rationality and 'knowledge' that are the foundation of the normalising strategies of the new public health. The discourse therefore represents an even greater extension of the new public health strategies of continual monitoring and calculation of the population's health status. The men's health discourse, like that of the women's health movement that preceded it, underlines the 'voluntary' nature of such surveillance, because the calls for the increased 'medicalisation' of men's bodies through greater access to health care services and medical screening technologies are not emerging from the state, but from community groups and individuals.

CONCLUDING COMMENTS

In this chapter we have emphasised the centrality of citizenship to the discourses of the new public health. Furthermore, we have sought to underline the ways in which judgments of morality, as they are constructed through the discourses and practices of citizenship, are gendered in both the 'old' and the 'new' public health.

The chapter also demonstrated the extent to which the 'public' and the 'private' spheres are merged more and more seamlessly in the context of notions of contemporary citizenship and the philosophies and strategies of the new public health. For Waldby (1994, p. 389) the concept of citizenship 'depends upon the public; the term has no significant meaning in the private'. Yet, as we have demonstrated in relation to the notion of the 'healthy' citizen, the state cannot fully be separated from either the individual or the family, and neither can the public be separated from the private. Why should the concept of citizenship be linked to the public sphere and not, for example, the domestic setting? Under the imperatives of public health, personal/individual and public welfare are one and the same. One engages as a healthy citizen by participating in self-care practices that are often intensely private; for example, teeth-brushing, condom use and restrained dietary habits. Since the emergence of germ theory, the home has been constructed as a site where intervention is required regarding health problems and where the spread of disease can be prevented via the domestic labour of women. While these practices may not often be articulated or overtly represented by those who engage in them as 'public' activities that contribute to 'public' health goals they are, nonetheless, inextricably linked to governmental goals and imperatives. Furthermore, health promotional materials are often directly targeted at individuals in the home setting, whether they are televised public service announcements, pamphlets mailed to householders, or health promotion advertisements in newspapers and magazines and on radio.

The concepts of 'risk' and 'the environment' have become increasingly integral to notions of the 'healthy' citizen. The next chapter discusses the ways in which these interrelated problems are constructed and dealt with in the new public health and examines the consequent rights and duties of citizens.

4 Risk discourse and 'the environment'

In its focus on moving away from biomedical care and towards a preventive understanding of health states, the new public health has directed much attention to the 'environmental' dimensions of health. A concern with 'the environment' has become increasingly prominent over the past two decades in most countries. Environmental discourse has become a central part of policy, business, planning and politics, moving from fringe groups to the centre:

> We have entered an era in which not only marginal social groups but also political parties, industrialists, religious leaders, scientists of all descriptions, even the legal and accountancy professions, all seek to reflect a sensitivity to 'environmental' priorities, whatever the other commitments they may aver. (Grove-White 1993, p. 18)

It is not surprising, therefore, that issues relating to health and the environment are integral to the new public health. In new public health discourses the types of environmental problems discussed include the emergence of new communicable diseases; the thinning of the ozone layer of the earth's atmosphere (predicted to cause climatic change and greater exposure to solar ultraviolet radiation); humans' exposure to ionising radiation and to the heavy metals, toxins and organic chemicals produced by industrial production; intensive farming; the dumping of hazardous wastes; and domestic chemical use. The new public health also pays attention to non-material aspects of the environment, particularly in relation to urban living, in developing a 'holistic' approach; that is, incorporating interpersonal, psychological and spiritual dimensions.

The representation of the environment as an entity that requires careful management and control is a traditional modernist approach. The environment has become represented as a set of physical resources that requires the rationalised strategies of governmentality, including continual surveillance, monitoring and regulation on the part of experts—just as the human population is conceptualised as a resource that depends on the environment. Environmental discourses also tend to rely upon traditional modernist assumptions in suggesting that the future may be rationally predicted, that the gathering of information is enough to control future effects as long as the appropriate 'rational' strategies are employed. Discussions about human health and environmental risks are thus a means by which individuals and social groups attempt to control and exert 'rational' dominance over a situation that appears to be moving out of control. To deal with anxieties about the environment, a range of governmental strategies employing specialised knowledges have been set in place in the attempt to 'manage' it (Rutherford 1994, p. 40). These strategies both construct and regulate the 'problems' of 'the environment'.

While there are strong overlaps between the environmental and green movements and the tendency in the new public health to focus on environmental health issues, there are also important differences. As we go on to demonstrate in this chapter, contemporary public health discourses, like those of the environmental and green movements, rely upon particular notions of 'the environment' and 'nature' when discussing the relationship between human health and non-human phenomena. Furthermore, the new public health as well as the environmental and green movements, often draw attention to the ways in which humans contribute to the 'sickening' of the planet and how in turn their health is negatively affected at the global level. This represents the apotheosis of the globalising tendencies of the new public health. However, as demonstrated later in this chapter (and also in Chapter 5), discussions of human health and the environment in the new public health tend not to take up the oppositional and sometimes radical political emphasis that forms an important arm of the environmental and green movements. Rather, the new public health adopts a largely neo-liberal approach, focusing on the citizen as rational consumer, one who engages as an autonomous individual in activities to prevent or reduce environmental damage and to protect herself or himself from health risks believed to be generated by the environment.

In the new public health discourses on the environment, therefore, there still remains a preoccupation with the individualistic and localised aspects of the human–environment encounter, particularly in relation to the ways in which individuals are asked to respond to health risks. While the 'environmentalist movement' as defined by that term has existed only since the 1950s, gaining force in the 1960s and 1970s, concerns about the health effects of environmental conditions to the public have been evident since antiquity, in relation to the problems of miasma, dirt and odour and the effects of the climate upon the balance of humours in the body. This chapter examines in depth the complexities of the contemporary use of the term 'the environment' vis-à-vis a description of the ways in which the nineteenth-century (the 'old') public health conceptualised and dealt with the problem of the environment. The chapter goes on to discuss the concept of the 'environmental citizen', the symbolic use of the terms 'risk' and 'nature', and the notion of the 'social environment'. It ends with an analysis of the 'at risk' and the 'risky' self in relation to the multiple understandings of the environment.

'THE ENVIRONMENT' IN NINETEENTH-CENTURY PUBLIC HEALTH

As in every other sphere of public health (both 'old' and 'new'), moral meanings—often related to binary categories—are central to discussions about human health and the environment. Some obvious binary oppositions routinely drawn upon include clean/dirty, pure/contaminated and rural/urban. Mary Douglas's (1980) argument about the symbolic nature of cleanliness is readily applicable to understanding the discourses of environment and health. That which is 'dirty', 'contaminating' or 'polluting' is morally reprobate, produced by an 'other' who is viewed as threatening the health of the self through greed or ignorance. As Bauman notes, strategies of hygiene that promise to keep disease at bay 'boil down in most cases to an activity of separating and maintaining distance. One should steer clear of "filthy places" and "unsavoury substances"' (1992b, p. 155). These strategies were a central feature of the nineteenth-century public health movement's approach to containing illness and disease.

Environmental health problems associated with the growth of populations in large urbanised areas became an issue of major importance to public health reformers in the late eighteenth and nineteenth centuries, when the effects of industrialisation and rapid urbanisation began to make themselves felt in the living and working conditions of the European and colonial cities. At that time the major concerns of public health reformers were the state of the streets, housing and sewerage in towns and cities, and the increasing burdens placed by the ever-growing populations of the poor upon welfare institutions. A 'medico-administrative' knowledge developed in the eighteenth and nineteenth centuries to isolate and treat problems of urban spaces and populations (Foucault 1984a, p. 283). 'Hygiene' was introduced as a regime of health at the population level, involving the surveillance and control of urban spaces, which were deemed 'perhaps the most dangerous environment for the population' (Foucault 1984a, p. 282). Space and place were therefore the dominant features of the discourses of nineteenth-century public health, which tended to pathologise certain regions, to render them sites of filth and toxicity to be avoided by 'decent citizens' if at all possible. Geography was used to construct 'maps' of disease and illness, providing a visual comparison of the parts of a region such as a city or country.

In nineteenth-century public health, therefore, the town or city itself was identified as a 'medicalisable object' (Foucault 1984a, p. 282). By the mid nineteenth century, the city was represented as 'the locus of fear, disgust and fascination' in health reformers' texts (Stallybrass & White 1986, p. 125). The sewer was a particular site of disgust, as the conduit of filth lying beneath the veneer of civilisation of the city, as the symbol of the body's waste tract. The rat, as the transgressor of the sewer and the city streets, was also an object of fear and loathing, the demonised 'other' (Stallybrass & White 1986, p. 143). It was not just the locations themselves that were understood to be contaminating, but also their human inhabitants. The threat posed by space and place and that posed by the human inhabitants of a 'dirty' physical environment were conflated. This was particularly evident in British, Australian and North American public health discourses of the time, which portrayed the slum areas of large industrial cities such as London, Manchester, Sydney, San Francisco and New York as dangerous, not only because of the inadequate housing, sewerage and garbage-disposal facilities found there but also because of the members of the working class, the poor and (in North America and Australia) the non-white ethnic minorities, such as the Chinese, who lived there. Public health writing on the polluted city in the nineteenth century was pervaded with moralistic judgments about members of these social groups, who were deemed to be 'contagious', the 'breeding grounds' of filth and squalor. They were constructed as bestial, incapable of self-regulation, while members of the white bourgeoisie were positioned as the neutral observers of their degradation (Stallybrass & White 1986, p. 132; Craddock 1995).

Public health strategies at this time, therefore, were directed at regulating the spaces between the bodies of the poor, the working class and the ethnic minorities and at preventing these groups from mingling with members of the bourgeoisie. Relying upon the theory of miasma, or the notion that foul odour in itself bred disease, public health reformers believed that as long as external dirt and detectable odour could be reduced or eliminated, then the spread of disease could be halted. The bourgeoisie lived in fear and disgust of the contaminating touch of the 'Great Unwashed', of being forced to mingle with them in the streets, of having to breathe-in their smell. It was not just urban space that was constructed as a site of intervention in public health, but also domestic space. Public health reformers believed that overcrowding led not only to the increased spread of infectious diseases but also to the risk of non-infectious diseases, crime, mental illness and other social problems (Rosen 1973; Lindheim & Syme 1983, p. 337). Vice and incest were constructed as both moral and health problems related to over-crowding, with particular concern expressed by public health and other authorities about working-class children sharing beds with their siblings or parents, or sleeping in the same room as their parents, thus being exposed to sexuality at an early age (Finch 1993, Ch. 3).

The move to 'disinfect' the poor, the working class and the ethnic minorities, to rid their bodies and their domiciles of filth and odour, also incorporated the notion that such hygienic strategies would promote their capacity for discipline and hard work (Corbin 1986, pp. 145–6). To deal with the problems of squalor, dirt, pollution and illness that were spread through close contact with others, members of the nine-teenth-century public health movement proposed ideas for utopian communities in which all houses had natural ventilation, sunlight and gardens (Lindheim & Syme 1983, p. 336). Parks and gardens were portrayed as the 'lungs' of town and cities, bringing in fresh air and 'natural' spaces to refresh and reinvigorate jaded urban dwellers. Both urban and domestic spaces, therefore, were understood as living organisms; like human bodies, requiring fresh air and cleanliness to function efficiently.

By the nineteenth century, and gaining impetus with the discovery of the microbe at the end of that century, a particular focus began to be placed upon 'the home' as a site of regulation, the cleanliness and management of which were considered vital to the health of its inhabitants, particularly infants and children. Public health reformers believed that not only should individual bodies be healthy, clean and fit, but the domestic space also must be 'purified, cleansed, aerated' (Foucault 1984a, p. 280). One example of public health literature of the time is a pamphlet written by James Russell during his term as Medical Officer of Health for the City of Glasgow, entitled *The House in Relation to Public Health* (1887). In his text Russell placed a great deal of emphasis on urban and domestic space as contributing to health states. He described the problems of density for human morbidity and mortality thus:

> In the process of living man [sic] defiles air, earth, and water. This defilement only becomes dangerous when his environment cannot cleanse itself, and this may happen either by shutting in the individual with some impervious structure or by the packing of individuals too closely together. (1887, p. 5)

It is not just proximity itself that is integral to health states, Russell argued. It is also important to bear in mind other considerations, such as the intensity of smoke and noxious emanations. He then discussed the importance of the house, in relation to the closed-off space that the 'householder acquires as his own' and over which he therefore exercises a degree of control:

> In this way may a man's house not only express in the properties of space many things about himself, such as his social position, his moral character, his intelligence, but it provides, so to speak, a material leverage to those abstractions which enables them to act upon the health of all the inmates. (1887, p. 9)

As Russell's text suggests, the domestic environment was constructed in late-nineteenth-century public health texts as an extension of the self. If one's house was dirty or smelly, this was a reflection upon one's personal characteristics as well as detracting from the inhabitants' health status. Therefore, in nineteenth-century public health the actions expected of citizens to protect their health in relation to 'the environment', for the bourgeoisie at least, centred around avoiding those places and people that were singled out by the experts as 'dirty' and potentially 'contaminating'. The importance of maintaining domestic cleanliness was also emphasised as a duty of all citizens, particularly those constructed as 'dirty': immigrants, members of the poor and the working class. However, as explained in Chapter 3, this duty was largely represented as the responsibility of women, as wives and mothers.

RISK AND 'THE ENVIRONMENT'

The major difference in the contemporary conceptualisation of human health and the environment in the new public health compared with nineteenth-century public health is the ways in which health threats and hazards are now understood to have multiplied and extended beyond the local environs of the home, town or city. Any contemporary discussion of health and the environment incorporates the notion of 'risk'. In previous chapters we discussed the ways in which health risk is individualised in epidemiological discourses, constructed as being the personal responsibility of people to manage. Discourses on environmental risk expand this understanding of health risk. Current environmental risks are understood to be far larger in scale and more far-reaching in their future effects than risks that have been identified previously. In the new public health and other discourses the meaning of environmental risk has broadened from a danger that threatens an individual or community to one of far greater magnitude, which threatens humans as a species. Concerns about human health and the environment, therefore, incorporate a sense of time that is evolutionary and long term (Lash & Urry 1994, p. 249). The 1986 Chernobyl nuclear disaster in the Ukraine, for example, exemplified the ramifications of particular countries' environmental disasters for other countries.

The new public health has played an integral part in this broadening of risk, particularly through such global organisations as the WHO, which, as pointed out in Chapter 1, frequently makes pronouncements on how nations should recognise that 'almost every aspect of the environment potentially affects health for good or ill' and how they should therefore take steps to 'properly manage' the environment, not simply to improve health but to ensure human survival (WHO 1990a, p. 21). As one public health textbook described it: 'Environmental health is the aspect of public health concerned with all the factors, circumstances, and conditions in the environment or surroundings of humans that can exert an influence on human health and well-being' (Last 1987, p. 131). In this discourse, environmental risks are diffuse and ever-present, understood to lurk in almost any activity or region, making it difficult for individuals to identify, conceptualise and therefore deal with them: 'In its most compelling and characteristic incarnations, the now unspecified enemy is infinite' (Massumi 1992, p. 184).

Several sociologists and cultural theorists have recently written about a growing trend in the late twentieth century for individuals to become highly aware of, and anxious about, environmental risks. In his book *Risk Society* (1992), Ulrich Beck described the constant state of concern, anxiety and even dread people in Western countries feel in relation to such environmental risks to human health as air and water pollution, ionising radiation, and food contamination, in the context of the break-down in industrial production following the end of the Cold War and the collapse of communism and socialism in Europe (see also Beck et al. 1994; Beck 1996). For his purposes Beck defines risk as 'a systematic way of dealing with hazards and insecurities induced and introduced by modernization itself' (1992, p. 21). Beck argues that the progress prom-ised by early modernity has at the end of the twentieth century turned into apparent self-destruction, not through class struggle or revolution, but rather as an unintended consequence of the inexorable and incre-mental processes of modernisation itself. For Beck, the naive certainties of early modernity and its claims to human progress have disintegrated, resulting in the need of individuals to seek and invent new certainties for themselves (Beck et al. 1994, p. 14). He suggests that compared with the 'natural' hazards of pre-industrial society, such as fires, famines and floods, which were understood as random acts of fortune generated by an 'other'—gods, demons or Nature—environmental risks are largely regarded as the outcome of human decisions, and are therefore calculable and predictable. From this perspective we have only ourselves to blame for the situation in which we now find ourselves. Beck (1992, p. 176) asserts, therefore, that the 'risk society' is also potentially a self-critical, or self-reflexive society, because anxieties about external risks serve to pose questions about current practices. Judgments on environmental risk represent implicit moral judgments—albeit masked in the discourse of objective, quantitative 'facts'—on the ways in which human societies have developed. Risk is closely linked to accountability and responsibil-ity. Risk is thus a central feature of a society that has come to reflect upon itself, to critique itself.

People living in contemporary Western countries have become highly aware of the hazards produced by industry largely through their coverage in the mass media. Media reports frequently employ the rhetoric of apocalypse, accompanied by images of oil spills, dying animals and disfigured humans. An article published on the front page of one Sydney newspaper in late 1995, for example, was headlined 'Apocalypse soon, say forecasters'. The writer went on to describe the contentions made at a conference of international scientists that due to global warming, within 100 years up to half of the world's glaciers will melt, there will be changes in the pattern and intensity of rainfall, and deserts will spread irreversibly. The ramifications for human health described in the article included an increase in the incidence of infectious diseases spread by insect vectors, starvation from crop failure and death from exposure to temperature extremes (Dayton 1995a). Incidents involving nuclear power stations, such as the Three Mile Island meltdown in the United States in 1979 and the Chernobyl disaster, have received high levels of media coverage. Media representations of nuclear risk have tended to demonstrate the 'silent' nature of danger lying-in-wait in apparently 'normal' settings: a ticking Geiger counter in the seemingly benign location of an agricultural field is a standard visual representation of the hazards that lurk nearby. The rhetoric of excess is also frequently employed to represent the intractable problem of nuclear waste and radioactivity (Corner et al. 1990, pp. 110–12).

The texts produced by activist and consumer advocacy groups similarly detail horrific visions of the future. One example is a document published by Greenpeace Australia, entitled *Solutions for Clean Healthy Cities*, which constructs the American city of Los Angeles as the ultimate urban nightmare, 'a mirror to an unsustainable future' from which Australia should learn: 'Eight million vehicles pollute the Los Angeles basin; 20,235 hectares of cropland give way to housing or shopping malls each year; urbanisation and farmland have destroyed 90 per cent of the state's wetlands; and more than 300 beach closings are recorded a year' (Greenpeace 1993, p. 3). Such texts clearly demonstrate cynicism towards the myth of human progress via the processes of industrialisation and urbanisation.

As a result of the increasing emphasis placed on health risk and the environment by the popular media and by environmental activism and the new public health literature, a concern for the ways in which humans are changing the ecosystem has become a central theme of modern subjectivity. The spectre of climate change evoked through the term 'global warming', for example, 'has come to haunt the political soul of popular consciousness', replacing the threats of nuclear devastation and global cooling that were prevalent from the 1950s to the early 1980s. It is now used to account for almost any kind of environmental anomaly, including fierce storms and floods and droughts and warmer-than-usual winters (Ross 1991, p. 197). One study carried out in the Lancashire region of northern England of people's personal experience and understandings of global environmental change found that they were highly anxious and concerned about environmental problems, particularly local pollution. The participants were disaffected with and cynical about both local and federal politics and official institutions in their ability to deal with these problems. They felt a sense of 'impending doom', believed that 'the system' and remote pressures were shaping their lives and expressed little sense of personal agency in ameliorating the situation (MacNaghten 1995). Madden (1995) used interviews to explore the perceptions of environmental risk among people living in the Australian city of Brisbane. She also found that her participants expressed a high degree of pessimism about environmental risks, combined with confusion and anxiety over how best to deal with the risks, the role they should personally take in alleviating the risks and who should be considered responsible for the generation and control of the risks.

As this research suggests, the risks engendered by industrialisation create ambivalence and anxiety because of their seemingly limitless spread and the difficulty in defining their effect. These risks threaten to cause irreversible harm throughout the ecosystem (Beck 1992, pp. 22–3). Their effects may resonate well into the future. They tend to be invisible and therefore all the more frightening: 'Everywhere, pollutants and toxins laugh and play their tricks like devils in the Middle Ages. People are almost inescapably bound over to them. Breathing, eating, dwelling, wearing clothes—everything has been penetrated by them' (Beck 1992, p. 73). Domestic space is now regarded as being equally as invaded by 'unnatural' chemicals detrimental to human health as is urban space. For example, an article published on air pollution in 1995 in an Australian consumers' magazine described in detail the pollutants found in homes, such as formaldehyde emitted from building materials and disinfectants; radon gas released from the soil; cigarette smoke; dust mites in carpets and furnishings; and ammonia and chlorine from household cleaning products. According to the article, 'staying inside won't necessarily lower your chances of exposure to air pollutants. The air quality of our homes can often be worse than outdoors' (Australian Consumers' Association 1995, p. 21).

Given the assumed pervasive and insidious nature of health risks, the identification of such risks has come to be viewed as beyond the capacity of most individuals. Risk identification is increasingly regarded as the preserve of those who have access to technology and expert knowledges, for example scientists and members of the medical profession. These experts are responsible for constructing a web of knowledges around environmental hazards, and for interpreting risk for members of the lay population. It is difficult for lay people to know how much trust they should invest in these experts, however, given the constantly shifting state of scientific and medical knowledge (Giddens 1992, p. 148). Global warming, for example, is subject to continuing expert dispute over whether or not it is 'really' happening. There are also continuing debates among expert authorities over the relative threat posed to human health by such phenomena as electromagnetic radiation from electric power cables and mobile telephones; herbicides such as Agent Orange; water fluoridation; the pollutants from car emissions; and so on. As one new public health document has noted, most potentially harmful chemicals and physical agents 'are at such low concentrations in air, water or food that it is often difficult to identify specific adverse health effects in epidemiological studies' (Nutbeam et al. 1993, p. 179).

THE 'ENVIRONMENTAL' CITIZEN

Contemporary discourses on the environment and health construct a new kind of citizen, the global citizen with a global world-view, who is concerned about planetary survival and how actions in one region affect all other regions (Ross 1991, pp. 212–13). This type of citizenship expands the debate over the rights of humans to those of other living things, incorporating as important the need for humans to consider how their actions affect non-human creatures and flora. In the context of risk society, citizens are required to be ever-vigilant, seeking both to protect themselves from the risks generated by others and to reduce the damage they inflict upon the environment. The 'risk-avoiding' individual in relation to environmental health is as dominant a figure in the new public health as is the physically active or dieting individual. Everyone is expected to be involved in identifying and dealing with the potential hazards that surround them. As we mentioned earlier, however, to do so they cannot often rely upon their own assessment or identification of risk, but must rely largely upon expert interpretations. As a result:

> Private life becomes in essence the plaything of scientific results and theories, or of public controversies and conflicts. The questions of a distant world of chemical formulas burst forth with deadly seriousness in the inmost recesses of personal life conduct as questions of self, identity and existence and cannot be ignored. (Beck et al. 1994, p. 45)

The contemporary concern for the 'health' of the environment finds expression in many practices of the self. One of these practices is vegetarianism. For some vegetarians, a moral/ethical stance is taken which contends that eating meat is both harmful for the environment and an abuse of humans' power over other animals. Some individuals who have not gone so far as to adopt vegetarianism as a protest have instead embraced organic meat, or meat that is produced through practices that avoid the use of 'artificial' fertilisers, in this way aiming for 'sustainability' through mixed rather than intensive farming, eschewing unnecessary cruelty to animals and encouraging consumers to develop their cognisance of the interdependence of the human and animal world (James 1993, p. 209). An even greater number of consumers have sought out organically produced foods not because of ethical or political qualms but because of their belief that such foods are more conducive to good health, being free of pesticide residues, other 'artificial' substances and disease-carrying agents such as salmonella, listeria and botulin (James 1993, pp. 213–14; Lupton 1996, Ch. 3).

In Western societies individuals *qua* citizens are encouraged by governments at all levels and by environmental organisations to participate actively in efforts to 'save the environment'. This entails a range of diverse activities, with a particular concentration on the domestic context and the need to 'pull together'; as a Greenpeace Australia text asserts, 'It's time to work together—to build a better future and establish lifestyles that don't ruin our planet' (Greenpeace 1993, p. 2). In a booklet entitled *Environmental Information Directory* and subtitled '*Everything You Need to Know to Protect Your Environment*', distributed to a local government area of Sydney by its council in mid-1995, a long and complicated list of strategies was provided for readers to help them fight 'environmental damage'. The foreword by the Mayor argued that he was sure that residents would agree that the control of such damage 'is the greatest challenge facing us all today'. He went on to argue that: 'The next century must be characterised by a degree of restraint in our abuse of the environment and this will take a considerable adjustment of public attitudes'. The reader, hailed as 'the environmental resident', was exhorted in the booklet to adopt such strategies as fixing leaking taps, using low-watt light bulbs, recycling household plastics and waste-paper, avoiding the use of pesticides on gardens, refraining from littering, using biodegradable detergents, using public transport rather than cars to travel to work, and monitoring the activities of pets. The list of activities extended to the conduct of the body and personal relationships; readers were encouraged to 'adopt a healthy lifestyle', in ways such as eating 'healthy food', engaging in regular exercise, developing 'positive attitudes' and forming 'healthy relationships'.

As this suggests, a major part of the governing of the environment is phrased through the concept of the 'environmental' citizen. The document takes a cosy consensual view, suggesting that all readers will share this vision of idealised citizenship and that there is little room for debate about the strategies it proposes. As is common with most texts on the 'environmental citizen' there is little or no recognition of social differences such as gender, ethnicity, age, or of physical or economic capacity to engage in the suggested activities. Such an approach to environmentalism positions the problem firmly in the context of individual actions. Many of the popular discourses and practices of environmentalism are directed at individuals' consciences as 'careful consumers' and exhort individuals to protect their own health status by acting as environmental citizens; by buying 'organic' vegetables rather than those grown using pesticides, for example. The 'rights' of citizens both to consume commodities and to enjoy good health are inextricably bound up with their consonant 'duties' in promoting a 'healthy' environment and engaging in consumption in certain prescribed ways. This approach suggests that 'saving the environment' is simply a process of heightened awareness leading to eternal vigilance, incorporating good household management and wise consumption choices.

In its focus on the individual choices and behaviours of citizens and its representation of the 'environmental citizen' as consumer rather than activist, the new public health draws attention away from the structural features of industrialised societies that shape work and production patterns and thereby contribute to large-scale pollution and the massive consumption of resources. As this individualistic focus on environmentalism routinely emerges from state agencies, it does little to challenge the role played by the state in regulating industrial production. Instead of seeking to dissuade consumption or change patterns of production, such texts seek to encourage a thoughtful, ethical and self-disciplined consumer who takes time to consider each purchase she or he makes for its possible harm to the environment. Indeed, the abovementioned *Environmental Information Directory* included many advertisements for local businesses, positioning it as both a commercial and pastorally caring text. Consumerism is portrayed as a prerequisite of citizenship in relation to the environment. New public health discourses on health and the environment, therefore, are predominantly privatised and individualised, directed at the conduct of the individual in his or her everyday life rather than at alleviating risks through political activism and the challenging of vested interests. The 'environmental citizen' is represented as the entrepreneurial subject, endowed with the freedom to regulate the self via a series of prudent consumption activities underpinned by expert knowledges.

Lash and Urry (1994, p. 299) identify three levels of environmental politics: the first directed at the preservation of certain features of the

physical or built environment; the second interested in reforming particular kinds of what are considered to be environmentally damaging
social activities; and the third (and most radical) directed at the proposed
ecological transformation of industrial societies, including their work and
consumption patterns. The 'environmental citizen' position concentrates
on the first and second levels rather than the third, most radical, level,
which is generally regarded as the extreme or fringe end of
environmentalism. This third approach tends not to be encouraged by
governments, for it challenges social, political and economic structural
features and is far more destabilising. It is not surprising, therefore, that
this approach is found in 'Deep Green' documents directed at challenging and changing the state's policies and activities, but is far less often
articulated in new public health texts that are generated by state
agencies. When it is articulated, as in some of the documents related to
the Healthy Cities project, the rhetoric is rarely translated into action
(see Chapter 5).

Risk discourse in relation to health and the environment, particularly
as it is employed in official risk reports, tends to speak about risks in
the absence of social differentiations. It is suggested that, at its most
extreme, environmental risk cannot be avoided, regardless of one's level
of socioeconomic privilege, if, for example, the risk is in the air or the
water supply. Beck argues that 'poverty is hierarchic, smog is democratic',
and therefore environmental risks are regarded as having a 'democratising' effect (1992, p. 36). This focus on the 'democratising' of risk,
however, tends to obscure the ways in which there remain differentials
in potential exposure to hazards. As Williams et al. (1995, p. 116) point
out, while most of the members of environmental groups are middle
class, it is the working class whose health is most threatened by environmental hazards. Factors such as age, gender, level of education,
occupation and place of residence continue to play a major role in
exposure to localised hazards. Wealth may buy safety from danger while
poverty attracts danger (Beck 1992, p. 35). In illustrating the importance
of geographic region in exposure to environmental hazards, Phillimore
(1993) contrasts the mortality rates in Middlesbrough and Sunderland,
two large towns in north-eastern England which have similar levels of
high socioeconomic disadvantage in their working-class areas. Middlesbrough had consistently high premature mortality in the early 1980s,
while similarly deprived areas of Sunderland had moderate premature
mortality. Phillimore argues that the major contributor to this differential
in mortality was the concentration of heavy industry in Middlesbrough,

accompanied by occupational exposure to dusts and toxic fumes and high exposure to air pollution in that town.

Williams et al. (1995) point out that social disadvantage, while directly associated with level of exposure to environmental hazards, is also associated with fewer opportunities to escape these hazards or attempt to do something about them. In an interview study carried out with residents of a disadvantaged inner-city area of Salford (in the north-west of England), participants expressed their concern about the physical and emotional problems caused by living in high-rise accommodation or damp housing; exposure to chemical pollution from local industries; unemployment; poverty; and the threat of crime. These people defined 'environmental risks' as those related to their immediate living situation. These risks were considered so overwhelming that they felt they had little personal agency over the situation (Williams et al. 1995). In another study carried out in northern England (in the Tyneside region), local residents expressed concerns about the possibility of ill health caused by pollution from a nearby coking works. They ranked air pollution and smell as more serious causes of stress or anxiety than any other issue, including money problems, their own health problems, work problems and family problems, and considered industrial pollution as the most serious health risk to which they were exposed (Moffat et al. 1995). As these studies suggest, acute awareness of environmental dangers and ambivalence about science and technology are not necessarily translated into political action or into change, particularly when individuals have few resources to act, or feel as if the situation is so overwhelming that little can be done (see also Wynne 1996).

THE DISCOURSE OF 'NATURE'

The symbolic meanings of 'nature' are central to discourses about 'the environment' and 'health', in which the term 'nature' tends to be used in different ways according to the context. These different uses of 'nature' point to its complexity. As Raymond Williams has argued, there are three major meanings of 'nature'. First it is understood as 'the essential quality and character *of* something', second as 'the inherent force which directs either the world or human beings or both' and third as 'the material world itself, taken as including or not including human beings' (1988, p. 219 [original emphasis]). Williams points out that the last two meanings in particular are used variably and in contradictory ways. In the discourses linking the environment and human health, the first meaning tends to emerge in discussions of the ways in which essential or primitive 'human nature' is subverted or distorted by the 'urban environment' in which many people now live, causing ill health. The second meaning is often used to denote the forces of an abstract 'Nature', as in the term 'Mother Nature'; that which drives inexorable forces, sometimes destructive, which affect the health of humans. The third major meaning of nature is typically employed to denote aspects of 'the environment' that exclude the urban or built world, as in the 'wilderness' or the 'countryside'.

Environmentalists draw extensively upon their preferred meaning of 'nature', representing it as an embattled entity which it is their duty to protect for the sake of humanity. In this discourse the environment is transposed with nature, both of which are portrayed as being at the mercy of humans. The concerns of the environmentalist and green movements are generally directed at the ways in which the 'health' of the 'natural' environment (including other living species and non-living phenomena not manufactured by humans) is affected by the actions of humans and the uncontrolled growth of human populations. This approach is a turn-about from the nineteenth-century modernist view of nature, which saw it as something that should be subdued and controlled, as external and inferior to humanity. Those who adopt this approach often take a sentimentalised view, tending towards an anthropomorphism of the environment in referring to the 'health' of the 'sick' or 'dying' planet. The 'innocence' of nature is frequently depicted as having been despoiled by the false premises of human progress, with seemingly little to counter this destruction.

Such discourses employ the language and rationale of 'New Age' approaches, which tend to privilege emotion and feeling over reasoning, the rural over the urban, the natural over the artificial. Nature, in this conceptualisation, is thus a largely benign entity: the 'Mother Nature' or 'Gaia' approach. The status of nature is that of absolute normalcy and good health; the wilderness is a place to be revered as 'pure' (Short 1991, p. 6; Evernden 1992, p. 22). In eco-feminist writings in particular, there is often a direct comparison drawn between the fertile, nourishing bodies of women and productive 'Mother Nature' or 'Gaia', and the way in which each is violently exploited by capitalistic, patriarchal societies: 'Ecofeminism calls for an end to all oppressions, arguing that no attempt to liberate women (or any other oppressed group) will be successful without an equal attempt to liberate nature' (Gaard 1993, p. 1). In such discourses nature is represented as sinned against by her children (humans), who seek to destroy her in their rush for domination of other species and the non-living environment. Nature is portrayed as 'outside' humanity and humans are depicted as having walled themselves off from nature. All things 'natural' are 'real' and 'good'; all things 'unnatural' are 'artificial' and 'bad'. Thus, when many popular environmentalist texts refer to the ways in which humans 'damage' the environment, it is 'nature' as the non-human material world that is usually denoted as 'the environment'; the 'rural', rather than the 'urban', is the environment.

The new public health literature often gives a slightly different emphasis by focusing on the effects of the environment upon humans. This approach does not ignore the role played by humans in influencing their environment, but it directs more attention to the effects of environmental damage on people's health. Thus the individual is represented as being at risk *from* the environment as well as posing a risk *to* the environment. The terms 'the environment' and 'nature' in this discourse are not necessarily synonyms. In the new public health, for example, the environment is now understood in far broader terms. 'The environment' in this context usually includes, as well as the 'natural', the 'non-natural' or the human-made, including human-generated pollution and chemicals such as pesticides and insecticides. The health effects of the environmental damage wrought by humans are thus understood as a ricochet effect: humans are regarded as abusing the environment through their thoughtless actions, causing its delicate balance to be upset; which leads to the environment 'sickening'; which in turn leads to ill-effects upon humans in their position as part of the ecosystem. This approach to the environment, often describing itself as the 'ecological' or 'holistic' approach, seeks to incorporate humans into nature rather than constructing them as separate. Thus humans are taken from their 'outside' stance as the penetrators and destroyers of nature and placed within the ecosystem as biological entities sharing the results of environmental change.

This approach to human health and the environment sometimes seeks to identify and adopt the cosmology of non-Western cultures, such as the cosmologies of traditional Australian Aboriginal or Native American cultures, as thought systems that are deemed more sensitive to and aware of the subtle and spiritual relationship between the land, its non-human inhabitants and humanity. The emphasis is placed on the 'interconnectedness' of all things, in which humans are just one part of a vast network (Slack 1994, p. 10). Humans, it is argued, need to 'live in harmony with the environment' (Greenpeace 1993, p. 2). The new public health has to some extent taken up this perspective on the human/nature interface. One example is an article published in a British health education journal, entitled 'Health education, ecology and the shamanic world view' (Money 1992). The author argued that health education should incorporate a shamanic perspective, defined as 'an ancient world view' that is based on myth and, among other things, relies upon an 'intuitive perception of the universe and all its inhabitants as being of one fabric'. He went on to assert that for humans, 'authentic' good health depended upon '[m]aintaining communication with the animals and plants and minerals and stars' and the development of rituals which recognise the 'sacredness of the land' (Money 1992, p. 302). The romantic, anodyne vision of nature in such accounts ignores the 'nature red in tooth and claw' alternative conceptualisation; the nature that is responsible for death, destruction, disease, the nature that enforces the 'survival of the fittest' and thus allows species to die out (Coward 1989). The notion of 'wilderness' as a space of mortal terror, an area of waste and desolation that is 'out there' away from human civilisation (Short 1991, p. 6), is submerged in the sentimental representation of nature.

While the environmentalist and green movements demonstrate a strong tendency towards the romanticisation of nature, not all representations of nature in contemporary discourses on public health and the environment portray it as passive and beneficent. Some portray nature as vengeful, 'striking back' for the damage it/she has received at the hands of humans. For example, Ross has observed that discourses on global warming betray a moral approach based on Christian principles of retribution, punishment and penitence. Humanity as a whole is represented as sinning against nature in its greed for an industrialised lifestyle. Indeed, Ross argues,

> certain elements of the new world-view that is being constructed to accommodate the global warming theory resemble pre-Enlightenment conceptions of Nature as a providential interpreter of human affairs, repaying the whole of humanity for its sins with the visiting of meteorological scourges. (1991, p. 198)

Other examples are the news reports, Hollywood films such as *The Plague, Outbreak* and *Congo*, and books that have emerged in the past few years centring around the theme of devastation wrought by uncontrollable epidemics on Western societies. Many of these popular texts implicate humanity's 'interference' with nature as the ultimate cause of the epidemic. Richard Preston's book *The Hot Zone* (1994), which details the threat posed by the Ebola virus to the United States, is one example.

The Ebola virus, which is spread—like hepatitis and HIV—through body fluids, causes haemorrhaging, fevers and vomiting. It is a virulent virus: approximately 90 per cent of those infected die from the illness, and as with HIV/AIDS, no effective treatment or vaccine have yet been developed. In his book, Preston argues that the Ebola virus emerged because of humans' destruction of the jungles and rainforests. Preston details the effects of the disease with phrases taken from Gothic horror; for example, he describes the virus as 'a perfect parasite because it transforms virtually every part of the body into a digested slime of virus particles . . . Ebola attacks connective tissue with particular ferocity . . . Spontaneous rips appear in the skin, and haemorrhagic blood pours from the rips' (excerpt published in the *Sydney Morning Herald*, 13 May 1995).

The concept of globalisation is strongly related to this discourse about the 'new killers'. It is argued that such viruses would have remained confined to their niche in the ecosystem (generally sited as a dank rainforest in Africa), were it not for urbanisation and industrialisation occurring on a global scale, the movement of humans around regions and countries, and mass air travel. All these social changes, it is suggested, bring humans together in more crowded conditions, encourage intimate contact between more people (including sexual contact) and allow bacteria and viruses to travel from region to region via their human hosts. As one Australian newspaper article argued, 'the emergence of the Ebola virus in Zaire is more than just a disease plaguing a remote community'. An American scientist was quoted in this article as asserting that '"with more and more human crowding and ecological infringement", ever more microbes would break the species barrier' (Dayton 1995b). At the same time, progress in medical science and the overuse of drugs such as penicillin have been linked to the development of 'mutant' bacteria that are resistant to antibiotics. Another newspaper article on these new microorganisms claimed that: 'Infectious diseases are returning with a potency never seen before. Scientists are already calling the 1990s the Post-Antibiotic Age' (da Silva 1995).

Contemporary public health writings similarly interpret the emergence of new diseases or re-emergent outbreaks of long-contained diseases as evidence of a 'sick' ecosystem fighting back. An article published in the *American Journal of Public Health* (Epstein 1995) described 'environmental distress syndrome', or the situation by which changes in the ecosystem such as loss of 'natural' predators, deforestation and the use of fertilisers have encouraged pests and pathogens to flourish, thus breeding disease in unprecedented ways. Epstein argued that '[e]nvironmental change and pollutants stress individuals and populations, and this may be reflected in the global resurgence of infectious disease as these stresses cascade through the community assemblages of species' (1995, p. 168). He attributed two 'new' diseases emerging in 1993—a virulent strain of hantavirus carried by rodents manifested in the south-western region of the United States, and a novel cholera variant appearing in India and Bangladesh—to this 'environmental distress syndrome'. Epstein called for epidemiological efforts that go beyond national boundaries by monitoring changes in the environment in order to deal with the emergence of such diseases, efforts including the recording of global meteorological trends and the surveillance of the non-human vectors of communicable disease, such as rodents and insects. Here again, the anxieties associated with globalisation are evident, related to the porous boundaries of nation-states; the loss of diversity; the interconnected nature of all apparently local actions; ephemerality; the disintegration of tradition; and the apparent escalation of social, economic and ecological changes that appear to be out of local control.

THE DANGERS OF THE 'SOCIAL ENVIRONMENT'

As noted above, the 'ecological' or 'holistic' approach to human health and the environment goes beyond the notion of the environment as 'nature' in its focus on the effects upon human health of living in complex urbanised societies. The holistic approach directs its attention at an 'environment' that includes not only the material world, but also social, economic and political aspects, incorporating human relationships and their spatial, temporal, emotional, psychological and social dimensions. The approach regards humans as placed at risk not simply from their material surroundings but also from other humans. The 'social', therefore, is viewed as an important subset of a more general conceptualisation of 'the environment'. Kickbusch has described this perspective as emerging from 'a new understanding of ourselves and our bodies . . . bodies are not just biological but social entities' (1986, p. 324). In one public health textbook, for example, the 'social environment' is described as including social class; the economy; culture; political, legal and administrative frameworks and institutions; health services; and lifestyles (Marmot & Morris 1984).

As noted earlier in .this chapter, a focus on the 'spiritual' nature of health is becoming evident in the new public health literature, sometimes under the rubric of 'holistic health promotion'. In such accounts it is argued that because the origins of health states are holistic and developed within an ecological framework, new public health strategies should be directed at such an approach. One example is an article published in the *American Journal of Health Promotion* that addressed the issue of the 'spiritual dimension as a vital component of human wellness' and its implications for health promotion (Hawks et al. 1995). The authors argued that a greater focus on the ways of helping people to 'connect' with self, others and a 'higher power', and to seek meaning and purpose in life, would enhance health promotional programs of disease prevention. They suggest that individuals' participation in such activities as meditation, yoga and prayer may result in 'healthy behavioural changes' such as giving up smoking and adhering to a low-fat diet.

Literature in this area typically represents 'holistic' approaches to health promotion as engaging such goals and values as 'human development', 'real needs and aspirations', 'mutual exchange relationships', self-help and local action, and as employing 'intuitive, experiential and empathetic' strategies versus the supposedly capitalist, anthropocentric, economically oriented, dependency-fostering and masculinist values and goals of the current health care and public health systems (de Leeuw 1989, p. 1284). The concept of empowerment is presented as an integral part of 'holistic' or 'ecological' health promotion. As Miner and Ward (1992, p. 429) assert: 'Those who share an ecological vision believe in the capacity of individuals to act collectively, on their own behalf, to promote health-enhancing social change'. Lindheim and Syme (1983, p. 354) similarly call for people to 'connect to the future' and engage in 'active participation' as a means of 'strengthening resistance to disease' (see Chapter 6 for a detailed discussion of community participation as a major strategy of the new public health).

In discourses on 'ecological' or 'holistic' health, humans are represented as essentially biological beings, with the social or cultural dimensions of human existence represented as part of their adaptation or maladjustment to their physical environment. Individuals' health status is viewed as emerging from a dynamic and symbiotic, rather than linear, relationship between people, their 'internal' environment (or psyche/spirit) and their 'external' environment (or social and material milieux). As a chapter on the 'social environment' in a public health textbook described it, health is affected by the 'on-going interactions of host, the individual, with environment; the former with his or her inherited and acquired dispositions; and plainly, the economic, cultural, and political pressures of the latter' (Marmot & Morris 1984, p. 99).

Drawing upon this dynamic notion of the self/environment relationship, public health researchers who have attempted to go beyond the socio-psychological explanation for the causation of illness have sometimes relied upon a 'noble savage' thesis. This thesis contends that humans in modern developed societies are living in conditions that deny their genetic inheritance, a situation that then causes illness. For example, Thomas McKeown, in his book *On the Origins of Human Disease* (1988), argued that humans are biologically adapted to the conditions they experienced in palaeolithic times, when they engaged in the 'hunter-gatherer' mode of existence. Humans today, he asserted, participate in activities and live in conditions that are estranged from humankind's biological inheritance: they are exposed to artificial light, consume overly refined diets too high in energy value, lack exercise and are exposed to pollution. The author of one textbook on public health and human ecology adopted this perspective to argue that:

> Recent changes in the social environment, associated with the growth of cities, the use of mechanized transportation, the explosion of mass media as the source of information, ideas, entertainment, and political and emotional stimulus, and dramatic changes in patterns of work from primarily manual to primarily clerical and service oriented, have transformed human existence from its primeval hunter-gatherer origins into something that we may not be well equipped by our evolution to cope with. (Last 1987, p. 24)

Contemporary discourses on environmental health risks thus return to the mid-nineteenth-century concern with the link between urban and domestic conditions and health status. The issues have, however, broadened far beyond those relating to the control of odour, dirt, infectious diseases and the 'unwashed masses', in drawing attention to the psychosomatic, spiritual or emotional effects of urbanised modern life on human health states. Illness and disease are represented as emerging from the alienating dimension of living in the city. In this discourse, the city is typically portrayed as a 'non-natural' or 'artificial' space generating 'unnatural' stresses which serve to repress or distort the 'true nature' of humanity. For many people living in developed societies at the end of the twentieth century, the 'wilderness' has come to be viewed as the blighted landscape of large cities, the 'concrete jungles', the wastelands, the slums, the skyscrapers, the stretches of alienating spaces filled with people they cannot trust: 'The big city is now the modern equivalent of the medieval forest populated by demons' (Short, 1991, p. 26).

As observed earlier in this chapter, this ambivalent response to the great cities was emerging in the late nineteenth century, when the view of the city as an evil, filthy growth was widespread in popular, literary and official texts. A focus on the negative and potentially health-damaging psychological effects of urban dwelling is more recent, however; it emerged in a significant way only in the early twentieth century, influenced by the emergence of psychological and psychoanalytic thought. It is found most famously in the works of the German sociologist Georg Simmel (1969), who referred to the impersonal, disorienting and overwhelming nature of urban living. Simmel argued that humans living in cities experience an excess of 'psychic stimulation', causing them to respond defensively by repressing their emotions and fragmenting their lives into small compartments so as to deal more easily with the complex nature of everyday life. As a result, he contended, humans in the urban environment experience a non-coherent and non-authentic selfhood. The urban environment, therefore, is regarded not simply as a physical or material space that is polluted with industrial waste, but is a conceptual space, contributing to a particular state of mind and selfhood.

This perspective emphasising the psychological effects of the urbanised environment has become more and more pervasive in the new public health literature. In their article entitled 'Environments, people, and health', for example, Lindheim and Syme (1983, p. 34) contend that good health is achieved by 'living in harmony with biological laws'. They identify four types of 'environment': 'the man-made [sic] environment' (that is, the 'built environment'), 'the social environment', 'the natural environment' and 'the symbolic environment'. They suggest that all these types interact with one another to form 'the environment': 'the environment is a result of the constant interaction between natural and man-made [sic] spatial forms, social processes, and relationships between individuals and groups' (1983, p. 337). The authors argue that one of the central 'environmental problems' for people living in Western societies is not overcrowding, as is seen to be the problem in developing societies, but rather alienation, isolation, loneliness and lack of social support. All of the latter are described as features of urban or modern rather than rural or traditional life. These problems, Lindheim and Syme contend, are combined with other social problems such as individuals' feelings of lacking autonomy over the conditions of their lives, low self-esteem and not belonging to a community, as well as the disruption of 'biological rhythms', exposure to artificial light and air conditioning, and a lack of 'connection to nature', 'connections to the life cycle' and 'connections to place'.

These authors therefore construct the archetype of the atomised urban dweller who is effectively cut off ('disconnected') from those elements of life that are considered to be vital to good health, and who is thus unable to express the authentic self. Urban living, except for the economically privileged, is represented as pathological and 'unnatural'. Lindheim and Syme note, for example, that exposure to artificial light and lack of contact with 'fresh air' and the seasons is potentially undermining of good health by disrupting 'natural' habits and rhythms:

> Children have been placed in windowless schools, workers in windowless factories, and secretaries in windowless offices. By so doing, people have been subjected to possibly harmful exposures and have been deprived of awareness of the time of day, the weather, the seasons of the year, and colours and motion of the natural landscape. (1983, p. 349)

Discussions of the imputed pathological effects of the contemporary 'social environment', therefore, often conflate the 'social' with the 'urban'. Rural living, it is implied, is far closer to a state of 'nature', and is therefore conducive to good health, while urban living is too far removed from 'nature', 'distorted' by society and culture. Thus, a disease such as cancer is phrased as a product of largely 'social/environmental' factors (that is, non-genetic or 'non-inherent' factors) related to 'modern' or 'urban' living, including a diet rich in fat, overindulgence in alcohol and tobacco, and exposure to radiation and chemicals. It is suggested that if only humans were to return to a more 'natural' state by casting off the pathological burdens of urbanisation ('society'), they would achieve good health. This discourse constructs individuals' relationship with their social and physical settings as an 'inside/outside' binary opposition. The body is represented as under attack from 'industrial society'; from without by artificial light, pollution and radiation and from within by the chemicals in food (Coward 1989, p. 79). Good health is portrayed as the 'natural' and 'normal' state of human embodiment with which 'culture' has interfered (Coward 1989, p. 24).

The concept of 'social stress', which is unique to the late twentieth century, has become a popular way of describing a sense of malaise, fatigue, depression, anxiety or tenseness in individuals in contemporary Western societies. This concept similarly relies upon the representation of humans as living in an 'unnatural' setting created by modern industrial society. As a cover story published in *Time* magazine on the stresses of the modern world asserted:

Whether burdened by an overwhelming flurry of daily commitments or stifled by a sense of social isolation (or, oddly, both); whether mired for hours in a sense of life's pointlessness or beset for days by unresolved anxiety; whether deprived by long work-weeks from quality time with offspring or drowning in quantity time with them—whatever the source of stress, we at times get the feeling that modern life isn't what we were designed for. (Wright 1995, p. 62)

Given the prevalence of 'stress discourse' in both medical or public health and popular forums, it is not surprising that an interview study of people living in the English city of Nottingham found that the great majority 'felt that the experience of stress was an inevitable and ubiquitous condition of modern living, and that stress could be a direct cause of illness', particularly 'heart attacks' and 'nervous breakdowns'. The respondents considered physical or mental overexertion (as in the stereotype of the harassed executive) or disrupted interpersonal relationships to be the primary causes of stress (Pollock 1988, p. 382).

The discourse of stress assumes that humans today are affected by far more fears and anxieties than in previous centuries, and are subject to rapid sociocultural change which causes 'dislocation', 'imbalances' and 'identity confusion'. Popular explanations of 'stress' often argue that humans were 'designed' for the 'flight or fight' mechanism in response to situations of fear, anger or anxiety: tensing muscles and secreting hormones such as adrenalin in order to deal physically with the situation (such as running away from a dangerous wild animal). It is contended that in the 'civilised' world, however, individuals are expected not to respond physically to situations in which they feel threatened, but must contain their emotions and physical responses, channelling them inwards. Ill health is therefore caused through a 'build-up' of stress, by weakening the immune system or raising blood pressure, or promoting recourse to alcohol use or suicide in order to 'cope'.

Similarly, a new concern for the health effects of lack of sleep reported in the news media in the 1990s argues that most people are 'chronically sleep-deprived' or have a 'sleep debt' caused by the demands of living in modern society, to which electric lights and the allures of television sets are said to contribute. Ironically, such understandings of the causes of ill health, with their use of the hydraulic terminology of 'pressure', 'steam' or being 'run down' or having a 'breakdown', rely as much on the mechanical model of the human body—conceptualising it as a system of gauges, pumps, energy flows, conduits and valves—as they do on notions of the 'natural/organic' body.

In its focus on the essentialist nature of human biology and its emphasis on the negative aspects of 'culture', conceptualised as 'intruding upon' or 'distorting' nature, this discourse ignores the ways in which biology and culture are inseparable. An individual's genotype is not simply an internal, individual phenomenon, but is itself the result of evolutionary changes that are the products of humans' encounters with non-human phenomena. While there are clearly some biological phenomena that are constant across time, space and cultures—all humans need to sleep, all humans bleed when cut, all human bodies are formed of organic matter which eventually dies and rots—the meanings and practices associated with 'biological' phenomena such as blood, death, ageing, birth, eating, excreta, menstruation, and illness and disease vary widely over time and between human cultures. So too, this perspective on human health and the urban environment tends to use the concept of 'nature' as it is equated with 'healthy', in a highly selective, culturally and historically specific manner.

An alternative perspective is to understand the human body and the spaces and places it occupies as constructed through discourse and practice, often in ways of which we have little conscious awareness. As Shields argues, '[t]here is a tremendous complicity between the body and the environment and the two interpenetrate each other' (1991, p. 14). Social relations and bodily practices take place within spaces and in places; they shape and are shaped by space and place. Expectations and assumptions about the appropriateness of space and place to human health are culturally and historically contingent. The ways in which we view space and place are constructed through sociocultural understandings which then underlie the strategies of regulation and control that contribute to public health knowledges. The space and place that individuals inhabit, then, cannot simply be categorised as either conducive or damaging to health status, but rather should be seen as contributing to individuals' sense of what is 'well-being', 'health' or 'illness' in the context of their everyday lives and embodied experiences. What may be experienced as extreme privation for one individual accustomed to a particular kind of space and place, for example, may be experienced as luxurious for another, with clear implications for that individual's sense of physical comfort, well-being and health. There is nothing essentially 'healthy' or 'unhealthy' about these responses. (These issues of space and place in relation to new public health knowledges are taken up in further detail in Chapters 5 and 6.)

THE 'AT RISK' AND 'RISKY' SELF

We have argued that the notion of environmental risk as expressed in the new public health goes well beyond identifying and dealing with material hazards to human health. This broadening of risk has had the effect of constructing a risk continuum, ranging from those risks that are perceived as completely out of individuals' control to those risks that are regarded as purely the responsibility of the individual. Inherent within this continuum is an equivalent and directly associated continuum of moral judgment. When environmental hazards are viewed as not amenable to the individual's conscious choice (for example, as radiation emitted from a nuclear power plant or toxic chemicals released by a nearby factory), as caused by others rather than the self and therefore as 'external' to the individual, the individual is represented as 'at risk' from these threats. The control of such risks is often phrased as a political issue, something with which individuals cannot deal alone and which therefore must be addressed via community action against vested interests. This is essentially the risk/subject dynamic that is presented in Beck's work on 'risk society'.

If, however, the risks are viewed as amenable to change on the part of the individual (for example, the 'lifestyle' choices relating to diet, smoking, alcohol use and exercise), it is the individual who is charged with the responsibility of acting to protect him- or herself; people become 'at risk' from their own ignorance or lack of self-control (see Chapter 2). Failing to protect oneself from this kind of 'internally imposed' risk is understood as an individual moral issue, highlighting personal failures or weaknesses (Lupton 1995, pp. 89–90). Susan Sontag drew attention to this differential in the moral meanings ascribed to 'risky' behaviours when she noted:

> Getting cancer . . . is sometimes understood as the fault of someone who has indulged in 'unsafe' behaviour—the alcoholic with cancer of the oesophagus, the smoker with lung cancer; punishment for living unhealthy lives. (In contrast to those obliged to perform unsafe occupations, like the worker in a petro-chemical factory who gets bladder cancer.) (1990, p. 113)

The extent to which a risk is understood to be within the realm of individual agency therefore influences the degree of moral culpability assigned individuals. The new discourses on 'stress' and 'holistic' health have had the effect of portraying more and more 'environmental' risks as being related to personal management. Unless a risk is understood to be overwhelmingly beyond an individual's control, people are understood as not simply being passively 'acted upon' by their environment. Instead, they are now often positioned as being in an interactive relationship with the external environment and their own inner self. Different types of people are understood as responding in different ways to the same environmental conditions, depending on such factors as age, culture and life-history (Lindheim & Syme 1983, p. 337).

The use of psychological models of behaviour has been important in constructing this mediation between self and environment. These models have begun to weaken the notion that environmental risks are out of an individual's control. Personality-based concepts such as self-efficacy, self-esteem and the 'addictive personality', as well as the emergent focus on 'spirituality' and 'stress' mentioned earlier in this chapter, emphasise this focus on the ways in which people deal individually, or 'cope', with the same types of environmental factors. They are used to explain, for example, why some people take up smoking or overindulge in alcohol in response to 'stress' while others desist, or why some people succumb to heart attacks while others remain healthy.

In such understandings of the self/environment, there is a symbiotic relationship posited in which the environment is regarded as both posing certain risks and influencing the extent to which an individual responds to these risks. As Greco notes:

> Stress exists as a function of the individual experience of environment, rather than as a totally 'environmental' or 'individual' phenomenon: the *pathogenic value* of a given environment is only ever a function of an individual's interpretation of it. Similarly, the pathogenic value of an individual's interpretive tendencies is relative to the quality and quantity of demands made by the environment. (1993, p. 360 [original emphasis])

This concept of the self/environment dynamic constructs a typology of internal responses (ranging over the physiological, the psychological, the cognitive and the behavioural) to a typology of situations and events. Risk, therefore, is directly associated with biography, with the ways in which individuals experience, respond to and interpret risks, and with the extent of self-knowledge they possess (Greco 1993, pp. 360–1). The notion of the environment as including social, psychological and spiritual as well as material phenomena has been important in the development of this understanding of the self/environment interaction. While urbanised society may be the site and primary generator of stressors and other threats to human health, it is ultimately the individual who is charged with dealing with these threats.

A further extension of the moral economy related to risk, health and individual behaviour is the construction of the individual as the cause of health risks to others. This understanding is evident in the ways in which smokers are exhorted not to 'share their smoke' with others to protect them from the effects of passive smoking, or in which people with HIV and other communicable diseases such as measles, hepatitis or tuberculosis are encouraged to protect others from infection by quarantining themselves, publicising their infected status or using such devices as condoms to prevent transmission of the disease agent (see Chapter 3). Again citizens are expected to engage in self-regulation, but this time for the sake of others' health rather than their own health. The 'risky' persona is placed in the position of being the source of contamination.

As we have pointed out in previous chapters, historically the representation of this 'risky' persona in medicine and public health discourses has been phrased through such aspects as gender, social class, ethnicity and sexual identity: women, the feminised gay male, non-white peoples, the poor and members of the working class have been portrayed as more contaminating, and therefore more morally culpable, than privileged groups. On a more individualistic level, the 'risky' self finds clear articulation in discourses on the 'environmental citizen'.

CONCLUDING COMMENTS

In this chapter we have identified the complex uses of the term 'the environment'. A common theme is the use of concepts of space and place in public health discourses describing the interrelationship between individuals and the environment. As we have shown, where nineteenth-century· and early-twentieth-century public health was largely concerned with the hygiene of urban and domestic spaces, the relationship between environmental risks and human health is now constructed through the new public health as a multi-sited phenomenon, including interpersonal, spiritual and psychosomatic dimensions. 'The environment' is used in different contexts to denote, among other things, the following:

- the home
- the family
- the city
- the workplace or school

- non-urban areas
- urbanised areas
- the globe
- the natural world
- the non-natural world
- the physical or material world
- the social world
- personal lifestyle
- human relationships

People themselves are differently positioned in relation to 'the environment', not only as members of social groups, but also through ascriptions of individual risk. When individuals are constructed as being 'at risk' from environmental hazards such as air or water pollution or radiation they are not considered responsible for any health problems that might arise, for the risk is regarded as too overwhelming, as beyond their personal control. When, however, individuals fail to take up their duties and responsibilities as 'environmental citizens' in relation to consumer activities—by not engaging in recycling, for example, or by wasting water—they are portrayed as culpable, as failing not only themselves but also their fellow citizens, other living creatures and generations of humans to come. We have argued that more and more 'environmental' risks are now conceptualised as amenable to personal control.

There are many contradictions in the concepts of the environment that have been taken up in the new public health. A continuing tension in discourses on the environment and health is the critique of the knowledge of science. While science related to industry is routinely positioned as the 'cause' of environmental damage, the 'objective' knowledges of the natural sciences are also constantly used to support most critiques of the damages believed to be wrought upon the environment by humanity. These knowledges are employed to construct the 'problems' of 'the environment' which are conceptualised as existing objectively in nature, their authenticity guaranteed by expert scientific investigation and confirmation (Grove-White 1993, p. 19). Arguments concerning the ways in which pollution affects human health, for example, are based almost exclusively upon the findings of scientific research. In environmental discourses the inevitable contingencies, indeterminacies and uncertainties, the socially constructed nature of scientific knowledge, tend to be glossed over for a reliance upon 'objective facts' (Grove-White

1993, p. 22). In turn, most solutions constituted to deal with environmental problems draw upon science and rational action. It is not the knowledge base of science per se that is challenged, therefore, but rather the effects of a 'misused' science.

Most of the new public health agencies, as we have pointed out, are funded and run by governments. It is perhaps not surprising, therefore, that discourses on the environment in the new public health literature tend to focus on 'collaboration', 'consultation' and 'partnership' with other sectors and organisations (both government and non-government), on attempting to 'work with' vested interests rather than directly challenge them. The new public health is also very supportive of the notion of 'community participation' to achieve goals and targets in relation to environmental health. Chapters 5 and 6 explore these issues in more detail in relation to the notion of 'community participation' and more specifically the 'Healthy Cities' project.

5 The 'healthy' city

People in a healthy city would be living in an unpolluted, safe environment; the built environment, particularly housing, would be of high quality. The city would be supported by, and contribute to, the development of a stable and sustainable ecosystem. Social life would be rich and political participation highly developed. Thus, if you lived in a healthy city you would feel that you were supported by a community in which there was mutuality in human relations and the absence of exploitation. Decisions which directly affected the well-being of individuals would not be taken only by some remote bureaucrat or planner, but would be reached after widespread public debate; decentralization of decision-making would devolve power and give people greater control over the decisions which affected them. (Curtice 1993, p. 38)

The concept of the 'healthy' city is gaining increasing currency within the discourses of public health. Since the mid 1980s, there has been a proliferation of expert commentary on the theme of the 'healthy' city, and hundreds of cities around the world have come to designate themselves 'Healthy Cities' and developed attendant programs of action. Health promoters have reported a 'booming conference industry' around the theme of the 'healthy' city (see de Leeuw 1994, p. 1). The discourse of the 'healthy' city illustrates a number of the integral features of the new public health we have discussed to this point. These include the adherence to modernist notions of the social and of change, the focus on 'the environment' (as it is broadly understood) and particularly environmental risk, the emphasis on active and individualistic citizenship, and the tendency to pathologise certain spaces and places through their identification as sites of risk.

120

All these dimensions of the new public health are manifest in the policies and strategies of the Healthy Cities project which has developed since 1986, initially in Western Europe under the auspices of the European Office of the WHO, and increasingly in other parts of the world, including North America, Australia, Eastern Europe, Central and South America, the Middle East, South-East Asia and the Pacific. Healthy Cities has been described by its proponents as 'the local expression of the new public health'. That is, the project is seen to translate new public health principles into local practice: redressing inequalities in health, increasing access to services, developing personal skills, 'creating supportive environments', and involving 'the community' in defining and resolving problems (Milio 1986; WHO 1988). The project's method and philosophy are seen to mark a decisive shift in ways of thinking about health in urban environments, and its programs are viewed as political programs that involve a change in power relations in respect to health and illness (Davies & Kelly 1993, pp. 3, 7). In this chapter and the next, we critically appraise some of the claims that have been made for the Healthy Cities concept and project, and examine some of the unacknowledged implications of related knowledges and practices.

We begin this chapter by tracing the historical antecedents of present conceptualisations of the 'healthy' city to efforts in the late eighteenth and early nineteenth centuries to control urban populations through rational scientific means. As we argue, the present context of concerns about the 'healthy' city is dominated by anxiety about 'eco-crisis' and about managing the risks arising from the impact of populations, particularly urban populations, on the 'natural' environment. In the policies and programs of Healthy Cities and the new public health one can see the continuation of the nineteenth century focus on the city as an organism and as a 'medicalisable object'. Despite rhetoric about the need to develop a new 'holistic' framework of analysis and new modes of social organisation, their philosophies, policies and practices reflect a conventional, modernist understanding of society and of reform. An overriding faith in the ability of science to resolve problems and to provide a basis for their rational management and control is manifest in conceptions of the 'healthy' city, in the planning strategies of the WHO, and in the development of specific projects. This chapter provides the background for the next chapter where we examine in more detail the notions of active citizenship and 'community participation', which are seen as central to Healthy Cities both as a concept and project and to the new public health more generally.

THE 'HEALTHY' CITY AS A MODERNIST CONCEPT

The foundations for contemporary conceptualisations of the 'healthy' city were laid between the late eighteenth century and early nineteenth century when the project of controlling populations began to be linked with the Enlightenment project (Rosen 1993, pp. 107–67). During this period, society was beginning to be seen as a unique object, 'with its own laws, its own science, and eventually its own arts of government' (Rabinow 1989, p. 11). Individuals' actions came to be viewed as a function not of their moral character but rather of their place within the social whole. Consequently, it made little sense to reform the individual separately from the social milieu within which actions were formed. With the emergence of modern society, people were no longer born into their places, but 'had to be trained, drilled or goaded into finding the place that fitted them and which they fitted' (Bauman 1992a, p. xv). As Bauman notes, urban planning and architecture provided the vehicles and master-metaphors for providing the perfect order and eliminating disorder. Detailed attention was given to segregating places and establishing a hierarchy of spaces and buildings. There remained, however, a view that 'man-made' order was 'an artificial imposition on the unruly natural state of things' and for this reason would 'forever remain vulnerable and in need of constant supervision and policing' (Bauman 1992a, p. xv).

Leading up to the period of Enlightenment, the city began to provide the model for the governmental rationality that was to apply to the whole of a territory. Michel Foucault has commented that from the seventeenth century one begins to see

an entire series of utopias or projects for governing territory that developed on the premise that a state is like a large city; the capital is like its main square; the roads are like its streets. A state will be well organized when a system of policing as tight and efficient as that of the cities extends over the entire territory. At the outset, the notion of police applied only to the set of regulations that were to assure the tranquillity of the city, but at that moment the police become the very type of rationality for the government of the whole territory. The model of the city became the matrix for the regulations that apply to the whole state. (1984b, p. 241)

The concept of police used in this quote is not the present-day sense of the term; that is, the authority charged with maintaining order and preventing dangers. Rather, it is a term employed in the eighteenth century to denote a body of knowledge and practices known as both 'the science of happiness' and 'the science of government'. The science of police was concerned to protect and promote the happiness and well-being of the population for the ultimate benefit of the state as a whole (Pasquino 1991, p. 108).

The Enlightenment 'medical police' strategy for the body politic can be seen as the forerunner of 'health and towns' drives in the nineteenth century, when the city and disease became inextricably linked (Porter 1993, p. 588). During the eighteenth century, a range of new knowledges, social categories and subcategories emerged, posing their different problems and requiring different forms of intervention. It was during this period that the health of the population attained a new value, and became a new object of analysis and intervention (Pasquino 1991, p. 115). In Chapter 4, we described how the town or city became a 'medicalisable object' and how urban spaces and their inhabitants became of increasing concern because of the threats they posed. Space was seen as a 'fact' of nature, to be subject to conquest and rational ordering as an integral part of the modernising project. The project of dominating space was part and parcel of 'the liberation of "Man" as a free and active individual, endowed with consciousness and will' (Harvey 1990, p. 249). Notwithstanding acknowledgments of the limits of the theory and practices of the sanitary idea in the new public health, the reforms of the mid to late nineteenth century provide a strong point of reference for the reform efforts of Healthy Cities. This is evident in references to 'the revival of public health in towns and cities' and to 'rediscovering the environment' (see, for example, Draper 1991, p. 7; Ashton 1992a, p. 5). Many of these early reforms, however, stemmed from fear among the elite of the revolutionary movements brewing in Europe in 1848 as much as from the dread of diseases (Rosen 1993, pp. 227–51). Rosen has described the widespread pressure for social reform building up throughout Europe in the years leading up to, and during, 1848. In England, a number of important reports directly or indirectly bearing on public health were undertaken, including Edwin Chadwick's 1842 report and the parliamentary reports of the Royal Commission for Inquiry into the State of Large Towns and Populous Districts (1844 and 1845). These reports helped to highlight the nature and extent of problems, and provided an avenue for moulding public opinion, as well as increasing pressure on governments to effect remedial legislation.

When action did take place it reflected a belief in the ability to rectify the dysfunctions of urban, industrial society through limited state involvement, rational planning, the application of science to problems, and the education of the population. Although in practical terms these reforms had undeniable and significant effects on the mortality levels in the population as a whole, they never challenged the core principles of economic and social policy. In the event, it is clear that there was a strong ideological bias in concerns about diseases. Although tuberculosis was a far greater killer, for example, it was seen as less of a threat than cholera and typhoid since it was less likely to respect class boundaries (Rosen 1974, pp. 71–7; 1993, p. 201). The persistence of the organic conception of the city that developed during the nineteenth century is immediately suggested by the neologism, the 'healthy' city. In line with the mechanical and systemic view that dominates biological and physiological understanding, the discourse of the 'healthy' city contains much reference to city systems, functions and adaptations. In a review of its Healthy Cities project, for example, the WHO begins its response to the question 'what is a healthy city?', with the comment that 'a city is a living, breathing, growing, changing complex organism', and so on. More than this, 'cities are players in promoting and maintaining health and have a unique capacity to implement ecological health plans' (Tsouros 1990a, p. 20). The development of organic images for human society also has a long history, dating back to the ancient Greeks, who saw the city, the citizen and the cosmos as being built according to the same organic principles (Haraway 1991, p. 7). But it would seem to have reached its apotheosis in the 'functionalist' theories of the modern human sciences, where the body politic is reduced to physiological explanations. For example, in Freud's *Civilization and Its Discontents* (1929), the body politic is seen to evolve as a result of the interplay between instinctual tendencies, particularly the instincts of aggression, which must be conquered to make possible the cultural group (Haraway 1991, p. 9). The use of such metaphors is clearly evident in the following description of the list of 'requirements for a healthy city':

> First of these is that the city's responses to its developmental needs, its organizations, and its people be appropriate and effective. Second is that the city should have the ability to cope with breakdowns of the system and its members. The third, then, is that the city should have the ability to modify itself and change to meet the always emerging, changing

requirements for life. This then leads, fourth, to the city's competence to enable its inhabitants to use it to their advantage. Finally, it must be understood that this cannot be accomplished unless the city is able to educate its inhabitants. (Duhl 1986, p. 55)

This writer goes on to describe in some detail 'the needs' and 'actions' 'required in the development of a healthy city', and what the city 'needs' in order to 'develop into a healthy organism which, itself, will allow others to grow and flourish' (Duhl 1986, p. 55). He concludes that, 'as in the healthy organism, the health of the parts as well as the vigour of the connections is essential to make the organism work at its highest level of competence' (1986, p. 59). The image portrayed of an organism of interacting, interdependent parts which strives to maximise its functioning, reveals the influence of both a mechanistic view of organic functioning and a Darwinian evolutionary model of adaptation and change.

It is interesting to note the individualistic and managerialist emphasis evident in the reference to the city-organism as a self-reflexive entity, capable of monitoring its own state of health and of learning to respond and change in appropriate and effective ways. This mirrors the conception of the individual-as-enterprise, who is charged with managing his or her own relationship to risk and taking whatever evasive or remedial action is required. However, like the health of the individual, the health of the city cannot be accomplished without education and appropriate support. As this commentary implies, if health is to be achieved there is .a need for the continuing involvement of expert advice so that inhabitants can use resources of the city most effectively to their own advantage.

As Donna Haraway (1991) has pointed out, the employment of the organic metaphor in descriptions of human society has set limits on permitted explanations of the body politic, the most important being the functionalist requirement of an ultimate explanation in terms of equilibrium, stability and balance. Explanations of social functioning are couched in terms of physiological parts or subsystems working in a coordinated way for the overall stability and harmony of the hierarchical whole. Within this scheme, there is no recognition of conflict and social inequality (Haraway 1991, p. 24). Such explanations have provided a major source of justifications for social inequalities—such as those that exist between men and women, between socioeconomic groups, and between different ethnic groups—which are seen as natural, given, inescapable and therefore moral. It has also reinforced a technical-rational and instrumentalist orientation towards ecological and social systems. In the discursive construction of the city as an organism, one can see a preoccupation with systems that can be dissected, analysed and repaired (Kelly et al. 1993, p. 160). If the organism suffers a 'breakdown' through 'maladaption', then it can be modified and rebuilt to bring it into harmony with its new environment. Following from the idea that the organism comprises specialist functioning components, it is assumed that specialist knowledges should be developed and applied for making those components 'more functional' for the organism as a whole:

> If a breakdown occurs, the city must have all the complex, scientific, human and other necessary skills to assist the individual or organization to return to paths of competence and health. Often another problem is created because the means or institutions that were used which were successful for coping in the past do not meet the needs of the present. The city must know when that time, the breakdown, comes and be flexible enough to meet new, emerging conditions. (Duhl 1986, p. 57)

The discourse of the city as a unified whole implies that problems can be resolved through a politics of consensus, and thereby obscures the conflicting interests and politics therein. In this description, questions about what counts as 'competence' and 'health', or who defines these outcomes, are not raised. Nor is the validity of the means for achieving these outcomes raised. From the start, Healthy Cities has proceeded on the assumption that the health of the city 'organism' could be achieved through rational administration. If problems are clearly defined and enough 'facts' are accumulated about how the city 'works' (or rather, does not work), then expert knowledge could be applied for bringing it to a 'healthier' state. The adoption by Healthy Cities of this rational and technical approach, which is premised upon the power of experts to define and solve problems, should not be surprising in light of the WHO's role in the project. As Kelly et al. point out, 'WHO in its practice and personnel has generally been an ultra-modernist organisation, favouring technical expertise as a means of solving clearly defined problems' (1993, p. 160). In virtually all discussions about Healthy Cities, belief in the scientific method and scientific progress, and in the ability of technical expertise to solve problems, is taken as given.

This belief is reflected in project descriptions that draw heavily on the metaphors and language of science. For example, Healthy Cities are described as ' "field laboratories" for testing HFA (Health for All) initiatives at local level [which] give important feedback to WHO and Member States that can be used to update and refine the HFA strategy'

(Tsouros 1994, p. 1). One of the leading and early proponents of Health for All principles has referred to the Healthy Cities project as a whole as a 'policy laboratory' where 'new policy approaches can provide a vision of the whole, a framework for leading and guiding projects and ongoing programs, using incentives to encourage new options, and controls to retain health-nurturing directions' (Milio 1990, p. 295). When the Healthy Cities project was launched, it was seen as a means whereby participating cities could 'collaborate in the development of urban health promotion initiatives', thereby providing 'models of good practice' which would inspire other municipal administrations in their health promotion efforts. As Ashton and Seymour put it,

> by concentrating on concrete examples of health promotion based on a commitment to equity, to community participation and intersectoral action, the Healthy Cities project was seen as making the point at which the Health for All strategy was taken 'off the shelves and into the streets of European cities'. (1988, pp. 153–5)

The reference to 'laboratories', and 'models of good practice' implies that the components of the city can be manipulated and controlled like variables in a scientific experiment, so that the experts can determine with certainty which strategies 'work' and which strategies 'do not work' in a particular situation, and then generalise the findings to other situations. This obscures the power relations, uncertainties and ambiguities that underlie the development and implementation of policies, and conveys the impression that national, cultural and local differences, competing interests and inequitable access to resources are irrelevant to policy outcomes.

RATIONALE AND APPROACH OF THE HEALTHY CITIES PROJECT

The Healthy Cities project, which is a joint initiative of the health promotion and environmental health programs of the WHO Regional Office for Europe, was launched ostensibly in order to 'put health on the agenda of decision-makers in the cities of Europe and to build a strong lobby for public health at the local level' (Tsouros 1990a, p. 11). Healthy Cities was seen to be a practical component of these programs in that it was intended to demonstate the application at local (city) level of the WHO strategy of Health for All by the Year 2000, the principles of health promotion outlined in the Ottawa Charter for Health Promotion and the principles of the European Charter on

Environment and Health (Tsouros 1990a, p. 11). According to one WHO publication, Healthy Cities was part of a deliberate strategy of 'networking and coalition building', and sought 'to bring together political and community leaders, local citizens, community organizations, professional associations and national and international agencies in a collaborative, intersectoral and community-based effort to achieve health for all at the local level' (WHO 1991, p. 1). Project documents explain that the role of the WHO is to coordinate the project, provide international leadership in innovative action for health, link and diffuse the ideas to national Healthy Cities 'networks' and build coalitions of international bodies for Healthy Cities. The Regional Office of the WHO describes its main tasks as providing political leadership, mobilising support and resources, and building strategic alliances (Draper et al. 1993, p. 132).

Although the project started in Europe, it has quickly grown into an international 'network' of Healthy Cities throughout other parts of the world, a development that has been nurtured and supported by the WHO in line with its stated objectives. While the WHO and its supporters frequently depict Healthy Cities as a spontaneous international social movement, it is clear that the overall direction and goals of the project have been defined by the WHO and collaborating bodies of expertise. From the outset, Healthy Cities in Europe was seen to be a prototype for other city-based projects worldwide, and to be part of a 20- to 30-year process of initiating a 'new public health movement' (Draper et al. 1993, p. 131). The stated intention behind the original project was that it would last five years and involve a small number of European cities that would demonstrate the principles of health promotion, and particularly the WHO's Health for All by the Year 2000 objectives, so that other cities might be inspired to develop projects in an autonomous way along similar lines. According to official histories, the WHO was to act as a catalyst in the process of setting the agenda for health, raising public awareness of new public health issues and 'establishing models of good practice' (see, for example, Ashton et al. 1986; Ashton & Seymour 1988, Ch. 9; Ashton 1992a).

A few comments should be made about the WHO's general objectives and modus operandi in order to clarify its particular approach and role in relation to Healthy Cities. Since 1946, when it was set up at a Conference of the United Nations as the single directing and coordinating authority on international health work, the WHO has played a key role in coordinating international public health efforts and in offering member states technical advice and managerial support. Its involvement in the Healthy Cities project is seen as consistent with its mandate of advancing the health of all peoples, with its commitment to primary health care and, more specifically, with its policy of achieving Health for All by the Year 2000 (or simply Health for All). Although the policy of Health for All was originally agreed upon by member states in 1977, in 1980 a commitment was made by the governing body, the World Health Assembly, to concentrate the WHO's activities over the coming decades—as far as possible in the light of all its constitutional obligations—on support to national, regional and global strategies for attaining Health for All (Commonwealth Dept of Community Services and Health 1988, p. 7).

The WHO encompasses six regions: Africa, the Americas, the Eastern Mediterranean, Europe, South-East Asia and the Western Pacific. In order to fulfil its objectives, the WHO adopts a managerial process that involves a continuous process of programming by objectives and budgeting by programs. The process includes such components as policy formulation, formulation of the general program of work, medium-term programs, program budgeting, implementation, evaluation and information support (Commonwealth Dept of Community Services and Health 1988, p. 29). The Executive Board of the WHO is required by the WHO's Constitution to submit to the World Health Assembly for consideration and approval a general program of work covering a period of approximately six years. The Global Strategy of Health for All by the Year 2000 spans three general programs of work. All programs are the end-product of an assessment of global and regional health policies and the needs of member states, and of an evaluation of previous general programs of work. They are based upon an assessment of information derived from a variety of sources including member states, statistical year books and reports of the Director-General and Regional Directors. The program of work describes global themes as well as objectives, targets and approaches in general terms. General programs of work comprise a number of individual programs, each consisting of organised activities directed towards the attainment of specific objectives (Dept of Community Services and Health 1988, p. 30).

In line with this planned, rational approach, the WHO, through the Healthy Cities project, has sought to translate the WHO Health for All strategy and the so-called '38 European targets for health for all' into local programs (Ashton 1992a, p. 5). The vocabulary that is adopted in its published documents reflects the WHO's strategic planning strategy, involving reference to 'mission statements' ('to build a new public health movement in the cities of Europe and to make health everyone's business at the city level'), 'five-year plans', and 'multi-city action plans' (Tsouros 1990a, pp. 23–9). At the time of its inception, it was announced that a 'minimal set of indicators for cities involved in the project' was to be developed in respect to such aspects as the extent of intersectoral collaboration and emphasis on 'healthy public policy', the quality of the physical environment and of infrastructure and housing, the quality of the social environment 'including levels of psychosocial stress and qualities of social support services and integration', 'traditional health indicators' (mortality and morbidity), and 'new health promotion indicators' such as dietary habits and participation in physical exercise (Ashton et al. 1986, pp. 320–1). Project cities have been designated according to their commitment to formulating and implementing 'intersectoral health promotion plans with a strong environmental health component, based on WHO policies and strategies and with active community involvement', reporting back regularly on the progress achieved and sharing information and experience with other participating cities, supporting the development of national 'networks' of healthy cities, carrying out population health surveys, developing active working links with other project cities fostering technical and cultural exchange, and hosting Healthy Cities meetings and events (Tsouros 1990a, p. 22; Draper et al. 1993, p. 9).

The first phase of the Healthy Cities project, involving 30 cities from 16 countries, was implemented between 1987 and 1992. Although the WHO Europe had initially planned to reduce its role after 1992 to one of partnership with a 'free-standing office/organisation', it decided to continue funding of the project for another five years. An increase in the number of participating cities (to 42) and countries (to 23) in the second phase of the project covering the period 1993 until 1998, gives only a very partial indication of the growing momentum of the Healthy Cities phenomenon. Many more cities than the Healthy Cities project could manage showed interest in the concept of the healthy city, and have demonstrated their support for it by undertaking activities similar to those of the WHO project, and by their involvement in national and international 'networks' of healthy cities. Although there are varying estimates of the total number of cities linked via these 'networks', available figures suggest that, by 1994, there were between 500 and 600 cities throughout Europe and between 200 and 300 cities in other parts of the world, spanning North America, Latin America,

South-East Asia, the Middle East, Africa and the Pacific region (Tsouros 1994, pp. 1, 4; Goldstein 1995, p. 3).

Because the Healthy Cities concept and project has been so popular, and because there has been the rapid development of 'networks' between cities, some commentators have begun to talk of a healthy cities movement (for example, Goumans 1992, p. 274). The use of the language of the 'new' social movements, the adoption of the ecological view of health, and the appeal to subjective health and to 'grass-roots' action all help support the view that Healthy Cities is a social movement for change (see, for example, Burgmann 1993). As Baum warns, however, the appeal to universalism and altruism in professional discourses should be treated with some caution since it can serve to conceal the expansion of bureaucratic and professional control (1993, p. 36). The development of Healthy Cities 'networks', which is widely seen as tangible evidence of a social movement, is a clear case in point. Ostensibly established for the sharing of information, knowledge and skills between participating cities, national and international 'networks' can be seen to have extended the panoptic gaze of experts to the global level, and to have strengthened links between decision-makers at all levels (see Goumans 1992). The WHO has developed a program of action, and an accompanying vocabulary, in respect to the development of these 'networks'.

National networks are seen by the WHO as a way of expanding the Healthy Cities 'movement' and of serving and supporting the needs of cities participating at the national level. They are considered to be a means of linking the participating cities to key national organisations and ministries and of adapting the project to the specific cultural and social characteristics of each nation. This is justified on the basis that it enhances the employment of national resources for the project as a whole. International networks establish links both between individual cities and between national networks. WHO publications refer to 'twinning networks', whereby cities establish links with at least one and often several cities, not only in their own WHO region (for example, the Russian city of St Petersburg and the Spanish city of Barcelona) but also with other regions (for example, Europe and North America). The 'networks' of the Healthy Cities project bring together a vast number of agencies, both at the national and international level. At the national level, 'networks' bring together such groups as public health associations; municipal authorities; universities; non-government organisations; and ministries with responsibility for municipal affairs, planning, housing, environment, social services and other key sectors. At the international level, 'networks' have been established between the WHO Europe and such bodies as the Council of Europe, the Economic Commission for Europe, the Organization for Economic Cooperation and Development (OECD), the United Nations Development Program (UNDP) and the World Bank. The Healthy Cities project is also linked, via 'networks', to international organisations that deal specifically with cities or that are organisations of cities, such as the World Association of the Major Metropolises (WHO 1991, pp. 15–25).

This whole edifice has facilitated the exchange of information and resources among experts, and between experts and politicians and top decision-makers in cities. The WHO openly acknowledges the potential of the 'networks' to strengthen collaboration between project cities and other agencies in the health and environment area (for example, the OECD's 'ecological city' project and the Sustainable Cities campaign that was launched by the Directorate General 11 of the European Union) (Tsouros 1995, p. 138). In the wake of the United Nations Conference on Environment and Development (UNCED) in 1992 (the 'Earth Summit '92'), these organisations are increasingly involved in collaborative efforts to improve the capacity of municipal government to manage the urban environment (see Goldstein 1995, p. 7). The WHO has supported these networking efforts by providing technical staff, 'fact-finding' and 'consultation missions', training, and information and literature to countries that are developing new national networks or strengthening existing ones (Goldstein 1995, pp. 6–7; Tsouros 1995, p. 135). It has also set up 'collaborating centres' that provide information to 'network' members on Healthy Cities research, projects, policies, conferences, and so on, via a regular printed newsletter (*Research for Healthy Cities*) and the electronic services of the Internet.

The term 'network' has strong democratic overtones, which has strong appeal for those seeking alternatives to expert and bureaucratic control, since it implies equitable access to information, mutual support, and a spirit of solidarity and collaborative effort. However, rather than broadening access to information and other resources, these 'networks' reinforce the control of knowledge and resources in the hands of experts, administrators and politicians, and serve to widen the gap between the 'information rich' and the 'information poor'.

THE PROBLEM OF MANAGING 'ECO-CRISIS'

The level of interest in Healthy Cities both as a concept and project has been rather phenomenal, and stands in need of explanation. What then is the particular context that has given rise to concerns about the 'healthy' city and that has shaped the development of policy? Of crucial importance has been the growing concern, evident since the mid 1980s, about global 'eco-crisis' and its influence on health. During this period an increasing number of government inquiries and expert commissions were set up to inquire into and report upon the dimensions of this crisis. A significant early event in the development of the Healthy Cities concept, according to documented histories, was a conference in Lisbon, Portugal, in 1986 at which representatives of 21 cities met to explore ideas about the 'healthy' city and ways in which the project might usefully proceed. As the authors of a 1986 article prophesied, the Lisbon symposium was to be something of a watershed in the development of the new public health, but perhaps not in quite the ways or to the extent envisaged by the proponents of Healthy Cities. In this article, there was reference to 'crisis in cities throughout the world' which 'pos[ed] the possibility of real change at the present time', although details of the nature of this 'crisis' were not spelt out in this particular article (Ashton et al. 1986, p. 322). A few years later, in a more detailed discussion, Ashton and Seymour refer to a number of conditions influencing the policy environment: the global fuel crisis of the mid 1970s, the growing awareness of the limits of technologically based medical care, the publication of the Health for All strategy in a more accessible form in 1983 and a growing awareness of the benefits to be had from an environmental approach to health (1988, p. 153). These specific concerns can be seen to be manifestations of a more general concern that the global ecological system had just about reached the limit of its sustainability.

Pressure for changes to established patterns of production and consumption linked to rich urban lifestyles had been building up throughout the 1970s and 1980s. The Ottawa Charter for Health Promotion (1986), and the Earth Summit '92 are significant indications of international concern about resource depletion, pollution and the creation of unhealthy living conditions and environments, especially in urban areas. As explained in Chapter 4, this generalised anxiety about risks resulting from the influence of modern industrial processes and lifestyles on the global ecosystem is reflected in a number of sociological writings published in the English-speaking world in the early 1990s (for example, Giddens 1991; Beck 1992; Beck et al. 1994). Concern about such issues as global pollution, loss of biodiversity, 'acid rain', global warming and the 'greenhouse effect' was becoming more evident throughout the 1980s and early 1990s both in expert discourse and in the popular media. McMichael's comment that these environmental problems 'reflect the systemic overloading of the "carrying capacity" of Earth's natural systems' (1993b, p. 1) reflects a widely shared view on the origins of the 'eco-crisis'.

In many discussions, including the sociological contributions of Beck and Giddens, processes of modernisation, including technological innovation and rapid population growth, have been implicated either implicitly or explicitly in the creation of environment risk and of a general climate of uncertainty. In the WHO report, *Potential Health Effects of Climatic Change*, it is stated that

> human activities have influenced the environment since the first settlements were built and the land cultivated. At that time, the changes were relatively small and were absorbed by the resilience of the environment. Today, however, it is clear that the effects of the unlimited growth of the human population, and of recent unrestricted technological advances, have had a much greater impact on the environment and may well exceed its capacity to absorb them. The human race is the sole protector of the environment, with the capability to plan wisely, to conserve providently, and to develop prudently. Conversely, it is also capable of polluting or even destroying the environment through greed, ignorance, or indifference. (WHO 1990b, p. 1)

In the 1980s and early 1990s, many government inquiries, WHO reports and other expert commentaries began to draw attention to the links between 'systemic overloading' and urban processes, particularly industrial processes and patterns of consumption. The city was being seen as both a major component, and a microcosm, of 'natural' systems 'gone wrong', and consequently became a focus for generalised concerns about managing the 'eco-crisis'. More specifically, it was the 'lifestyles' of city citizens that were of major concern. As Ashton observes, there has been increasing recognition that 'crises' such as those described above 'are, in large part, the results of the lifestyle and expectations of city-dwellers and of the way in which they affect patterns of agriculture and world development' (1992a, p. 7). While public health experts have derived hope and inspiration from the nineteenth-century environmental reformers, they have recognised the limits of the theory and practice implied by their predecessors' sanitary ideal; that is, using engineering solutions to control the influence of the 'natural' environment on humans. In a context of heightened concerns about rapid urban growth and the resulting incapacity of biological systems to cope, a new model of public health reform was needed.

Inverting the nineteenth-century concerns about the incursion of 'nature' into bodies, attention shifted to concerns about the intrusion of those bodies into nature (see Chapter 4). The Ottawa Charter for Health Promotion, and the WHO Healthy Cities project, both launched in 1986, signalled the beginnings of systematic institutional responses to these perceived risks of human intrusions into the 'natural' environment. Since then, there has been a burgeoning of expert interest and activities (publications, conferences, and government inquiries and commissions) focusing on the environmental threats posed in particular by industrial activities and rapid population growth, especially in urban areas; for example, the health effects of energy use and of land degradation (Ewan et al. 1991; National Health and Medical Research Council 1992; WHO 1992a; National Commission on the Environment 1993).

The First European Conference on Environment and Health articulated some of these major concerns (WHO 1990a). It adopted a broad definition of 'environmental health' to include 'both the direct pathological effects of chemicals, radiation and some biological agents, and the effects (often indirect) on health and wellbeing of the broad physical, psychological, social and aesthetic environment, which includes housing, urban development, land use and transport' (WHO 1990a, p. 18). As we pointed out in Chapter 4, this definition leaves few areas of the 'built' and 'natural' environment not relevant to the environmental health agenda. As an outcome of this conference, member states of the European Region of the WHO adopted a European Charter on Environment and Health which avowedly signalled their commitment to action. The Charter's list of 'priority areas for action' gives some insight into the nature and scope of issues of concern:

- global disturbances to the environment such as the destruction of the ozone layer and climatic change;
- urban development, planning and renewal to promote health and wellbeing;
- safe and adequate drinking-water supplies . . . together with hygienic waste disposal for all urban and rural communities;
- water quality in relation to surface, ground, coastal and recreational waters;
- microbiological and chemical safety of food;

- the environment and health impact of:
  — various energy options
  — transport, especially road transport
  — agricultural practices, including the use of fertilizers and pesticides, and waste disposal;
- air quality on the basis of the WHO *Air Quality Guidelines for Europe*, especially in relation to oxides of sulfur and nitrogen, the photochemical oxidants ('summer smog') and volatile organic compounds;
- indoor air quality (residential, recreational and occupational), including the effects of radon, passive smoking and chemicals;
- persistent chemicals and those causing chronic effects;
- hazardous wastes including management, transport and disposal;
- biotechnology and in particular genetically modified organisms;
- contingency planning for and in response to accidents and disasters;
- cleaner technologies as preventive measures. (WHO 1990a, pp.12–13)

All these problems are thought to be linked to some degree to distinctly urban resource use and patterns of living. Problems are attributed in particular to rapid urban growth which is seen to lead to 'overconsumption', depletion of non-renewable resources, and degradation of soil and water; in short, 'systemic overloading'. Recognition of the contribution of the urban environment has provided something of a dilemma for authorities, however, since it carries the politically unpalatable implication that there is a need for radical changes in economic policies and in the lifestyles of a large segment of the population in the wealthier urban centres. The various expert commissions that have been appointed to report on the 'eco-crisis' have tended to offer qualified appraisals of the contribution of urbanisation to environmental and health problems.

A number of expert commissions have noted that it is not urbanisation per se that is the problem, but rather the processes of managing the city environment. In some cases, urbanisation has been depicted as beneficial for both health and the environment, although this remains a minority position. The WHO Commission on Health and Environment, for example, comments that:

Rapidly growing urban centres pose a particular challenge for environmental health. As well as being an essential part of economic development, urbanization can bring major benefits to health and the environment. The concentration of production and of population lowers unit costs for the supply of piped water and health services, for many forms of sanitation system, and for the collection and treatment of household and commercial wastes. But in the absence of government action to provide the infrastructure, services, and control of pollution on which health and environment depend, environmental health problems are greatly increased, because of the high concentration of industrial, commercial, and residential wastes. (WHO 1992a, pp. 197–8)

As this suggests, control of risks to 'the environment', and hence to humans, has been seen to be achievable through rational administration. However, cities are seen to be ungovernable because responses are locked into old conceptions of problems. In order to understand the systemic and ecological complexity of the current urban society, the public health experts argue, there is a need to view the city as an ecological whole and develop appropriate techniques of governance (Duhl 1993, p. 113). What is needed are new forms of social organisation, and policies that take the 'green' message seriously and put health on the agenda of a whole range of different activities.

It was against the background of these particular configurations of concerns and events that the 'healthy' city emerged as an object of a particular kind of understanding and action. The stated rationale for focusing on the city in the Healthy Cities project is that, as the local accountable administrative level, it has access to a wide range of resources and networks and 'can act as a facilitator, mediator and advocate for improving its citizen's health' (see, for example, Ashton & Seymour 1988, p. 154). More specifically, it is seen to be the most effective site for engaging citizens in the active pursuit of their own and others' health and well-being. Because the city is a place with which its citizens strongly identify, it is believed to offer good prospects for participation harnessed to 'the neighbourhood' or 'civic pride' (Ashton et al. 1986). In city planning processes, the value of making health a reference point for all decision making can be demonstrated in the development of 'healthy public policy' (Curtice 1993, p. 38). As the Ottawa Charter states, healthy public policy

> puts health on the agenda of policy makers in all sectors and at all levels, directing them to be aware of the health consequences of their decisions and to accept their responsibilities for health . . . The aim must be to make the healthier choice the easier choice for policy makers as well [as for individuals]. (WHO 1986)

Nancy Milio, who has been one of the most articulate advocates of 'healthy public policy', and has in fact been widely credited with coining this term, sees the task of public policy as 'creating environments' so that 'individuals would be better able to develop and pursue their personal views of "health"'. As she puts it, although governments cannot assure that every individual attains personally defined 'health', they at least have the responsibility to 'establish environments that make possible an attainable level of health for the total population' (Milio 1986, pp. 4–5). In her view, 'healthy' cities provide visible, tangible evidence of how resources may be mustered and utilised in 'health-supporting ways'. That is, 'their efforts are the focus of research on not only *what* they do but *how* they do it' (Milio 1990, p. 295 [original emphases]).

According to the rhetoric, 'healthy public policy' involves 'intersectoral' action; that is, it is not confined to the conventional sphere of health policy. It is also collaborative in strategy, involving many levels and areas of government, voluntary, economic and community groups (Milio 1986, p. 9). In a review of Healthy Cities as it operated between 1987 and 1990, the WHO reaffirmed its

> political support for the strengthening of intersectoral action on the broader determinants of health and for exploring with our city councils or other city authorities ways to make health and environmental impact assessment part of all urban planning decisions, policies and programmes. (Tsouros 1990a, p. 14)

In the review report, it was noted that present systems of organisation are based on nineteenth-century concepts of bureaucracy, disciplinary specialisation, and sectoral analysis, which needed to be jettisoned in favour of 'new, holistic, flexible approaches' (1990a, p. 19). As is explained in this report,

> the old system of organization by professional department and by sector has to be complemented by new approaches to such health issues as equity, sustainability, safety and mobility. These issues cut across the old departmental lines and indeed across the different sectors—public, private, voluntary and community. None can be addressed by one department of government alone, nor indeed by city government alone. The whole community has to be mobilized and the efforts of all sectors and departments have to be combined and focused. (Tsouros 1990a, p. 19)

This new holistic approach calls on everyone to play their part in the collaborative effort of advancing the population's health. The achievement of the Healthy City, as this quotation implies, calls for nothing short of the total reordering of society.

THE 'GREENING' OF PUBLIC HEALTH

The 'greening of public health', as some writers have dubbed this broad environmental and policy project, has led to the targeting of such diverse areas of activity and policy as food production, parenting practices, economic policy, workplace practices, media policy, energy use, transport policy, the global arms trade, Third World debt, town planning and building design (see Badura & Kickbusch 1991; Draper 1991). It implies a large-scale reorganisation of institutions, and cooperative endeavours between members of 'the community' and experts drawn from such diverse areas as transport planning, engineering, architecture, agriculture, banking, social work, media and communication, community arts, town planning and local government. Its emergence in Healthy Cities would seem to imply a rethinking of 'the political', in particular about how the non-party politics of the environmental and policy aspects of public health can be defined (Draper 1991, p. 19). Thus far, this has proved difficult in practice, according to at least one account, because of entrenched interests of traditional sectors and because of difficulties in gaining political acceptance for the idea and in shifting resources (Tsouros 1990a, p. 62). Nevertheless, these ideals continue to hold sway in the discourse of the 'healthy' city, and are seen as fundamental to the fulfilment of the goal of Health for All.

The adoption of the language and rhetoric of ecological politics in Healthy Cities has ensured broad political support for the concept and project both among politicians and among members of the general public. The holistic credo of Healthy Cities is seen to be congruent with the ecological philosophies of the international 'green movement' and of 'responsible environmental management'. The fact that tends to be overlooked, however, is that 'green' has many shades, and that there are different political positions on the determinants of and solutions to the current 'eco-crisis'. When examined closely, many current eco-political positions carry implications that would seem to be greatly at odds with the stated ideals of Healthy Cities and the new public health; particularly the Health for All emphasis on reducing inequalities in health. A number of ecological feminists have pointed out that many 'mainstream' ecological movements fail to establish connections between forms of domination—particularly the domination of women—and the domination of the non-human 'natural' environment. Warren argues that any environmental philosophy that fails to include the recognition of all ecosystems ('whether understood as organisms, individuals, populations, communities and their interactions, or as nutrient flows among entities

"in the biospherical net of relationships"') is inadequate (1994, p. 2).
An adequate environmental philosophy, she argues, needs to attend to
the connections between all systems of domination, including racism,
classism, ageism, ethnocentrism, imperialism and colonialism as well as
sexism (1994, p. 2).

'Deep Ecology', one school of radical ecological thought popular
among many white, middle-class activists and academics in the United
States, Europe and Australia, has been criticised for its failure to adequately theorise connections of this kind. According to one eco-feminist
commentator, its emphasis on the 'population problem' as the central
causative factor in the destruction of the biosphere and wilderness areas
can be seen to involve a 'one-dimensional characterisation' of the
problem (Plumwood 1994, p. 93). In this perspective, because of their
inability to appreciate the earth's 'natural carrying capacity', 'humans'
selfishly reproduce more of their species than can be supported by the
biosphere. There is no critical analysis of the complex factors contributing to the size of population or of the concepts of 'carrying capacity'
and 'standard of living' which are always based on evaluations about
how 'humans' will have an influence on particular habitats (Plumwood
1994, p. 93).

As Plumwood points out, Deep Ecologists tend to register the ill-
effects of population growth as a consequence of a battle between
'humans' and 'nature'. 'Humans', however, are not an undifferentiated
group. Arguments about population size have tended to be advanced by
certain dominant groups in the wealthy Western world who are concerned about the ultimate impact of growth of the populations of poorer
developing countries on their own lifestyles, and who show ignorance
of the economic and other factors that underlie and sustain high
population growth; for example, the importance of large families for
economic survival in a context of high infant mortality. Such arguments
are often underpinned by racism, and do nothing to advance the position
of people, mainly women, who frequently live in poor socioeconomic
circumstances and suffer various forms of sexual abuse. Arguments about
the 'population problem' have often been used to support coercive
policies such as forced sterilisation of poorer peoples, and have led some
ecologists to propose that the global HIV/AIDS epidemic and the
outbreak of famine in developing countries are 'necessary solutions' to
the 'population problem' (Plumwood 1994, p. 92; Petersen 1994a,
pp. 43–5).

So too, as we argued in Chapter 4, the concept of 'nature' is by no means stable, varying through time and across society. In the modern, industrially developed Western world, 'nature' is seen as something that is outside 'society', that should be subdued and controlled but also protected. Modernity has involved the belief that human progress should be measured and evaluated in terms of human domination of 'nature' rather than in terms of the transformation of the relationship between humans and 'nature' (Lash & Urry 1994, p. 293).

The complexity of eco-political positions *not* acknowledged in the discourse of Healthy Cities has become apparent during discussions about 'ecologically sustainable development' (ESD) (or simply 'sustainable development'). An examination of some of the debates about ESD underlines just how contentious is the notion of 'responsible environmental management', especially when the dominant Western model of development is put under scrutiny. The question of exactly what ESD means in practice, particularly for the mass of the population who live in urban areas, is the subject of continuing political dispute. Any definition of sustainable development depends upon the definition of development and of its desirability, and of what is to be sustained: high levels of 'development', or the fulfilment of human needs. Definitions of wealth, need, scarcity, well-being, and so on, vary according to culture (Braidotti et al. 1994, p. 113).

In a report by the American National Commission on the Environment, it is noted that

> economic and environmental well-being are mutually reinforcing goals that must be pursued simultaneously if either is to be achieved. Economic growth cannot be sustained if it continues to undermine the healthy functioning of the Earth's natural systems or to exhaust natural resources. By the same token, only healthy economies can generate the resources necessary for investments in environmental protection. (National Commission on the Environment 1993, 'Summary statement', p. 5)

In this view, it makes no sense to separate economic and environmental goals, since 'long-term growth depends on a sound environment, and resources to protect the environment will be forthcoming only from a strong economy' (National Commission on the Environment 1993, p. 14). Significantly, in this report 'poverty' is identified as 'the enemy of the environment' and consequently, it is argued, 'one of the principle objectives of environmental policy must be to ensure a decent standard of living for all' (1993, p. 5). The underlying theory of development here is 'the trickle-down' effect, which assumes that all economic and social problems can be solved within existing capitalist arrangements. Given the long history of the Western model of development in the United States, it is hardly surprising that there has been a guarded response by authorities to suggestions that existing economic processes themselves might be implicated in environmental problems and should therefore be curtailed.

A competing, and less economically constrained, conception of ESD has been proposed by the Brundlandt report; that is, development that 'meets the needs of the present without constraining the ability of future generations to meet their own needs' (World Commission on Environment and Development (WCED) 1987). The Brundlandt report refers to 'Our Common Future', underlining the global character of certain of the threats posed to 'nature', in particular the 'nuclear' threat. This definition carries the implication that the conventional model of 'development' does need to be curtailed and that its underlying assumptions need to be questioned. It implies that present citizens assume responsibility for the health and well-being of future generations by collectively adopting the role of 'environmental stewards', which implies some degree of collective 'self-sacrifice'.

This particular definition has strong appeal within sections of the new public health, implying as it does a global or 'holistic' philosophy and a concern with cross-generational solidarity (that is, the future of 'our children and their children') (Lash & Urry 1994, pp. 298–9). The Brundlandt definition, however, is based on an abstract (that is, universal) notion of the citizen, without allowing any recognition of the fact that there are many different current subject positions vis-à-vis 'development' and 'the environment' both within and between countries. For a start, there is no consensus among present governments about the seriousness of problems concerning environmental degradation and loss of biodiversity, and about what needs to be done to redress them. We have already discussed some of the problems and implications of the emphasis on the 'population problem' as the cause of environmental problems, such as the failure to examine the factors underlying population growth, and the underlying racism informing the discourse. In the event, many developing countries do not see why their economic development should be limited by constraints imposed by wealthier countries who are seen to have largely contributed to problems of environmental degradation in the first place. The governments of many developing countries have linked changes to bring about 'sustainable development' to other needed changes, such as the net transfer of resources from developed to developing countries, and to the deteriorating terms of trade. Understandably, they baulk at the financial commitment that is required for energy-saving measures and forest protection (Ewan et al. 1993, p. 9).

Many of these competing conceptions of sustainable development were evident at the Earth Summit '92 and the parallel conference, the Global Forum. The Earth Summit was to provide the opportunity for affirming the responsibility of all peoples to protect the planet for present and future generations. As Porras explains, 'the environment' provided a rallying point in calls for a 'new globalism' based upon ideals of sharing, common interests and long-term perspectives (1993, p. 21). Political positions on the relative importance of 'the environment' and 'development', however, soon polarised around various axes. Negotiations of the Rio Declaration took on an essentially bipolar North–South character. Arguments assumed that a country was either 'developed' or 'developing' holding either a developed (pro-environment/anti-development) position or a developing (anti-environment/pro-development) position. This had the effect of stifling debate about other possible alignments and dichotomies that did not fit in with the primary North-South divide (Porras 1993, p. 23).

A large contingent of non-government representatives, including the business community, churches, youth groups, different United Nations institutions and women's groups, held differing and often contradictory positions that often did not correspond to the North–South divide. For example, the international business community sought ways of integrating environmental concerns into industry in order to establish a niche market of 'green' production and consumption in the North; while women across all divides pointed to the inextricable link between the crisis in development and the 'eco-crisis', on the one hand—and militarism, the nuclear threat, violation of human rights and the domination of women, on the other (Braidotti et al. 1994, p. 5). All these different political positions carry very different implications for 'the environment', for relations between nations and for relations between different social categories. As it turned out, although the conference did result in consensus about large measures that may result in 'environmental protection' and sustainable development, the text of the Rio Declaration reflects 'uneasy compromises, delicately balanced interests, and dimly discernible contradictions', that offered no fundamental threat to the dominant Western model of development or to the dominant relations of power both within and between 'developed' and 'developing' countries (Porras 1993, p. 23).

These complexities and implications of different eco-political positions do not figure in the discourse of Healthy Cities. As argued in Chapter 4, in the new public health as a whole there has been a tendency to view human society and the 'natural' environment as conceptually distinct, as is evident in calls for efforts to 'save the environment'. Its ecological politics is based upon a view that problems can be solved through scientific understanding of issues, the management of 'the environment', and the structuring of individual choices through public policy ('healthy public policy'). Despite claims that Healthy Cities represents a departure from nineteenth-century (modernist) conceptions of society and of approaches to problems, its ecological and rational approach to problems draws heavily upon modernist assumptions. As such, it offers no fundamental challenge to the hierarchies of power that underpin many of the problems that have come to be identified as part of the crisis of modern urban life, such as inequalities in health and environmental degradation.

CONCLUDING COMMENTS

In the above analysis of Healthy Cities as both a concept and project, we have sought to underline and illustrate a number of points that we have made in earlier chapters, particularly the new public health's deployment of modernist conceptions and strategies, and the context of concerns about 'the environment' and environmental risk. The assumption that problems can ultimately be controlled through expert knowledges and the ordering of bodies and spaces within the 'organism' of the city was shown to have emerged with the Enlightenment, and to have effectively set limits on explanations of the body politic. Although the rhetoric of the new public health suggests a break with the traditions of nineteenth-century thinking about the city and its processes, we have emphasised a continuing modernist preoccupation with the functioning of city systems, with scientific explanations, and with the search for technical–rational 'fixes'. Thus, despite the use in policy documents of language generally associated with radical social movements, such as 'collaboration' and 'networks', the rationale and approach of the Healthy Cities project show that this new public health initiative has been very much in line with the conceptions and goals of the chief sponsoring organisation, the WHO, which adopts a fundamentally modernist approach to problems.

In examining the global context shaping contemporary concerns about the 'healthy' city, we have emphasised the significance of perceived threats posed by urban growth and unsustainable patterns of resource use. A sense of 'crisis' about the incapacity of natural systems to cope ('systemic overloading') has lent urgency to the effort to find rational solutions to problems. In this context, the rhetoric of 'green' politics has obvious broad appeal and helps give legitimacy to new public health initiatives. As we have pointed out, however, the discourse of Healthy Cities does not acknowledge the complexity of contemporary eco-political positions that may conflict with stated new public health ideals. Concerns about 'eco-crisis', particularly among peoples living in the privileged developed world, have led, not to a radical reassessment of the concepts of the social and social change, nor to the widespread abandonment of modernist ideals, but rather to a concentration of efforts on new, more effective forms of social regulation that continue to support privileged groups over disadvantaged groups. In expert discussions, it is assumed that problems can be solved through a politics of consensus and the engineering of social conditions particularly so as to encourage individuals to manage their own relationship to risk. Healthy Cities advocates have made no effort to rethink the concept of the city itself or to critically appraise the politics of the new public health as a whole. Indeed, as we go on to explain in the next chapter, there has been a noticeable absence of critical reflection upon the utility and implications of one of the basic concepts of Healthy Cities and the new public health: 'community participation'.

6 The duty to participate

Health for all will be achieved by people themselves. A well informed, well motivated and actively participating community is a key element for the attainment of the common goal. (Principle, WHO, Health for All)

Community participation is one of the key planks of the new public health, figuring prominently in both the Ottawa Charter for Health Promotion and the WHO's Health for All strategy. The focus on 'communities' and on 'participation' is neither new nor restricted to the new public health. In fact, within Western thought these concepts have long informed discussions regarding the development of democratic processes. Recently, however, there has been something of a revival of interest in 'community participation', and this is nowhere more apparent than in discussions surrounding Healthy Cities. The focus on 'community participation' is seen as evidence of the democratic nature of Healthy Cities and the new public health and of the close alignment of the new public health with other social movements. By allowing 'the community' to have a greater say in the shaping of all policies influencing health, so its advocates claim, it represents a break with earlier traditions of public health which have had more to do with 'top-down' social engineering and the management of the physical environment.

In this chapter we ask what 'participation' means in a context dominated by expertise, competitive individualism, and neo-liberal democratic structures and values. Participation has become not simply a right, but a duty, and great efforts have been made, increasingly through strategies such as the Healthy Cities project, to engage all citizens in the task of creating a 'healthier', 'more sustainable' environment. Although public health experts have reported problems with this strategy, they have not reflected upon the limitations and implications of their own discourse. As we argue, the discourse of active citizenship has constrained thinking about alternative forms of political intervention, and has served to obscure the personal and interpersonal demands and responsibilities required of those who are called upon to conform to the participatory ideal. We also make some critical observations on the assumed 'community' that is called upon to 'participate'. We suggest that while reference to 'community' can be usefully employed by groups in seeking to making visible their identity and in advancing their claims to disadvantage and marginalisation, the particular concept of community adopted in the new public health is narrowly defined and imposed, giving priority to locality over other criteria as the basis for identity. In conclusion, we argue that 'community participation' is part of a discourse of liberation that needs more critical scrutiny by those in the new public health for its unacknowledged implications, its potential for discrimination and its regulatory effects.

THE PARTICIPATORY IMPERATIVE

Within liberal democratic societies the concept of participation has a long history, but its meanings and implications are by no means uncontested. As it is typically used in the dominant discourse of democracy, 'participation' implies full and open debate of issues and decentred processes of decision making, allowing for a broad base of citizen involvement in a range of activities, including service delivery, management of resources, and cultural activities. Both Young (1990) and Pateman (1970) have discussed at some length the liberal democratic assumptions underlying the contemporary concept of participation. As Young argues, according to liberal democratic theory citizenship rights are demonstrated through exercising the opportunity for citizens to 'participate' in processes of collective decision-making. It is seen as important that democracies foster the development of citizens' capacities for appreciating their needs in relation to the needs of others and for appreciating the relation of others to social institutions. Only through 'participation' can citizens gain a sense of their relationship to social institutions and an appreciation that social relations are not natural and immutable but are subject to construction and change.

According to Pateman, the major function of participation in the theory of participatory democracy is an educative one: to instil in citizens the very qualities necessary for a democratic polity, such as individual attitudes and psychological qualities, and to enable citizens to gain practice in democratic skills and procedures. The existence of representative institutions at national level is not sufficient for democracy (Pateman 1970, pp. 42–3). Participatory democracy is seen as a prerequisite for distributive justice. This is because the only ground for claiming that a policy or a decision is 'just' is that it has been arrived at by virtue of all those who are affected by the decisions being free to express their needs and points of view (Young 1990, pp. 92–3). Many groups have, however, expressed scepticism about the justice of participatory democracy because they doubt that its processes in fact lead to just outcomes. The assumption that local decision-making necessarily leads to distributive justice has, in particular, been questioned. Permitting autonomous local control over resources when resources are unequally distributed among locales is likely to produce exploitation rather than justice (Young 1990, p. 94).

Participation often amounts to little more than tokenism, where affected people may be consulted to a limited extent but have no real power to affect decisions, and may even be co-opted into the power structure that they set out to oppose (Ife 1995, p. 113). This is evident, for example, in those government-sponsored programs going by the name of 'community development'. Citizens have often been encouraged to partake in decision-making processes only insofar as this is in line with predefined and delimited governmental objectives (see our comments on this below.) Feminists have drawn attention to the limitations of a conception of participation that implicitly excludes women from a role in the most important areas of public decision-making. As Pateman and other feminist political theorists have stressed, the abstract actor of liberal democratic theory is a male subject who, unlike the female subject, is regarded as relatively unconstrained in public life and relatively unburdened by the demands of private life (for example, Pateman 1989; Young 1990). Gay men and lesbians have also emphasised the restricted and exclusive nature of the discourse of participation. Their struggle for civil rights and entrée to electoral politics forcefully underlines just how limited is the conception of 'participation' for those who do not subscribe to dominant heterosexual norms (see, for example, Adam 1995). With the winding back of the welfare state from the mid 1970s onwards, and with the concerted attacks of conservative forces on even fundamental citizen rights (that is, the right to a basic standard of living), welfare activists have joined the chorus of those who have challenged the orthodoxy of neo-liberal democratic discourse. In light of these criticisms, the notion of participatory rights begins to look flimsy. Indeed, close examination of Healthy Cities and new public health literature shows that the discourse of participatory rights has been circumscribed by a discourse of citizen duties.

During the 1980s and early 1990s, 'participation' came to be seen as imperative to the enterprise of public health, especially to Health for All. The WHO Regional Office for Europe's Target's for Health for All notes that: 'It is a basic tenet of the health for all philosophy that . . . health developments in communities are made not only for but with and by the people' (WHO 1985, p. 11). This concern finds its clearest expression in the discussions and activities relating to Healthy Cities. Throughout much of Europe, North America, Australia, and increasingly in developing countries, Healthy Cities is seen as the key means by which 'participation' can be realised. The Health for All approach of Healthy Cities is distinguished from earlier 'top-down', 'paternalistic' town planning—the 'environmental determinism' characteristic of the period of sanitary reform—in terms of the emphasis on 'citizen control', 'citizen participation' or 'active citizenship' (Ashton & Seymour 1988, p. 157; Bracht & Tsouros 1990; Pike et al. 1990, p. 17; Bracht 1991). A 'healthy' city is defined not merely by the absence of disease, but also by the involvement of all citizens in creating conditions for the promotion of health and well-being. On the face of it, the emphasis on 'participation' in Healthy Cities and the new public health would indeed seem to represent a departure from the nineteenth-century approach to urban reform. It does not appear to utilise the organic conception of city functioning (that is, the identification and segregation of pathological spaces) described in the last chapter (but see our later comments under 'Community, space and place'), and it rejects the physical engineering approach to problems that distinguished the period of sanitary reform. However, neither does the Health Cities project signal a rejection of the rational administrative approach to problems that characterises modernity. The Healthy Cities project has become one of the most important administrative mechanisms by which authorities have sought to encourage citizen 'participation'. Cities wishing to be designated as WHO Healthy Cities are required by the WHO to demonstrate 'commitment to establish mechanisms for public participation' (Draper et al. 1993, p. 9).

The importance of 'participation' to the task of creating a 'healthier' and 'more sustainable' environment is underlined in the Report of the

WHO Commission on Health and the Environment. As the Report notes:

> Participation can promote health and environmental quality because it provides a means of organizing action and motivating individuals and communities. It enables individuals and communities to shape policies and projects to meet their priorities. Involvement in planning gives people the possibility to influence choices about the use of limited resources. Primary environmental care is one way of helping communities to apply their skills and knowledge to satisfy their own needs, improve their own environment, and promote the sustainable use of resources. Participatory political structures are a check on the abuse of the environment, since citizens with clear rights and knowledge and access to a legal system that allows speedy redress can exercise a powerful restraint on those contravening health and environmental regulations. (WHO 1992a, p. xxxi)

This quotation reveals a number of key assumptions underlying thinking on 'participation', such as the idea that it is an 'enabling' process, which will be the focus of discussion in the following section. The broad point that it forcefully underlines is just how central 'participation' has become to the environmental project of the new public health. If cities are to be made 'healthier' and the environment 'more sustainable', so it is argued, it is incumbent on individuals to work actively to shape policies and projects through collaborative efforts with others. It is significant that, in this quote, 'participation' is couched in terms of citizenship rights and implied obligations (citizens with clear rights can exercise a restraint over others, and so on). As argued earlier, many contemporary societies with developed welfare states are witnessing a redefinition of citizenship rights, with a greater emphasis on duties implied by rights. Citizens, it is argued, should consider the effect of their own 'freedoms' on others and, where necessary, curb and change their own 'unhealthy', 'risky' and 'ecologically damaging' consumption (Roche 1992, p. 239). This rights discourse, implying as it does a furthering of democratic processes and the exercising of greater responsibility towards the 'natural environment', clearly has broad appeal in many contemporary societies. As will become apparent, however, it serves to obscure certain operations and effects of power, particularly as they pertain between experts and non-experts.

One of the ways in which the WHO seeks to advance 'participation' is through the hosting of annual Healthy Cities symposia, where project cities debate and exchange ideas about mechanisms for encouraging 'participation'. From published proceedings of these symposia, it is clear that 'participation' increasingly is expected to take place at the outset, in the development of a 'city health plan' which is conceived of as 'the city's vision of health and the steps it intends to achieve it' (WHO 1994, p. 11). The importance of 'participation' to this process was emphasised, for example, at the 1994 Polish symposium, which was convened in order to clarify the role and the skills required of all cities in the Healthy Cities network to produce 'city health profiles' and 'city health plans'. In the resulting report it is stated that

> A key aspect of city planning is the involvement of the community. Participation is particularly important in all the development phases. Community participation in health promotion has some basic require-ments concerning the organisation of the work [of city planning], including the following four:

- that the citizens know where to apply for participation;
- that authorities are co-operative;
- that the citizens know how to make themselves heard or how to get involved;
- that participation should be attractive to the citizen. (WHO 1994, p. 15)

Given this rhetoric, it is curious that these symposia themselves have remained largely inaccessible to all but the experts. Attendance at the symposia is by invitation only and travel costs can be prohibitively expensive. Moreover, the language tends to be restricted to English or the language of the host country or both, and discussion tends to be couched in the exclusivist jargon of the public health experts (personal communication, Ruth Shean, Coordinator, Camden Healthy Cities Proj-ect, London). The failure of the WHO to make its symposia open to the involvement of a broader (non-expert) public reflects its unwilling-ness to democratise its own processes in line with its espoused philosophies. These symposia are not intended for critical reflection upon and debate about the desirability of the WHO approach. They are strategic planning sessions comprising largely senior politicians, directors of health, city officials and project coordinators.

Project cities and other 'network cities' have sought to show how they have 'involved' 'the community' in the development of city health plans and in other health-promoting strategies. The Healthy Cities literature reveals the adoption of a wide variety of mechanisms, reflect-ing somewhat different conceptions of what 'participation' entails in practice. These include providing 'information and documentation from different sources' through 'direct communications ("phone, meetings, lunches, etc.") with potentially interested people on every possible occasion'; posting 'newsletters to every household to inform people and encourage consultation of the public'; using local print media to 'promot[e] the philosophy of Healthy Cities as well as projects which Healthy Cities was associated with'; placing 'information posters [detailing city health plans] in areas where there is frequent public access, such as libraries, health centres, leisure centres, area offices, etc.'; facilitating '[community] participation in provincial conferences and conventions of municipalities and community health organizations (presentations, workshops, exhibits, or just . . . chatting in hallways)'; setting up 'Task Groups', 'working groups' and 'forums' with 'community input'; and providing access to 'community representatives' on existing district and regional 'councils' (see Baum, et al. 1990, p. 56; Fryer 1991, pp. 187–8; Lacombe & Poirier 1992, p. 8; Chittagong City Corporation 1993, p. 34; City of Liverpool undated, p. iii). In some instances (for example, Glasgow in Scotland and Sheffield in England), 'Community Support Units' have been established, and 'facilitators' have been recruited, to hold 'discussion groups' and 'focus groups' with members of 'the community' and to design and distribute questionnaires. In other cities (for example, Liverpool in England), emphasis has been placed on making materials more 'accessible' by providing copies of the draft city health plan in Braille, in languages other than English, on audio cassette and in large print (see, for example, WHO 1994, p. 15; Laughlin & Black 1995, p. 118; City of Liverpool undated). Regardless of the specific techniques adopted, it is considered important that cities wishing to be designated 'Healthy Cities' demonstrate their commitment to the ideal of participation by setting up formal mechanisms for 'involving' 'the community' in decisions about health planning.

EXPERTS' ROLE IN THE 'EMPOWERMENT' OF CITIZENS

Against the background of the imperative to 'participate', the public health experts have spent a great deal of effort exploring ways to motivate and engage citizens. Adopting a vocabulary consistent with what they see as their role in this democratising process, many experts speak of 'enabling' or 'empowering' individuals and groups (for example, Wallerstein 1993; Yeo 1993). More often than not, these terms are left undefined, or are at best loosely defined, both as concepts and as processes. The Ottawa Charter for Health Promotion (WHO 1986), which is a widely cited source of reference in discussions of empowerment, has been criticised for its lack of specificity in defining basic terms. As Stevenson and Burke point out, while the Charter equates community empowerment with the community's 'ownership and control' of its 'own endeavours and destinies', the means of effecting empowerment are not specified by the Charter (1991, p. 284).

The experts have identified a number of 'barriers' to 'participation'. In the literature, a significant cluster of such barriers refers to a lack of individual or community 'awareness', 'know-how' and 'problem-solving capacities'. These 'knowledge problems' are seen to comprise such faults as a lack of 'awareness of the extent of the problem', or a lack of 'awareness of other agencies and groups' activities', or ignorance about how to gain access to information, use the media, lobby decision-makers, chair meetings, and so on (for example, Bracht & Tsouros 1990, pp. 204–5; Hawe 1994, pp. 205–7). Another commonly identified source of difficulty, however, is the 'misunderstandings' and 'conflicts' that arise between experts and lay people resulting from differences in the way they approach decision making. Whereas health professionals base their judgments on scientific 'objective' knowledge, so one argument goes, lay people employ common sense, 'subjective' evaluations. This view is evident, for example, in Piette's discussion of 'problems of community participation in formal mechanisms of decision-making' in relation to Community Health Councils (CHC) in England and Wales. As she observes:

> Health professionals base decisions on scientific grounds which may or may not be well understood by CHC members. Similarly, health authorities may misunderstand the reasons underlying CHC proposals. Conflicts are likely to arise in situations where lay people face an expert consensus in routine decisions. (1990, p. 190)

In an expert-dominated culture, it is inevitable that many 'knowledge problems' will be attributed to the scientific ignorance or naivety of 'participants', or to problems with lay knowledge or lay rationality or both. An unstated assumption in much writing is that scientific knowledge is superior to lay knowledge. Thus, it should not be surprising that among her conclusions for promoting 'participation', Piette calls for the 'training' of community representatives so that they may better 'understand [sic] how experts approach problems' (1990, p. 195). Significantly,

Piette makes no reference to the need to train experts to better understand and accommodate the perspectives of lay people.

A number of these problems, and others, have come to light in the WHO's evaluations of its Healthy Cities project. In one such review, encompassing the period between 1987 and 1990, 'community participation' was described as 'one of the most problematic areas in the development of local Healthy Cities projects' (Tsouros 1990a, p. 61). The problems associated with 'community participation' were seen to be related to:

- a lack of understanding of what community participation is and the variety of means that can be used to achieve it;
- resistance by politicians and professional and managerial groups to accept the views and knowledge of community representatives;
- mistrust of city administration and the projects themselves, frequently based on the relationship between government and the community in the past;
- a research orientation that under-emphasizes community knowledge and does not consult the community in developing research projects; and
- a lack of resources that adequately support and encourage community initiatives. (Tsouros 1990a, p. 61)

Reviews of individual Healthy Cities projects in different countries have revealed that considerable difficulties have been encountered in putting the rhetoric of participation into practice. Some cities report 'non-existent' or low levels of 'participation', and others have identified such problems as lack of citizen access to formal decision-making positions, poor project visibility, loss of ongoing 'community' commitment to projects, and continuing professional dominance (Tsouros 1990a, p. 53; Fortin et al. 1992, pp. 21–2; Nuñez et al. 1994; Ouellet et al. 1994). Questions have been raised about the tokenism of much 'participation', about the extent to which government employees can work with community groups that may be critical of government actions, and about whether or not community representatives can ever be truly representative (see, for example, Baum et al. 1990, pp. 56–63). These difficulties and doubts, however, have tended to be down played or set aside in discussions about 'how to improve participation'. According to the reckoning of experts, all these problems and impediments are subject to an administrative solution, involving a combination of rational knowledge and personal enlightenment (that is, education), both of which involve continuing expert advice and direction. As expressed in one of the earlier cited quotations, individuals need to 'know where to apply for participation' and 'how to make themselves heard or how to get involved'. Furthermore, they need to see participation as 'attractive'.

On all these counts, and others, the experts see themselves as playing a key role both in terms of highlighting the nature of the problems and in terms of offering advice and support. In fact, in their 'enabling' role, the experts see it as their duty to redress these problems. They do not see themselves as simply inculcating knowledge or skills in passive subjects, however. In their efforts to distance themselves from 'blaming the victim' strategies, experts have been careful to describe their role in non-directive terms: as 'nurturing' 'freedom' and 'self-responsibility' (see, for example, Yeo 1993, p. 231). In the words of one commentator, 'instead of seeing the professional as the expert whose influence and reach must be maximised, the health professional [is] seen as a resource, someone whose job is to enhance natural helping and problem-solving capacities within the community' (Hawe 1994, p. 201).

An important way in which experts seek to further the goal of citizen involvement is through the development of theory. Public health commentators frequently lament the 'absence of theory' and lack of conceptual specification in discussions of 'community participation' or 'community empowerment'. Better theory, so it is argued, will lead to more effective practice since concepts and outcomes can be better 'operationalised' (usually meaning quantified) and measured (see, for example, Rissel 1994, p. 40). On the face of it, it is difficult to argue with the overall thrust of this objection. In policy documents and academic commentary, basic terminology often remains undefined, or loosely defined. It is evident from even a cursory review of public health and health promotion literature, that explicit, well-articulated theory of any kind is thin on the ground. When it is made explicit, theory tends to be narrowly conceived of as 'a model of behaviour', based upon particular scientific or behaviourist principles, rather than as a form of sociological analysis and social critique (see Lupton 1995, pp. 54–8).

Given the rational administrative framework within which problems are defined, this is hardly surprising. As we explained in the last chapter, the health promotion effort as manifest in Healthy Cities has been oriented to the development of 'models of good practice'. In this scheme, theory is merely an instrument for achieving predefined objectives, and offers little scope for any substantial analysis and critique of basic principles and practices. In the public health literature there has been little reflection upon the implicit social and political theory that informs all public health thinking and practical action, or upon the kind of theory that may be required for a more just, equitable, 'healthier' society. Theory tends to be 'positivist', in that it establishes a strict distinction between 'facts' and 'values', 'object' and 'subject', and 'theory' and 'practice'. This is most evident in the calculation of risk profiles (see Chapter 4), where there is a fetishism with enumerating, counting, calculating, and establishing 'the norm'. However, the argument applies throughout all domains of public health, even where 'qualitative' approaches, such as 'grounded theory', have been adopted. As with theories developed in other substantive areas of research and practice, theories of 'participation' in the new public health are constructed through 'dualisms'—mind/body, individual/society, nature/culture, and so on—that reinforce, rather than challenge, existing power relations. There has been little recognition of how expert knowledge constitutes and 'fixes' the objects of study, and in the process serves to exclude, and render invisible, certain categories from analysis and understanding.

In an attempt to challenge the power relations of 'positivistic' (that is, 'top-down', objectifying) research, some commentators have advocated the use of 'participatory action research'. This kind of research supposedly involves 'working with communities' rather than 'working on communities' and arriving at a definition of problems after consultation with members. It is therefore seen to produce theory that better reflects the interests and perspectives of 'participants', and is regarded as 'more democratic'. But what exactly is meant by 'democratic' research in a culture that is dominated by rational, science-based expertise and bureaucratic structures? Few questions have been raised about what 'participation' means in a neo-liberal democratic context where the values and practices of competitive individualism and representative decision-making predominate.

Expert commentary in this area strongly evokes the ideal of the Greek *polis*, involving the exercise of 'popular power' by sovereign subjects. Suggested models, however, presume the engagement of citizen representatives with formal hierarchical structures, 'top-down' decision-making processes, and professional expert advisers. A clear example of this is to be found in Laughlin and Black's (1995) report, *Poverty and Health: Tools for Change*. As a poverty strategy, the authors argue the need for 'community development as a way of working' as opposed to 'work[ing] with communities'; that is, the 'real involvement and empowerment of the community, sharing of power and decision making, not just basing a worker in a locality' (1995, p. 44). In their subsequent discussion of 'community participation', however, they uncritically posit a model of 'participation' that assumes varying 'degrees of control' by 'the community' over decision making, spanning full consultation with 'the community' at one end of the continuum through to no consultation at all at the other (1995, p. 48). The legitimacy of the representative model of the decision-making process is never questioned, and consequently the role of that process in sustaining inequality and poverty is left unchallenged.

Commentators also frequently refer to 'modes' or 'levels' of citizen participation, employing metaphors of ladders or continua. Bracht and Tsouros, for example, draw upon Arnstein's (1969) work to posit 'eight rungs on a ladder of citizen control', ranging from 'manipulation' ('non-participation') at the bottom of the ladder through to 'citizen control' (the highest 'degree of citizen power'), at the top (1990, p. 202). Here, as elsewhere, an increasing level of 'participation' is assumed to be bound up with a general process of democratisation. Experts see themselves as centrally involved in promoting this process through developing or advocating structures or practices that 'accommodate' or 'facilitate' 'citizen involvement' (see, for example, Bracht 1991). There is little recognition of how these hierarchical and idealised models of 'participation' constrain thinking about other possible forms of political intervention, or of how expert discourses themselves define and delimit the sphere of 'participation' and the subjects who are the 'participants'. (For a notably self-reflective exception to this observation see Fortin et al. 1992, pp. 16, 21–2.)

Authorities have frequently sought to mobilise citizen involvement through programs known as 'community development'. 'Community development' is a highly disputed term whose meanings vary across time and space, but among those working in the new public health arena it has increasingly come to be used as a synonym for 'community participation'. The history of community development underlines how the discourse of empowerment is employed for utilising the agency of citizens in fulfilment of particular governmental objectives. Programs going by the name of 'community development' were originally instigated by British, French and Belgian colonial administrations in Africa and Asia as a means of stimulating local leadership and drawing local factions into cooperation, and for securing resources (Marris 1985, p. 137). In the 1960s, however, the term began to be used in countries with a strong welfare tradition to designate those projects designed to foster 'participation' in local area service delivery, and to encourage 'self-help', voluntarism and cost-saving decentralisation. Attempts at cost saving and voluntarism are, for example, evident in the 1960s urban reform programs in the United States and Britain, and in the Community Health Program in Australia (Dixon 1989).

Although a number of limited reforms were achieved through this piecemeal social engineering, such as improved services and facilities and some increased involvement of local groups in formal decision-making processes, there has been a failure to move beyond local concerns to nurture an intergroup movement for broader change. Programs have not challenged established power relations and control has remained centralised within the institutions of state (Petersen 1994b, p. 215). As Labonte (1990a, 1990b) indicates, in the absence of any specific analytical framework of power the discourse of empowerment is liable to appropriation by dominant groups in order to defend their own interests. It has been used to support New Right economic policies by justifying the cutting back of state policies in the name of increasing community control. While the focus on decentralised decision-making does allow for the development of solutions tailored to the unique needs of local groups, it diverts attention from the fact that most economic and social policy is national and transnational in character. Direct decision-making and control by local citizens over programs and resources is used by health promoters and community developers as the acid test of empowerment. It is seen as more efficient and effective than, and as an antidote to, state centralism. However, it has served to localise global problems and to obscure macro-level systems of power and decision making (Labonte 1990b, p. 79–80). (For an overview of a range of perspectives on 'empowerment' as it is used in discussions on 'community development', see Ife (1995, pp. 56–64).)

That 'participation' is an idealised construct whose meanings can vary across contexts and between different parties is underlined by the findings of a study involving interviews with Healthy Cities organisers in two cities with vastly different democratic and cultural traditions: Barcelona in Spain and Sheffield in England. This case study found that organisers of the two project cities adopted very different conceptions of participation which were seen to reflect differences both in democratic tradition and in the degree of centralisation in the respective political systems (Smith 1991). In Sheffield, while the conception of participation is well established, reflecting centuries-old democratic traditions, action is constrained by strong lines of accountability to a central government that views participation only in the consultative sense. In Barcelona, on the other hand, while 'participation' is a less familiar concept and there are few precedents for action after a 40-year dictatorship that only ended in the 1970s, a more decentred political system allows great scope for experimentation with participatory mechanisms. These very different histories and political structures were found to influence both definitions of what constitutes 'participation' and expressions of commitment to the ideal. Even within cities, there were also found to be differences among organisers in perception and expressed commitment, according to their positions within the hierarchy (Smith 1991, pp. 114–16).

This case study strongly underlines the point that it makes little sense to speak of 'community participation' in any abstract, transcultural sense. The meanings and implications are always dependent on the contexts of use, and on the structural location and continuing commitments of parties who are involved. This point tends to be overlooked both in academic discussions of 'participation' and in the health promotion literature. It is often assumed that an abstract set of principles can be developed and applied across a range of settings irrespective of cultural practices, existing political structures and values, and the personal commitments and positions of those involved.

'PARTICIPATION' AS PRACTICE OF SELF-DISCIPLINE

The idealisation of the process of democratisation—involving a shift in focus from parliamentary and electoral politics to the wider sphere of civil society, and from passive to active citizenship—has served to obscure the fact that 'freedom' is a set of practices inseparable from ascetic constraint and self-discipline and a related set of skills in negotiation (Minson 1993, p. 206). Techniques deployed for maximising the involvement of members 'presuppose myriad forms of small-scale disciplinary work on the self'; for example, the ability to work with and negotiate with others, to attend regular meetings, to 'manage' one's time required for regular attendance at meetings and for reading up on and mastering the issues, and so on (Minson 1993, p. 203). Individuals are called upon to discipline themselves in conformity with the administrative model of decision making, which assumes a disposition, willingness and ability to engage with hierarchical structures, to adhere to strict time management and to be able to discriminate among clearly defined alternatives. It is assumed that if appropriate 'participatory structures' are developed, and if individuals are instilled with enough 'know-how' and skills, then the democratic ideal of 'participation' can be realised.

A clear example of how these assumptions inform thinking on 'participation' is to be found in one item of 'self-help' literature prepared by the WHO, *Twenty Steps for Developing a Healthy Cities Project*, which is worth examining here in some detail. This booklet is intended to provide guidance for cities wishing to introduce a Healthy Cities project or to review and expand an existing one, and is ostensibly 'based upon the insights and experience gained from the first implementation phase [that is, 1987 to 1992] of the World Health Organization (WHO) Healthy Cities project' (WHO 1992b, editorial preface). By the end of 1994, this booklet had been translated into nineteen languages and more versions were in preparation (Tsouros 1994, p. 4).

In the booklet, readers are presented with detailed information on how to get started and how to organise the project, and on areas for action and strategic work. In the chapter entitled, 'Getting Started' (Chapter 4), advice is offered under the following headings: 'Building a support group', 'Understanding Healthy Cities ideas', 'Getting to know your city', 'Finding project funds', 'Deciding organisational location', 'Preparing a project proposal' and 'Getting City Council approval'. For each of these areas, detailed information is given on the resources, inclinations, commitments and demands required of members. These include: 'strong interest in social issues, public health and innovation' and 'close links to the political system and [the ability to] represent as many sectors of city life as possible'; the ability to contribute 'significant time and effort to the project in its early stages and enjoy working in an informal and flexible manner'; the commitment, ability and time to 'gather and analyse information, make contacts, convince potential supporters and ultimately prepare a project proposal'; familiarising oneself with established health promotion principles and exploring and utilising available resources (for example, Healthy Cities 'networks'); undertaking research and analysis of one's city (for example, its important health problems, the effect of economic and social conditions, city politics, and so on); preparing estimates of project costs and locating potential sources of funding; and securing city council support.

After describing the qualities required of group members, and the need for members to familiarise themselves with the 'principles, strategies and practices that are part of the Healthy Cities movement', the chapter informs the reader about the importance of 'getting to know your city'. It is suggested that research and analysis can be organised around 'ten important questions about your city', which include 'what are important health problems in the city?', 'how do economic and social conditions affect health?', 'whose support is essential for project success?' and 'how do city politics work?'. Members of the support group are advised that they should set up a subgroup to gather information, and that faculty members and students from local academic institutions be asked to help (WHO 1992b, pp. 15–17). While it is not assumed that each and every individual will become expert in 'knowing their city', it is taken for granted that 'the city' can be objectively known, and that some individuals (the 'representatives') can gain access to this knowledge, through contact with experts, to the overall benefit of the group. The section's reference to the need for 'extensive documentation' that 'should be well organized from the beginning' underlines the faith in the power to be had from rationally collecting and organising information. It is assumed that, armed with systematically accumulated and detailed data about the economic, political and social context, 'participants' can accurately identify problems and then resolve them. In subsequent sections, information is presented on identifying sources of funds, deciding on the location of the project within the organisational hierarchy of the city, preparing a project proposal for presentation to the city council, and obtaining city council approval. In conclusion, the chapter outlines the importance of achieving bipartisan support among politicians and senior executives (to 'avoid the project being weakened if city government changes') and of developing skills for presenting the proposal in council and defending it from sources of potential opposition (1992b, pp. 17–20).

As should be apparent, involvement in these activities presupposes a whole range of personal attributes, skills, attitudes and commitments as well as detailed work upon the self. Few individuals—without a great deal of 'free' time, personal inclination and commitment, and specialist training—would be able to follow through with more than a small proportion of this agenda, even if they had time to read and assimilate the mass of published material. This example reveals much more about the way bureaucrats and professional experts approach problems in their bureaucratic settings than about how lay people make decisions and initiate action. There is no recognition of how formal structures constrain action, or of the nature of the power relations with which individuals are expected to engage when they are 'participating' in this way. There is no acknowledgment of the fact that different individuals and groups have varying degrees of 'freedom' to fulfil their participatory responsibilities and obligations. Many of those who have been the target of participatory strategies live in disadvantaged circumstances that make it difficult to attend regular meetings or to become involved in activities that entail financial outlays and so on; they may not enjoy even basic rights, such as the rights to work and to shelter, which are denied many young people and members of indigenous populations. Despite its egalitarian overtones, 'participation' is always contingent upon some 'trade-off', whereby, clearly, some have a lot more to trade with than others.

This is not to argue against individual involvement in any of these activities, or to deny the benefits, 'personal' and 'social', that may be derived from them. Rather, it is simply to highlight certain structures and operations of power, and effects of power/knowledge relations, that tend to be overlooked in rather abstract and generalised discussions among experts about 'how to improve participation' or 'overcoming barriers to participation'. With the legitimacy of neo-liberal democratic processes and of expert definitions taken for granted, the equation of 'participation' with the process of democratisation is never questioned. As Minson points out, it is a mistake to automatically assume that limits on people's interest and preparedness to take responsibility are an obstacle to a totally politicised or actively involved 'community' (1993, p. 206). On the contrary, evidence of 'failures' may be seen to indicate 'participants"' successful resistance to imposed relations aimed at their 'liberation', as well as individuals' recognition of the personal and interpersonal demands of 'participation' and of the limits of negotiation.

Faced with the imperatives associated with being a responsible, active citizen, individuals can perhaps most effectively assert their agency and autonomy by simply not engaging with those processes that attempt to regulate them. Public health experts have proceeded on the assumption that there is an objectively existing 'community' 'out there' that can be readily defined, located, and acted upon or engaged in ways that will necessarily be 'empowering' for 'participants'. The 'community' of the new public health, however, is a constructed concept, the meanings of which are shaped by a context of shifting relations of power. In the remainder of this chapter we examine this constructed community in some detail, drawing particular attention to the context of its emergence and to the specific ways in which the concept is articulated in Healthy Cities and new public health discourses.

COMMUNITY, SPACE AND PLACE

Although the term 'community', like 'participation', has a long history in Western social and political thought, it began to gain increasing currency from the mid 1970s in the context of the state's efforts to reduce the costs of health and welfare services by shifting the burden of responsibility for services from the state onto 'the community'. As the more critical commentators have pointed out, the use of the term 'community', as in 'community-based services', has served to obscure the return to reliance on the market, on families (particularly women), and on individuals themselves to meet basic needs (Ife 1995, pp. 12–14). The 'community'-based health promotion approach of the new public health is seen to offer the antidote to costly, centralised and bureaucratised medical care. In new public health discourse one can identify a number of dichotomies in which 'community' provides the focal point for debates about how to make health delivery less costly, more democratic and more effective: community care versus hospital care, community control versus professional control, community empowerment versus bureaucratic regulation, and community responsibility versus state mismanagement. For many groups, 'community' has come to signify the very antithesis of all that is wrong with state-sponsored medicine. This is the broad context that has shaped concerns about, and evaluations of, 'community' in the 1980s and 1990s.

How exactly has 'community' been deployed in public health discourse? The term 'community' in the new public health is generally used to designate some supposedly fixed space or place, and more specifically a geopolitical entity defined, or circumscribed, by local government administration. In the European, North American and Australian contexts at least, this place-based conception of community is reflected in both the philosophy and the practical strategies of the Healthy Cities project. As explained in the last chapter, Healthy Cities is seen to translate new public health principles into practice 'at the local level' and to demonstrate 'models of good practice' that would be copied and developed by other municipal administrations. By focusing on concrete examples of health promotion based on a commitment to equity, community participation and intersectoral action, the Healthy Cities strategy has been seen as the means whereby the Health for All strategy is 'taken off the shelves and into the streets of European cities' (Ashton & Seymour 1988, p. 154). As we pointed out in the last chapter, the city is seen as the place with which citizens identify and is therefore considered to offer good prospects for participation linked to the 'neighbourhood' or 'civic pride'. Within the literature on Healthy Cities and the new public health there has been little questioning of the politics of this place-based conception of community.

In a context of increasing concern about centralised control of health by the state, calls for local government involvement over matters affecting health clearly have broad political appeal. Local government is seen to be 'the level of government closest to the people', and hence more sensitive to 'local concerns'. The notion that locality provides the basis for shared sentiments and collective identity among citizens would seem to reflect, at least in part, nostalgia for the idealised *Gemeinschaft* 'community' of the Greek *polis*, involving the immediate co-presence of subjects and based upon consensus, and shared and agreed values, attitudes and goals (see Plant 1974). This ideal has proved alluring to advocates of the new public health, as well as supporters of other social movements, who seek alternatives to the impersonality, alienation and bureaucratisation of modern systems of government. Critics of welfare capitalist society repeatedly invoke the model of local face-to-face direct democracy as the ideal. This ideal has, however, been subject to a great deal of criticism by feminist philosophers such as Iris Marion Young (1990). These critics argue that the ideal is a metaphysical illusion in that it incorrectly presumes that social relations are unmediated, and that mediation equates with alienation. Face-to-face relations are privileged because they are conceived as immediate and mutually transparent. It is assumed that each party understands the other and recognises the other as they understand themselves (Young 1990, p. 231). The ideal of community denies differences, and basic asymmetry, between subjects. Relations between individual subjects are always mediated by voice and gesture, spacing and temporality, and the presence of third parties. The mediation of relations among persons by the speech and actions of other people is an inescapable aspect of sociality. The greater the time and the distance between subjects the greater the number of persons who stand between other persons (Young 1990 p. 233).

Despite the widely reported difficulties associated with 'community participation', noted earlier, the WHO and many city governments continue to express faith in the locality-based strategy of the Healthy Cities program and related Healthy Cities 'networks'. For instance, in the summary report of the first-five-year (1987–1992) review of the Healthy Cities project it is noted optimistically that:

> Healthy Cities projects, with their focus on local action, have made progress in increasing participation. This meant that local people had a

stronger voice in the decisions of city government that affect health, within an environment that could support change. Projects have enabled groups of city residents working to take direct action to promote their health. (Draper et al. 1993, p. 71)

Nearly all the evidence that is mustered in support of this contention refers to 'resident' 'involvement' in Healthy Cities projects located in 'neighbourhoods' (see Draper et al. 1993, pp. 72–9). These 'neighbourhoods', or their cultural equivalent (for example, 'villages', in Canada), are the primary object of expert knowledge and intervention in nearly all cities that seek to promote the participatory ideal. In large cities, a common method of 'encouraging local action' has been to divide the city into smaller districts and 'neighbourhoods'—or both—for project development, and then to have 'residents' in these areas undertake the gathering of data through community surveys as well as participate in the planning and implementation of projects; for example, through representation on steering committees, management committees, and working groups (Chamberlin 1992, p. 367; Draper et al. 1993, pp. 72–9). Although the methods that have been adopted for identifying 'neighbourhoods' vary somewhat between cities, 'neighbourhoods' tend to be defined according to measures of socioeconomic deprivation such as housing standard or housing type. They may, however, simply describe all 'residents' within an electoral ward of the city government.

The Glasgow Healthy Cities Project is a clear example of the use of this locality-based approach. Applying a technique developed by the Greater Glasgow Health Board, Glasgow has been divided into various 'neighbourhood types' that are area-based distinctions made according to housing type and quality (Black & Womersley 1993, pp. 36–9). In one of these more 'deprived neighbourhoods', Drumchapel, which is classified according to its 'post-war local authority housing with young families, high unemployment and mainly unskilled workers', the assumed identity of interest linked to this locality has been employed in a number of local strategies. These include most notably the training of a pool of 'community health volunteers' who help in the work of the project by undertaking such tasks as giving presentations and seminars to local residents, helping in the community health library, and conducting surveys of children's playgrounds (Draper et al. 1993, p. 79; Niven & Kelley 1994, p. 12). It can be argued that projects such as these merely focus on the symptoms of inequality (that is, 'poverty') rather than on processes sustaining inequality that operate well beyond the local 'neighbourhood' at the regional, national and international levels. They give the impression that 'something is being done', while failing to address broader issues such as regional disparities in wealth, trade imbalances, militarism, racism, unemployment, exploitative work practices, and indeed problems inherent in the Western model of development. In light of failure to address these issues, the locality-based strategy of Healthy Cities can be criticised for simply shifting the blame for problems from individuals onto 'communities'.

In projects such as these, it is assumed at the outset that there is a shared identity of interest among people, and that this can and should be deployed in project development. There is often little recognition of other broader shared experiences and identities of interest linked to class, 'race', ethnicity, age, sexual preference, and so on, that cut across, intersect, or even conflict with, place-based identities. Although Healthy Cities literature acknowledges the importance of other, non place-based affiliations, strategies continue to give priority to place, thereby denying the likely practical and political significance of these other affiliations that transcend particular locales. This is not to deny the shared affiliations, and identities of interest, that exist among those who inhabit defined areas in the city, or to denigrate the efforts of the Healthy Cities workers who strive to improve the situation of those people who have been identified as 'disadvantaged'. Rather, it is to simply draw attention to the importance of other possible bases for identity and action that tend to be excluded, or rendered marginal, in assumptions about the primacy of the place-based sentiments and affiliations.

In their focus on the locality-based 'community' and the consequent denial of other non place-based identities, Healthy Cities and the new public health can be seen to involve the imposition of identity on subjects. The assumption that place has some essential, fixed character whose meaning is transparent to and shared by co-residents denies the fact that space reflects and is a product of social relations and involves continuing political disputation over the meanings and uses of different spaces and places. (On the social relations of space, see the works of Harvey 1990; G. Rose 1993; Lash & Urry 1994; Massey 1994; Hanson & Pratt 1995; Urry 1995). The essentialism of community operates as a device that homogenises, suppresses internal differences, separates and excludes (Woodward 1995, p. 237). It reflects the modernist preoccupation with the rational ordering of space in which a conception of 'otherness' can be admitted only as long as everyone knows their place (see Harvey 1990, pp. 249–52).

The 'politics of exclusion' associated with the essentialism of community, whether by place or other criteria, has been an important topic of feminist analysis and critique (see, for example, Young 1990; hooks 1991; Pettman 1992; Phelan 1994). As has become increasingly apparent, those who make reference to a community in staking their claims to disadvantage and marginalisation have frequently unwittingly adopted the same generalising and 'totalising' strategies they have set out to challenge. Attempts to build solidarities based on assumed harmony and wholeness deny the power relations that always exist between members on the basis of such criteria as place, class, 'race', gender, sexuality and age (that is, their already existing 'communities'), and the ways in which these relations change through time and space. The local community, it is clear, is a site for exclusions. Sociological studies underline the point that those who consider themselves the authentic 'locals' (for example, the 'born and bred') tend to mark a boundary between those with whom they feel they belong and others. Groups gain identity and solidarity by defining themselves in relation to 'outsiders', or even 'incomers' ('newcomers') whom they frequently seek to exclude (Payne 1994).

Richard Sennett (1974, Ch. 2) and Iris Marion Young (1990) have discussed how the idea of the local community operates in American society to produce and legitimate racist and classist behaviour and policy. In many towns, suburbs and neighbourhoods people have an image of their locale as one in which people know each other, and are bound together by a sense of belonging, and by shared values and lifestyles. Yet, as Young indicates, this image is nearly always partial in that it usually represents an image promoted by a dominant group. This image has served to produce 'defensive exclusionary behaviour: pressuring the black family that buys a house on the block to leave, beating up the black youths who come into "our" neighbourhood, zoning against the construction of multi-unit dwellings', and so on (1990, p. 235). In his Australian study, *Smalltown*, Dempsey (1990) describes how particular groups are marginalised or excluded for breaching core Smalltown values or challenging the position of its community. Various categories of 'deviant' individuals who reside either within the neighbourhood or outside it serve as foils for facilitating Smalltown's definition of itself as a community. These include the 'no-hopers' (for example, those who are constantly in trouble with the police, who drink excessively or are alcoholic, or who fail to work); the 'blockies' (recent arrivals who are attracted to the area by the subdivision of land into hobby farming blocks, but who find it difficult to make a living from the land or to find work locally and hence register for unemployment benefits, as a consequence being stereotyped as 'dole bludgers'); deviant women (mainly women who do not fulfil the stereotypical respectable roles as mothers and wives); and the transients (otherwise known as 'two-bob blow-ins', who are criticised for not 'fitting in' or for not 'becoming one of us'; for example, schoolteachers) (1990, pp. 43–52).

Similar sorts of defensive exclusionary practice have also been reported in the United Kingdom. Doreen Massey (1994), for example, has described how 'certain East End communities in the Docklands of London', have deployed particular definitions of place to resist encroachment of new developments, and more particularly of 'yuppies', into what was considered to be 'a working class area'. As Massey argues, reference by the 'locals' to the area's timeless authenticity (that the area is working class and, by implication, should therefore not be changed) denies the early history of the area (the Isle of Dogs), and underplays the political nature of the struggle over ownership of, or rights to, the area. A few centuries earlier, before the industrial revolution, the area consisted of fields and farmland. Fifteen years before the struggles against the 'yuppie' invasion, there were struggles of a similar kind waged in nearby areas. At that time, groups of 'locals' had sought to resist an 'invasion' by ethnic minority groups, and had based their claims for exclusion on the basis that the area was white and working-class. While the political left, on the whole, supported 'the local residents' against the 'yuppies', they resisted the racist version of their claims to exclusive ownership of, or right to live in, that place. Yet, in each case, the conceptual basis of the claim was identical, and involved an 'essentialist' definition of place. As Massey observes, 'the real issue was the politics and social content of the changes under way, including their spatial form, rather than a fight over "the true nature" of a part of east London' (1994, p. 122).

The idea that places have an essential character has become increasingly problematic as the process of globalisation has proceeded. Although there are a number of different conceptions of globalisation, and of its causes and manifestations, it may be sociologically understood as referring to the development of symbolic flows that link diverse localities across the globe in ways that defy both socially constructed boundaries and borders and geography itself (Waters 1994, p. 229; see also Featherstone 1990; Lash & Urry 1994). The development of new communication technologies, including electronic communications such as the World Wide Web, has radically altered time–space relations such that, for an increasing number of people (in the industrially developed world at least) their 'imagined communities' have expanded beyond both the local area and the nation-state.

As a number of commentators have pointed out, 'globalisation' has effectively led to the dissolution of the nation-state, and indeed to the dissolution of the concept of 'society', giving rise to profound questions about the capacities and responsibilities of governments, citizenship and democracy (see, for example, Hindess 1994; McDonald 1994; Waters 1994; Yeatman 1994). This has not undermined the significance of the local or the search for authenticity of place, however. On the contrary, as Lash and Urry have indicated, as spatial and temporal barriers have collapsed there has been greater sensitivity by businesses, governments and 'the general public' to variations of place across time and space and to those factors that define the uniqueness of place (1994, p. 323). With the increasing mobility of capital and of people, places are forced to compete to attract investment, workers and visitors. Consequently there has been a greater concern 'to make places different from each other and to make them consistent with particular images of place' (Lash & Urry 1994, p. 303). People have sought to discover what is authentic in a place, and governments have encouraged activities designed to emphasise local distinctiveness through planning policies. Harvey (1993) has commented that as competition between regions to attract capital has increased, there has been little room left for definitions of place outside of capitalist norms. In order to capture and retain capital investment, places have had to adopt an antagonistic and exclusionary stance vis-à-vis other places.

The image of the local community has been extensively commodified by many urban developers for the purpose of marketing residential properties; with the support of local authorities, these developers have imposed detailed regulations and restrictions on developments in order to ensure the purity of their 'product'. The residential community, along with the marketplace, has been the primary source for most of the dominant images of urban life, past and present. Residential communities have been portrayed as 'constantly changing, free-flowing networks of human relationships centred in the home and family' (Judd 1995, p. 145). This ideal has been exploited by residential developers in the creation of 'new walled communities' or 'gated communities', so-called because of a passing or imagined resemblance to the walled cities of the Middle Ages. Although Judd's analysis is centred on the United States, where the enclosure of commercial and residential space has become a ubiquitous feature of cities, it is evident that similar developments are occurring in the cities of other countries, thereby creating spatially segregated environments. As Judd observes, 'whereas historical notions of community evoke images of organic complexity and change, developers have learned to fine-tune their projects to achieve segregation and isolation' (1995, p. 159). Employing sophisticated methods of 'market segmentation', involving the 'packaging' of 'products' with extremely specialised groups in mind, such as single people, retirees and wealthy couples, developers have in effect created 'ghettoes' of homogenised neighbourhoods.

The partitioning of urban space into these exclusive enclaves has been a potent means of reinforcing ethnic, class, sexual and other divisions, and has been made possible by the appropriation of the idea of the local community. The ultimate irony of this attempt to create a unique sense of place is that planners and developers have ended up creating places that share a certain sameness in their appearance and character (Harvey 1993, p. 8). In their calculated attempts to attract capital to their areas, local governments have supported these developments through their planning processes. It is these very same planning processes that, according to the new public health philosophies, are supposed to bring about the 'healthy' city by creating 'healthy public policy' and promoting citizen 'empowerment'.

The model of the good society based upon decentralised, self-sufficient, face-to-face 'communities' is not only unrealistic and politically undesirable, but avoids the political question of just relations among such decentralised 'communities'. It denies the material conditions presently affecting people's lives (for example, widespread unemployment, unsatisfactory working conditions, physical isolation, and the practical consequences of the emphasis on entrepreneurialism and commodity consumption), and leaves completely unaddressed the question of how such small 'communities' relate to one another. In light of the increasing trend towards the development of segregated spatial communities, referred to above, the idea that there is a shared identity of interest even within a single city is highly problematic. Politics needs to be conceived of as a relationship, across time and space of strangers who do not understand one another in a subjective and immediate sense (see Young 1990, pp. 233–4).

It also needs to be acknowledged that 'communities' can exist without being in the same locality—from networks of close associates or friends to major religious, ethnic or political entities (Massey 1994, p. 153). The notion of 'imagined communities', proposed by Benedict

Anderson, acknowledges that a 'community' can involve 'comradeship' and 'fraternity' and yet members may never know most of their fellow members, or meet or hear them (1991, p. 7). With the aforementioned developments in new communications technologies, a whole range of new networks of relations are developing on the basis of shared interests and positions that do not involve a shared 'sense of place' or direct, face-to-face encounters. In the global economy, populations are highly mobile, and locality may provide only a minor basis for identity. Different categories of people have varying degrees of access to, and mobility within, different spatio-temporal configurations according to gender, 'race', ethnicity, age, socioeconomic status, sexuality, and so on, and therefore construct diverse meanings around space and place (for example, levels of 'safety', opportunities for personal mobility, degrees of 'homeliness', and so on).

There is a growing body of geographical literature highlighting the unique conceptions and uses of spaces by gay and lesbian people (for example, Binnie 1995; Rothenberg 1995; Woodward 1995). These spaces are often invisible to the dominant heterosexual 'community' because they have been excluded from the hetero-dominant narratives on the city and its spaces and are 'written out' of mainstream academic theory. Some groups, such as young people, may not be invisible as such but may be vigorously policed and therefore have a sense of having 'no space of their own' (White 1990). The persistent identification of 'community' with place, conceived of as a single, fixed, authentic entity, diverts attention from the power relations of space and from the diverse constructions of place and the way these constructions change through time and across different contexts.

These comments, it should be stressed, should not be interpreted as an outright dismissal of the strategic uses of 'community', which have proved useful for those seeking to make visible their identity and to press their claims to disadvantage and marginalisation. 'Community' is a site of shared injustice, of a sense of solidarity and of resistance. The strategy of strategic essentialism (Spivak 1988; 1993, pp. 3–5) that has been adopted in relation to the identity politics of feminists, blacks, and gay and lesbian people, and which involves the strategic use of essence as a mobilising slogan or master word, deploys some notion of a material or 'imagined' community. The dichotomies relied on to conceptualise spatial notions of community in Healthy Cities and the new public health, however, serve to deny identities that transcend place, in effect rendering them invisible. In particular, they serve to deny the fact that everyone always already belongs to, and is defined by, a multitude of 'communities'. As Phelan (1994) notes, there is no such thing as being without 'community', nor does 'the community' exist beyond the 'being-in-common' of particular people. She proposes that 'community' be viewed in processual terms; that is, as simultaneously constituted by and constitutive of persons. Our 'communities' are constantly in flux, and therefore we will have many overlapping and shifting identities. Consequently, the attempt to delimit community by way of prescribing or imposing a criterion of membership can have oppressive implications and serve to restrict possibilities for identity and experience (Phelan 1994, pp. 81, 90).

CONCLUDING COMMENTS

The use of the term 'community participation' in the new public health has lent weight to the claim that the project is a progressive social movement for change, in that it is in opposition to dominant relations of power. Our analysis, which has focused on a number of unexamined regulatory implications of the imperative to 'participate', casts doubt on this claim. The deployment in health promotion and the new public health of the terms 'participation', 'community', and 'empowerment', all of which have strong positive associations, has served to obscure the ways in which power operates by maximising the utility of subjects for the fulfilment of certain rational administrative goals. It is no 'accident' that at the very same time as there have emerged widespread concerns about 'eco-crisis', there has also been a focus on active citizenship. The responsible citizen is one who is able to demonstrate her or his commitment to 'the environment' through 'participation' in 'healthy', 'sustainable' practices.

Calls for the development of a more democratic body politic have obvious broad appeal. Few would quibble with the argument that all citizens should have the opportunity to shape the circumstances in which they live. The question of exactly what sort of society is prefigured by the use of the particular interventions prescribed by the discourses of the new public health, however, has yet to be considered in any detail. It is significant that the question of how one might begin to challenge established hierarchies of power, such as those that exist between experts and non-experts, has not been explored to any real extent in the new public health literature. Neo-liberal democratic structures and values, and the dominance of scientific, rational knowledge, are taken as givens and as necessarily supportive of efforts towards 'liberation' and 'self-actualisation'.

Within the neo-liberal democratic framework, 'community participation' is represented as 'empowering' (pre-social) subjects through the deployment of rational knowledge and rational techniques of administration. This discourse does not recognise the 'constitutive' and regulatory power of expert knowledges which have remained largely immune to critical scrutiny. Subjects are called upon to regulate themselves in conformity with the demands of neo-liberal democratic structures and values, not in opposition to them. There is no recognition of the full extent of demands and responsibilities required of those who do 'participate' in prescribed ways, nor acknowledgment of the regulations and exclusions that operate in respect to those who for whatever reason do not or cannot 'participate'. That there has been little analysis and critique of the concept of 'community participation' in the new public health literature attests to its strong evaluative force and to the difficulty of articulating theories and developing social practices that do not conform to the norms of neo-liberal democratic discourse.

An obvious starting point for the development of an alternative discourse is to critique the assumption of the autonomous rational subject whose identity is stable and pre-social and therefore unmediated by relations of power and knowledge. As we have explained in our discussion of 'community', identity is by no means fixed, stable and unitary. We occupy a multiplicity of constantly shifting subject positions and corresponding selves. This is effectively denied by the discourse of the new public health, which adopts idealised and romanticised notions of the social actor and of social relations. The task of thinking about and working towards the development of alternative forms of association that allow for a diverse range of being, thought and action is difficult given the constraints and dichotomies of neo-liberal discourse. It is important, however, that those who are serious about developing a more equitable, tolerant society begin to develop a language and practices that acknowledge the complex interactions between power, knowledge, community, subjectivity and embodiment.

LIBRARY, UNIVERSITY OF CHESTER

Conclusion

In this book we have analysed a number of discourses, practices, strategies and assumptions central to 'the new public health', seeking to show how they are located within certain ways of seeing subjectivity, embodiment, and the material and social world. A strong theme emerging from the discussions in this book is the manifold ways in which the new public health is directed, overtly or covertly, towards the 'making up' of specific kinds of individuals. We began our discussion by noting that the new public health is at its core a moral enterprise that involves prescriptions about how we should live our lives and conduct our bodies, both individually and collectively. The new public health contributes towards understandings of citizenship and communities, and of the relationship of individuals to other humans, other living things and the non-living world. We have also drawn attention to the dominant concept of 'risk' and how it is phrased as a property of individuals or as an external threat, and emphasised the importance of risk for the ontology and conduct of selves and bodies. We have addressed the central role played by concepts of place and space in the new public health discourses, particularly in relation to notions of the 'healthy city', the 'community' and 'the environment'. We have further shown how certain social groups—the poor, the working class, women, gay men and lesbians, non-Europeans—and geographical locations—for example, the city, the slums, working-class areas, the continent of Africa—have historically been designated in Western societies as the contaminating 'other', against which public health measures are undertaken. Despite its rhetoric of egalitarianism, the new public health continues this routine of distinguishing between 'clean' or 'safe' and 'dirty' or 'risky' places and people. The central monitoring strategies of the new public

174

LIBRARY, UNIVERSITY OF CHESTER

health—epidemiology, statistical surveys, and the calculation and attribution of risk—serve to define and delimit notions of 'normality' and 'pathology' for both groups and individuals.

Many people have thrown their support behind the new public health because they are genuinely concerned about such issues as inequalities in health, lack of access to health care services, the constraints of bureaucracy, professional dominance, the limits of biomedicine, and environmental degradation, and are seeking an alternative vision of a 'healthier', 'more sustainable' society and ecosystem. Part of the broad appeal of the new public health is undoubtedly due to its adoption of a language of 'empowerment' and a rhetoric advocating social and environmental change. We have argued, however, that the moral and political implications of the new public health apparatus tend to be obscured by a post-Enlightenment modernist discourse that emphasises the role of science and rationality in social progress and the liberation of the human condition. The arguments and evidence presented in this book indicate the need for a more critical appraisal of the new public health, whose agenda has been largely set by professional experts and is closely aligned with official objectives. New public health knowledges and related practices have implications that may not be in accordance with what its supporters envisage.

One central tension emerging from our sociological analysis of the new public health is the relationship between the state and the individual. Although much of the apparatus of the new public health is invested in state-funded and state-run organisations, particularly within local and federal bureaucracies, it is clear that the discourses of the new public health seek constantly to shift the responsibility of the state for protecting the public's health from the state to members of the public themselves. This shift, as we have argued, is supported by the neo-liberal humanist philosophies held by governments in contemporary Western societies. While new public health authorities and agencies continue to adopt overtly coercive strategies such as quarantine, isolation and enforced medical treatment when they seem required and most justified (such as in the face of a serious epidemic of infectious disease), they are equally, if not more, reliant upon the use of strategies that position citizens as acting of their own free will and in their own interests to protect their own health. These discourses are particularly articulated in the goals and practices of health promotion and community participation. Discourses of personal responsibility and good citizenship have potentially great appeal to the late modern subject, who has been acculturated to accept and privilege the notion of autonomous individuality, not simply through health-related discourses and institutions but also through such institutions as the family, the mass media, and the education and legal systems. As a result, the new public health philosophies tend to make eminent 'sense' because of their emphasis on people participating in activities to improve their own health status. It is for this reason, among others, that the new public health philosophies, discourses and strategies have been little challenged thus far.

We have argued, however, that the strategies of self-care that have become central to the philosophy of public health can lead to a narcissistic preoccupation with the self. The notion that individuals should conduct themselves like an enterprise implies that they should be in competition with others and seek to maximise their own potential even when, as is invariably the case, this is at the expense of others who are less able or less willing to conform to dominant sociocultural norms. A strong emphasis on the ethic of self-care would seem to be directly at odds with the stated ideals in the new public health of nurturing social support, redressing inequality, and creating a tolerant, democratic polity. It can serve to divert attention from increasing inequalities in wealth and power and from attacks on established rights during a period of retreat from welfare provision. Although the development of a new duties discourse implies empathy and concern for fellow citizens and 'the environment', it is not clear how this can be reconciled with competitive individualism and entrepreneurial ideals.

Science itself has been directly implicated in systems of domination and there is now abundant research, particularly from feminist perspectives, that analyses the ways in which science reinforces inequalities in power and knowledge at the local and global levels (see, for example, Harding 1986; Haraway 1991; Braidotti et al. 1994). This work highlights the role of underlying dualisms—subject/object, mind/body, male/female, nature/culture, truth/falsity, public/private, clean/dirty, and so on—in sustaining relations of power through processes of exclusion and hierarchical ordering. In the view of Braidotti et al.,

> Dualism, in the masculinist hegemonic thinking that marks the production of Western science, is a system of exclusion of 'others' from patriarchal subjectivity. The very definition of 'the scientific mind' is coterminous with rationality, masculinity and power. The scientist as model for the subject of knowledge is therefore defined in a set of hierarchical relations to others: the non-scientists. Feminists have criticized scientific discourse as an account of the world that systematically

devalues every category that is 'other' than the male, Western, bourgeois self: women, children, other races, foreign cultures, lower classes, handicapped people and nature. (1994, p. 31)

As Braidotti et al. point out, the dualistic ordering of reality affects individuals' sense of their identity and of their place in the world, whether they are men or women. It is a hierarchical ordering that gives priority to male over female, mind over body, culture over nature, subject over object, and so on. The principles of hierarchy, domination and control are deeply inscribed in Western thinking, yet are made to appear 'normal', 'natural', and altogether neutral (Braidotti et al. 1994, p. 30).

This important work has so far made little impact on mainstream public health thinking about how problems might be constituted, conceptualised and solved. We have emphasised the continuing belief in the power of science, in social progress through science, and in the rational control of problems as they are evident in the discourses and strategies of the new public health, at many points in our discussion. Belief in science is manifest in the use of metaphors such as those applied in descriptions of the 'healthy' city (Chapter 5), in the rational ordering of space (Chapters 2, 4, 5 and 6), in theories of disease aetiology and in the calculation of risk (Chapters 2, 3 and 4). As we have suggested, the use of natural metaphors in the government of the social has a long history in modernist discourse and has been an important means of setting limits on permissible explanations of the body politic. The idea that social systems are 'naturally' harmonious, stable and equilibrant denies conflict and power relations and serves to 'naturalise' inequality. A questioning of science must entail consideration of how science presently operates within existing systems of power to 'normalise' certain patterns of action and systems of thought, such that they appear self-evident, given and therefore beyond dispute.

If the groundwork is to be laid for a society that is more equitable, more tolerant of difference and more likely to protect and ameliorate the health status of individuals, then priority must be given to challenging the dominance of science in social explanation and in the control of problems. We are not arguing that science as a system of knowledge and action should be rejected wholesale. We are simply challenging its position as the most privileged way of approaching social problems, by showing how science works to construct these problems and by seeking to identify its often unintended outcomes. As we have shown, situated or lay knowledges have far less opportunity to compete with privileged science in defining and dealing with public health problems, and this has often meant that lay individuals have felt far less able to challenge 'expert' knowledges or to act when they perceive problems to exist. As Wynne (1996) argues, the objectivist discourses and rationales of science are often experienced by lay people as alien and impoverished models of human nature, values and social relations, clashing with people's own lived and embodied experiences, values and localised knowledges.

The work of Foucault has been of great assistance to those who seek to develop new perspectives on the workings of science in modern systems of governance and on developing ways of utilising, subverting or resisting it. As Foucault (1980) explains, science has been used not simply to 'explain' reality, but to produce, control and normalise it. One of the important insights of Foucault's work, and indeed of those scholarly writings that fall under the rubric of 'poststructuralism', is in drawing attention to the interrelationship between discourses, knowledges, practices and power relations when conducting sociopolitical analysis and critique. It is important that the representational practices of such hegemonic knowledges as science and medicine be laid open to scrutiny wherever they appear so that their assumptions can be examined for their moral and political effects.

Poststructuralist theory has also questioned the notions of the unified self and of fixed subject positions that we have identified as central to new public health understandings. Belief in the knowledges of science and medicine is closely tied to faith in the discourse of liberation which, we have argued, should also be opened up to more thorough scrutiny. In our discussion, we drew particular attention to the unexamined implications of the neo-liberal notion of 'freedom' which is pegged to a concept of the autonomous, unified and rational subject who approaches life as if it were an enterprise. As we suggested, this is an idealised concept which should be rejected in favour of a view of the self as unstable, multifarious and (at least in part) discursively constructed. The idealisation of the 'normal', 'healthy' subject as one endowed with certain 'natural' capacities and inclinations fails to recognise the multiplicity of possible subject positions, and can serve to coerce, marginalise, stigmatise and discriminate against those who do not or cannot conform with the ideal. This ideal denies difference—whether this is based on social class, gender, sexuality, 'race', ethnicity, physical ability, or age—and the kinds of personal commitments and demands that are required of those who are called upon to conform to it. There are real political and material effects that may emerge from the employment of such discourses, including social and economic discrimination, disadvantage and exclusion.

In Chapter 6 we outlined some of the problems with the notion of a fixed subjectivity in our discussion of 'community'. As we argued there, reference to a single, shared basis for identity by those seeking to make visible an identity or to press their claims to disadvantage and marginalisation can be strategically useful. One should seek, however, to challenge imposed identities on the grounds that they reinforce intolerance of difference and of diversity. In particular, the assumption that 'health' should be a priority for all, and act as a marker of self-control and a criterion for citizenship, should be questioned. We have pointed to some of the exclusions associated with the assumption that everyone should work and live to maximise their health. 'Healthism' contributes to a general intolerance of those who are unable or unwilling to subscribe to the dominant sociocultural norms, and it should therefore be challenged. If society is to be tolerant of difference, provide scope for the full expression of all our identities, and offer support for all its members regardless of background, disposition or ability, then the status of this type of knowledge itself must be questioned.

In our discussions of the ways in which the new public health seeks to construct specific subject positions, we do not argue for a view that sees individuals as passive, manipulated dupes. Whether or not public health strategies are overtly coercive or reliant upon the alignment of individuals' personal objectives, we need to acknowledge the way that individuals often fail to conduct themselves according to the goals of public health. Foucault's reflections on the 'practices of the self' in his later writings suggest that although individuals constitute themselves as subjects in relation to external imperatives, there is a complex relationship between dominant norms and individual behaviour and actions, leaving much room for playful engagement with norms and even for resistance (see, for example, Foucault 1988, 1991). Foucault was interested in the possibilities that this presented for the development of modes of existence that broke with the 'normalising' tendencies in contemporary society, particularly the endless examination of one's inner self which he saw as a dominant characteristic of modern society (see Best & Kellner 1991, p. 63; McNay 1992, pp. 63, 86). The idea of one's life as the enterprise of oneself would suggest that there is some degree of open-endedness and indeterminacy at play in the process of privately managing risk. Public health interventions are consequently liable to produce outcomes at variance with what the experts may have intended. Thus, although rules for personal conduct are recommended to the individual by the social context, often issuing forth from dominant institutions such as public health, different contexts provide different degrees of freedom to act and to interpret, negotiate and resist norms: 'bodies are active creators of new power relations, and sustain individuals in their confrontations with and against systems of power' (Outram 1989, p. 23). Individuals routinely turn imposed laws, practices and representations to their own ends as a way of 'making do' within, and of subverting, the dominant relations of power (de Certeau 1984).

While there is much evidence of many people's conformity at either the conscious or the unconscious levels to the imperatives of health issuing forth from the state and other sites, it is also clear that people frequently either directly resist these imperatives, ignore them or fail to take them up in favour of other practices of the self. The attempts of public health reformers to enshrine legislation directed at restricting individual freedom has historically been met with opposition on the part of citizens up in arms about a 'Nanny' state. At the more mundane level, people's desire to engage in pleasurable or playful activities, such as their continued consumption of tobacco, their refusal to give up favourite foods to lose weight or their choice not to engage in condom use when participating in sexual activities, is evidence of lack of conformity to public health imperatives, despite widespread knowledge and acceptance of these imperatives. Such activities may be conscious floutings of public health advice or may simply represent attempts to construct subjectivity through alternative practices, privileging the pleasures of smoking, for example, over its imputed long-term health effects (see Lupton 1995, Ch. 5 for an expansion of this argument).

In writing this book we have not sought to prescribe alternatives for the new public health, to construct ways of developing a 'newer' (and by implication 'better') public health. We have simply attempted to suggest different ways of viewing the rationales and practices of the new public health, seeking a more reflexive way of viewing it through disruption of its taken-for-granted beliefs and approaches. Thus, for example, we have pointed out that attempts to 'emancipate' or 'empower' marginalised groups through such strategies as community participation, based on humanistic, neo-liberal principles, may be regarded as ever more complex ways of defining, regulating and normalising the members of such groups. As Usher and Edwards assert: 'Oppression and emancipation are not polar opposites, the one excluding the other . . . they are co-implicated in ever shifting patterns arising from on-going struggles' (1994, p. 226). As this suggests, attempts at emancipation, well meaning as they are, often serve to further constrain and disadvantage those individuals to whom they are directed by prescribing specified ways of behaving. Some readers who are engaged as workers in the new public health may decide that in the absence of viable alternatives their activities remain worthwhile, despite the questions we have raised. Nonetheless, the very raising of these questions, we hope, may serve to unsettle some of the often unexamined assumptions prevailing in those who support the new public health initiatives. This may lead to more reflexive practice and ways of engaging with the 'public', and to a recognition of the tendency towards totalising statements and judgments and of the uncertainties and contradictions in the area that are often left unacknowledged.

References

Adam, B. (1995) *The Rise of a Gay and Lesbian Movement* (revised edition), Twayne Publishers, New York

Anderson, B. (1991) *Imagined Communities: Reflections on the Origin and Spread of Nationalism*, Verso, London

Armstrong, D. (1983) *Political Anatomy of the Body: Medical Knowledge in the Twentieth Century*, Cambridge University Press, Cambridge

——(1993) 'Public health spaces and the fabrication of identity', *Sociology*, vol. 27, no. 3, pp. 393–410

Arnstein, S. (1969) 'Eight rungs on a ladder of citizen participation', *AIP Journal*, July, pp. 216–24

Ashton, J. (1992a) 'The origins of Healthy Cities', in J. Ashton (ed.), *Healthy Cities*, Open University Press, Milton Keynes

——(ed.) (1992b) *Healthy Cities*, Open University Press, Milton Keynes

Ashton, J., Grey, P. & Barnard, K. (1986) 'Healthy cities: WHO's New Public Health initiative', *Health Promotion*, vol. 1, no. 3, pp. 319–24

Ashton, J. & Seymour, H. (1988) *The New Public Health: The Liverpool Experience*, Open University Press, Milton Keynes

Atrens, D. (1994) 'The questionable wisdom of a low-fat diet and cholesterol reduction', *Social Science & Medicine*, vol. 39, no. 3, pp. 433–47

Australian Consumers' Association (1995) 'Something in the air', *Choice*, vol. 36, no. 7, pp. 16–19

Backett, K. & Davison, C. (1992) 'Rational or reasonable? Perceptions of health at different stages of life', *Health Education Journal*, vol. 51, no. 2, pp. 55–9

Badura, B. & Kickbusch, I. (eds) (1991) *Health Promotion Research: Towards a New Social Epidemiology*, WHO Regional Publications, European Series No. 37, WHO, London

Balshem, M., Oxman, G., van Rooyen, D. & Girod, K. (1992) 'Syphilis, sex and crack cocaine: images of risk and morality', *Social Science & Medicine*, vol. 35, no. 2, pp. 147–60

Bassuk, E. (1986) 'The rest cure: repetition or resolution of Victorian women's conflicts?', in S. Suleiman (ed.), *The Female Body in Western Culture: Contemporary Perspectives*, Cambridge, MA, Harvard University Press

Baum, F. (1993) 'Healthy Cities and change: social movement or bureaucratic tool?', *Health Promotion International*, vol. 8, no. 1, pp. 31–40

Baum, F., Cooke, R., Crowe, K., Traynor, M. and Clarke, B. (1990) *Healthy Cities Noarlunga Pilot Project Evaluation, July 1990*, Southern Community Health Research Unit, South Australian Health Commission, Adelaide

Bauman, Z. (1992a) *Intimations of Postmodernity*, Routledge, London

——(1992b) *Mortality, Immortality and Other Life Strategies*, Polity, Cambridge

Beck, U. (1992) *Risk Society: Towards a New Modernity*, Sage, London

——(1994) 'The naturalistic fallacy of the ecological movement', in A. Giddens, D. Held, D. Hubert, D. Seymour & J. Thompson (eds), *The Polity Reader in Social Theory*, Polity, Cambridge

——(1996) 'Risk society and the provident state', in S. Lash, B. Szerszynski & B. Wynne (eds), *Risk, Environment and Modernity: Towards a New Ecology*, Sage, London

Beck, U., Giddens, A. & Lash, S. (1994) *Reflexive Modernization: Politics, Tradition and the Aesthetics in the Modern Social Order*, Polity, Cambridge

Becker, M. (1987) 'The cholesterol saga: whither health promotion?', *Annals of Internal Medicine*, vol. 106, pp. 623–6

Bell, D. & Valentine, G. (eds) (1995) *Mapping Desire: Geographies of Sexualities*, Routledge, London

Berger, J. (1972) *Ways of Seeing*, Pelican, London

Best, S. & Kellner, D. (1991) *Postmodern Theory: Critical Interrogations*, The Guilford Press, New York

Binnie, J. (1995) 'Trading places: consumption, sexuality and the production of queer space', in D. Bell & G. Valentine (eds), *Mapping Desire: Geographies of Sexualities*, Routledge, London

Black, D. & Womersley, J. (eds) (1993) *Glasgow's Health, Old Problems—New Opportunities*, Health Information Unit, Department of Public Health, Glasgow

Bland, L. (1992) 'Feminist vigilantes of late-Victorian England', in C. Smart (ed.), *Regulating Womanhood: Historical Essays on Marriage, Motherhood and Sexuality*, Routledge, London

Bloor, M. (1995) *The Sociology of HIV Transmission*, Sage, London

Bloor, M., Goldberg, D. & Emslie, J. (1991) 'Ethnostatistics and the AIDS epidemic', *British Journal of Sociology*, vol. 42, no. 1, pp. 131–9

Bloor, M., Samphier, M. & Prior, L. (1987) 'Artefact explanations of inequalities in health: an assessment of the evidence', *Sociology of Health & Illness*, vol. 9, no. 3, pp. 231–4

Bordo, S. (1993) *Unbearable Weight*, University of California Press, Berkeley

Bracht, N. (1991) 'Citizen participation in community health: principles for effective partnerships', in B. Badura & I. Kickbusch (eds), *Health Promotion Research: Towards a New Social Epidemiology*, WHO Regional Publications, European Series No. 37, WHO, London

Bracht, N. & Tsouros, A. (1990) 'Principles and strategies of effective community participation', *Health Promotion International*, vol. 5, no. 3, pp. 199–208

Braidotti, R., Charkiewicz, E., Hausler, S., & Wieringa, S. (1994) *Women, the Environment and Sustainable Development: Towards a Theoretical Synthesis*, Zed Books in association with INSTRAW, London

Broom, D. (1989) 'Masculine medicine, feminine illness: gender and health', in G. Lupton & J. Najman (eds), *Sociology of Health and Illness: Australian Readings*, Macmillan, Melbourne

——(1994) 'Taken down and used against us: women's health centres', in C. Waddell & A. Petersen (eds), *Just Health: Inequality in Illness, Care and Prevention*, Churchill Livingstone, Melbourne

Bruce, N. (1991) 'Epidemiology and the new public health: implications for training', *Social Science & Medicine*, vol. 32, no. 1, pp. 103–6

Bunton, R. (1992) 'More than a woolly jumper: health promotion as social regulation', *Critical Public Health*, vol. 3, no. 2, pp. 4–11

Bunton, R., Nettleton, S. & Burrows, R. (1995) *The Sociology of Health Promotion: Critical Analyses of Consumption, Lifestyle and Risk*, Routledge, London

Burchell, G. (1991) 'Peculiar interests: civil society and governing "the system of natural liberty"', in G. Burchell, C. Gordon & P. Miller (eds), *The Foucault Effect: Studies in Governmentality*, Harvester Wheatsheaf, Hemel Hempstead

Burchell, G., Gordon & Miller, P. (eds) (1991) *The Foucault Effect: Studies in Governmentality*, Harvester Wheatsheaf, Hemel Hempstead

Burgmann, V. (1993) *Power and Protest: Movements for Change in Australian Society*, Allen & Unwin, Sydney

Burrows, R., Bunton, R., Muncer, S. & Gillen, K. (1995) 'The efficacy of health promotion, health economics and late modernism', *Health Education Research: Theory & Practice*, vol. 10, no. 2, pp. 241–9

Cartwright, L. (1995) *Screening the Body: Tracing Medicine's Visual Culture*, University of Minnesota Press, Minneapolis

Castel, R. (1991) 'From dangerousness to risk', in G. Burchell, C. Gordon & P. Miller (eds), *The Foucault Effect: Studies in Governmentality*, Harvester Wheatsheaf, Hemel Hempstead

Chamberlin, R. W. (1992) 'Think globally act locally: the WHO Healthy Cities Project', *Developmental and Behavioural Pediatrics*, vol. 13, no. 5, pp. 366–7

Chittagong City Corporation (1993) *Chittagong Healthy City Project, Health for All—All for Health, City Health Plan 1993*, Chittagong City Corporation and World Health Organization, Chittagong

City of Liverpool (undated) *The City Health Plan: The Context for the Plan*, Section One (First of Three Sections), Liverpool Healthy City 2000, City of Liverpool, Liverpool

Comaroff, J. (1993) 'The diseased heart of Africa: medicine, colonialism, and the black body', in S. Lindenbaum & M. Lock (eds), *Knowledge, Power and Practice: the Anthropology of Medicine and Everyday Life*, University of California Press, Berkeley

Commonwealth Department of Community Services and Health (1988) *World Health Organization: A Brief Summary of Its Work*, AGPS, Canberra

Commonwealth Department of Human Services and Health (1996) *Draft National Men's Health Strategy*, AGPS, Canberra

Corbin, A. (1986) *The Foul and the Fragrant: Odour and the French Social Imagination*, Harvard University Press, Cambridge, MA

Corner, J., Richardson, K. & Fenton, N. (1990) 'Textualizing risk: TV discourse and the issue of nuclear energy', *Media, Culture & Society*, vol. 12, pp. 105–24

Coward, R. (1989) *The Whole Truth: the Myth of Alternative Health*, Faber & Faber, London

Craddock, S. (1995) 'Sewers and scapegoats: spatial metaphors of smallpox in nineteenth century San Francisco', *Social Science & Medicine*, vol. 41, no. 7, pp. 957–68

Crawford, R. (1977) 'You are dangerous to your health: the ideology and politics of victim blaming', *International Journal of Health Services*, vol. 7, pp. 663–80

——(1994) 'The boundaries of the self and the unhealthy other: reflections on health, culture and AIDS', *Social Science & Medicine*, vol. 38, no. 10, pp. 1347–65

Curtice, L. (1993) 'Strategies and values: research and the WHO Healthy Cities project in Europe', in J. Davies & M. Kelly (eds), *Healthy Cities: Research and Practice*, Routledge, London

da Silva, W. (1995) 'The plague bomb', *Australian Financial Review Magazine*, September, pp. 38–45

Davey Smith, G., Phillips, A. & Neaton, J. (1992) 'Smoking as "independent" risk factor for suicide: illustration of an artefact from observational epidemiology?', *The Lancet*, no. 340, pp. 709–12

Davies, J. & Kelly, M. (eds) (1993) *Healthy Cities: Research and Practice*, Routledge, London

Davison, C., Davey Smith, G. & Frankel, S. (1991) 'Lay epidemiology and the prevention paradox: the implications of coronary candidacy for health education', *Sociology of Health & Illness*, vol. 13, no. 1, pp. 1–19

Davison, C., Frankel, S. & Davey Smith, G. (1992) 'The limits of lifestyle: re-assessing "fatalism" in the popular culture of illness prevention', *Social Science & Medicine*, vol. 34, no. 6, pp. 675–85

Davison, C., Macintyre, S. & Davey Smith, G. (1994) 'The potential social impact of predictive genetic testing for susceptibility to common chronic diseases: a review and proposed research agenda', *Sociology of Health & Illness*, vol. 16, no. 3, pp. 340–71

Dayton, L. (1994) 'It's a biological fact: women need more sleep', *Sydney Morning Herald*, 15 August

——(1995a) 'Apocalypse soon, say forecasters', *Sydney Morning Herald*, 28 October

——(1995b) 'Killer virus jumps the species barrier', *Sydney Morning Herald*, 13 May

Dean, M. (1994) '"A social structure of many souls": moral regulation, government, and self-formation', *Canadian Journal of Sociology*, vol. 19, no. 2, pp. 145–68

de Certeau, M. (1984) *The Practice of Everyday Life*, University of California Press, Berkeley

de Leeuw, E. (1989) 'Concepts in health promotion: the notion of relativism', *Social Science & Medicine*, vol. 29, no. 11, pp. 1281–8

——(1994) 'Healthy City Conferences booming industry?', *Research for Healthy Cities*, 6 (January), pp. 1–4

Dempsey, K. (1990) *Smalltown: A Study of Social Inequality, Cohesion and Belonging*, Oxford University Press, Melbourne

de Swaan, A. (1990) *The Management of Normality: Critical Essays in Health and Welfare*, Routledge, London

Detels, R. & Breslow, L. (1984) 'Current scope', in W. Holland, R. Detels & G. Knox with E. Breeze (eds), *Oxford Textbook of Public Health, Volume 1*, Oxford University Press, Oxford

Dietz, M. (1994) 'Context is all: feminism and theories of citizenship', in B. Turner & P. Hamilton (eds), *Citizenship: Critical Concepts*, Routledge, London and New York

Diprose, R. (1994) *The Bodies of Women: Ethics, Embodiment and Sexual Difference*, Routledge, London

Dixon, J. (1989) 'The limits and potential of community development for personal and social change', *Community Health Studies*, vol. 13, pp. 82–92

Donzelot, J. (1979) *The Policing of Families*, Pantheon Books, New York

Douglas, M. (1980) *Purity and Danger: An Analysis of Concepts of Pollution and Taboo*, Routledge & Kegan Paul, London

Douglas, M. (1992) *Risk and Blame: Essays in Cultural Theory*, Routledge, London

Dow, S. (1995) 'Push for prostate screening', *Sydney Morning Herald*, 2 January

Draper, P. (ed.) (1991) *Health Through Public Policy: The Greening of Public Health*, Green Print, London

Draper, R., Curtice, L., Hooper, J. & Goumans, M. (1993) *Healthy Cities Project: Review of the First Five Years (1987–1992)*, WHO Regional Office for Europe, Copenhagen

Duden, B. (1991) *The Woman Beneath the Skin: A Doctor's Patients in Eighteenth-Century Germany*, Harvard University Press, Cambridge, MA

Duhl, L. (1986) 'The healthy city: its function and its future', *Health Promotion*, vol. 1, no. 1, pp. 55–60

—— (1993) 'Conditions for healthy cities: diversity, game boards and social entrepreneurs', *Environment and Urbanization*, vol. 5, no. 2, pp. 112–24

Dutton, K. (1995) *The Perfectible Body: the Western Ideal of Physical Development*, Cassell, London

Easthope, A. (1990) *What a Man's Gotta Do: the Masculine Myth in Popular Culture*, Unwin Hyman, Boston

Elias, N. (1978) *The Civilizing Process*, Urizen, New York

Epstein, J. (1995) *Altered Conditions: Disease, Medicine, and Storytelling*, Routledge, New York

Epstein, P. (1995) 'Emerging diseases and ecosystem instability: new threats to public health', *American Journal of Public Health*, vol. 85, no. 2, 168–72

Evans, D. (1993) *Sexual Citizenship: the Material Construction of Sexualities*, Routledge, London

Evernden, N. (1992) *The Social Creation of Nature*, Johns Hopkins University Press, Baltimore

Ewan, C., Bryant, E. & Calvert, D. (eds) (1991) *Health Implications of Long Term Climatic Change*, AGPS, Canberra

Ewan, C., Bryant, E., Calvert, D. & Garrick, J. (eds) (1993) *Health in the Greenhouse: The Medical and Environmental Health Effects of Global Climate Change*, AGPS, Canberra

Falk, P. (1994) *The Consuming Body*, Sage, London

Featherstone, M. (1990) *Global Culture: Nationalism, Globalization and Modernity*, Sage, London

Figlio, K. (1989) 'Unconscious aspects of health and the public sphere', in B. Richards (ed.), *Crises of the Self: Further Essays on Psychoanalysis and Politics*, Free Association Books, London

Finch, L. (1993) *The Classing Gaze: Sexuality, Class and Surveillance*, Allen & Unwin, Sydney

Finkelstein, J. (1991) *The Fashioned Self*, Polity Press, Cambridge

Fleck, L. (1979/1936) *Genesis and Development of a Scientific Fact*, University of Chicago Press, Chicago

Fletcher, R. (1994) 'Prostate cancer screening and men's health', *Australian Journal of Public Health*, vol. 18, no. 4, pp. 449–51

Fortin, J-P., Groleau, G., O'Neill, M. and Lemieux, V. (1992) *An Instrument for Evaluating Healthy Communities Projects in Quebec*, Université Laval, Quebec City

Foucault, M. (1980) *The History of Sexuality. Volume One: An Introduction*, Vintage Books, New York

——(1984a) 'The politics of health in the eighteenth century', in P. Rabinow (ed.), *The Foucault Reader: An Introduction to Foucault's Thought*, Pantheon Books, New York

——(1984b) 'Space, knowledge, and power', in P. Rabinow (ed.), *The Foucault Reader: An Introduction to Foucault's Thought*, Pantheon Books, New York

——(1988) 'Technologies of the self', in L. Martin, H. Gutman & P. Hutton (eds), *Technologies of the Self: A Seminar with Michel Foucault*, University of Massachusetts Press, Amherst

——(1991) 'The ethic of care for the self as a practice of freedom', in J. Bernauer & D. Rasmussen (eds), *The Final Foucault*, MIT Press, Cambridge, MA

Frankenberg, R. (1993) 'Risk: anthropological and epidemiological narratives of prevention', in S. Lindenbaum & M. Lock (eds), *Knowledge, Power and Practice: the Anthropology of Medicine and Everyday Life*, University of California Press, Berkeley

Fraser, N. & Gordon, L. (1994) 'Civil citizenship and civil society in Central Europe', in B. van Steenbergen (ed.), *The Condition of Citizenship*, Sage, London

Frenk, J. (1993) 'The new public health', *Annual Review of Public Health*, no. 14, pp. 469–90

Fryer, P. (1991) 'Healthy cities', in P. Draper (ed.), *Health Through Public Policy: The Greening of Public Health*, Green Print, London

Fujimura, J. & Chou, D. (1994) 'Dissent in science: styles of scientific practice and the controversy over the cause of AIDS', *Social Science & Medicine*, vol. 38, no. 8, pp. 1017–36

Gaard, G. (1993) 'Living interconnections with animals and nature', in G. Gaard (ed.), *Ecofeminism: Women, Animals, Nature*, Temple University Press, Philadelphia

Garner, D., Garfinkel, P., Schwarz, D. & Thompson, M. (1980) 'Cultural expectation of thinness in women', *Psychological Reports*, no. 47, pp. 483–91

Giddens, A. (1991) *Modernity and Self-Identity: Self and Society in the Late Modern Age*, Polity Press, Cambridge

——(1992) *The Consequences of Modernity*, Polity, Cambridge

Gifford, S. (1986) 'The meaning of lumps: a case study of the ambiguities of risk', in C. Janes, R. Stall & S. Gifford (eds), *Anthropology and Epidemiology: Interdisciplinary Approaches to the Study of Health and Disease*, D. Reidel, Dordrecht, the Netherlands

Gilman, S. (1989) 'AIDS and syphilis: the iconography of disease', in D. Crimp (ed.), *AIDS: Cultural Analysis, Cultural Activism*, MIT Press, Cambridge, MA

——(1993) 'Touch, sexuality and disease', in W. Bynum & R. Porter (eds), *Medicine and the Five Senses*, Cambridge University Press, Cambridge

Goldstein, G. (1995) 'WHO Healthy Cities—an interregional programme framework', paper presented at the International Healthy and Ecological Cities Congress, Madrid, March

Gordon, C. (1991) 'Governmental rationality: an introduction', in G. Burchell, C. Gordon & P. Miller (eds), *The Foucault Effect: Studies in Governmentality*, Harvester Wheatsheaf, Hemel Hempstead

Gordon, D. (1988) 'Tenacious assumptions in western medicine', in M. Lock & D. Gordon (eds), *Biomedicine Examined*, Kluwer, Dordrecht, the Netherlands

Goumans, M. (1992) 'What about healthy networks? An analysis of national healthy cities networks in Europe', *Health Promotion International*, vol. 7, no. 4, pp. 273–81

Greco, M. (1993) 'Psychosomatic subjects and the "duty to be well": personal agency within medical rationality', *Economy & Society*, vol. 22, no. 3, pp. 357–72

Greenpeace Australia (1993) *Solutions for Clean Healthy Cities*, Greenpeace Australia, Sydney

Grosz, E. (1994) *Volatile Bodies: Toward a Corporeal Feminism*, Allen & Unwin, Sydney

Grove-White, R. (1993) 'Environmentalism: a new moral discourse for technological society?', in K. Milton (ed.), *Environmentalism: The View from Anthropology*, Routledge, London

Hacking, I. (1986) 'Making up people', in T. Heller, M. Sosna & D. Wellberg (eds), *Reconstructing Individualism: Autonomy, Individuality, and the Self in Western Thought*, Stanford University Press, Stanford

——(1990) *The Taming of Chance*, Cambridge University Press, New York

——(1991) 'How should we do the history of statistics?', in G. Burchell, C. Gordon & P. Miller (eds), *The Foucault Effect: Studies in Governmentality*, Harvester Wheatsheaf, Hemel Hempstead

Hannaway, C. (1993) 'Environment and miasmata', in W. Bynum & R. Porter (eds), *Comparative Encyclopedia of the History of Medicine*, Routledge, London

Hanson, S. & Pratt, G. (1995) *Gender, Work and Space*, Routledge, New York

Haraway, D. (1991) *Simians, Cyborgs, and Women: The Reinvention of Nature*, Routledge, New York

Harding, S. (1986) *The Science Question in Feminism*, Cornell University Press, Ithaca

Harper, A., Holman, C. & Dawes, V. (1994) *The Health of Populations: An Introduction*, Churchill Livingstone, Melbourne

Harvey, D. (1990) *The Condition of Postmodernity: An Enquiry into the Origins of Cultural Change*, Basil Blackwell, Oxford

——(1993) 'From space to place and back again: reflections on the condition of postmodernity', in J. Bird, B. Curtis, T. Putnam, G. Robertson & L. Tickner (eds), *Mapping the Futures: Local Culture, Global Change*, Routledge, London

Hawe, P. (1994) 'Capturing the meaning of "community" in community intervention evaluation: some contributions from community psychology', *Health Promotion International*, vol. 9, no. 3, pp. 199–210

Hawks, S., Hull, M., Thalman, R. & Richins, P. (1995) 'Review of spiritual health: definition, role, and intervention strategies in health promotion', *American Journal of Health Promotion*, vol. 9, no. 5, pp. 371–8

Health Targets and Implementation Committee (1988) *Health for All Australians*, Australian Government Publishing Service, Canberra

Hearn, J. (1995) 'Imaging the aging of men', in M. Featherstone & A. Wernick (eds), *Images of Aging: Cultural Representations of Later Life*, Routledge, London

Herzlich, C. & Pierret, J. (1987) *Illness and Self in Society*, Johns Hopkins University Press, Baltimore

Hindess, B. (1994) 'The world we have lost?' (Symposium: Globalisation, multiculturalism and rethinking the social), *Australian and New Zealand Journal of Sociology*, vol. 30, no. 3, pp. 234–9

hooks, b. (1991) *Yearning: Race, Gender, and Cultural Politics*, Turnaround, London

Hooper, C.-A. (1992) 'Child sexual abuse and the regulation of women: variations on a theme', in C. Smart (ed.), *Regulating Womanhood: Historical Essays on Marriage, Motherhood and Sexuality*, Routledge, London

Howson, A. (1994) 'The cervix and surveillance: issues for a sociology of the body', paper presented at the BSA Medical Sociology Group Conference, University of York, England, September

Hulley, S., Walsh, J. & Newman, T. (1992) 'Health policy on blood cholesterol: time to change directions', *Circulation*, vol. 86, pp. 1026–9

Ife, J. (1995) *Community Development: Creating Community Alternatives—Vision, Analysis and Practice*, Longman, Melbourne

Illich, I. (1976) *Limits to Medicine: Medical Nemesis: the Expropriation of Health*, Marion Boyers, London

Jackson, D. (1990) *Unmasking Masculinity: A Critical Autobiography*, Unwin Hyman, London

Jackson, P. (1994) 'Passive smoking and ill-health: practice and process in the production of medical knowledge', *Sociology of Health & Illness*, vol. 16, no. 4, pp. 423–47

Jacobus, M., Fox Keller, E. & Shuttleworth, S. (eds) (1990) *Body/Politics: Women and the Discourses of Science*, Routledge, New York

James, A. (1993) 'Eating green(s): discourses of organic food', in K. Milton (ed.), *Environmentalism: The View from Anthropology*, Routledge, London

Janowitz, M. (1994) 'Observations on the sociology of citizenship', in B. Turner & P. Hamilton (eds), *Citizenship: Critical Concepts*, Routledge, London

Johnson, T. (1993) 'Expertise and the state', in M. Gane & T. Johnson (eds), *Foucault's New Domains*, Routledge, London

Jones, A. (1993) 'Defending the border: men's bodies and vulnerability', *Cultural Studies from Birmingham*, vol. 2, pp. 77–123

Judd, D. (1995) 'The rise of the new walled cities', in H. Liggett & D. Perry (eds), *Spatial Practices: Critical Explorations in Social/Spatial Theory*, Sage, Thousand Oaks

Kaufert, P. & O'Neil, J. (1993) 'Analysis of a dialogue on risks in childbirth: clinicians, epidemiologists, and Inuit women', in S. Lindenbaum & M. Lock (eds), *Knowledge, Power and Practice: the Anthropology of Medicine and Everyday Life*, University of California Press, Berkeley

Kelly, G. (1994) 'Who needs a theory of citizenship?', in B. Turner & P. Hamilton (eds), *Citizenship: Critical Concepts*, Routledge, London

Kelly, M., Davies, J. & Charlton, B. (1993) 'Healthy cities: a modern problem or a post-modern solution?', in J. Davies & M. Kelly (eds), *Healthy Cities: Research and Practice*, Routledge, London

Kickbusch, I. (1986) 'Health promotion: a global perspective', *Canadian Journal of Public Health*, vol. 77, pp. 321–6

Kleiner, K. (1995) 'Why low cholesterol can get you down', *New Scientist*, 29 April, p. 10

Koval, R. (1986) *Eating Your Heart Out: Food, Shape and the Body Industry*, Penguin, Ringwood

Kriegler, N. (1994) 'Epidemiology and the web of causation: has anyone seen the spider?', *Social Science & Medicine*, vol. 39, no. 7, pp. 887–903

La Berge, A. (1992) *Mission and Method: The Early Nineteenth-Century French Public Health Movement*, Cambridge University Press, Cambridge

Labonte, R. (1990a) 'Empowerment: notes on professional and community dimensions', *Canadian Review of Social Policy*, no. 26, pp. 64–75

——(1990b) 'Ecology: health and sustainable development', paper prepared for the Integrating Health and the Environment Conference, Australia, April

Lacombe, R. & Poirier, L. (1992) 'The Quebec Network of "Villes et Villages en Santé"', paper prepared for the annual meeting of Healthy Cities National Networks Coordinators—Eindhoven, Holland, August 1989 (updated January 1992)

Lash, S. & Urry, J. (1994) *Economies of Signs and Space*, Sage, London

Last, J. (1987) *Public Health and Human Ecology*, Appleton & Lange, East Norwalk

Latour, B. & Woolgar, S. (1979) *Laboratory Life: the Social Construction of Scientific Facts*, Sage, Beverly Hills

Laughlin, S. & Black, D. (1995) *Poverty and Health, Tools for Change: Ideas, Analysis, Information, Action*, The Public Health Alliance, Birmingham

Lawrence, S. & Bendixen, K. (1992) 'His and hers: male and female anatomy in anatomy texts for US medical students, 1890–1989', *Social Science & Medicine*, vol. 35, no. 7, pp. 925–34

Lear, D. (1995) 'Sexual communication in the age of AIDS: the construction of risk and trust among young adults', *Social Science & Medicine*, vol. 41, no. 9, pp. 1311–23

Levine, M. (1992) 'The implications of constructionist theory for social research on the AIDS epidemic among gay men', in G. Herdt & S. Lindenbaum (eds), *The Time of AIDS: Social Analysis, Theory, and Method*, Sage, Newbury Park

Lewis, J. (1992) 'Women and late-nineteenth century social work', in C. Smart (ed.), *Regulating Womanhood: Historical Essays on Marriage, Motherhood and Sexuality*, Routledge, London

Lilienfeld, A. & Lilienfeld, D. (1982) 'Epidemiology and the public health movement: a historical perspective', *Journal of Public Health Policy*, vol. 3, pp. 140–9

Lindheim, R. & Syme, S. (1983) 'Environments, people, and health', *Annual Review of Public Health*, vol. 4, pp. 335–59

Lupton, D. (1993) 'Is there life after Foucault? Post-structuralism and the health social sciences', *Australian Journal of Public Health*, vol. 17, no. 4, pp. 298–300

——(1994a) *Medicine as Culture: Illness, Disease and the Body in Western Societies*, Sage, London

——(1994b) *Moral Threats and Dangerous Desires: AIDS in the News Media*, Taylor & Francis, London

——(1995) *The Imperative of Health: Public Health and the Regulated Body*, Sage, London

——(1996) *Food, the Body and the Self*, Sage, London

Lupton, D. & Gaffney, D. (1996) 'Discourses and practices related to suntanning and solar protection among young Australians', *Health Education Research: Theory & Practice*, in press

Lupton, D., McCarthy, S. & Chapman, S. (1995) '"Panic bodies": discourses on risk and HIV testing', *Sociology of Health & Illness*, vol. 17, no. 1, pp. 89–108

McDonald, K. (1994) 'Globalisation, multiculturalism and rethinking the social' (Symposium: Globalisation, multiculturalism and rethinking the social) *Australian and New Zealand Journal of Sociology*, vol. 30, no. 3, pp. 239–47

MacInnes, A. & Milburn, K. (1994) 'Belief systems and social circumstances influencing the health choices of people in Lochaber', *Health Education Journal*, vol. 53, pp. 58–72

Martin, C. & McQueen, D. (eds) (1989) *Readings for a New Public Health*, Edinburgh University Press, Edinburgh

McKeown, T. (1988) *On the Origins of Human Disease*, Blackwell, Oxford

McKinlay, J. (1993) 'The promotion of health through planned sociopolitical change: challenges for research and policy', *Social Science & Medicine*, vol. 36, no. 2, pp. 109–17

McMichael, A. (1993a) *Planetary Overload: Global Environmental Change and the Health of the Human Species*, Cambridge University Press, Cambridge

——(1993b) 'Global environmental change and human population health: a conceptual and scientific challenge for epidemiology', *International Journal of Epidemiology*, vol. 22, no. 1, pp. 1–8

MacNaghten, P. (1995) 'Local responses and global environmental change', paper presented at the 2nd Theory, Culture and Society conference, Berlin, August

McNay, L. (1992) *Foucault and Feminism: Power, Gender and Self*, Polity Press, Cambridge

Madden, K. (1995) 'Householders' experiences of "save the environment" messages', *Australian Journal of Communication*, vol. 22, no. 3, pp. 82–102

Marmot, M. (1994) 'The cholesterol papers: lowering population cholesterol concentrations probably isn't harmful', *British Medical Journal*, vol. 308, pp. 351–2

Marmot, M. & Morris, J. (1984) 'The social environment', in W. Holland, R. Detels & G. Knox with E. Breeze (eds), *Oxford Textbook of Public Health, Volume 1*, Oxford University Press, Oxford

Marris, P. (1985) 'Community development', in A. Kuper & J. Kaper (eds) *The Social Science Encyclopaedia*, Routledge & Kegan Paul, London

Massey, D. (1994) *Space, Place and Gender*, Polity Press, Cambridge

Massumi, B. (1992) 'Everywhere you want to be: introduction to fear', *Warwick Journal of Philosophy* (Deleuze and the Transcendental Unconscious issue), pp. 175–216

Metcalfe, A. (1993) 'Living in a clinic: the power of public health promotions', *Anthropological Journal of Australia*, vol. 4, no. 1, pp. 31–44

Milio, N. (1986) *Promoting Health Through Public Policy*, Canadian Public Health Association, Ottawa

——(1990) 'Healthy Cities: the new public health and supportive research', *Health Promotion International*, vol. 5, no. 4, pp. 291–7

——(1991) 'Making healthy public policy; developing the science by learning the art: an ecological framework for policy studies', in B. Badura & I. Kickbusch (eds), *Health Promotion Research: Towards a New Social Epidemiology*, WHO Regional Publications, European Series No. 37, WHO, London

Miller, P. and Rose, N. (1993) 'Governing economic life', in M. Gane & T. Johnson (eds), *Foucault's New Domains*, Routledge, London

Miller, T. (1993) *The Well-Tempered Self: Citizenship, Culture, and the Postmodern Subject*, Johns Hopkins University Press, Baltimore

Miner, K. & Ward, S. (1992) 'Ecological health promotion: the promise of empowerment education', *Journal of Health Education*, vol. 23, 7, pp. 429–32

Minson, J. (1993) *Questions of Conduct: Sexual Harassment, Citizenship, Government*, Macmillan, Basingstoke

Moffat, S., Phillimore, P., Bhopal, R. & Foy, C. (1995) '"If this is what it's doing to our washing, what is it doing to our lungs?" Industrial pollution and public understanding in north-east England', *Social Science & Medicine*, vol. 41, no. 6, pp. 883–91

Monaem, A. (1989) 'An orientation to health promotion', in G. Lupton & J. Najman (eds), *Sociology of Health and Illness: Australian Readings*, Macmillan, Melbourne

Money, M. (1992) 'Health education, ecology and the shamanic world view', *Health Education Research: Theory & Practice*, vol. 7, no. 2, pp. 301–3

Moscucci, O. (1990) *The Science of Woman: Gynaecology and Gender in England, 1800–1929*, Cambridge University Press, Cambridge

Mrozek, D. J. (1989) 'Sport in American life: from national health to personal fulfilment, 1890–1940', in K. Grover (ed.), *Fitness in American Culture: Images of Health, Sport, and the Body, 1830–1940*, University of Massachusetts Press and the Margaret Woodbury Strong Museum, Amherst and New York

Mullen, K. (1992) 'A question of balance: health behaviour and work context among male Glaswegians', *Sociology of Health & Illness*, vol. 14, no. 1, 73–97

——(1994) 'Control and responsibility: moral and religious issues in lay health accounts', *Sociological Review*, vol. 42, no. 3, pp. 414–37

Mundell, I. (1993) 'Peering through the smoke screen', *New Scientist*, 9 October, pp. 14–15

National Commission on the Environment (1993) *Choosing a Sustainable Future, The Report of the National Commission on the Environment*, Island Press, Washington

National Health and Medical Research Council, Australia (1992) *Ecologically Sustainable Development: The Health Perspective*, NH&MRC, Canberra

Nettleton, S. (1991) 'Wisdom, diligence and teeth: discursive practices and the creation of mothers', *Sociology of Health & Illness*, vol. 13, no. 1, pp. 98–111

New South Wales Health Department (1991) *A State of Better Health*, Health Promotion Unit, NSW Health Department, Sydney

Niven, S. & Kelly, M. (1994) 'The new public health and health promotion in the context of the healthy settings approach: a briefing paper', manuscript prepared for the South Western Research and Development Directorate, School of Social Sciences, University of Greenwich, Greenwich

Nuñez, A., Colomer, C., Peiro, R. & Alvarez-Dardet, C. (1994) 'The Valencian Community Healthy Cities Network: assessment of the implementation process', *Health Promotion International*, vol. 9, no. 3, pp. 189–98

Nutbeam, D. (1986) 'Health promotion glossary', *Health Promotion*, vol. 1, no. 1, pp. 113–27

Nutbeam, D., Wise, M., Bauman, A., Harris, E. & Leeder, S. (1993) *Goals and Targets for Australia's Health in the Year 2000 and Beyond*, AGPS, Canberra

Oliver, M. (1992) 'Doubts about preventing coronary heart disease', *British Medical Journal*, vol. 304, pp. 393–4

Oppenheimer, G. (1995) 'Comment: epidemiology and the liberal arts—toward a new paradigm?', *American Journal of Public Health*, vol. 85, no. 7, pp. 918–20

Ouellet, F., Durand, D. & Forget, G. (1994) 'Preliminary results of an evaluation of three Healthy Cities in the Montreal area', *Health Promotion International*, vol. 9, no. 3, pp. 153–9

Outram, D. (1989) *The Body and the French Revolution: Sex, Class and Political Culture*, Yale University Press, New Haven

Packard, R. and Epstein, P. (1991) 'Epidemiologists, social scientists, and the structure of medical research on AIDS in Africa', *Social Science & Medicine*, vol. 33, no. 7, pp. 771–94

Parsons, E. and Atkinson, P. (1992) 'Lay constructions of genetic risk', *Sociology of Health & Illness*, vol. 14, no. 4, pp. 437–55

Pasquino, P. (1991) 'Theatrum politicum: the genealogy of capital—police and the state of prosperity', in G. Burchell, C. Gordon & P. Miller (eds), *The Foucault Effect: Studies in Governmentality*, Harvester Wheatsheaf, Hemel Hempstead

Pateman, C. (1970) *Participation and Democratic Theory*, Cambridge University Press, London

——(1989) *The Disorder of Women: Democracy, Feminism and Political Theory*, Polity Press, Cambridge

——(1994) 'Feminism and democracy', in B. Turner & P. Hamilton (eds), *Citizenship: Critical Concepts*, Routledge, London

Patton, C. (1990) 'Inventing "African AIDS"', *New Formations*, vol. 10, pp. 25–39

Payne, G. (1994) 'Community and community studies', *Sociological Review*, vol. 4, no. 1, pp. 16–19

Peele, S. (1993) 'The conflict between public health goals and the temperance mentality', *American Journal of Public Health*, vol. 83, no. 6, pp. 805–10

Petersen, A. (1994a) *In a Critical Condition: Health and Power Relations in Australia*, Allen & Unwin, Sydney

——(1994b) 'Community development in health promotion: empowerment or regulation?', *Australian Journal of Public Health*, vol. 18, no. 2, pp. 213–17

——(1996) 'Risk and the regulated self: the discourse of health promotion as politics of uncertainty', *Australian and New Zealand Journal of Sociology*, vol. 32, no. 1, pp. 44–57

Petersen, A. & Winkler, A. (1992) 'The contribution of the social sciences to nurse education in Australia', in J. Daly & A. Kellehear (eds), *Annual Review of Health Social Sciences*, La Trobe University, Bundoora

Pettman, J. (1992) *Living in the Margins: Racism, Sexism and Feminism in Australia*, Allen & Unwin, Sydney

Phelan, S. (1994) *Getting Specific: Postmodern Lesbian Politics*, University of Minnesota Press, Minneapolis

Phillimore, P. (1993) 'How do places shape health? Rethinking locality and lifestyle in North-East England', in S. Platt, H. Thomas, S. Scott & G. Williams (eds), *Locating Health: Sociological and Historical Explorations*, Avebury, Aldershot

Piette, D. (1990) 'Community participation in formal decision-making mechanisms', *Health Promotion International*, vol. 5, no. 3, pp. 187–97

Pike, D., O'Keefe, E. & Pike, S. (1990) 'Camden in the WHO Healthy Cities project', *The Planner*, no. 21 (September), pp. 17–20

Plant, R. (1974) *Community and Ideology: An Essay in Applied Social Philosophy*, Routledge & Kegan Paul, London

Plumwood, V. (1994) 'The ecopolitics debate and the politics of nature', in K. Warren (ed.), *Ecological Feminism*, Routledge, London

Pollock, K. (1988) 'On the nature of social stress: production of a modern mythology', *Social Science & Medicine*, vol. 26, no. 3, pp. 381–92

Porras, I. M. (1993) 'The Rio Declaration: a new basis for international cooperation', in P. Sands (ed.), *Greening International Law*, Earthscan, London

Porter, D. & Porter, R. (1988) 'The enforcement of health: the British debate', in E. Fee & D. Fox (eds), *AIDS: The Burdens of History*, University of California Press, Berkeley

Porter, R. (1993) 'Diseases of civilization', in W. Bynam & R. Porter (eds), *Comparative Encyclopedia of the History of Medicine*, Routledge, London

Potter, J., Wetherell, M. & Chitty, A. (1991) 'Quantification rhetoric—cancer on television', *Discourse & Society*, vol. 2, no. 3, pp. 333–65

Prior, L. & Bloor, M. (1993) 'Why people die: social representations of death and its causes', *Science As Culture*, vol. 3, no. 3, pp. 346–75

Rabinow, P. (1989) *French Modern: Norms and Forms of the Social Environment*, MIT Press, Cambridge, MA

Rapp, R. (1993) 'Accounting for amniocentesis', in S. Lindenbaum & M. Lock, (eds), *Knowledge, Power and Practice: the Anthropology of Medicine and Everyday Life*, University of California Press, Berkeley

Ravnskov, U. (1992) 'Cholesterol lowering trials in coronary heart disease: frequency of citation and outcome', *British Medical Journal*, no. 305, pp. 15–19

Rissel, C. (1994) 'Empowerment: the holy grail of health promotion?', *Health Promotion International*, vol. 9, no. 1, pp. 39–47

Roche, M. (1992) *Rethinking Citizenship: Welfare, Ideology and Change in Modern Society*, Polity Press, Cambridge

Rose, G. (1993) *Feminism and Geography: The Limits of Geographical Knowledge*, Polity Press, Cambridge

Rose, H. (1990) 'Activists, gender and the community health movement', *Health Promotion International*, vol. 5, no. 3, pp. 209–18

Rose, N. (1990) *Governing the Soul: the Shaping of the Private Self*, Routledge, London

——(1993) 'Government, authority and expertise in advanced liberalism', *Economy & Society*, vol. 22, no. 3, pp. 283–99

Rose, N. & Miller, P. (1992) 'Political power beyond the state: problematics of government', *British Journal of Sociology*, vol. 43, no. 2, pp. 173–205

Rosen, G. (1973) 'Disease, debility, and death', in H. Dyos & M. Wolff, (eds), *The Victorian City: Images and Realities*, Routledge & Kegan Paul, London

——(1974) *From Medical Police to Social Medicine: Essays on the History of Health Care*, Science History Publications

——(1993/1958) *A History of Public Health*, Johns Hopkins University Press, Baltimore

Ross, A. (1991) *Strange Weather: Culture, Science and Technology in the Age of Limits*, Verso, London

Ross, E. (1993) *Love and Toil: Motherhood in Outcast London 1870–1918*, Oxford University Press, New York

Rothenberg, T. (1995) '"And she told two friends": lesbians creating urban social space', in D. Bell & G. Valentine (eds), *Mapping Desire: Geographies of Sexualities*, Routledge, London

Rushton, J. & Bogaert, A. (1989) 'Population differences in susceptibility to AIDS: an evolutionary analysis', *Social Science & Medicine*, vol. 28, no. 12, pp. 1211–20

Rutherford, P. (1994) 'The administration of life: ecological discourse as "intellectual machinery of government"', *Australian Journal of Communication*, vol. 21, no. 3, pp. 40–55

Saltonstall, R. (1993) 'Healthy bodies, social bodies: men's and women's concepts and practices of health in everyday life', *Social Science & Medicine*, vol. 36, no. 1, pp. 7–14

Sawicki, J. (1991) *Disciplining Foucault: Feminism, Power and the Body*, Routledge, New York

Scarry, E. (1985) *The Body in Pain: The Making and Unmaking of the World*, Oxford University Press, Oxford

Scheper-Hughes, N. & Lock, M. (1987) 'The mindful body: a prolegomenon to future work in medical anthropology', *Medical Anthropology Quarterly*, vol. 1, pp. 6–41

Scott, S. & Williams, G. (1991) 'Introduction', in S. Scott, G. Williams, S. Platt & H. Thomas (eds), *Private Risks and Public Dangers*, Avebury, Aldershot

Sears, A. (1992) '"To teach them how to live": the politics of public health from tuberculosis to AIDS', *Journal of Historical Sociology*, vol. 5, no. 1, pp. 61–83

Sennett, R. (1974) *The Fall of Public Man*, Random House, New York

Sevenhuijsen, S. (1992) 'Mothers as citizens: feminism, evolutionary theory and the reform of Dutch family law 1870–1910', in C. Smart (ed.), *Regulating Womanhood: Historical Essays on Marriage, Motherhood and Sexuality*, Routledge, London

Shields, R. (1991) *Places on the Margin: Alternative Geographies of Modernity*, ·Routledge, London

Shilling, C. (1993) *The Body and Social Theory*, Sage, London

Short, J. (1991) *Imagined Country: Society, Culture and Environment*, Routledge, London

Shuttleworth, S. (1990) 'Female circulation: medical discourse and popular advertising in the mid-Victorian era', in M. Jacobus, E. Keller & S. Shuttleworth (eds), *Body/Politics: Women and the Discourses of Science*, Routledge, New York

——(1993/94) 'A mother's place is in the wrong', *New Scientist*, 25 December/1 January, pp. 38–40

Simmel, G. (1969) 'The metropolis and mental life', in R. Sennett (ed.), *Classic Essays on the Culture of Cities*, Meredith Corporation, New York

Singer, L. (1993) *Erotic Welfare: Sexual Theory and Politics in the Age of Epidemic*, Routledge, New York

Skolbekken, J.-A. (1995) 'The risk epidemic in medical journals', *Social Science & Medicine*, vol. 40, no. 3, pp. 291–305

Skrabanek, P. (1993) 'The epidemiology of errors', *The Lancet*, vol. 342, p. 1502

Slack, J. (1994) 'The environment matters: complicity, ethics, theoretical rigour, intervention', *Australian Journal of Communication*, vol. 21, no. 3, pp. 1–13

Smart, B. (1990) 'Modernity, postmodernity and the present', in B. Turner (ed.), *Theories of Modernity and Postmodernity*, Sage, London

Smith, L. (1991) 'Community participation in health: a case study of World Health Organization's Healthy Cities project in Barcelona and Sheffield', *Community Development Journal*, vol. 26, no. 2, pp. 112–17

Sontag, S. (1990) *Illness as Metaphor and AIDS and its Metaphors*, Anchor, New York

Spensky, M. (1992) 'Producers of legitimacy: homes for unmarried mothers in the 1950s', in C. Smart (ed.), *Regulating Womanhood: Historical Essays on Marriage, Motherhood and Sexuality*, Routledge, London

Spivak, G. (1988) *In Other Worlds: Essays in Cultural Politics*, Routledge, New York

——(1993) *Outside in the Teaching Machine*, Routledge, New York

Stallybrass, P. & White, A. (1986) *The Politics and Poetics of Transgression*, Methuen, London

Stein, H. (1990) 'In what systems do alcohol/chemical addictions make sense? Clinical ideologies and practices as cultural metaphors', *Social Science & Medicine*, vol. 30, no. 9, pp. 987–1000

Stevenson, H. & Burke, M. (1991) 'Bureaucratic logic in new social movement clothing: the limits of health promotion research', *Health Promotion International*, vol. 6, pp. 281–9

Strandberg, T., Slomaa, V., Naukkarinen, V., Vanhanen, H., Sarna, S. & Miettinen, T. (1991) 'Long term mortality after 5-year multifactorial primary prevention of cardiovascular diseases in middle-aged men', *Journal of the American Medical Association*, no. 266, pp. 1225–9

Susskind, A. (1992) 'Is health care for women sex discrimination against men?', *Sydney Morning Herald*, 12 March

——(1994) 'Injection of reality', *Sydney Morning Herald*, 12 November

Sweet, M. (1994) 'Life in womb will be written on your tomb', *Sydney Morning Herald*, 29 October

Terris, M. (1992) 'Healthy lifestyles: the perspective of epidemiology', *Journal of Public Health Policy*, vol. 13, no. 12, pp. 186–94

——(1993) 'The society for epidemiologic research and the future of epidemiology', *Journal of Public Health Policy*, vol. 14, p. 2, pp. 137–48

Theweleit, K. (1987) *Male Fantasies. Volume 1: Women, Floods, Bodies, History*, Polity, Cambridge

Thomas, J. (1993) 'Citizenship and historical sensibility', *Australian Historical Studies*, no. 100, pp. 383–93

Treichler, P. (1989) 'AIDS, homophobia, and biomedical discourse: an epidemic of signification', in D. Crimp (ed.), *AIDS: Cultural Analysis, Cultural Activism*, MIT Press, Cambridge, MA

——(1992) 'AIDS, HIV, and the cultural construction of reality', in G. Herdt & S. Lindenbaum (eds), *The Time of AIDS: Social Analysis, Theory, and Method*, Sage, Newbury Park

Trostle, J. (1986) 'Early work in anthropology and epidemiology: from social medicine to the germ theory, 1840 to 1920', in C. Janes, R. Stall & S. Gifford (eds), *Anthropology and Epidemiology: Interdisciplinary Approaches to the Study of Health and Disease*, D. Reidel, Dordrecht, the Netherlands

Tsouros, A. D. (ed.) (1990a) *World Health Organization Healthy Cities Project: A Project Becomes a Movement (A Review of Progress 1987 to 1990)*, Sogess, Milan

——(1990b) 'Healthy cities means community action', *Health Promotion International*, vol. 5, no. 3, pp. 177–8

——(1994) *The WHO Healthy Cities Project: State of the Art and Future Plans*, WHO Regional Office for Europe, Copenhagen

——(1995) 'The WHO Healthy Cities Project: state of the art and future plans', *Health Promotion International*, vol. 10, no. 2, pp. 133–41

Tulloch, J. & Lupton, D. (1997) *Television, AIDS and Risk: A Cultural Studies Approach to Health Communication*, Allen & Unwin, Sydney

Turner, B. (1987) *Medical Power and Social Knowledge*, Sage, London

——(1990) 'Outline of a theory of citizenship', *Sociology*, vol. 24, no. 2, pp. 189–217

——(1994) 'Postmodern culture/modern citizens', in B. van Steenbergen (ed.), *The Condition of Citizenship*, London, Sage

Urry, J. (1995) *Consuming Places*, Routledge, London

Usher, R. & Edwards, R. (1994) *Postmodernism and Education*, Routledge, London

van Steenbergen, B. (1994) 'The condition of citizenship: an introduction', in B. van Steenbergen (ed.), *The Condition of Citizenship*, Sage, London

Vogel, U. (1992) 'Whose property? The double standard of adultery in nineteenth-century law', in C. Smart (ed.), *Regulating Womanhood: Historical Essays on Marriage, Motherhood and Sexuality*, Routledge, London

——(1994) 'Marriage and the boundaries of citizenship', in B. van Steenbergen (ed.), *The Condition of Citizenship*, Sage, London

Volinn, I. (1989) 'Issues of definitions and their implications: AIDS and leprosy', *Social Science & Medicine*, vol. 29, no. 10, pp. 1157–62

Waldby, C. (1993) 'Biomedicine and the body politic', paper presented at the Sex/Gender in Techno-Science Worlds conference, Melbourne, July

Waldby, C., Kippax, S. & Crawford, J. (1995) 'Epidemiological knowledge and discriminatory practice: AIDS and the social relations of biomedicine', *Australian and New Zealand Journal of Sociology*, vol. 31, no. 1, pp. 1–14

Waldby, S. (1994) 'Is citizenship gendered?', *Sociology*, vol. 28, no. 2, pp. 379–95

Wallerstein, N. (1993) 'Empowerment and health: the theory and practice of community change', *Community Development Journal*, vol. 28, no. 3, pp. 218–27

Warren, K. (1994) 'Introduction', in K. Warren (ed.), *Ecological Feminism*, Routledge, London

Waters, M. (1994) 'A world of difference' (Symposium: Globalisation, multiculturalism and rethinking the social), *Australian and New Zealand Journal of Sociology*, vol. 30, no. 3, pp. 229–34

Watson, J. (1993) 'Male body image and health beliefs: a qualitative study and implications for health promotion practice', *Health Education Journal*, vol. 52, no. 4, pp. 246–52

Weber, M. (1976 [1930]) *The Protestant Ethic and the Spirit of Capitalism*, George Allen & Unwin, London

White, P. & Gillett, J. (1994) 'Reading the muscular body: a critical decoding of advertisements in *Flex* magazine', *Sociology of Sport Journal*, no. 11, pp. 18–39

White, R. (1990) *No Space of their Own: Young People and Social Control in Australia*, Cambridge University Press, Cambridge

Williams, G., Gabe, J. & Kelleher, D. (1994) 'Epilogue: the last days of Doctor Power', in J. Gabe, D. Kelleher & G. Williams (eds), *Challenging Medicine*, Routledge, London

Williams, G., Popay, J. & Bissell, P. (1995) 'Public health risks in the material world: barriers to social movements in health', in J. Gabe (ed.), Medicine, Health and Risk: Sociological Approaches, Blackwell Publishers, Oxford

Williams, R. (1988) Keywords: a Vocabulary of Culture and Society, Fontana, London

Willis, P. (1990) Common Culture: Symbolic Work at Play in the Everyday Cultures of the Young, Open University Press, Milton Keynes

Woodward, D. (1995) '"Surveillant gays": HIV, space and the constitution of identities', in D. Bell & G. Valentine (eds), Mapping Desire: Geographies of Sexualities, Routledge, London

World Commission on Environment and Development (WCED) (1987) Our Common Future, Oxford University Press, Oxford

World Health Organization (1985) Targets for Health for All, WHO Regional Office for Europe

——(1986) The Ottawa Charter, WHO Regional Office for Europe, Copenhagen

——(1988) Priority Research for Health for All, WHO, Copenhagen

——(1990a) Environment and Health, The European Charter and Commentary (First European Conference on Environment and Health, Frankfurt, 7–8 December 1989), WHO Regional Publications, European Series No. 35, WHO, Geneva

——(1990b) Potential Health Effects of Climatic Change, Report of a WHO Task Group, WHO, Geneva

——(1991) City Networks for Health: Technical Discussions on Strategies for Health for All in the Face of Rapid Urbanization, May 1991, WHO, Geneva

——(1992a) Our Planet, Our Health, Report of the WHO Commission on Health and Environment, WHO, Geneva

——(1992b) Twenty Steps for Developing a Healthy Cities Project, WHO Regional Office for Europe, Copenhagen

——(1994) City Health Profiles—City Health Plans (Report on a WHO Healthy Cities Technical Symposium, Poznan, Poland, 23–24 September 1994), WHO Regional Office for Europe, Copenhagen

Wright, P. (1988) 'Babyhood: the social construction of infant care as a medical problem in England in the years around 1900', in M. Lock & D. Gordon (eds), Biomedicine Examined, Kluwer, Dordrecht, the Netherlands

Wright, R. (1995) 'The evolution of despair', Time, 11 September, pp. 62–8

Wynne, B. (1996) 'May the sheep safely graze? A reflexive view of the expert–lay knowledge divide', in S. Lash, B. Szerszynski & B. Wynne (eds), Risk, Environment and Modernity: Towards a New Ecology, Sage, London

Yeatman, A. (1994) 'Multiculturalism, globalisation and rethinking the social' (Symposium: Globalisation, multiculturalism and rethinking the social), Australian and New Zealand Journal of Sociology, vol. 30, no. 3, pp. 247–53

Yeo, M. (1993) 'Toward an ethic of empowerment for health promotion', Health Promotion International, vol. 8, no. 3, pp. 225–35

Young, I. (1990) Justice and the Politics of Difference, Princeton University Press, Princeton

——(1994) 'Polity and group difference: a critique of the ideal of universal citizenship', in B. Turner & P. Hamilton (eds), Citizenship: Critical Concepts, Routledge, London

Index

Aboriginal culture, Australian, 105
Acheshon Report on the Public Health
  (1988, British), 27
acid rain, 133
acquired immune deficiency syndrome
  see HIV/AIDS
advocacy, health, 5
Africa, racism, 56; HIV/AIDS, 36–7,
  56–8
Agent Orange, 99
AIDS see HIV/AIDS
alcohol, 55, 71; advertising and sale of,
  5; alcoholism, 54; drink-driving
  and, 5, 70, 71
alternative therapies, 7
American National Commission on
  the Environment, 141
antivivisectionist movement, 7
arms trade, global, 139
atherosclerosis, 44; see also
  cardiovascular disease; heart disease
Australian Health Ministers'
  Conference (1988), 20

bacteria, 100, antibiotic resistance, 107;
  necrotising fasciitis, 7
biodiversity loss, 2, 133, 142
biomedicine, iatrogenic, as, 7; limits of,
  175; see also medicine
biostatistics, xi, 5, 27; see also
  epidemiology; statistics
birth, home, 7
birth control, 5
body, ix, xii; child's, 74; consuming,

body cont.
  23; fat, 50–1; feminine, xiv, 24–5,
  65, 72, 76–8, 83, 85; health risk
  management, 22; health status, ix;
  healthy, 23, 25; lifestyle and, 1;
  masculine, xiv, 81–4; monitoring,
  65, 72, 78; normality, 25; public,
  84–5; risk and, 22, 50–2;
  self-regulation, ix, 22–6, 51, 69; see
  also embodiment
body industry, 24
bodybuilding, 81, 82
botulin, 100
breast cancer, 45, 79–80, 86
Brundlandt report (WCED 1987), 142

cancer, 2, 54; breast, 45, 79–80, 86;
  cervical, 69, 86; curable, as, 38;
  epidemiology and, 30, 31; lung, 31,
  59; prostate, 86; screening, 69, 86;
  skin, 83; testicular, 86
cardiovascular disease, 2, 43–4, 54; see
  also cholesterol; heart disease
chemicals, hazardous, 1, 89
Chernobyl nuclear disaster (1986,
  Ukraine), 95, 96
child, abuse, 76, 77; body, 74; health,
  3, 73–5; immunisation, 69; welfare,
  74
chlorosis, 35–6
cholera, 108, 124
cholesterol, blood, 38–9, 43–5, 69
cigarettes see smoking
cities see city; Healthy Cities project

citizenship, ix, x, xiv, xv, 13, 61–5, 70, 87, 149, 172, 175, 179; civility and selfhood, 62–5; consumerism and, 101; cultural, 63; dutiful and governable, as, xiii, xiv, 88, 149, 176; environment and, ix, xiv, 99–103; expert empowerment role, 152–9; global, 99; health status of others, 69; Healthy Cities project, xvi, 149; healthy citizen, xiii, xiv, 60, 61–88; middle class women and, 75; morality judgements and public health, 87; neo-liberalism and, 64; participation, xvi, 147, 149, 150, 157; rights, xiii, 11, 12, 88, 147, 148, 150; self help health and, 69, 175; self-control, xiii, 64; social, 13–14; women and, xiv, 72–80

city, xv; eco-crisis, 134–5; environmental risk and, xv; healthy, xv, 120–45; medicalisable object, as, 123; organic concept of, xv, 124–6, 144, 149; see also urbanisation

civility, 62–5, 71; see also citizenship

class see social class

climate change see global warming

collaboration, 5–6, 11, 19

communications, new technologies and, globalisation, 132, 168–71

communities, power relations and, 167; segregated spatial, 169

community, xvi, 139, 163, 172, 173; advocacy health groups, 4; citizenship and, 70; control, 11; empowerment, 155; essentialism of, 166–8; exclusionary, as, 167–8; fixed subjectivity and, 179; identity, xvi, 163, 166, 169–71, 173, 179; new communications technologies and, 170–1; politics of exclusion and, 167; processual definition, 172; space and place, 163–72; state health coercive regulations and, 72; strategic essentialism strategy and, 171; urban development and, 169

community arts, greening of public health and, 139

community development, 19, 20, 148, 157–8

Community Health Councils (CHC), 153

Community Health Program (Australia), 158

community participation, xvi, 5, 8, 18, 145, 146–73, 175, 180; barriers to, 153–4; Healthy Cities project and, xvi, 145, 146, 151–2; liberation discourse, as, 147; men's health and, 87; neo-liberal democracy and, 156–7, 173; non place-based affiliations and, 166

community-based health, new public health and, 163

computer technology, 47; communications, 170–1

condom use, 88, 180; risky self and, 117

consumption, 15, 23; citizenship and, 67, 101, 150

Council of Europe, 132

death, 2, 29, 40–1, 49

Deep Ecology, 102, 140; eco-feminist critiques of, 140

degradation see environmental degradation

democracy, 172; citizenship rights and, 147; direct face-to-face ideal, 164; participation and, xvi, 147–8, 157, 159–60, 162; self-care and, 176

democratic research, 156

dental hygiene, 70–1, 88

developing countries, sustainable development and, 142–4

diabetes, 54

diet, 15, 50–1, 69, 88, 109, 180

discrimination, 178; new public health morality and, xvi; risk groups and, 58–9

diseases, xi, 34–6, 59, 177; aetiology theories, 177; agents of, 100; atherosclerosis, 44; communicable, 89, 117; contagious, 28; environmental distress syndrome and, 107–8; epidemiology and, xiii, 29, 30–2, 38, 59; Huntington's chorea, 54; infectious, 2, 5, 7, 29, 30, 107, 175; internment, 71; isolation, 5, 7, 175; legionnaires' disease, 31; lung, 39–40; malaria,

diseases *cont.*
  36; measles, 117; muscular
  dystrophy, 54; new, 7, 89, 107–8;
  non-infectious, 2; osteoporosis, 69;
  quarantine, 5, 7, 175; re-emergence
  of, 107; respiratory, 54; sexually
  transmitted, 51–2, 56, 65, 78;
  smallpox, 65; stress and, 51;
  syphilis, 51–2, 56, 78; tuberculosis,
  78, 117, 124; typhoid, 124;
  venereal, 65; *see also* bacteria;
  cardiovascular disease; heart disease;
  hepatitis; viruses
disease–gene link, 54
domination, 139, 143, 175–7
Down's syndrome, 54
Drug Offensive, The (Australian), 55
drugs, illicit, 5, 55, 71, 76–7; cocaine,
  71; crack cocaine, 51–2, 56; heroin,
  71; HIV/AIDS and, 37
drugs, licit, 71
duties discourse, 12–13; *see also*
  citizenship

Earth Summit '92, 5, 132, 133, 143.
Ebola virus, 7, 106–7
eco-crisis, ix, xv, 143, 145, 172;
  Healthy Cities project, 139;
  management, 132–8; *see also*
  eco-politics
eco-feminism, 104; Deep Ecology
  critique, 140; domination critiques,
  139; environmental philosophy
  critique, 139–40; *see also* feminist
  critiques
eco-politics, 139–45; Healthy Cities
  project and, 139
ecological cities project (OECD), 132
ecological citizenship, 63; *see also*
  citizenship
ecological crisis *see* eco-crisis
ecological health, 105, 108, 109
ecological politics *see* eco-politics
ecologically sustainable development
  (ESD), 141–2; *see also* sustainable
  development
ecology *see* environment
ecology movement, 12; *see also* Deep
  Ecology; environmental movement
Economic Commission for Europe, 132

economic development, ESD and,
  141–2
economic discrimination, 178
economics, xi, xiii, 5, 8, 139
education, x, 5, 176
electric power cables, 99
electromagnetic radiation, 99
electronic communications,
  globalisation and, 168–9
emancipation, marginalised groups, of,
  180–1
embodiment, x, xi, 81–4, 87, 173; *see
  also* body
empowerment, 9, 11, 109, 152–9, 172,
  175; community development and,
  157, 158; marginalised groups, of,
  180; neo-liberal democracy and,
  173; *see also* power
energy use, 5, 135, 139, 143
Enlightenment project, 122
entrepreneurial subject, 10, 12, 17,
  170, 176; neo-liberalism and, xiii
environment, ix, xiv, xv, 4, 5, 16,
  88–90, 117–18, 133, 144, 176;
  ecologically sustainable *see*
  ecologically sustainable
  development (ESD); health risks *see*
  environmental risk; natural, 5, 16,
  104, 150; resource depletion, 16,
  133; risk discourse and, 89–119;
  social, 108–14
environment, save the, 100–1
environmental citizen, 99–103
environmental degradation, 5, 142,
  144, 175; land, 5, 135
environmental distress syndrome, 107–8
environmental management, Healthy
  Cities project and, 139, 144
environmental movement, 90, 106; *see
  also* Deep Ecology; ecology
  movement; environmentalists
environmental politics, 101–2
environmental pollution *see* pollution
environmental protection, 13, 142,
  145; Rio Declaration and, 143
environmental risk, xv, 5, 94–9, 102–3,
  115–16, 118, 133–4, 144; *see also*
  pollution

environmentalism, government
    regulation of industrial production,
    101
environmentalists, 91, 97; nature and,
    104–5
epidemiology, xi, xii, xiii–xiv, 5, 27–60,
    175; contamination of data, 42–3;
    death and, 29, 40–1, 49; disease
    and, 7, 28, 29, 30; health risk, 48;
    health status registers, 31;
    knowledges, 37–47, 54, 59; lay, xiv,
    51–2, 53, 56, 59; life tables, 29;
    mortality rates, 29, 40–1; policy
    role, 30; political function, 59; risk
    and, 19, 47–55; sociocultural
    dimension, x, 33–7, 39–42, 55–9;
    web of causation, 32–3, 47
essentialism strategy, strategic, 171
ethnicity differences, normal subject
    and, 178
ethnostatistics, epidemiology and, 37
eugenics, genetic testing discourses and,
    54–5
European Charter on Environment and
    Health, 13, 16, 127–8, 135–6
exclusion, 178
exercise, 15, 69
expert/community cooperation,
    greening of public health and, 139
expertise, xii–xiii, 14–18, 146
experts, xiv, 4, 18, 98–9, 120, 139,
    153, 155–7, 172; citizen
    empowerment role, 152–9; Healthy
    Cities project and, 126, 127, 151,
    141; knowledges, xii–xiii, 15, 18,
    144, 156, 172, 173, 175, 177–8

family, 73–4, 176
farming, intensive, 89
feminism, 12, 24–5, 86, 148, 164, 171
feminist critiques, x, xvi, 139–40, 167,
    176; see also eco-feminism
firearms use, 5
First European Conference on
    Environment and Health, 135
fluoridation of water, 99
foodstuffs, 5, 96, 139
forest protection, 143
fuel crisis, global (1970s), 133

'Gaia', 104
gay and lesbian rights movement, 11

gay men (homosexuality), 59, 72, 148,
    171, 174; HIV/AIDS and, 37, 41,
    42, 46, 58, 85
gay-related immuno-deficiency (GRID),
    37; see also HIV/AIDS
gender, xiv, 24–5, 75–6, 83, 178
genetic testing, 54–5
germ theory, 88
ghettos, 169; see also spatial segregation
global citizenship, 63, 99
global ecosystem, 133–4
Global Forum, 143
global warming, 1–2, 96, 97, 106, 133;
    expert knowledge and
    environmental risk, 98
globalisation, ix, xii, 13, 90, 143,
    168–9; body and, 22–3;
    environmental risk and, xv, 13,
    142, 145; nation-state and, 169;
    new killer diseases and, 107–8;
    place and, 168, 169
Greater Glasgow Health Board, 165
green movement, 11, 90, 106; Healthy
    Cities project and, 139; see also
    Deep Ecology; ecology movement;
    environmental movement
green politics, 145
greening of public health, 139–44
greenhouse effect, 2, 133
Greenpeace Australia, 97, 100
gynaecology, 85

hantavirus, 108
hazardous chemicals, 1, 15, 89, 96–7, 99
health care, 30, 175
Health for All (HFA), 20, 126–9, 133,
    139, 146, 149, 163
health literacy, 69
Health of Towns Association (British
    1840s), 9
health planning, epidemiology and,
    xiii–xiv
health professionals, 153, 155; see also
    expertise; experts; knowledge;
    science
health promotion, xi, 15, 24, 47, 88,
    175; healthy body and, 23–4; media
    and, 67, 88
health science see science
health skills, 69

health status, 1, 31; personal responsibility for, 51
health visitor system, 74–5
healthism, 25–6, 179
Healthy Cities project (WHO), xv, xvi, 8–9, 14, 102, 121–2, 124, 126–33, 135, 137, 139, 144–5, 149, 154, 160–2, 165; community as place, 163–4, 171–2; community participation, 146, 151–2, 154–5; eco-politics and, 139, 141, 144, 145; Health for All, 149; holistic approach, 138; locality-based community and, 164–6, 171–2; neighbourhoods, 165; networks, xv, 131–2, 164; participation, 149–51, 158–62; symposia, 150–1
healthy city, xv, 120–45, 149; post-Enlightenment modernist concept, as, xv, 122–7, 141
healthy public policy, 17–18, 137–8
heart disease, alcohol consumption and, 40; blood cholesterol and, 38–9, 43–5; coronary, 69; men's health and, 86; smoking and, 39–40; see also cardiovascular disease
heavy metals, 75, 89
hepatitis, 69, 107, 117; C, 58
herbicides, 99
heroin, 71
hierarchy, 177
HIV/AIDS, 7, 4, 24, 35–7, 42, 46, 59, 107, 140; African epidemic, 36–7, 56–8; citizenship and, 69–70; confidentiality rights and, 37; epidemiology and, 31, 41–2, 46–7; feminine body as contaminating, 78–9; heterosexual men and, 79; HIV virus, 5, 7, 35, 46, 117; masculine body and, 85; racist stereotyping and, 56–8; risk group discrimination, 58–9
holism, ecological environmental approach, 105; environmental protection and new public health, 142
holism and health, 89, 105, 108, 115, 109; Healthy Cities project and, 138, 139; spirituality and, 108–9
home birth, 7

homosexuality, 54, 55; HIV/AIDS epidemiology, 37, 41, 42; see also gay men; lesbians; sexuality
Human Genome Project, 54; see also genetic testing
human immunodeficiency virus (HIV) see HIV/AIDS
human rights, 143
Human Rights and Equal Opportunities Commission (Australian), 86, 87
humanism, 180
Huntington's chorea, 54
hygiene, 2, 74; see also sanitation
hysteria, 35–6

immigrants, 72
immunisation, 5, 69; see also vaccination
impotence, 86
industrialisation, 5, 8, 16, 91–2, 133, 135, 107
inequality, 165–6, 175–8
infant health, 31, 75; see also child
Infant Welfare movement (British), 74–5
infectious diseases see diseases, infectious
Internet, 132, 168; see also communications
ionising radiation, 96

knowledge, x, xi, xii, xiv, 3–6, 69, 173, 175; epidemiological, xiii, xiv, 43–7, 59; expert, 15, 18, 98–9, 144, 173, 177–8; expertise and power and, xii–xiii; governance and, 10, 18; lay, 153, 177–8; neo-liberalism and, 10; power and, xii–xiii, 10, 14, 162, 177–8; science and, 118–19, 153, 172, 176–8

land degradation, 5, 135; see also environmental degradation
lay knowledge, 153–4, 177–8; challenges to medicine, 6; epidemiology and, xiv, 51–3, 56, 59
lead levels, blood, 75
legionnaires disease, 31
legislation, health, 5, 65–6
lesbians, 11, 72, 80, 148, 171, 174
liberal democratic theory, 147
liberation, xvi, 172, 178

life expectancy, 2
life tables, 29
lifestyle, ix, xiii, 2, 4, 15–16; class and,
    16; eco-crisis and, 134; ethnicity
    and, 16; gender and, 16; health
    promotion and, 15; risks and, xiii,
    15, 21, 53–4, 133, 134
listeria, 100
locality, community base, 163–6,
    169–72; contaminating other, as,
    174; neighbourhoods, 165; see also
    place
lung disease, 31, 39–40, 59; respiratory
    disease, 54

mammographic screening, 4
male see body, masculine; masculinity;
    men
malaria, 36
market economics see economics
Marxist critiques, x
masculinity, 83–4
maternity, child health and, 5; health
    status, 5, 31; see also motherhood
measles, 117
media and communication, 139, 176;
    consumption campaigns, 67;
    contested knowledges, 43–5;
    electronic communications, 168–9;
    environmental risks and industrial
    hazards, 96–7; health promotion,
    67, 88; men's health and, 86
medical care, limits of, 133
medical treatment, enforced, 71, 175
medicine, lay challenges to, 6;
    liberation and, 178; negligence
    litigation, 7; scientific see scientific
    medicine; sociopolitical analysis and
    critiques, 178; see also biomedicine;
    science
meditation, 109
men, embodied, as, 81–4; healthy
    citizenship and, xiv, 80–7;
    heterosexual, AIDS and, 78–9;
    male domination, 177; medical
    surveillance of, 85, 87; middle class,
    85; see also gay men
men's health, 85–7; accidents and, 86;
    disembodiment, 87; resource
    allocation and services for, 86–7

Men's Health Conference (1995,
    Australia), 85–6
men's movement, 85
methadone programs, 71–2
miasma, theory of, 93
middle class, men, 85; women, 75
militarism, 143, 166
mobile phones, 99
modernism, new public health
    discourses and, 175, 177; statistics
    and, 29
modernist concept, environment as, 89,
    90; Healthy Cities project as,
    144–5, 149; healthy city as, 122–7,
    141; new public health and, xii,
    xiv–xvi, 7–8
modernity, 96; Healthy Cities project,
    149; healthy city, 141; nature and,
    141; post-, 7–8; public health and,
    6–10; scientific medicine and, 6–10
morality judgements, public health
    and, xii, xvi, 1–26, 60, 87, 174
mortality rates, 2, 29
'Mother Nature', 104
motherhood, 74–5; see also maternity;
    women
muscular dystrophy, 54

National Heart Foundation, Australian,
    45
National Men's Health Strategy (1966,
    Australia), 86
Native American culture, 105
nature, xiv, 103–8, 141; vengeful, as,
    106–7
neighbourhood, xvi, 165; see also
    community
neo-liberalism, xiii, xiv, 10–15, 90,
    175, 178, 180; citizenship and, 64;
    democracy and, xvi, 148–9, 162,
    172–3; participation and, xvi, 146,
    156–7, 162, 173
networking, Healthy Cities project
    and, 131–2; see also electronic
    communications
new diseases see diseases, new
'New Age', 104
new public health, agencies, 119;
    apparatus, 175; biomedical
    emphasis, 4; citizen concept, 61,

new public health *cont.*
71–2, 87–8; coercive strategies and state health regulation, 71; community as place, 171–2; community participation and, xvi, 146–73; community-based health and, 163, 166; concepts and strategies, xvi, 2, 5; conformity to imperatives, 180; consumption and aesthetics, 67; critical appraisal of, 175; definition of, ix; discourses, 11–12, 67; discrimination and, xvi; economics and, 5; empowerment and, 175; environment and, 89, 90, 97; environmental citizen, 100–1; epidemiology and, x, 27, 60; green politics and, 139, 145; Healthy Cities project, 121–2; healthy citizens and, 67–8; holistic approach, 89, 105, 108; individual body and, 23; knowledges, x; legislation, 5, 71; lifestyle emphasis, 4; modernist, as, xii, xvi, 7; monitoring strategies, 87, 174–5; morality and, xii, 1–26, 60, 174; neo-liberalism and, 175; participation philosophies, 175, 176, 179; population as health category, 4; power and, 26; public opinion and, x; regulation and surveillance, 3; risk discourses, xii; science-based, as, xii, xvi, 2, 6, 177; self-regulation and control philosophies, 68–9, 71; sociocultural practice, as, x, xii, 4; state and, 119, 175; *see also* public health
New Right, 11, 12, 158
new social movements, 11; *see also* gay and lesbian rights movement; green movement
nineteenth-century public health, xvi, 65–6, 91–4, 109; epidemiology, 28–30; hygiene and sanitation, 2, 23, 92–4; urban reform, xv, 92–4, 123–4, 149; women and family, 73–4
non place-based identity, xvi, 166; *see also* place
non-Europeans, 174
normal subject, age differences and, 178; social class differences, 178

normality, xiii, 25, 66, 156, 175, 178, 180–1; *see also* epidemiology
nuclear threat, 95–7, 142, 143
nuclear waste, 97
nursing, xi

obesity, 50
occupational health and safety, 5
old public health *see* nineteenth-century public health
Organization for Economic Cooperation and Development (OECD), 132
osteoporosis, 69
other, contaminating, 174; epidemiology and, 55–9
Ottawa Charter for Health Promotion (1986, WHO), 127, 133, 135, 137, 146, 153
ozone layer, thinning of, 89

participation, xvi, 11, 146–73; barriers to, 153–4, 162, 173; citizenship and, xvi, 150, 157; demands and responsibilities of, xvi, 173; democracy, 147–8; enabling process, as, 150; Healthy Cities project and, 149–51, 154–5, 164–5; imperative, 147–52, 162; new public health philosophies, 176; self-discipline and, 159–62; *see also* community participation
passive smoking, 36
pathology, 175; *see also* diseases
patient advocacy groups, 7
peace movement, 11
penicillin, 107
personal health services, 5
pesticides, 100
place, space and, 163–72; authenticity of, 169; community and, xvi, 163–72; diverse constructions of; essential character of, 168; fixed character of, 166; health status and, 114; *see also* locality
place-based affiliations, 166
planning, healthy city and, xv; epidemiology and, xii–xiv; town, 139, 149; transport, 139; urban, 122
pollution, 1, 118, 133; air, 16, 95, 98, 103; car emissions, 99; chemical,

pollution *cont.*
 103; environmental, 133; social
 differentiations and, 102–3; water,
 16, 95
poor, the, 72, 174; *see also* poverty
population growth, 140, 142; Deep
 Ecology and, 140; environmental
 risk, as, 5, 135; nineteenth-century
 public health and, 91–2; urban, 16,
 91–2
populations, ix, xiii, 1–5, 66; censuses,
 28; control of, 122; ESD and urban,
 141; epidemiology and, 27, 28,
 53–4; priority populations, 21;
 regulation and normality in, 22
poststructuralism, x-xi, 10, 178
poverty, 165; economic development,
 141–2; *see also* poor, the
power, xi, xiii, 173; citizenship and,
 xiii, 3, 150, 153; eco-politics and,
 143–4; hierarchies of, 144, 172;
 knowledge and expertise, xi-xiii, 14,
 176; participation and, 148, 161,
 162; relations, 9, 156, 167, 176–7;
 science and, 176; space and, 171;
 see also empowerment
pregnancy, 76–7
preventive action, ix, x, 5; new
 diseases and, 7
privacy and personal liberty, 71–2
private sector health care, 3
probability statistics *see* biostatistics;
 statistics
promotion, health *see* health promotion
prostitution, 29, 65, 72; HIV/AIDS,
 37, 79; risk group discrimination,
 58–9
psychiatric disorders, 54
public health, coercive strategies, 65–6;
 definitions of, xi, 3–6, 6–10;
 greening of, 139–44; imperatives,
 88; movement, 66; policy, 43, 137–8
public policy, 5, 17–18; Healthy Cities
 project and, 144

quarantine, 5, 7, 175

racial differences, normality and, 178
racism, 166; epidemiological risk
 factors and, 56–8; population
 problem and, 140, 142

radiation, ionising, 89; solar UV, 89
radioactive nuclear waste, 97
rationality, epidemiology, 34, 59;
 governmental, 122–3; health
 economics, 8; public health, 6, 27,
 29; role in social progress, 175;
 scientific medicine, 6; space
 ordering, 166; *see also*
 epidemiology; science
respiratory disease, 54; *see also* lung
 disease
right to health, 65
rights, 12–13; citizenship, xiii, 11, 12,
 88, 147, 148, 150; human, 143;
 welfare state and, xvi
Rio Declaration, 143–4
risk, xii, xiv, 18–22, 49–50, 58–9,
 88–119, 175, 177; assessment,
 18–21; environmental, ix, xiv, xv,
 1, 16–17, 89–119; epidemiology
 and, xiii, 2, 20, 30, 32–3, 38–9,
 41–2, 45–9; HIV/AIDS and, 41–2;
 lay epidemiology and, 51–3, 56;
 lifestyle and, xiii, 15, 16, 21;
 management, 22, 24, 47; profiles,
 18–21, 156; subjects at, xiii, 115–17
risk society, 20, 96
risky self, xiii, 1, 16, 20, 115–17, 180;
 see also self
Royal Commission for Inquiry into the
 State of Large Towns and Populous
 Districts (1844, 1845 England), 123
rural environment, health and, 112

safe sex, ix; *see also* condom use
safety helmets, 5
salmonella, 100
sanitation, 2, 5, 8, 9, 23, 149; *see also*
 hygiene
science, xi, xii, xiv, 2, 178; actuarial,
 47; environment and health,
 118–19; Healthy Cities project and,
 126–7, 144; healthy city and, 177;
 knowledge, 118–19, 153, 172,
 176–8; lay knowledges and, 177–8;
 power and, 176, 177; public health
 and, xi, xii, xvi, 2, 6, 177; social
 progress and, 175, 177
scientific knowledge, 172; *see also*
 knowledge

scientific medicine, xi, 3, 6–10; *see also* medicine
screening, diagnostic, 4, 5, 69, 78, 86
seatbelts, compulsory wearing of, 5, 70, 71
self, ix, x, xiii, xiv, 23, 55–9, 62, 64, 70–1, 80–2, 99–100, 111, 112, 116, 178, 179; risky *see* risky self
self-actualisation, 172
self-care, 80, 88, 176
self-control, xiii, 64, 179
self-discipline, 159–62
self-help, 7, 11, 69, 175
self-identity, 10
self-regulation, ix, 22–6, 29, 51, 66, 68–9, 71
sexual citizenship, 63
sexual difference and normality, 178
sexual discrimination, 86–7
sexuality, bisexuality, 43; racist stereotyping and epidemiology, 56–9; women's, 78
sexually transmitted diseases, 51–2, 56, 65, 78
sleep deprivation, 113
smallpox, 65
smoking, 109, 180; cigarettes, 5, 69, 71; epidemiology and, 39–40, 47–8; lung disease, 39–40; passive, 117; risk and, 47–8; risky self and, 117; tobacco, 180
smoking-related disease, 4
social class, normal subject and class differences, 178
social differentiations, environmental hazard exposure, 102–3
social discrimination, 178
social environment, dangers of, 108–14
social groups, categorisation, epidemiological, 55–9; contaminating other, as, 174; underprivileged, x
social marketing, 5
social stress, 51, 112–13
social support, self-care and, 176
social surveys, lifestyle and risk, 21
social work, 139
socio-economic status, xii, 18, 164–5
sociocultural theory, x, xii
South Australian Health Foundation, 68

space/spatiality, 114, 123; healthy city and, xv; power relations and, 171; rational ordering of, 177; social relations and, 166; urban, 123, 149
spaces and places, 2; city, xv; community, 163–72
spatial segregation, gated communities and, 169–70
spirituality, 105–6, 108–9
statistical surveys, 175
statistics, curable cancer, 38; epidemiology, 28–9, 31–2, 37; ethnostatistics, 37; modernism and, 29; probability, 47; *see also* biostatistics
sterilization, forced, 140
strategic essentialism strategy, 171
stress, 112–15; men's health and, 86
subjectivity, xi, 10, 13, 173
sudden infant death syndrome (SIDS), 41
Sustainable Cities campaign, 132
sustainable development, ix, 19, 143, 145, 175; healthy cities and, 150; Rio Declaration and, 143; *see also* ecologically sustainable development (ESD)
Sydney Breast Cancer Institute, 79
syphilis, 51–2, 56, 78

therapies, alternative, 7
Third World debt, 139
Three Mile Island nuclear meltdown, (1979, US), 97
tobacco *see* smoking
town planning, 122, 139, 149
toxins, 89
trade imbalances, 166
transport, 21; car emissions, 99; planning, 139; policy, 139
tuberculosis, 78, 117, 124
typhoid, 124

ultraviolet radiation (UV radiation), solar, 89
unemployment, 166
United Nations Conference on Environment and Development (UNCED) (1992), 5, 132, 133, 143

United Nations Development Program
(UNDP), 132
urban planning, 122
urban population growth, 16, 91–2, 141
urban reform, xv, 92–4, 123–4, 149, 158
urban space, 123, 169
urbanisation, x, 2, 8, 91–2, 145, 169;
eco-crisis and, 134–7; risks of, 5,
107, 110–11; see also city
urbanism, health and, xv, 89, 133, 144;
psychosomatic effects of, xv, 111–12

vaccination, 65, 71; see also
immunisation
vegetarianism, 99–100
violence, 86
viruses, Ebola, 7, 106–7; hantavirus,
108; human immunodeficiency virus
(HIV), 5, 7, 35, 46, 117

War on Drugs (US 1980s), 55
wastes, hazardous, 17, 97
welfare state, retreat from, xiii, xvi, 11,
148, 176; neo-liberalism and, xiii,
10–11, 12
women, 24–5, 140, 148; citizenship
and, xiv, 72–80; contaminating, as,
79, 81, 174; domination of, 143;
embodied, as, 81; family health and

women cont.
welfare, 73–5, 77–80, 88, 94;
middle class, 75; pregnancy and,
76–7; public role of, 75; working
class, 74–5; see also body, feminine;
feminism; lesbians; maternity;
motherhood
women's health, 7, 72–80
women's movement, 11
women's sexuality, 78
work practices, exploitative, 166
working class, 2, 74–5, 174
workplace practices, 139
World Association of the Major
Metropolises, 132
World Bank, 132
World Commission on Environment
and Development (WCED), 142
World Health Assembly, 129
World Health Organisation (WHO),
xv, 68, 95, 124, 126–32, 138,
144–5, 164; Commission on Health
and the Environment, 136–7,
149–50; Regional Office for Europe,
127, 128, 149; see also European
Charter on Environment and
Health; Health for All (HFA);
Healthy Cities project (WHO)
World Wide Web, 168

Lightning Source UK Ltd.
Milton Keynes UK
07 April 2010

152453UK00002B/21/P